Library of
Davidson College

Travels on the Lower Mississippi
1879–1880

Travels on the Lower Mississippi 1879–1880

A Memoir by Ernst von Hesse-Wartegg

**Edited and translated by
Frederic Trautmann**

University of Missouri Press
Columbia and London

Copyright © 1990 by
The Curators of the University of Missouri
University of Missouri Press, Columbia, Missouri 65211
Printed and bound in the United States of America
All rights reserved
5 4 3 2 1   94 93 92 91 90

Library of Congress Cataloging-in-Publication Data
Hesse-Wartegg, Ernst von, 1854–1918
  [Mississippi-Fahrten. English]
  Travels on the lower Mississippi, 1879–1880: a memoir /
Ernst von Hesse-Wartegg; edited and translated by Frederic
Trautmann.
     p.   cm.
  Translation of: Mississippi-fahrten.
  Bibliography: p.
  Includes index.
  ISBN 0-8262-0709-X (alk. paper)
  1. Mississippi River Valley—Description and travel. 2.
Louisiana—Description and travel—1865–1950. 3. Plantation
life—Louisiana—History—19th century. 4. Hesse-Wartegg, Ernst von.
1854–1918—Journeys—Mississippi River Valley. I. Trautmann,
Frederic II. Title.
F354.H5813   1989   89-4847
917.6304'61—dc20   CIP

First published as *Mississippi-Fahrten: Reisebilder aus dem
amerikanischen Süden, 1879–1880.* Leipzig: Verlag von Carl
Reissner, 1881.

∞™ This paper meets the minimum requirements of
the American National Standard for Permanence of Paper
for Printed Library Materials, Z39.48, 1984.

Designer: Liz Fett
Typesetter: Connell-Zeko Type & Graphics
Printer: Thomson-Shore, Inc.
Binder: Thomson-Shore, Inc.
Typeface: Baskerville

*To the great translators
once, now, and hence
and especially*
Cicero
Martin Luther
George Smith
Jean-François Champollion
Georg Friedrich Grotefend
Henry Creswicke Rawlinson
Constance Garnett
Robert Fitzgerald
Richard Wilbur

Descriptions by [Ernst von Hesse-Wartegg] of the life on the Mississippi and in its towns will be read with interest in every part of the Union.

New York Times, 30 January 1882

Contents

Preface *xi*
Acknowledgments *xv*
Introduction *1*

Travels on the Lower Mississippi
Preface *13*

Part I. South to the Land of Cotton
1. St. Louis *17*
2. The Mississippi Fleet *22*
3. Southward Bound! *29*
4. Cairo and the Ohio River *33*
5. River Vignettes *38*
6. Memphis *45*
7. Yellow Jack! *54*
8. Grenada and the Yazoo Country *64*
9. Through the State of Mississippi *72*
10. Ku Klux Klan and Judge Lynch *78*
11. Days on the River *86*
12. The Negro Exodus *98*
13. King Cotton! *107*
14. Arkansas *116*

Part II. Louisiana
15. Louisiana *123*
16. Controlling the Mississippi *129*
17. Arrival at the Port of New Orleans *136*
18. International Port *141*
19. The Metropolis of the South *151*
20. A Black Government *165*
21. Carnival *169*
22. A Cockfight *176*
23. My Steamboat Excursion to the Sugar Plantations *182*

24. Plantation Life in Southern Louisiana *192*
25. A Sugar Plantation *201*
26. A Rice Plantation *206*
27. Progress and Prosperity in Agriculture and the Basic Industries *211*
28. The Lives of Women in Creole Land: Louisiana and the Caribbean *219*
29. The Mouths of the Mississippi *230*
30. To Mobile *235*

Bibliography *241*
Index *251*

Preface

By Frederic Trautmann

I have tried to be the good housekeeper and the faithful steward. In translating I have hewed to the original and tried to set forth the meaning in clear, graceful English. Thereby I have reached my goal of literal rendition—often but not always, as the purposes sometimes crossed. Unfortunately, literal meanings sometimes oppose clear renditions. Worse, made clear, they may defy grace. As Bruno Bettelheim has written: "Expression that in English would be scorned as muddleheaded and confused is quite acceptable in German. While English authors, particularly in scientific writings, shun ambiguities, German writing is full of them" (*Freud and Man's Soul,* 44). My goals may thus be at odds, so I have on occasion had to forsake the literal for the accurate in order to be clear. But never have I sacrificed accuracy and clarity to rhetorical flourish or stylistic conceit.

For example, I abandoned *natürliche Bedingungen,* "natural conditions," and went to "climate, weather and soil": it is clearer, more precise, and more expressive of the phrase in context. When subjunctives signify direct discourse, I usually rendered them as quotations. *U.s.w.,* the German equivalent of "etc.," is more legitimate in literary German than in equivalent English, so I usually replaced it with what English favors: the specifics, sometimes to the extent of a list. "That" as an independent reference (as in "He did just that!") may have the currency to claim legitimacy in defiance of clarity in English, but I have saved the reader's hunting up what "that" stands for. (Even the foggiest English rarely goes to the German excess of a "that" to refer to something complicated enough to be expressed by one or even several paragraphs.) I have added transitions and strengthened weak ones, providing "accordingly," say, or "therefore" to help the reader, or substituting a phrase such as "This discussion shows what happens if . . ." as a better bridge than the one there. When an important fact appears only once and late in a passage, I have improved clarity and retained accuracy by inserting the fact early and perhaps several times before its original appearance. As German is more agreeable to closely successive shifts in tense and especially to the historical present, I have not always been able to honor them. Instead clear, graceful English has sometimes demanded English past for German present, and English present for German past. If the translation seems exclamatory at times, it is less so than the original, where enthusiasm sounds agreeable in a language that accepts—even expects—the exclamation point after any imperative. (Hesse-Wartegg uses two or three where one hurts the American ear but seems subdued in German.) I have usually found equally disagreeable and changed to the positive the common German use of litotes: "a not inconsiderable elevation" becomes "a considerable elevation" or "a height."

And then how to translate *Neger*? The 1880s translator would have made it "Negro" without a second thought. But, disfavored through association with oppression, it has declined; it sounds too much like "nigger." We usually hear "black" as the noun, sometimes as the motto of liberation, for dark-skinned Americans of African descent. "Negro" still retains some currency, however, among blacks and whites, especially in the South. Compounding the problem, Hesse-Wartegg also used the German for "black," noun and adjective. My solution is to do as he did and use both, the word of the 1880s and the word of the 1980s, each as it obeys the text, serves the context, and respects history and semantics.

In editing I have checked Hesse-Wartegg's against the Census Bureau's *Historical Statistics* and Dodd and Dodd's *Historical Statistics of the South*. I have usually found his accurate enough to stand without change or note. I have moved most of his footnotes into the text to which they refer. Those kept as notes I have labeled as such. I have added notes to correct, explain, expand, sustain, or illuminate the text, and to connect it to the literature of the lower Mississippi. I have tried to steer between the Scylla of too few annotations and the Charybdis of too many, between a raw mass and an overloaded opus, toward a handsome text enhanced by editorial apparatus.

Hesse-Wartegg's English, including his quotations of speech and writing, I have retained as he had them: in quotation marks and italicized. I have corrected misspellings and grammatical errors in this English only when they seem to be his mistakes. Especially when it records an unusual spelling or catches a peculiar turn of phrase, the English adds the color and flavor he intended and preserves examples of the American language of 1880.

I have inserted the original chapter 30 as 27, increasing by one the number of each that follows. I have also transposed the order of several others. Sentences and paragraphs I have usually kept in original order. Seeking clarity, coherence, and emphasis, however, I have now and then shifted paragraphs within chapters and sometimes reassigned sentences, phrases, and words among and within paragraphs. For the same reasons I have rearranged more extensively chapters 2, 4, 6, 10, and 25. Parts of them I have had to recompose to retain accuracy while gaining economy and clarity. Thus I have tried to follow the motto of housekeeping and stewardship: a place for every right word, and every right word in its place.

Acknowledgments

It has been a delight to prepare this book for its true audience. It would have been a pain, if not impossible, to do it alone. Of the many who helped, I must name: Lady Luck: always there, smiling, when needed; Elizabeth Delano Whiteman: still my best reader; Maxwell Whiteman: bookman and man of books; John C. Van Horne's staff of the Library Company of Philadelphia: every other page would have been less without those helpful, friendly, knowledgeable, generous keepers of treasure; Cathy Meany, Betty Denkins and Liz Romano of Inter–Library Loan, Temple University Libraries: this time they had to work harder and they worked better than ever; Jean Thorsten, Manager, Faculty Offices, Ambler Campus, Temple University: her congenial manner and capable hand turn "the office" into a pleasant and well-run workplace; Judy Shatz of the same Offices: always helpful; Mary Dunn, Manager, and Priscilla Jackson, of the Information Processing Center, Temple University: their knowledge and skill brought the manuscript out of the Dark Ages and into the Age of the Computer; Renate Merrick and the Library of the German Society of Pennsylvania: they provided *Mississippi-Fahrten* and much else besides; Sandi Thompson, Library, Ambler Campus, Temple University: she dispenses information and radiates vivacity, each in full measure; Estelle Zafran and Elly Daymont: they didn't know how much they were helping, day in, day out; David M. Neigher: kind, wise, generous, thoughtful, considerate, and an inspiration always; Oskar: if he could talk, what tales he might tell; Beth: she knows, she understands, she helps, first and last and all the times, good and bad, and in between. Thanks be to them that I give this book with greetings and best wishes to my fellow Americans and all who read it everywhere.

Introduction

By Frederic Trautmann

I cannot rest from travel; I will drink Life to the lees.
Tennyson, "Ulysses"

Ernst von Hesse-Wartegg (1854–1918) may have journeyed farther and written more than any other travel memoirist in modern times. Slower but no less resourceful than Phileas Fogg in Jules Verne's *Around the World in Eighty Days,* Hesse-Wartegg used any means to circle the globe four times and roam in six continents. When conveyances broke down or blew up, when horses, mules, oxen, camels, dogs, elephants, llamas, or yaks balked, failed, or died, Hesse-Wartegg walked—through mud, sand, snow; under open skies and beneath jungle canopies; beside still waters and along foaming cataracts; in blizzards and heat waves. This Austro-German came to North America with insatiable wanderlust, traveling in nearly every state and territory of the United States, as well as Mexico and Canada. He toured the South when "travelers from abroad did not always venture across the Hudson, fewer still across the Potomac."[1] During that crucial time between Reconstruction and the rise of the New South, he followed the Mississippi from St. Louis to the Gulf and witnessed the agonized transformation of the region.

Hesse-Wartegg published over forty travel books and perhaps newspaper and magazine articles to supply the casual reader for life, though they remain uncounted and probably forever fugitive, like his reputation. We do not know how many articles were on the United States, but there are at least eight books, some multi-volumed and some in more than one edition. Many of the articles probably reappeared in the books, especially in *Nord-Amerika*'s four volumes. *Mississippi-Fahrten* (1881), the first full-length treatment of the lower Mississippi, remains the most interesting.

Of course, Mark Twain's *Life on the Mississippi,* which appeared a few years after Hesse-Wartegg's book, remains the classic on travel and culture along the river. In addition to personal experience, Twain took

---

1. C. Vann Woodward, *Origins of the New South,* 491.

material from published sources. He listed sixteen authors from whom he had borrowed, saying that "there are others."[2] One he did not list but quoted in the book was a writer on yellow fever in Memphis, "a German tourist who seems to have been an eye-witness of the scenes which he described." Thus, three paragraphs of Ernst von Hesse-Wartegg's *Mississippi-Fahrten* joined the 9,500 words Mark Twain admitted were "mainly stolen from books, tho' credit given."[3] He may have stolen 9,500 from Hesse-Wartegg alone. Hesse-Wartegg had "gathered an enormous amount of miscellaneous information," and Mark Twain "dredged it freely in the preparation of the second half of his *Life on the Mississippi*."[4] But the relationship between the writers was symbiotic: in chapter 3 below, Hesse-Wartegg paraphrases Twain's account of a steamboat landing, and in chapter 5 he notes the etymology of "Mark Twain" with good-humored irony.

Twain's listed sources comprised fifteen British authors and one French. Of those not listed, some were his countrymen; but the most American of authors drew predominantly from foreign writers for his American classic. He relied on them because they were plentiful and they knew what they were talking about: they were authorities. Travelers have taught Americans about America because tourists, out to escape the tedium and boredom of a workaday world, flee the ordinary and appreciate what they find new and interesting. Residents may think of home as humdrum and hackneyed; visitors write home about this fascinating place. Foreigners remark what residents assume. What locals dismiss, strangers take in. What natives make light of, foreigners ponder and judge.

So it amazed Americans that iced drinks and ice cream, restlessness and haste, tobacco-chewing and spitting on the floor, hurried eating and piggish manners, and the pursuit of dollars—dollars—dollars evoked pages of description and provoked evaluations of bizarre—bizarre—bizarre. Charles Dickens saw such details and dramatized them in *American Notes* (1842), which Allan Nevins praised as "the best of all works of American travel, from a literary point of view."[5] In *Domestic Manners of the Americans* (1832), Frances Trollope, novelist and mother of Anthony Trollope, jolted Americans into a sense of identity they would not feel again until the Civil War. She said, "I do not like

2. See the list in Willis Wager's edition of *Life on the Mississippi*, 402. For Twain on Hesse-Wartegg, see *Life on the Mississippi*, ch. 29. Twain may also have used Hesse-Wartegg in *Huckleberry Finn*. See Dewey Ganzel, "Twain, Travel Books, and *Life on the Mississippi*," 50.

3. *Mark Twain–Howells Letters*, 417.

4. Thomas D. Clark, "The Mississippi River in History," 188.

5. Allan Nevins, *America Through British Eyes*, 89.

their principles, I do not like their manners, I do not like their opinions."⁶ Like these writers, Hesse-Wartegg "sees things more picturesquely here than we can. He is more shocked by the special features of low life in the great Mississippi Valley towns. He is more impressed by the hugeness and majesty of the Mississippi steamboat."⁷ He was, as the *New York Times* put it, a "traveler of the stamp of Dickens and Mrs. Trollope."⁸

Their counterpart as traveler and writer, he resembled them little otherwise. He was upper-class and cosmopolitan, from the nobility and grand bourgeoisie represented in every country of Europe, the upper crust who floated in leisured enjoyment on the tranquil times between the Franco-Prussian and the Great War.⁹ Many other foreign writers on America were lower middle-class, they wrote for a living, and as much as for any other reason, they wrote well because the better the writing, the better the living. Many of their kind were artisans, shopkeepers, and officials; many of his, the idle rich. True, he wrote for money, so he wrote to attract an audience. But he also wrote readable books because, as a gentleman, one minded courtesy and taste. Besides, style was the last refinement of the civilized mind.

Well off but not inherently rich, yet wanting to live high and go everywhere, he could not be idle. He must write, and his books must sell. He did not want to be idle; idleness contradicted his nature. To satisfy curiosity and liberate energy, he craved motion, spectacle, adventure, excitement. Travel was the outlet. But travel did not mean what it meant to many; it was not mere tourism. He had to call it travel for lack of a better term. He wanted excursions around the world for the fun and the hardship and the terror, and for the struggle and the profit and the joy of writing about them.

He grew up among people who went in season according to taste—to the Riviera for the beaches in summer or the casinos in winter, and to the Alps for skiing or hiking. He followed in their footsteps as far as they went, then blazed trails. His trip to Syria and southern and east-central Europe at eighteen would have been *the* journey for someone

---

6. Ibid., 83.
7. "A German Traveler on the Mississippi," *New York Times*, 30 January 1882.
8. Ibid.
9. The biographical details here and below are drawn from *Wer ist's*, the *Deutsches Biographisches Jahrbuch*, and *Meyers Konversations-Lexikon* (1893), s.v. "Hesse-Wartegg, Ernst von"; *Berliner Tageblatt*, 20 May 1918; Hauk, *Memories; Dictionary of American Biography, Appleton's Cyclopedia of American Biography, National Cyclopedia of American Biography*, and *New Grove Dictionary of Music and Musicians*, s.v. "Hauk, Minnie"; and *New York Times*, 7 February 1929. On the life-style of the leisured upper classes in Europe in the late nineteenth century, see the early chapters of Felix Gilbert, *A European Past: Memoirs 1905–1945*.

else. For him the trip and his description of it only marked the beginning; travel for life and livelihood lay ahead. He trekked over much of the world. He was the first German in Korea. He wrote book upon book that sold well, brought the world to untold readers in several languages, and financed expeditions over the rest of the world. For the money he often went as the correspondent of German, Austrian, and Swiss newspapers and magazines. He dispatched scores of articles to be read throughout central Europe. His publisher welcomed the *Munich/Augsburg Abendzeitung*'s rave that his name on a book stamped it sterling. He belonged to the geographical societies of Vienna, Madrid, Hamburg, Metz, and Belgium, and to the German Atheneum of London. He deserves some of the credit for universal and standard time zones, and the practice, now routine, of signaling locations of icebergs and wrecks. He was a director of museums, held the title of Commandeur, and was knighted.

A member sometimes of another traveling profession, diplomacy, he served as consul in London. There the Baron de Wartegg—or the Chevalier as he was called in the French of the corps—belonged to the Grosvenor Club in Bond Street, an affiliation for a gentleman. In London he perfected his English. He came to the United States accomplished, mature, and articulate; a graduate of the best schools; accustomed to the long, Continental view of history; conversant in subjects that had engaged thoughtful minds since antiquity; equipped with the keener eye of the foreigner; seasoned in travel worldwide; and adept at writing about it.

Fitting, then, that a gentleman and the leading foreign writer on the United States should marry Minnie Hauk, a traveler nearly his match, the American prima donna who sang the first Carmen in the United States. She became an international operatic luminary, "a queen of song . . . of unnumbered triumphs," and perhaps the best Carmen anywhere ever.[10] After girlhood in Kansas, she went with her family from St. Louis to New Orleans by houseboat. There she lived until her parents appreciated that her talent warranted New York and the best teachers. In 1882 she married the man who had just written about his travels between St. Louis and the Gulf by steamboat. He became an American citizen at her request. She joined him to live where he had finished the book: the Villa Treibschen near Lucerne, Switzerland. Richard Wagner once occupied it and wrote parts of *Der Ring des Niebelungen* and *Die Meistersinger* in the villa's spacious beauty.

A. M. Williamson remembered the Hesse-Warteggs as "generous and hospitable and happy, and [they] had plenty of money. They knew

10. *New Orleans Picayune*, 21 January 1879.

all the traveling Royalties and distinguished people of every sort."[11] Celebrities and personages dropped in, generals, diplomats, and nobility—every rank of royalty below monarch. Nobody refused an invitation from Baron and Baroness de Wartegg. Luxury and ease were de rigueur at the villa and everywhere its proprietors went. Flowers filled the garden. The Christmas tree would be fine and big, "with many candles, gilded nuts, and appropriate presents."[12] In the winter the Hesse-Warteggs stayed at the grand hotel outside Nice.

Living, entertaining, and traveling in style could not be had for a song. Neither an aria nor a concert by Minnie at her best would suffice. Money ran out, friends ran away, and he died in 1918, leaving her destitute. She got the villa but also the debts. "How my poor, deluded husband managed it all I do not know. . . . Had I not sold my diamond jewelry, I might be at the starvation point."[13] Cold comfort that her eyes could not see the sparkle so well anymore anyway. The diamond that was Minnie Hauk was fading, too. She died in 1924, nearly blind. She had subsisted on charity from another great Carmen, Geraldine Farrar, and on the first pension granted by the Music Lovers' Foundation of New York.

But Minnie Hauk and Ernst von Hesse-Wartegg, the Baron and the Baroness, the Chevalier and his lady, had done as they wished and got what they wanted: success, fame, and a full life. Above all, they had traveled; they had gone everywhere and seen the sights and followed exotic ways to their hungry hearts' content. She had glittered on the world's stages and been applauded from Berlin to Buenos Aires to Bangkok. He had seen more of the world perhaps than anyone before or since. She was a great entertainer. He was "an entertainer of the highest order, a storyteller of appeal and substance, who had much to impart in his chatty tone of an experienced man of the world."[14] You might meet the likes of one such nonpareil in a lifetime. They were two together for thirty-six years.

Photographs show a dapper fellow tricked out in the finest. The air of puckish expectancy seems to say, "I'm ready for anything." The gleam of swashbuckling deviltry implies, "I pray it will happen!" A famous photograph shows him with hat, gloves, and stick in hand, ready to go. When Williamson met him on the Riviera about 1910, he had excelled at travel and the description of travel. He appeared to have enjoyed every minute. "A good-looking man," she said, "with

---

11. A. M. Williamson, Preface to Minnie Hauk, *Memories of a Singer*, 5.
12. Hauk, *Memories of a Singer*, 272–73.
13. *New York Times*, 7 February 1929.
14. *Berliner Tageblatt*, 20 May 1918.

brown hair turning slightly gray and very smart, miniature side whiskers." She was told, "There isn't a spot on earth he doesn't know!"[15]

He traveled for fun, for adventure. As much as any tourist he expected to see the "curiosa" and sample the entertainments and try the waters. But, to be satisfied, he must write a good book. It must appeal to readers and include, for those who would emigrate, an account of the region as a place to settle. So he must apprehend the fundamentals of the place and the traits of the people. He must be an eyewitness because readers expected it, emigrants needed it, the standards of the time dictated it, and he wanted it.

Motivated by these expectations and standards, he developed remarkable insight into the river, land, and people of the Mississippi valley. Another side of him, however, can outrage today's reader. At his worst, he endorses patronage, condescension, and prejudice. Indeed, he asserts them. He did not mince words. His points of view, neither unique nor original but nonetheless sharp, are not to be mistaken or missed; they puncture and cut. They are therefore not superficialities or mistakes for the editor to excise or correct. Such statements, though we gag on them, must be kept because they tell about the author and because ideological features belong here: what people thought counts as much as how they and the river looked and behaved. By setting forth ideas and revealing moral codes, his own as well as others', he depicts a mental landscape as significant as the physical.

Monarchist and anti-democratic, he sneered at "the empire of the ballot." Racist and anti-Semitic, he disdained Native Americans and Chinese, disliked the "lower races" of southeastern Europe and the Middle East, and despised Jews. Native Americans, a stumbling block to Civilization and Progress, were to be shoved aside. The Chinese built much of the transcontinental railroad, but he pronounced the race unfit for plantation labor. Jabs at Armenians, Turks, and Bulgarians, more jocular than serious, are as gauche now as they must have seemed then. The slurs on Jews are anything but jokes. Unlike his comments about blacks, they occur infrequently and reflect an anti-Semitism that seems universal rather than strictly southern. However strong southern anti-Semitism may have been, his few brief remarks tell us little about it.

It is the attitude toward blacks that resonates, illustrating an aspect of life on the Mississippi and contributing to the history of race relations. He expressed ideas held in the United States then and long after he died, and by people of intelligence, education, experience, and position that equalled and even exceeded his. At bottom to him a lower form of life, childlike, unfit for equality, capable of less than whites,

---

15. Williamson, Preface, 5.

better off as slaves with masters to look after them—blacks were shiftless ne'er-do-wells freed by a misguided policy imposed by the ignorant. He could be sympathetic, even compassionate to blacks, but still thought them inferior. To be pitied and helped, they could be liked but hardly respected. They ought to remain below whites in accord with divine will, human reason, and common sense.

In keeping with Hesse-Wartegg's beliefs, the mood of the United States, and public opinion in the region, he favored racism in a book about the South at the end of Reconstruction. True, neither he nor most Americans endorsed Pitchfork Ben Tillman's running of oratorical tines into blacks or approved the savagery of the Ku Klux Klan. His and perhaps much of America's was a genteel, paternalistic look down the nose with compassion at the lesser being. He and southerners sighed for the good old days of slavery: "Mostly, the slaveowners were kind to the darkies" and treated them "as children or as mentally incompetent adults." The slaves "loved their masters and refused to leave when freedom came."[16] (Hesse-Wartegg reported that he heard Negroes themselves wish for the same good old days.) If not prejudice, it was condescension and the message clear: blacks were inferior.

As another sign of aristocratic bias, his favorite southerner (perhaps his favorite American) was the "southern gentleman," the "human thoroughbred of the plantation regime,"[17] to use Samuel Eliot Morison's phrase. If that Olympian were gone, if the lord of white-pillared porticoes and ruler of empires of sugar and cotton and rice had been swept away on the winds of war, then the carpetbagger who aped the old-time planter would do. Indeed, by Hesse-Wartegg's measure transplanted carpetbaggers could be superior. Trying to strike northern roots in southern soil, they wanted to combine two worlds: the cultured leisure and grand hauteur of southern and Latin aristocracy with the acquisitive energy, ruthless aggressiveness, and economic productivity of the Yankee entrepreneur. When Hesse-Wartegg seems to oppose railroad interests and favor the Grangers, he does not hearken back to the Forty-Eighters and their support for liberal causes. He wants the best for economic efficiency, commercial expansion, and monetary success. His point of view is that of a European nobleman applied to the American situation. His best friend in the South was therefore Henry Clay Warmoth, late of the Union army, former northerner, owner of one of Louisiana's grandest plantations, and governor of the state.

16. Clyde Brion Davis, *The Arkansas*, 263. See also Eliza Ripley, *Social Life in Old New Orleans*, 192–96, 258, 260; William A. Percy, *Lanterns on the Levee*, 298–309; Ulrich Bonnell Phillips, *Life and Labor in the Old South*, 213–17; and "Plantations with Slave Labor and Free," 89–90.
17. Samuel Eliot Morison, *The Oxford History of the American People*, 501.

Except for his admiration of a kind of carpetbagger, Hesse-Wartegg subscribed to the "mythic view" of Reconstruction: a "tragic era" when the North unleashed upon the South a pack of villains from both sides of the Mason-Dixon line. Blacks were incompetent, he believed, yet black-white equality was forced upon the South; the region must submit to black rule in local and state government. In short, he thought the South writhed under fascist heels of Radical Republican jackboots. Corruption followed, and distress, terror, economic exploitation, and sectional subordination. Progress was arrested. Home rule (and concomitant white supremacy) being too little too late, the South remained benighted. Such was Reconstruction to Hesse-Wartegg in 1880.

The book has shortcomings that are less offensive. The attempt at comprehensiveness risks superficiality and may suggest randomness. A short time in a place, a fresh view by eyes new to it, and completion of the manuscript far from its subject can stimulate the imagination and produce vivid reportage—and mistakes. Some chronological references by Hesse-Wartegg raise questions. How is it that he seems to report the Memphis plague firsthand, whereas he suggests that the journey began months later? Why does he write as if it is February in one chapter and January later when but a few days seem to have elapsed? It must be that he traveled the South before the journey depicted here. Indeed, he may have taken no voyage the length of the lower river, but several on various parts of it, making this memoir a pastiche of visits. His title specifies *travels* or *journeys,* plural, and the preface mentions two in the South. Furthermore, he included details about the South in the earlier *Nord-Amerika,* written between 1875 and 1880. He may have set down in retrospect what he saw in the hell of the Memphis yellow-fever epidemic, as the dates and contents of the books suggest, as the fire and brimstone of his description urge, and as Mark Twain assumed.

At all events, neither the power of his prose nor the trenchancy of his reportage can be denied. What may be a pastiche amounts to a narrative portrait of the lower Mississippi. Though the first on the topic, it is not so original as comprehensive and unified. C. Vann Woodward has pointed out, "Of those [foreigners] who came South [and wrote about it], the greater number concentrated on the race question."[18] In Hesse-Wartegg's book, race is but one of a hundred topics that include the social, economic, political, cultural, and historical. Commerce, engineering, hydrology, agriculture, epidemiology, conservation, flood control, industrial technology, scenery, railroads, language, climate, sanitation, architecture, entertainment, journalism, law, and justice

---

18. Woodward, *New South,* 491.

join race relations in these pages. Hesse-Wartegg's writing on yellow fever, admired by Mark Twain, emphasizes how he treated important topics. Read him and get the latest and the best of knowledge in 1880. Accordingly, the discussion also summarizes the misguided reasoning, reports the scientific ignorance, and expresses the profound stupidity of that time. People were still burning tar and firing cannon to drive off the disease. The epidemic he witnessed was probably the last major one because he and others said that stagnant water exuded miasma and should be eliminated. They were urging the right thing for the wrong reason. The water bred the mosquito that spread the disease.

He treated a catalogue of topics, then, and many in detail, but not in the diary of a tourist. He sought not merely the sights, however significant, nor only the points of interest, however engrossing, but a panorama of the river, the valley, the people, and their way of life. Consequently, he often ignored tourist attractions, saying nothing for instance of dining in New Orleans, a magnet to visitors then as now. What might have evoked pages by another or constituted an essay in a Baedeker he passed with a line or two if mentioned at all. He wrote little on famous cathedrals in St. Louis and New Orleans. He had less to say about a monument than about the tattered Indian groveling under it. Steamboat travel on the other hand, vital to his purposes, called for exposition. Passenger sociology; crew morale; boat construction; pilotage; chances the boat might founder, run aground, or explode; the freight; the boat's looks, sounds, and smells; its place among world river craft and in the history of Mississippi navigation; steamboat-railroad competition as an economic factor—these he described and analyzed.

It followed that the *New York Times* called him a "conscientious observer" and the "careful modern reporter." He wrote "intelligently, if not profoundly, sometimes elaborately, sometimes humorously," and with "directness [of] the filth of many of the towns, their ragged black and white loafers, and insecurity of life among a rough population."[19] Much of what he wrote could be heard and read or observed as he observed it, feature by feature, item by item. But traits do not compose a portrait, nor components a whole. The genius sees what others miss and shows it to them, and they say, "Of course! Why didn't I think of that!" The lower valley seems definable if not obvious as a subject and at least as significant as any region in North America, yet others missed it. His was not only the first account but also ecumenical and balanced, and coherent because done by one mind and set forth in one work.

The *New York Times* praised Hesse-Wartegg and his books; scholars have praised them since. They remain meritorious because he rallied

---

19. "A German Traveler," *New York Times,* 30 January 1882.

to the standards of direct, accurate observation collated with what others had learned. He pushed on the public no weekender's scrapbook, recording the oohs and ahs of "now we saw this, and then we ate that." His is a study of a region, systematic and extensive, based on observation, experience, and interviews, as well as research into documents. He went to the places and told what he saw. He loved what he called "the exciting enterprise of study and observation."[20] Ignorance of English hindered some foreign travelers here. He knew the language well enough to conduct diplomacy in it. Eyewitness experience being essential but insufficient, he talked to people who knew the places, and he read up on them. Local papers told much about localities. Ignorance of German closed the largest foreign-language press to many who wrote about America. German was still the mother tongue to millions of Americans, and a bibliography of their press fills a volume.[21] As well as reading American newspapers and magazines in German, he read those in French and English and consulted the best books.

In the end let us remember but not dwell on his dark side. A child of his times and a creature of his class, he spoke accordingly. A European aristocrat unregenerate, he favored the old order (his) and a vanishing way of life (also his). He could be as archaic socially and politically as he was advanced in technology and economics. At times his analysis may be thin, his discussion scattered, his ideas reactionary, and his attitude patronizing, condescending, and prejudiced. But racial judgments and political interpretation are not his main ideas. Let us remember the erudite, perceptive, articulate observer who saw life in the Mississippi valley, and reported and interpreted it with excellence. Who else in 1880 observed dangers to the environment and realized the need for conservation? Who else foretold the rise of agribusiness before there was a word for it?

To write is to enlarge the field and sharpen the focus by choosing words for the thing discerned, thus to appreciate it more and understand it better. In this way, Hesse-Wartegg learned why Goethe exclaimed, "America, it is better with you than on our old continent!" He drew upon talent, education, and experience, and put America into words. He comprehended the immensity and the diversity, felt the loneliness, heard the hubbub, grasped a past and a present so different from Europe's, foresaw a future twinkling so various, so beautiful, so new as to dazzle the Old World. He conveyed that vision with epic sweep in a work of breadth, erudition, and insight.

20. Chapter 30 below.
21. See Karl R. J. Arndt and May E. Olson, *German American Newspapers and Periodicals, 1732–1955*.

**Travels on the
Lower Mississippi**
1879–1880

Preface

Literature on the southern states of the Mississippi valley has always been painfully inadequate. Worse, recent times have not seen a single work that depicts the part of the country so ravaged by the Civil War, the region that suffered the bloodiest battles and the worst destruction. Moreover, the South has attracted considerable attention and should be written about because its society, agriculture, and industry have lately been transformed.

The migration of Germans to Arkansas, Louisiana, and Alabama; the movement of blacks from there north; the new social status of former slaves; the position of cotton planters and the Creoles; and the entry of the Mississippi River into world commerce: those are matters that merit discussion in their own right, even apart from their broader significance. And there are many others of general interest, such as control of the "Father of Waters," the opening of its mouths to shipping, and the hideous yellow fever epidemics that repeatedly ravage the South.

Such matters caused me to travel twice during four years, each time for several months, through the southern states of the Mississippi valley and to devote myself to this book, recently updated and just finished, on what I learned in my travels. It is the one and only book exclusively about those very interesting states, an essential part of America.

Bearing fully in mind the serious nature and philosophical importance of the topics discussed, I have nonetheless deemed it practical to write in the same popular style that, in the view of the critics, helped my earlier works on America to unexpectedly great success.

Ernst v. Hesse-Wartegg
Nizza, January, 1881

I. South to the Land of Cotton

1. St. Louis

Day after day we speed from New York straightaway west. Winter submerges the lush gorgeous green of summer's prairie. Deep, steadfast snow levels everything. A million and a half square miles, enough for a nation, yet nothing but snow and ice. We race through a landscape ever the same, blanketed every inch by snow, blinding snow, and its crust of ice. Again and again we stall, stuck in a soft mountain of winter's mire. Our locomotive frees itself after hours of struggle. Sometimes the sun shines. It beams on thousands and thousands of miles of snow around us. It shimmers and glitters and blinds us hour after hour. Then we again negotiate dense clouds of snow that dim our day to twilight. The moon rises. Its pale light transfigures the night. In roomy Pullman beds we cannot sleep for noonday radiance.

The next day plays yesterday's scenes over again. The hollows are filled, the slopes leveled, the forests covered—as if somebody had spread a great white cloth. Only the cities provide the relief of remote oases in the desert of snow. We pass them with a rush.

Speeding through New York, New Jersey, Pennsylvania, Ohio, Indiana, and Illinois, each in its turn, our express brings us to the Mississippi at last.[1] We cross the "Father of Waters" on a huge, majestic bridge for trains to the capital of the Mississippi valley, St. Louis.[2] The river at our feet does not resemble an ice-covered body of water, but an elongated puddle of frozen mud—an expanse black in some places, dirty-yellow and gray in others, opaque, like dry and frozen land.

In February the metropolis of a million square miles of valley hereabouts has languished under weeks of siege by river ice. The great steamboats of the Anchor and Kountz lines lie at their wharves idle,

---

1. This journey is unlikely to have been as simple as it seems here. It probably meant traveling from New York to Chicago on the Pennsylvania Railroad and from Chicago to St. Louis on one of several lines.
2. Completed in 1874, the construction of Eads Bridge took seven years and cost $10 million. The entire bridge including approaches is 6,220 feet, or well over a mile long. In 1879, 719,178 railroad passengers crossed it, as did 186,311 freight and 3,349 stockyard cars (United States Treasury Department, *Report on the Internal Commerce of the United States*, 45–46). In addition to this bridge, Hesse-Wartegg encountered the work of engineer James B. Eads at the other extreme of his travels on the Mississippi; see chapter 29, note 5 below.

captains and pilots hibernating.[3] As long as ice grips the Mississippi, the commerce of St. Louis seems to stagnate. The sources might as well fail, the river dry up, and the city of a half-million have its Mississippi no more. The river town, the port city, becomes an inland village, landlocked, communicating with the rest of the world by railway alone.

This year the condition persisted until the beginning of February, when finally the long-desired dispatch from the hinterlands reported break-up. "*The ice-gorge begins to move*" raced along the telegraph lines beside the river, clacking in every station, rousing functionary and river dweller from winter's sleep, warning them to get ready—mobilize! At the waterfront they tie steamboats one to another and the shore with stout chains, irons as thick as the body of a man. Ferries, "*tugs*," and "*towboats*," once frozen somewhere in the river, are moved through the ice and nearer shore. The world awaits the icebergs from the North. During the night the lid blows. Ice no longer covers the river. A rise of muddy, coffee-colored water drifts south. Then we see a parapet of ice blocking the river above the bridge. It creeps closer. Thunder in the approaching mass strikes the ear like the boom of cannon. Fathom-thick slabs heave and subside, bunch up and dive apart, grind against each other like millstones, and crash and screech. Between steep, high banks the assault advances like a powerful, compact, angry mob. Huge, shifting, convulsive phalanxes reach the St. Louis bridge, rear against the massive stone piles, reshuffle themselves, and pass peaceably beneath the arches.

However colossal the icebergs, they do no harm. Old, rotten with age, they have been on the water since Christmas; they have warmed and been honeycombed and weakened. They do not hurt the steamboats but crumble against the smooth solid hulls. So they clear the harbor here, these old men of ice, and pass Carondelet, and float south in warmer water on an open river. Waves play with them, lap at them, submerge them, and bang them along rocky shores. Such sport diminishes the slabs. They shrink and keep shrinking until—where the first magnolias and oranges greet the river—the mute, resolute, stubborn, dirty-yellow Northside Gang has broken up, melted, and disappeared.

The Mississippi is open. Shipping on the West's main artery begins. Tiny vignettes of steamboats reappear at the head of announcement columns in the big dailies: steamboat X, Y, or Z will depart on such and such a day to Cairo and Cincinnati, to Memphis, Vicksburg and New Orleans—north and south, or east and west—round trips of hundreds of miles.[4] Has color dimmed and verve diminished on the

3. The Anchor Line was, strictly speaking, the St. Louis & New Orleans Anchor Line. See Leonard V. Huber, *Advertisements of Lower Mississippi River Steamboats,* 96.
4. For examples of these announcements, see Huber, *Advertisements.*

river and in the harbor at this big city since the proud, majestic bridge has been built? The European sees a scene nonetheless new to him, exotic, magnetic: dozens of palatial steamboats painted brilliant white, many little tugs, clumsy ferries of a peculiar design. On the other side of the river, grain elevators rise eight to ten stories where dirty black *"wharfboats"* tie up along shores roughly paved in stone; miles of giant warehouses, grim of outline, edge the perimeter of the broad quay opposite. Altogether a singular riverscape with thousands of figures: laborers, freight wagons, spectators, and tourists.[5]

When we look from the cathedral's tall spire, out over urban expanses, a fact strikes us as incredible. Wall after coal-smoke-blackened wall, chimneys beyond number, countless steeples—a sea of buildings, and the fathers of today's residents are supposed to have built them all! This city, one of America's oldest, continued to suffer long after the French founded it. A state of war persisted for years between the Osage Indians and the settlers. A settler could not venture very far outside the city without doing battle. The savage hordes precluded agriculture. The shortage of grain and other food prompted the French to name their settlement *"Pain Court."*[6] Accordingly, the city counted barely 1,000 citizens as late as 1788. When it passed to the United States in 1804, the population, largely French, numbered 1,500. Today, scarcely two generations later, 400,000 inhabit the largest, richest, most industrialized city in the million square miles of the Mississippi valley!

The city extends at least twelve miles along heights bounded by the Missouri, the Mississippi, and the Meramec. Many parks and gardens relieve [the expanses of urban architecture]. Thirty railways terminate in grand stations. The port of St. Louis covers more than a mile and a half of waterfront, home to steamboats that traverse a continent on thousands of miles of rivers. The old French city stood where today's business district comprises big hotels, splendid churches, and mammoth buildings of four and six stories. Little remains of the French element. A German presence of at least 150,000 has replaced it. To an extent corresponding to their numbers, they wield influence in commerce, industry, and finance. Probably Germans in no other American city cut the figure they cut here. The St. Louis German is aspiring and robust. His irrepressible conviviality, active societies, thriving

---

5. This description calls into question Twain's claim that Mississippi traffic had decreased to a sleepy fraction of its former exuberant self. See *Life on the Mississippi*, 193, 225. Unless otherwise noted, all references to *Life on the Mississippi* are from the Stormfield Edition.

6. "Pain Court," French for "short of bread," seems to have been a jab at the lack of agriculture rather than of food. Work Projects Administration, *Missouri: A Guide to the "Show Me" State*, 299.

clubs, cultivation of art and music, and diligent, able press are to be remarked even by comparison to the Anglo-American life that surrounds his.[7]

Yet St. Louis cannot be called beautiful. Of all cities in my experience, it most resembles London. I mean in situation and appearance, but in other respects too I could not better describe St. Louis than as the London of the American West. Commerce and industry in St. Louis have swelled to incredible size. No fewer than 40,000 passenger trains and 3,000 steamboats arrive each year. Produce of western prairie and output of southern plantation pour in, mounting to some 100 million hundredweights. Bituminous coal comes to about a fifth of it. Every year perhaps thirty million bushels of grain pass through the riverfront elevators, and out of it the mills grind about one and a half million barrels of flour. St. Louis, [as an international port of entry] like Chicago, Memphis, and New Orleans, has authority to collect duties on foreign imports and annually collects two or three million dollars' worth of tariffs.[8] The stockyards get 300,000 to 400,000 cattle a year and a million hogs. Cotton arrives loose and departs for New York in 80,000 to 100,000 bales. Other regions send equal amounts [of their products]. Lumber, having come on rafts from Wisconsin and the rivers of the upper Mississippi valley, piles up in hundreds of millions of board feet.

St. Louis, not only the commercial but also the industrial hub of this great valley, will become ever more industrialized. Ores occur nearby in unbelievable quantities. Neighboring Illinois and Indiana can match them with soft coal. St. Louis, now spending about $10 million to produce iron and steel, will spend ten times as much in a few years. The increase will not seem fabulous. The future of St. Louis and Missouri can be read in the fact that, despite the interruptions of war, the city nearly quadrupled its industrial output, from $27 million in 1860 to $100 million in 1870.[9] In 1870, St. Louis produced 54,000 tons of iron. Three years later the suburb of Carondelet alone produced three times as much![10]

---

7. According to Julius Chambers, *The Mississippi River and Its Wonderful Valley,* St. Louis was the "most German city in the American Republic, except Milwaukee" (294). There were 30,000 Germans before 1850: "professional men and scholars, skilled tradesmen, and cheap labor for the growing industries" (Work Projects Administration, *Missouri,* 302).

8. St. Louis collected customs only in a manner of speaking. The federal government had been collecting them since U.S. jurisdiction began, doing so in the famous custom house after 1851. See Work Projects Administration, *Missouri,* 308.

9. Prosperity and public improvement began during the Civil War and continued, despite setbacks, to 1900 and beyond (ibid., 304–5).

10. Lying south of St. Louis along the river, Carondelet became part of St. Louis

Thus the immense new wealth of the people of St. Louis. It shows in homes on the heights outside the city and in public buildings and parks. Horsecars criss-cross the city; they speed us from the grimy smoke-blackened commercial district to fashionable residential ones. There the splendor and elegance of homes—and especially their number—astound us. Street after street of them, on and on, far into the countryside. Along the routes to them, entertainment establishments crowd one another. Theaters. German clubhouses. Beer gardens.

St. Louis also has its seamy side, unfortunately the first the visitor sees. On the street or two along the river, filth flourishes and squalor prevails. Dilapidated buildings provide an apt setting for carousal that runs rampant there. St. Louis is not only the continent's foremost inland port, but also the city nearest the prairies, the Colorado mining districts, and the plains and steppes of New Mexico and Texas. At one time or another, all their riffraff visit St. Louis to spend their hard-earned money, to amuse themselves as they will be amused, and then to resume the rugged life of the frontier. In St. Louis they—together with Mississippi fishermen, mulattoes, sailors and local highwaymen—enjoy a district all their own, of infamous hotels and notorious casinos, saloons and dance halls, and houses of the lowest sort. Between Washington Avenue and Elm Street the situation gets downright horrid unless the police put a stop to dissipation. The fiend of gambling holds sway day and night. Three games of chance of the worst repute—faro, keno, poker—flourished during the slavocracy and retain their luster here and now. Fittingly, many miners, buffalo hunters, adventurers, and river pirates thus spend their time. Leading the exciting and eventful lives of vagabonds, they have long since lost touch with the better elements of the human race.

Time was, the burghers of a city easily got rid of such a district. They set it afire at the corners and burned it and its contents to the ground. Today such absolute methods are passé—unfortunately!

---

in 1871 under the city charter of 1867. It was the site of heavy industry, as Hesse-Wartegg describes it here and at the outset of chapter 3 below. See United States Department of the Interior, *Report on the Social Statistics of Cities,* 578.

2. The Mississippi Fleet

The river is the thoroughfare of St. Louis and the South. True, ice covers the river and blocks the port for the winter, the river often falls too low in summer and imperils shipping, and the river must sustain competition from a number of new railroads. Yet the river remains the most important artery of commerce in this giant nation.

Words cannot express the amount and vigor of river traffic at St. Louis. But the spectacle of what swarms over the river's broad back—hordes of cranes, barges, floating jetties, tugs, and steamboats—manifests the Mississippi's size, capacity, and significance here.

Before steam came to the river, rafts and flatboats carried everything, taking three to five months for the 1,200 miles.[1] At New Orleans they were dismantled as lumber and wood. Passenger boats now go between the river's two big cities within eight days.[2]

Today every sort of river craft anchors at the "levee"—*every* sort:[3]

- Powerful flat-bottomed Red River packets. Almost as big as the steamboats, they make their way via Louisiana to Arkansas and Texas.
- Small and fast passenger steamers of the upper Mississippi and the Missouri. They pierce Nebraska and Dakota, and penetrate the northwest of this huge continent.
- Big "*sternwheelers*" from Pennsylvania. Out of Pittsburgh, they have come hundreds of miles from home, via Cincinnati.
- Steam-powered cotton transports from the rivers of Tennessee and Arkansas.

---

1. "At the turn of the eighteenth century," flatboats "dominated the river trade." As late as 1830, 3,000 descended the river annually (Hodding Carter, *Lower Mississippi*, 215).
2. Running time between New Orleans and St. Louis was well within the eight days claimed by Hesse-Wartegg. Boats made the trip upstream to St. Louis and even Cincinnati in five to seven days. In the race between the *Robert E. Lee* and the *Natchez* in 1870, which excited "interest throughout the civilized world," the *Lee* reached St. Louis three days, eighteen hours, and thirty minutes out of New Orleans (John H. Morrison, *History of American Steam Navigation*, 247, 250, 252). See chapter 11, note 15 below for more on this race.
3. Cf. Twain, *Life on the Mississippi*, 87.

- Colossal, dusky barges, in long columns, bearing ore and coal from Illinois.
- Finally, the multitude of rafts and their thousands of logs, scattered at anchor about the river. From the bridge they look like chips afloat down there.

Altogether a diverse flotilla has massed: boats by the hundreds. Yet they practically disappear beside the river itself, sweeping high and wide among them.

The river's largest ports [if reckoned by the numbers of steamboats that call them home] include St. Louis (160 boats carrying 65,000 tons) and New Orleans (140 boats and 30,000 tons, plus 20 oceangoing steamships, 15,000 tons). Cincinnati and Pittsburgh on the Ohio [taken together] have 165 and 40,000. Smaller ports—such as Louisville, Cairo, Memphis, Vicksburg, Nashville and others—are each home for 25 to 60 boats.

The Southern Transportation Line is the most important firm working the river between Cincinnati and New Orleans.[4] In St. Louis the most important are the Anchor and the Kountz lines (passengers) and the Mississippi Valley and the Lowey transportation companies (freight).[5] Mississippi Valley's six *"towboats"* propel the company's fifty barges, each 200 feet long, 34 feet wide, and 6 feet in draft, able to take 30,000 to 50,000 bushels of grain at a load. In 1878 they moved five million bushels from St. Louis to New Orleans.[6] (On that route, many a coal barge is so big it covers ten acres!) Other firms in each Mississippi shipping town work their local rivers [Mississippi tributaries]. Therefore, the valley has been united into nothing less than one riverboat network that includes every state between the Allegheny Mountains and the Rockies, with Pittsburgh, St. Louis, and New Orleans as chief ports.

About 1,200 steamers with their quarter-million tons of capacity, and 1,000 barges with their 200,000 tons, ply the rivers in the valley of the "Father of Waters." Mississippi shipping therefore approaches half the capacity of the German merchant marine in four times as many steam-powered vessels! Indeed the boatbuilders of Jeffersonville, Indiana, and of Louisville and Cincinnati launch 100 to 150 vessels a year,

4. Probably the Cincinnati & New Orleans Southern Transportation Company. See Huber, *Advertisements*, 96.
5. The Anchor Line is probably the St. Louis & New Orleans Anchor Line. Huber does not list the Kountz, Mississippi Valley, and Lowey Companies. See Huber, *Advertisements*, 96.
6. The Mississippi Valley Transportation Company, the "Barge Line," "pioneered in the bulk grain trade from St. Louis to New Orleans." By 1881 it had thirteen towboats and ninety-eight barges and could move three million bushels a month (Louis C. Hunter, *Steamboats on the Western Rivers*, 573, 635).

with a total capacity of 15,000 to 30,000 tons.[7] A bizarre statistic may suggest the number of voyages undertaken in the valley. Boilers explode, fires rage, boats sink or run aground, and the number of these accidents total 500 annually![8]

Anchor Line operates the largest and most beautiful of the steamers, no doubt about it. Flat-bottomed and drawing but a few feet (dictated by the shallows), they look bigger than the biggest liners out of Southampton for the East Indies. They look bigger; they *are* bigger. The *Great Republic,* the *Robert E. Lee,* the *Richardson,* and several others would cover a Prussian morgen [about three-fourths of an acre].[9] Yet those Mississippi boats barely exceed the *Golden City,* the *Golden Rule,* and the *Golden Hour,* the Ohio's giants. These jumbos accommodate 500 to 1,000 passengers each. The *Golden Rule* even edits and prints its own newspaper on board, also called the *Golden Rule.* A crew consists of captain, purser, two pilots, a few engineers, thirty to forty "*hands*" or Negroes who load and unload the cargo, and that is all.[10] In other words, the seaman in the maritime sense does not exist on a riverboat. (A seaman has no place on a vessel without masts, and where pilots and engineers work the machinery of steering.) Boats are made of nothing but wood to increase buoyancy and reduce draft. What fits them to negotiate the shallows also exposes them to fire. They are firetraps.[11]

---

7. Many of the largest and finest steamboats of the era were built in Jeffersonville (ibid., 107). Though less known than shipbuilders of Cincinnati and Louisville, Howard Shipyards of Jeffersonville "built many of the Mississippi River packets of the early days" (Work Projects Administration, *Indiana: A Guide to the Hoosier State,* 393).

8. The careers of Mississippi steamers hardly averaged four years (Phillips, *Life and Labor in the Old South,* 149). For a "list of accidents on Western waters during the years 1886 and 1887" (about 150, groundings excluded), see U.S. Treasury Department, *Report on Commerce,* 104–7. Since Hesse-Wartegg includes groundings, it is hard to compare his figure to those which are less inclusive. One report cites 618 losses on western rivers "from the introduction of steam to the close of 1848" (Fred E. Dayton, *Steamboat Days,* 345–46; see also 341–45).

9. Hesse-Wartegg confuses the *Great Republic,* at 1,727 tons the largest boat of its type when constructed in 1867, with the *Grand Republic,* which was built in 1876 and displaced 2,600 tons. They are easily confused: the *Grand Republic* was the *Great Republic* enlarged and refitted. See Walter Havighurst, *Voices on the River: The Story of the Mississippi Waterways,* 199. The *Grand Republic* and the *J. M. White* set the standard for the largest class of steamboats. Though huge, these boats did not cover three-fourths of an acre (over 32,000 square feet). The *Robert E. Lee* (315 feet by 48.5 feet) covered a little more than 15,000 square feet. See Hunter, *Steamboats,* 608, and Morrison, *Steam Navigation,* 261.

10. Cf. Twain, *Life on the Mississippi,* 53.

11. Fires destroyed boats more frequently than explosions did; "wooden superstructures and hulls and the cotton cargoes were quick to ignite" (Carter, *Lower Mississippi,* 223). Unfortunately, "Steamers can not be built with boilers and fire-room far below the water-line and removed from the vicinity of an inflammable cargo, as

The *Great Republic,* for example, the world's largest riverboat, caught like tinder and burned to the waterline three times within a few years. The owners rebuilt it each time.

A problem challenged the designer of the Mississippi steamboat. Passengers must be comfortable amid gross and nasty freight. He solved it by designing the most practical and beautiful conveyance afloat in the world. Members of the crew occupy the lowest deck, together with animals, stacks of cargo, greasy barrels of oil, dripping barrels of molasses, oily machinery, coal, and hides. The engine and boilers of the colossus reside on this level. Provided with iron supports but without housing, this machinery can be readily seen between an empty boat's pillars and struts. Every boat carries a gangplank. Another steam engine, the small one called a "nigger," raises and lowers it.[12] All the lowest deck from the engine outward serves as cargo space for baled cotton and the various other freight. Six thousand bales can be stacked there.[13] Yet this mess is so well hidden, so separate from passengers, that one rarely suspects freight and never gets a whiff of the odors so redolent on most oceangoing steamers. Cleopatra's barge could not have been more cheerful, more luxurious, or more elegant than the Mississippi's waterborne palaces.

They are majestic, these grand steamboats. Approaching from a distance, one of them suggests a mosque taking shape against the blue of a southern sky, a floating mosque with tall slim minarets. It boggles the imagination, this floating, glittering palace in scintillating white, this phantasmagoria. As for the dozen together at St. Louis now—what a spectacle!

Imagine a three- or four-story structure, each story shorter and narrower than the one below, leaving room for the four levels of encircling deck. This wooden pyramid, 300 feet long by 100 high, rises from a keel that projects fore and aft, adding considerable open deck at the lowest level. The reception hall of this public mansion is the saloon, a large room on the second deck that extends from one end of the boat to the other. What could be more sumptuous than its soft carpets, satin-covered furniture, library, piano, buffet, and the like? Cabins along

---

in the case of ocean steamers. . . . The wonder is that loss by fire is not tenfold what it has proved to be during the last few years" (U.S. Treasury Department, *Report on Commerce,* 108).

12. These small hoisting engines, standard equipment on most steamboats, were also called "mickeys" (Hunter, *Steamboats,* 454). On *nigger* in this sense, see Mathews, *Dictionary,* 2:1117.

13. This was beyond the usual capacity for 1879 and must have been near the maximum. See Havighurst, *Voices,* 140–41. The *J. M. White* might have loaded 10,000 bales; when it exploded and burned it was carrying 3,500 bales, 8,000 sacks of cottonseed, and 200 pounds of oil (142).

either side open into the saloon or onto the outer deck. Each cabin has two or three berths, one above the other. On the *Great Republic* the grand hall also serves for dining. Just how big is it? Well, if you walk up and down six times [three times around], you will cover half a mile![14] Every boat offers one or two cabins done in princely luxury, the so-called "*bridal chambres.*"[15] A broad, open verandah circles the saloon and the cabins, and also goes around the purser's office at one end [of the boat] and the passenger kitchen at the other end. Usually the food cannot be praised.

Captain, stewards, and pilots occupy the third level. The hurricane deck is up there, too, its floor the ceiling of the saloon.

Finally, at the top is the glassed-in pilothouse, which is about fifty feet above the water. There is the giant wheel. There are the handles and levers for stopping the boat, for giving signals, and for other operations. In front of the pilothouse and to either side, the two smokestacks thrust dragon-toothed mouths into the air. In bow and stern, tall staffs and long poles for lanterns and flags also rise above the superstructure.

In short, riverboats would be perfect in every part, only they unfortunately incline to explosions in the boilers and devastation by fire.[16]

Relaxing on the hurricane deck of the *Vicksburg,* we watch the usual bedlam that greets a steamer. The black, rough-hewn "wharfboat," nothing more than a waterborne warehouse when tied-up ashore, brings cargo from the levee. "*Spring goods*" [so called because needed now] so cram that jerry-built freight-floater that we think the rickety roof ought to have been lifted up and off. Dozens of ragged Negroes rush about. They roll barrels of flour at us with astonishing ease and grace. The barrels will be unloaded at small places along the river, at southern cotton and sugar plantations. Other Negroes bring on their shoulders

---

14. This walk would cover the 300-foot length 12 times, a total of 3,600 feet.

15. The forty-eight bridal chambers of the *Eclipse* helped make it "the most decorative packet of the fifties," when "great main cabins, or lounges, resembled the ornate lobbies of metropolitan hotels, heavily carpeted, glowing with brilliant cut-glass chandeliers, hung with oil paintings on the outer doors of each stateroom," and with "dining rooms [that] boasted of 24 stewards and 13 desserts" (Carter, *Lower Mississippi,* 228). See also George Ward Nichols, "Down the Mississippi," 835; and Coleman O. Parsons, "Steamboating as Seen by Passengers and River Men, 1875–1884," 23–27.

16. "Explosions, as may naturally be supposed, are of very frequent occurrence." Thus "no one who is at all acquainted with the steam engine, can examine the machinery of one of those vessels, and the manner in which it is managed, without shuddering at the idea of the great risk to which all on board are every moment exposed" (Morrison, *Steam Navigation,* 222, 223). Dramatic in suddenness and devastating in force, explosions "held a morbid fascination for the public" and "outranked every other class of steamboat accidents" (Hunter, *Steamboats,* 282).

the farm implements that industrial St. Louis sends to the agricultural areas and newly settled lands of Kansas, Tennessee and Arkansas: plows, wheelbarrows, shovels. These things constitute most of what southbound steamers carry, together with tools and various household appliances—in short, all the commodities for life and work downriver. In fall and winter, boats will return with sugar and cotton from the plantations, upriver to St. Louis.

Our boat settles lower into the currents. Yet the ragged, sweaty Negroes load and load. The boat's belly has already engorged 1,500 tons! More, therefore, than some transatlantic ships can take! Half, though, of what this behemoth wants! An iota of what this monster river can carry!

"Wasp," our chief mate, so shouts and curses and drives the Ethiopians to their task that they fling themselves back and forth like madmen.[17] On the wharfboat the mountain of cargo shrinks like butter melting in the hand. The picturesque sight of these stevedores, or roustabouts (they are flat-nosed and as black as ravens), must delight any painter and sadden any humanitarian. Let us have a closer look at one of the dusky gentlemen. What at a distance looks like a parody of Burnam Wood, a lively bundle of rags with some spots of brilliant white, turns out to be a human being marked by the whites of the eyes and the double row of teeth. The back is crooked, the head bends forward, and the hands tremble at the sides. The clothing consists of loose rags, dangling where they please. A hat riddled with holes, dirty, brimless, huddles on the black, dusty wool of the head. As for the feet, our "*darkey*" probably found those remnants of shoes in a gutter years ago. A crust of dirt covers the face, neck, and hands: the skin looks like an alligator's. Behold a consequence of the Civil War! Look upon the Freed Man, the liberated Negro, the white man's equal at the ballot box and before the law! See what freedom has given him![18]

He and hundreds of other stevedores work for a contractor hired by the steamboat companies to load and unload. The contractor pays him a dollar a day, and he regularly hands it to the "*barkeeper*" for drinks. Europeans reckon a dollar a lot of money, about equal to five francs. But here in the West, dollar and franc stand at nearly one to one.[19] With this pittance these Ethiopians are to get clothing and shelter,

17. Mates could be rude, brutal, and insolent; they often drove men with curses and sticks or canes (Hunter, *Steamboats,* 458).
18. Hesse-Wartegg held, with many whites and some Negroes of his time, that the Negro had been better off under slavery.
19. The implication is that the West was experiencing runaway inflation, perhaps the last of that following the Civil War. But Hesse-Wartegg's assessment seems excessive. See *Concise Dictionary of American History,* s.v. "inflation."

support a wife and raise children—in a word they are to be *human*! Is it any wonder that herculean men, so well cared-for by planters in the slavocracy, have been reduced to misery and lack even a roof over their heads? Or that Negro women, forced to fend for themselves but too lazy to work, try to get their bread in easier but shameful ways? And that no children are born or, if born, are let live but grudgingly?

Loading continues in the flicker of "*torchbaskets*." We have moved from the cobbled riverfront of St. Louis to the giant elevators of East St. Louis. The "*roustabouts*" carry sack after sack into the cargo space of our bottom deck. They ease the travail by singing their exotic songs. At work early this morning, they work now at midnight, as doggedly now as then—all for a dollar![20]

Loading is done at last. Smoky torches had cast the scene in Rembrandtian half-light. They are put out and it gives way to darkness. A blast on our steam whistle roars and echoes the length of the valley, like the extended boom of a cannon. Softly, almost imperceptibly, we glide away downriver.

---

20. Hesse-Wartegg here seems to contradict his assertion of Negro laziness in the prior paragraph. Another racist called "the old-fashioned prime Negro . . . at his best" on a Mississippi steamboat: "chaffing and chattering, singing and swinging, lusty and willing freight handlers, whom a river captain plying out of New Orleans has called the noblest black men that God ever made." They rested and slept "only between landings" and carried loads "almost at running speed" (Ulrich Bonnell Phillips, *American Negro Slavery*, 292–93).

3. Southward Bound!

St. Louis from a steamboat at night looks anything but beautiful. Black smoke cloaks the city to the last precinct, wrapping everything in a gloom of profound depths, striking a fierce contrast to the clear, bright sky above.[1] The long rows of lights, burning in windows and illuminating stores—many lights, many windows, many stores—only sharpen the contrast between the heavens and the pollution. The city resembles a giant bed of coals, spewing smoke while glare and fire rage within. Gliding downstream, we glance into streets that end at the river—long, dim streets speckled with a few lamps. Finally, we pass them, too. But romance continues, the dusky romance of this voyage down the Mississippi at night.

As one city seemed wrapped in smoke, so a counterpart appears ablaze. Every flue, every door, every window, every last crack radiates incandescence. Cones of fire reach for the heavens. Colored according to the metal being smelted—scarlet, orange, bright green, violet, bluish white, blinding white—they cast a rainbow in those lurid tones across enormous smokestacks, and the stacks in turn thrust their big, bold features toward the city on the hills behind them.

We are looking at Carondelet.[2] Passing it like this on our journey downriver, we see only the city's fabulous exterior. But we paid it a visit earlier; we know its industrial significance. Furnaces abound. Dozens of mills crowd one after another. In those vast interiors, thousands of Cyclopes toil half-naked at smelters, rollers, steam hammers, and foundries, day in, day out, and night after night. In the early days, along the small Rivière des Pères, pious friars established their Catholic mission to the Osages.[3] Yet [after all those quiet years] the little waterway has seen these monstrous works take shape almost entirely since the recent war.

Carondelet's lights, the last to brighten the valley for us this night,

---

1. "I am sure there is not as much smoke in St. Louis now [1883] as there used to be. The smoke used to bank itself in a dense billowy black canopy over the town, and hide the sky from view. This shelter is very much thinner now; still, there is a sufficiency of smoke there, I think" (Twain, *Life on the Mississippi,* 191).
2. See chapter 1, note 10 above.
3. The Jesuit Mission of St. Francis Xavier, established in 1700.

fade in the distance and disappear. We have entered the wilderness of land and water that stretches from Rivière des Perès along the Father of Waters and reaches far below the mouth of the Yazoo.

We cruise downriver, tree trunks and blocks of ice our only companions. The whole night, passing Ste. Genevieve and all the way to Cape Girardeau, we meet no steamboats, not a boat of any kind.[4] The river seems to me as lonely and forsaken as it must have seemed to DeSoto, the man who discovered it. We steer amid numerous sandbars and among shallows—straight up to Cape Girardeau, the first town of some size. A row of substantial houses face the river and look down from steep banks. The banks have been melting like sugar into the river.[5] We approach the stone wharf and the *Ste. Genevieve.* So here is the only stone wharf on the 1,250 miles between St. Louis and New Orleans, a nonesuch, and beside it the steamboat named for the holy French nun. Our boat glides with divine grace between them. Incredible how the pilots in their crow's nest land us with confident ease: they swing us athwart the current and bring us to rest against the wharf.

The harbor at Cape Girardeau begins and ends with this wharf, 100-or-so paces of stone. The floating lady who preceded us has unloaded and piled on the steep slopes hundreds of barrels, washtubs, household appliances, and farm tools. We carry identical cargo for this destination. The plank has been dangling from our booms.[6] Our Negro crew stand in the bow, ready to unload. A bell rings; the plank lowers. No sooner has it touched than the black fellows leap diabolically to the wharf. They swarm like locusts upon pyramids of barreled flour and stacks of wood, and in a jiffy reduce them to nothing. One group carries boxes and assorted cargo ashore while another rolls barrels down the incline and aboard. The Negroes move the barrels with such speed and aplomb that we cannot tell them apart, Negroes from barrels. They alternate, Negro-barrel-Negro-barrel-Negro-barrel, descending the slope, barrels tumbling in an insane rush. Yet, no matter how fast they go, the drivers keep their vehicles under control, steering them with a push of the hand at one end or the other.

Here as at every such point, *"Mississippi loafers"* have assembled to watch lazily this dynamic drama. Indeed, for all inhabitants of these towns—or in river jargon, *"river landings"*—the arrival of the steam-

---

4. Ste. Genevieve is about 60 miles and Cape Girardeau about 150 miles below St. Louis.

5. At the town the banks are at least in part a rock ledge and should not have been subject to the degree of erosion implied here. See Work Projects Administration, *Missouri,* 199.

6. Booms may also be called spars. See Twain, *Life on the Mississippi,* 146.

boat is the day's event, or the week's.[7] Before an arrival and after departure, time drags. A town, desolate. A few clerks or shopkeepers at their doors, leaning back in their chairs with feet braced against a neighbor's chair, or in some other improbable position. Workmen dozing in the shade of the little pile of goods at the levee. Not a person in the street. The only sound is a ripple of wavelets breaking along the shore of the calm river. Across the majestic Mississippi, a forest covers the opposite shore. Above and below the town, the river disappears around bends, or "*points*."[8] At last, above a point, we see the smoke of a steamboat. A Negro, spying it, shouts: "*Steamboat coming!*" The scene explodes. Sleepers wake, the town wakes. Everybody hustles, everything bustles. People bestir to meet the boat. It lands and . . . but we have seen what happens when it lands.

We would rather go up and visit the town while they load and unload down at the waterfront. In Cape Girardeau—the name betrays French roots—we find little more than a settlement, in other words a large village in its tenderest years: streets unpaved and muddy, cut and furrowed by creeks that form in the rain, and houses not in rows but scattered sporadically to either side of a street. An occasional house of brick interjects luxury amid a picturesque array and disarray of wood houses. Brick or wood, all hug the ground as if the earnest builders feared earthquakes at any moment. The inevitable newspaper office identifies itself in big bold letters: *Democrat*. The practical eye peering through thin whitewash can read another word in equal letters underneath: *Republican*. (The editor proves himself a timeserver. To him politics and masthead mean no more than the stroke of a brush.) Several shops near the *Democrat* sell saddles and other tack, trunks, rubber coats, and the paraphernalia of "*general outfitting*." Finally, the everlasting newsstand, with *Frank Leslie's, Harper's,* the shameless *Police Gazette* and the *Police News,* along with *Under the Gaslight* and *Criminal News:* the chaste, demure journals that pour out of New York and flood

---

7. "In our town the *Pargo* landed regularly on Sunday, usually between eleven o'clock and noon. Everybody would be at church, but when she blew, the male members of the congregation to a man would rise and, in spite of indignant glares from their wives and giggles from the choir, make their exits, with a severe air of business just remembered. With the *Pargo* came the week's mail and gossip of the river-front from St. Louis to New Orleans and rumors from the very distant outside world" (Percy, *Lanterns,* 5). Hesse-Wartegg's description of the arrival of a steamboat in the rest of this paragraph must have been taken from the first installment of Twain's "Old Times on the Mississippi," which appeared in the *Atlantic,* January 1875, and later in chapter 4 of *Life on the Mississippi*.

8. Bends and points are not identical. *Bend* refers to the turn of the river, *point* to the land thus left sticking out. See Twain, *Life on the Mississippi,* 63–66.

the nation.[9] They—yes, these very ones—sell like hotcakes in the South. Remarkably, they find there a more avid audience than in the West. But Girardeau's *"leading store,"* the *"Ladies Fancy Store,"* displays its wares in an ingenious composition of stockings, corsets, and chignons in every color. The proprietors try to tempt a female clientele with this exhibit of trophies that resembles a showcase of military panache.

Cities begin thus in all the West. Culture can take hold and thrive only after settlers have secured their homes and established prosperous business. Pioneering, always and everywhere the hardest part of settlement, means every man for himself and no care for neighbor or the general welfare. With time comes organization into municipalities: officials, taxes, and concern about the community. Such things must happen in Cape Girardeau, too.

---

9. *Harper's* and any of Leslie's titles were family fare and not in a class with the sensationalistic *Police Gazette* and *Police News*. See Frank Luther Mott, *A History of American Magazines*. Mott does not mention *Under the Gaslight* and *Criminal News*.

4. Cairo and the Ohio River

The closer we got to the tip of Illinois, the less the pilots worried about sandbars and snags. We went straight downriver. The current seemed to slow gradually, creeping at last to a halt. Then—and no less true because only the pilots could perceive it—the normal flow yielded here and there to another that opposed us. It ran *upstream*. What was it that could bring to a standstill and then reverse the Father of Waters himself?

He submits twice to tributaries, his disobedient children, here the Ohio and [to the north] the Missouri. Deluges off the Alleghenies had swelled the Ohio to rare depths. After flooding the region below the mouth of the Tennessee, the Ohio struck its parent's flank with a force to block and overpower the Great River. Indeed, the Ohio created the reverse current by imposing itself upon the Mississippi and running over it in the opposite direction.

Cairo stands at the confluence of the two mighty streams, Mississippi and Ohio.[1] We lay twenty-four hours at the muddy waterfront. Is this the transatlantic namesake of the residence of the pharaohs? We could not have stopped anywhere more miserable, more desolate, more wretched on the Mississippi. Zealous boosters of America predict a bright future for Cairo because of its uniquely favorable position at the juncture of the country's chief rivers.[2] But he who has seen Cairo will blink at such stargazing. Successful at business—three Illinois railroads terminate here, delivering freight for transshipment, and we spent twenty-four hours loading our share of it—Cairo nonetheless presents one of the gloomiest and most deplorable aspects of any city on earth, if it can be said to be on earth.[3]

---

1. "Some say that [the Mississippi's] beauty ends where the blueness of the Ohio is drowned at Cairo in the green and yellow and brown of its merging" (Carter, *Lower Mississippi*, 5). "The Mississippi . . . changes sex at Cairo" from the svelte upper, feminine, to the "broad brute" of the lower, masculine (Willard Price, "The Lower Mississippi," 681).

2. "In many respects this is the most remarkable water center on the earth," located on the vast watershed where it can receive by rail as well as by water half a continent's raw materials, and being favorably "situated for the purposes of manufacture," disburse commodities to the other half at the finest harbor "on any stream in the United States" (U.S. Treasury Department, *Report on Commerce,* 89–90).

3. The railroads were the Illinois Central; Mobile & Ohio; and Cleveland, Cin-

At high water embankments hold the streets above the surrounding swamps: a checkerboard skeleton of a city seems afloat. Down in the enclosed squares, people are to build houses on so-called "*lots*." The muddy squares and all the myriad rubbish and filth that litter them lie below the level of the Ohio; only a few squares have buildings on them; and it must amaze the observer that the Ohio has not carried them off. You see poverty wherever you look. Muck and filth foul the streets a foot deep. Horses and wagons get stuck everywhere.[4] At the riverfront I despaired of fording the first street. I'd never reach the wooden sidewalk over there; I'd never survive the quagmire. A Negro, a loafer on my side of the obstacle, wore enormous boots as if his feet had been equipped for prevailing conditions. I asked whether, if I gave him a "*nickel*," he would loaf on the other side. He showed me his superb teeth in a grin. "*All right, sir. All the same to me.*" He ambled through the sea of muck, sinking to the knees. I followed hot at his heels, stepping carefully into the holes he left behind. I reached the far shore safe and sound.

Cairo exists only because three important railroads cross the river here. Cairo's income therefore consists mostly of what little originates in transshipment—shifting freight from railroad to steamboat and steamboat to railroad—and of the pittance for repairs to rolling stock and steamboats, and their outfits and equipment. Repair appears to be Cairo's passion. You see smithies and machine shops everywhere, mending old iron in this Vulcan of cities. Cairo fixes everything except what needs fixing most: itself.

This "city" is nothing more than one long row of buildings and a few shacks and brick affairs on side streets. Trains of dozens of cars run along the streets; stations are on the outskirts. Pedestrians must be careful at crossings not to be knocked down and crushed by one loco-

---

cinnati, Chicago & St. Louis (Work Projects Administration, *Illinois: A Descriptive and Historical Guide,* 169). Cairo was a community that failed after "great claims for its future" (Herman R. Lantz, *A Community in Search of Itself: A Case Study of Cairo, Illinois,* 3; see also 1). "A more disheartening place I never beheld than this same Cairo, which, from its location at the junction of the Ohio and Mississippi rivers, many people professed to believe would become a large city. I would not like to prophesy as to its future beyond that of a third-class graveyard" (Nichols, "Down the Mississippi," 839).

4. Cairo "is the vilest hole above-ground, if the streets formed by introducing foreign soil can be said to be above-ground; for the open lots formed by the streets were partially filled with water covered with green scum, and which was also the receptacle for offal, dead animals, and other offensive refuse. Turn which way you would the sight was unspeakably disgusting. The streets were knee-deep in mud, and it seemed impossible to transact business upon them when horses and wagons were required" (Nichols, "Down the Mississippi," 839).

motive or another. Every station posts the same signs, either "*BE-WARE OF CONFIDENCE MEN*" or "*DO NOT LEND YOUR MON-EY TO STRANGERS.*"

Cairo alleges 8,000 inhabitants, has 4,000 (Winter, 1879). Half seem to be Negroes. They do the work of the waterfront and therefore live nearby, on Front Street. "Homes" in this sense means a few miserable shacks on swampy blocks, shingles whitewashed, bearing signs. "*BOARDING HOUSE.*" "*BOARD AND LODGING.*" These places could also be called coffins for the living. One even advertised "*ROOM FOR ALL.*" Ironic yet true, as this black hostelry had not one guest.

Half of Front Street's houses boast eateries or "*restaurants*" for "*coloured gentlemen.*" When you walk through this beautiful neighborhood, the treat to your nose rivals what wafts to the innocent who strolls past the soggy blocks described above. Windows appetizingly display "*apple pies,*" boiled onions, tomatoes, old sausages, and even older hams studded with spikelets of seasoning like nails in the heel of a boot. The ancient Negress grinned at me: "*To make it spicy.*"

These establishments enjoyed no run of customers during our visit. The proprietors stood at the doors, smoking, chewing, or whittling at that obligatory little piece of wood.

"It must be quite unhealthy here in the summer," I said to one.

"*Not at all, sir,*" he replied indignantly. "No fever or cholera here, ever. One of the healthiest places on the whole river, sir. *Bound to be a big city, sir.*"

The good man proclaimed a healthy city while his face reported the city's health. Yellow skin, sunken eyes, and hollow cheeks spoke plainly. Besides, on every wall, every board, giant signs advertise CHILLS AND FEVER MEDICINE—JONES FEVER CURE—QUININE PILLS—FEVER DROPS, etc.[5]

In every small town of the South and West, shopkeepers use painted signs and carved wooden figures to lure customers. Shopkeepers here try to tempt their black clientele likewise. Here, as everywhere else, the decoys are individualistic and ludicrous. The typical tobacco-shop soldier or cigar-store Indian appears in nothing but flat profile, sawed out of a board and painted. On signs with the names of shops, representations of the merchandise often appear: fruit, say, or clothing, luggage, or tools. Few painters in Cairo have learned their art in school. So if you try to visualize these works, let fancy run; they exceed its every stretch.

Cairo has also been original with boats. I mean the "*snag boats,*" a

---

5. Except *Quinine,* Hesse-Wartegg has the signs in English.

pair so unusual they must be unique.[6] The city built them, and they operate out of here. They deal with trees that—uprooted, limbs stripped by ice—float downstream in the spring. Often these tramps establish themselves in the shallows and become snags. Outspread roots in soft sand, trunks pointed downstream, underwater, they pose a lethal hazard to shipping. Everyone knows how the hundreds of Mississippi and Ohio steamboats have to fear the ugly customers. Pilots carefully record snag positions in so-called "*snagbooks*," and steamboats carefully avoid the peril.[7] In midsummer, river at nadir, most snags show their crowns above water. The snagboats take action.

They are of singular design.[8] Few people have heard of them. Each is itself two boats, being two long narrow hulls fastened together with iron-reinforced beams. Two paddle wheels, one outside each hull, propel a "double boat." Away it goes in midsummer, hunting for snags, as I have said. Finding one, the boat rams it again and again, to free the roots. Then a two-armed, steam-powered crane hoists the snag by chains put under the head. The snag dangles, the crane swings it onto the ironbound crossbeams. There the crew saws off the heavy, dangerous fan of roots. It sinks of its own weight. Nothing to detain the trunk, the current carries it off. The boats do first-rate work.

As a rule the procedure is simple and easy, like the routine pulling of a tooth. The snagboat captains consult snagbooks, learn where pilots have spotted snags, and during the summer can readily pull whatever teeth the Old Man has sprouted during the spring.[9]

It took all evening and all night to bring our cargo aboard. Machines (steam-powered cranes) move every ounce of loads into ocean-going ships far smaller than our riverboat. Yet Mississippi and Ohio boats lack such equipment. Each carries forty or fifty Negroes to do

---

6. Henry Miller Shreve (1785–1851), Superintendent of Western River Improvement, perfected the snag boat. With it he cleared snags between Cairo and St. Louis fifty years before Hesse-Wartegg marveled at it. See Florence Dorsey, *Master of the Mississippi: Henry M. Shreve*, 146–54, and Havighurst, *Voices*, 71–72. Twain mentions "snag-boats" in *Life on the Mississippi*, 232.

7. "Every pilot makes a diary of his experiences and observations, and leaves his record at the next port for the benefit of the next to go over that course. . . . Sometimes so marked and unsafe is the alteration or obstruction that a telegram is sent to the following boat" (U.S. Treasury Department, *Report on Commerce*, 95).

8. These boats seem to have been a variation of the machine boat, which was designed by S. H. Long of the Topographical Engineers and perfected and patented by Shreve. Hesse-Wartegg's description fits Shreve's, except that Shreve's did not have outside paddle wheels. See Hunter, *Steamboats*, 193–95.

9. Shreve heard French boatmen call snags *chicots:* teeth. Shreve's boats would be "Uncle Sam's tooth-pullers." See Havighurst, *Voices*, 68, and Hunter, *Steamboats*, 194. Twain also spoke of "pulling the river's teeth" (*Life on the Mississippi*, 232).

what machines might do. Riverboats accordingly load slower no doubt, but therefore safer and better.

The Ohio meanwhile could be viewed in all its magnificence. I must confess, no river in the world has made a deeper or grander impression on me.[10] An expanse of water, an ocean, seemed to be rolling my way; and a forest, about the same size, appeared to float with it. In fact, the river—so wide the *Great Eastern* could easily turn around in it—had bloated until the bed looked too small for such excess, as if the flood had brimmed and bulged to a convex surface.[11] Limbs and trunks of trees of the most colossal size, together with logs, lumber, and other wood, crowded and covered the water. Ousted from the forests of the Monongahela or the Allegheny, ripped out and torn away by a river, they swam and swarmed in a mad rush past us. We saw this forested river when we arrived in the evening. We saw it next morning. Yet when we expressed astonishment to the pilot, he laughed. "Forests don't float by here for days—they float by for weeks!" Where do they come from, these legions of wood, these gigantic trees, these limbs and the underbrush? The Ohio appears to have overflowed timberlands, and uprooted and swept away every stick!

We descended the Mississippi, reached Memphis, and the hordes had disappeared. Nothing but a few trunks now. All the rest, what happened to them? To all that wood? It had been pulled gradually from the mainstream. Where the river twists and bends, it induces whirls, becoming eddies behind the turns. A whirl swings wood into its depths, and the eddies take it. In the eddies (pools that rotate independently of the mainstream) it floats, rotating too in its own harbor. In time it disappears. Sandbars and low islands also catch part of it, collect it, pile it into small mountains. I saw them. A picture of hideous destruction but at the same time an illustration of the power of water.

---

10. A considerable statement from a traveler who had seen many a river and all the great ones.

11. The British *Great Eastern*, 693 feet long and 82 feet wide, was "the world's largest ship up to its time" (*Concise Dictionary of American History*, s.v. "Great Eastern").

5. River Vignettes

One night we drifted along a lazy Mississippi toward the sunny South. The moon obliged with enough light for pilots. Everyone else saw only a ghostly riverscape, dim and mysterious, as if the moon did not so much illuminate as cast a veil over it.[1] I was up in the tiny pilothouse. Anxiously the pilots studied the surface of the water and monitored the progress of our large and loaded steamboat. A dangerous "piece of river" extends from St. Louis to the mouth of the Ohio and beyond, even to New Orleans. Feminine monsters like those of the Lorelei imperil every inch of this river, except they are neither so young nor so pretty, and they wreck the sailor without siren songs or other poetic compensation.[2] Our Mississippi sailor also has a crowd of passengers to worry about and hundreds of tons of cargo: a situation of greater risk and more serious consequences than Heinrich Heine could have imagined when he sang of the Lorelei. Besides, the romance of his beautiful poem would never have survived the steamboats, cotton bales, and Negro deckhands.

So far forward in the bow as to crowd the unguarded edge of the deck, a scant two feet above the turbid water, the "*leadman*" stood watch with his weight.[3] In monotones he shouted the depths to the watch on the hurricane deck. Louder but equally monotoned the deck repeated them.

"*Ma-a-a-rk three!*"

"*Half twain—quarter less twain—m-a-r-k twain!*"

1. "When the river was a dark gliding mirror reflecting the darkness above—when the forests of cypress and cotton-wood on the nearest bank were but a spectral line, and always the same, unvarying in its obscurity and monotony—when all human sounds had ceased, and only the deep solemn breathings of our river monster could be heard—then it was not difficult to believe that the silent figure standing there in the darkness, guiding us through the darkness and into darkness, was leagued with powers of the other world" (Nichols, "Down the Mississippi," 837).

2. In German legend a sirenlike fairy lived on the Lorelei, a cliff above a dangerous narrows in the Rhine. Her singing lured sailors to their deaths. German poet Heinrich Heine (1797–1856) wrote a famous ballad on the theme, included in his *Book of Songs* (1827).

3. "Soundings are always taken at doubtful points" where boats might run aground in shallows (U.S. Treasury Department, *Report on Commerce*, 96).

So they shouted, minute upon minute. I cannot translate their Mississippi-River English. Mark Twain's name in the mouth of the flat-nosed Ethiopian down there? Whatever did the name of the American humorist have to do with the muddy bottom of the Mississippi? Timidly I ventured the question to the captain.

"*Two fathoms*," said he.

Wasn't it modest of Mr. Clemens to sign his books with so shallow so superficial a nom de plume!

The Mississippi, but for perhaps the exception of its powerful tributary the Missouri, is the most tedious, most ennui-producing river in the world. Charles Dickens described it as "an enormous ditch, sometimes two to three miles wide, running liquid mud, six miles an hour."[4] Other, lesser authors, before and after him, have chosen more poetic terms for the river, as many have put his idea into more flowery language, but it remains the pithiest and truest description ever uttered about the most eminent of rivers.

It must have caused Longfellow trouble with his anthology, *Poems of Places*.[5] What poet ever found words to sing of this dilatory puddle? European waters have nymphs and sirens and mermaids, but could such poetic features be found hovering and flitting about the slowest and most tiresome of rivers?

That is, this broad Mississippi bends and twists and crawls like a snake through the primeval forest. Its course is south, but it seems too shy to go there direct. East it goes, and west, and to every point except South. It wants twenty or thirty miles in which to advance one mile. Inside of an hour, as we proceeded downstream, the sun shone now in our faces, now on our backs, now to the right, now left, while we steered always straight down the river's center. With the brashness of a fly, the river annoyed and tormented us. Only, here, a fly did not disport itself about us—we busied ourselves as if chasing a fly.

This convoluted river never shows more of itself than an area of water five miles long and two miles wide surrounded by dense virgin forest that hems in the water and blocks out the horizon. Hence the steamboat passenger, seeing the water moving, wonders *where does it go?* During the entire journey the five-mile tightly closed ring of virgin

---

4. Dickens, *American Notes*, 171. Dickens's language has been used in the translation, though Hesse-Wartegg's German does not translate exactly into what Dickens wrote.

5. Henry Wadsworth Longfellow's *Poems of Places* (31 vols., 1876–1879) gathers poetry from around the world on the theme of place. Five volumes concern the United States. See Newton Arvin, *Longfellow: His Life and Work*, 294. Hesse-Wartegg refers to the paucity of poems on the Mississippi.

forest stayed with and around us, enclosing us in its magic circle. For twelve days we steamed full ahead but on the twelfth seemed stalled in the middle of the muddy, forest-ringed lake of the first. The forest might have been our shadow hard after us for every mile of the 1,200. Under such surveillance and in this confinement, only one person could be happy: Peter Schlemiel.[6] The boat went right and left with the river. Let it go [either way and] fast or slow; let us stand on the main deck; let us stand on tiptoe on the roof of the pilothouse: we saw the same thing—water inside a dense, an impenetrable wall of forest. The Mississippi seemed to us the escaped prisoner's cell. He wants to get away but the cell races along with him. After a mad flight of hundreds of miles he finds himself still in its clutches.

The scenery did not, does not, will not change. Such a voyage is therefore more than boring; it is also dangerous. Indeed, the Mississippi ranks as the most sinister, the most perfidious river in the world. It is more deceitful than an Armenian! It wanted to destroy us, so it worked hard and persisted at destroying us. It set new traps everywhere. Time and again, no sooner did we believe we had spotted some, than in a flash and with a rearrangement like the turn of a kaleidoscope, the enemy shifted and reshuffled the devices to do us in. But it never removed them. Geographers have taken the greatest pains to plot the course. They might as well chase a will-o'-the-wisp. They mark a shoreline and in a moment—with treacherous speed—the river has reversed itself! A bay here, a point there, today! In two weeks they will trade places, swap identities, and become the bay there and the point here!

The river has even altered its route over the years since it found its way from Minnesota to the Gulf. A turn of weather along the headwaters, the melting of mountain snow in the spring, and floods without fail inundate hundreds of square miles. No dam in the world could prevent conquest by this giant of a river then. It never stops taking acres and square miles from one shore and putting them on the other. Riverside farmers and cotton planters watch year after year with horror as one field after another disappears into the muddy-yellow of the Mississippi—to reappear for the benefit of a dear neighbor on the other side.[7] Mississippi floods often wreak havoc in the hundreds of thousands and the millions of dollars, and the river neither redresses the balance nor pays reparations.

6. Title character of the 1814 novel by Adelbert von Chamisso (1781–1838). *Schlemiel*, referring to an awkward, luckless person, entered American English through Yiddish.

7. For a discussion of how the river alters its course and shortens itself, see Twain, *Life on the Mississippi*, 153–58.

We have gone to bed in our narrow cabins. Sleep eludes us. The engines pound. The huge, cockeyed paddle wheels splash. Often they strike one of those trees floating down from virgin forests at the headwaters. The monotonous shout of the leadman drones the depths. Above all, one time and another, the greeting to boats met as they go upstream, or the signal to postal officials at the next stop. I mean the screech, the shriek of the whistle, a bloodcurdling blast like the trumpets leveling the walls of Jericho. So *this* is the river we follow by steamboat south!

We are speaking of January and therefore the very low river of winter.[8] Anxiously the pilots sought their guideposts—tree trunks, hills, bends, other physical features. Often the engines must be shut off and the boat left to the current. But that precaution will not always do. A skiff, let down by chain and manned by two deckhands and the two pilots, precedes the heavy-laden boat and sounds with the lead for safe passage. Suddenly the news comes back: the pilotboat has found shallows, a sandbar. The obstruction intersects the width of the river and could have taken shape in the last few days. Pilots file reports at the end of the run so that other pilots may benefit from what they have observed. But this sandbar has not yet been mentioned.

Nothing remained to us but, as they say in river vernacular, "*to jump the bar.*" (We dared not stumble and thresh about in the middle of the river on a dark night.) Jump with a steamboat? This 3,000-ton vessel plus cargo, across that barrier of sand? Yes, it poses a delicate situation, a thorny problem. The danger did not escape the passengers. It left its mark on them. But it could not be dodged, it had to be faced. The boat, maneuvering slowly, positioned itself at the shoals of danger, then laid on all steam and struck the bar *full speed ahead.*

A jolt. A scraping. A grinding on the sand. They send a shiver through the boat and—we find ourselves on the other side in deep water! Danger remains, looms large. From the pilotboat suddenly the cry, "*Larboard snag!*"[9] At that moment our boat swerves to the right in a lunge, the great wheel in the pilothouse whirling like the smaller one that spins thread, and we drive perpendicular to the current—straight for the west bank. There the journey resumes. We have cleared the peril! The steersman has executed a masterpiece!

A landlubber cannot imagine what it means to be a pilot. The difficulties must be experienced. This peculiar fraternity has no sense whatsoever for scenery or the beauties of nature. Passengers admire a

---

8. Hesse-Wartegg is "speaking of January," though he was to have left St. Louis in February, a sign that he traveled the river more than once.

9. "The term 'larboard' is never used at sea, now, to signify the left hand; but was always used on the river in my time" (Twain, *Life on the Mississippi,* 99).

lovely sunset while pilots take warning of impending rain. Passengers gaze upon large, lone sycamores or moss-draped cypresses and marvel at their wondrously shaped foliage. Pilots study the same because they tell of shallows or a snag.[10] Should the pilot leave his post for a few minutes, woe unto us!

He must guide his boat every inch of the 1,200 miles from St. Louis to New Orleans. Responsibility for the boat rests with him. He steers at his discretion. The captain neither has the right nor would dare interfere. If the pilot decides to spend the day—or the day and the night—in one spot in the middle of the river, he does it and cares nothing for what the captain wants or the passengers would like. The pilot and the pilot alone must answer for mishaps. Consequently the pilot must, above all, be an authority on the river. He must know the location, the *exact* spot, of every tree for 1,200 miles. Every sandbar, every bend, every shallows, and each and every detail of the thousand landings besides. Bear in mind that up-passage and down-passage differ in the extreme. Steamboats going downstream prefer the broad main channel because the current will boost their speed. Those upstream take every cutoff, each bayou, every eddy, to shorten the distance and meet the current least able to impede.[11] His wealth of knowledge can be acquired in time, of course. Unfortunately these features do not remain the same. They change, year to year, month to month, week to week! The more you learn of Mississippi piloting, the more you must be amazed at what he remembers.[12]

Yet his salary is low. In times gone by he would get $1,000 for the run from New Orleans to St. Louis. Today's intense competition for jobs has depressed wages to food, lodging, and $5.00 a day.[13]

To illustrate the immensity and power of his memory, let one small sample suffice. Take Berlin's 10,000 buildings. Put them in a row. The pilot shall be expected to know each and state its location anywhere in the row. He can describe it. He knows height, design, condition. Furthermore, he will be acquainted with every merchant in this elongated

---

10. A "day came when I ceased altogether to note" the "glories and the charms which the moon and the sun and the twilight wrought upon the river's face. . . . The romance and beauty were all gone. . . . All the value any feature of it had for me now was the amount of usefulness it could furnish toward compassing the safe piloting of a steamboat" (Twain, *Life on the Mississippi,* 79, 80).

11. Morrison, *Steam Navigation,* 249, notes that upstream boats wanted to avoid currents, but "cut-offs are no advantage"; they "create a strong current."

12. The early chapters of *Life on the Mississippi* dramatize the encyclopedic detail the pilot must master even as he realizes that the river keeps changing and must be relearned and relearned. See especially 82–88.

13. Cf. Hunter, *Steamboats,* 445, which cites $100 to $150 a month in 1877; $40 to $100 in 1880.

Berlin and remember the names and addresses of their establishments, even if he calls on them once a month or once a year.

I witnessed in person the genius of pilots; my proofs are firsthand. For example, the federal government has put tiny lighthouses in great numbers along the banks, to mark shallows and sandbars.[14] They signal danger by day with their white-painted presence, by night with a white or red lamp. As the bars continually shift and shuffle, so the lighthouses must be changed. Rarely do they stay put for a month. How many in all? I asked the pilot of our *City of Vicksburg*. "I've never counted them," he laughed, "but I'll tell you in a jiffy." He started counting rapidly on his fingers. In five minutes he reported 220. I learned later that he had not erred. The number was exact. Again, on the 2,600 miles of shore between St. Louis and New Orleans, only a half-dozen cities occur. The boat also calls at plantations isolated in the wilderness and must stop by night as well as day, so he must know name and precise location of each. Maps or books to help? They do not exist.

One dark night the captain ordered a landing at Dr. Dickinson's plantation. To passengers the shore appeared as nothing but a dark line in the distance. Surprised, we wondered that the captain should expect the pilot to distinguish Dickinson's from a hundred other plantations. Astonished, we heard the pilot answer calmly: "Which end, Captain? Lower or upper?"

"*There,* as close as we can get to the house."

Ten minutes later our boat crowded the shore. The captain and Dr. Dickinson shook hands while the Negro crew, the so-called "*roustabouts,*" loaded bales of cotton.

Floods add still another peril to Mississippi steamboating south of Vicksburg. Louisiana's forests have been cleared for miles inland, low-lying sugar plantations have replaced them, and water in the spring covers the land for thirty or forty miles around. (Covered by forests, the shores north pose no problem in this regard.) Then planters burn bagasse, the refuse of sugar refining. Thick white smoke mixes with fog, and you can see nothing for the clouds. Inexperienced pilots in lakes they cannot see across often lose the channel and steam inland

---

14. The first of these "lighthouses," usually called beacon lights, began to aid navigation in 1875. More and more were added until lighted buoys and beacons on the Mississippi numbered in the hundreds and eventually in the thousands (Havighurst, *Voices,* 251–52). See also Hunter, *Steamboats,* 248. The "lights have proven to be of very great benefit, saving time and affording fixed and reliable marks by which pilots run without hesitancy where in former times it was necessary to lay by till next day or go ashore, build fires, and look for marks not discoverable at night. Steam-boat men only wish there were more of these lights" (U.S. Treasury Department, *Report on Commerce,* 96). See also Twain, *Life on the Mississippi,* 232–33.

somewhere.[15] Sometimes a pilot manages to find his way back. Just as frequently his boat runs aground. It is difficult to refloat it if the water recedes. Occasionally the bizarre spectacle may amuse you, of a grand Mississippi steamboat high and dry a mile from the river. But then, as we have seen, Mississippi steamboating has many charms.

---

15. Through the fog Deltans might perceive "a dull crash, a red-tongued explosion; and they have rushed to the river to find disaster in their front yards" (Harnett T. Kane, *Deep Delta Country,* xv).

6. Memphis

Our second day out of Cairo, rain fell in sheets and threw a pall over distant shores. The boat glided through rain on a calm river while we dallied to the heart's content in the saloon. At one end of the long space, male passengers played "*poker*," the West's infamous game of chance.[1] At the other end, females played the piano. Therefore at one we could lose our money; at the other, hearing and sight; so we avoided both. In the middle we remained in reasonable safety, thanks to the immense length.

We passed a dozen "*landings*" one after another and took the mail from each, in a tall limp leather sack. Our approach and departure would wash away some of the incipient city's vertical, sugarlike, dissolving shores—so much that we could fairly predict how many steamboats would call before the town tumbled into the river.

In forty-eight hours the *City of Vicksburg* arrived at Memphis. Gray clouds wrapped the sky from horizon to horizon. Rain fell, penciling the air from heaven to earth with lines that ended in drops and gurgled as they hit river. This atmosphere complemented Memphis, as the Memphitic panorama unrolled before us like the shadow of a passing cloud or the shades of witchcraft. Memphis appeared first as nothing but three long horizontal streaks, white below, yellow in the middle, dirty-brown above. Later they proved to be steep sandy bluffs, a row of steamboats at their feet, and Front Street's row of imposing houses asserting themselves on a height between. Our pilots blew the whistle with a blast of steam. A sandbar lay dead ahead, between us and Memphis. After lengthy maneuvers around it, the pilots landed us at last at the quay.

A few months before I arrived, yellow fever had turned Memphis into a giant hospital and a morgue of corpses.[2] But in this chapter I do not wish to dwell on the epidemic that ravaged here. My purpose is to

---

1. "Any narrative of a week's life upon a Mississippi steamboat without gambling experience would not possess the flavor of reality" (Chambers, *Mississippi River,* 189).
2. "The city's greatest calamity," the epidemic of 1878, "took an awesome toll of human life. It caused panic" (Sigafoos, *Cotton Row to Beale Street,* 55). The disruption of economic and social life had effects that lingered years after. See also Gerald M. Capers, Jr., "Yellow Fever in Memphis in the 1870s," 492–500.

sketch the city where only doctors, nurses, and traveling salesmen appeared since the onset of fever. We were the first tourists.

Cisatlantic and transatlantic Memphis contradict one another as places to visit. In the seat of King Rameses, I found as few hospital orderlies as I found tourists in the seat of King Cotton. I felt different, entering one and entering the other. True, initial feelings in each were responses to the past. But the past meant an antiquity of thousands of years in Memphis, Egypt. In Memphis, U.S.A, it asserted itself as something immediate. It so pressed itself upon us that we thought, "A few months ago, '*Yellow Jack*' staged his show in this sultry air, and now we are breathing it." We must have looked at this Memphis with corresponding jaundice, for we saw nothing but a terrible dourness at first.

Indeed, after traveling to the four corners of the world, I cannot remember impressions anywhere as disagreeable as those upon entering this Memphis.[3] There was the rain that trapped the smoke and the gloom and held them captive within the city's walls; and the foot-deep mire creeping down the slopes toward the Mississippi, slithering like a polypous creature with tentacles, threatening to pull our overshoes off; and especially, everywhere, taciturnity and silence. In all the dull faces we thought we could read Y-e-l-l-o-w F-e-v-e-r. Our rooms were damp and uncomfortable. We went to bed thinking of the recent epidemic.

Next morning the sun of the South shone warm through our window and lit up our world. To our eyes, in that bright and cheerful light, what a difference from the day before: a room far less uncomfortable, the Hotel of the Gruesome Past not nearly so gruesome, and the yellow faces not at all so yellow as imagined. A short stroll through the city now showed us new marvels at every step and partially reconciled us with Memphis. Of the epidemic, not a trace. Streets bustled. Faces glowed. Doubt could honestly arise: was the calendar right? Had we arrived before the epidemic, not after?

Truth be told, though, it seems incredible. A mere three or four months previously, Memphis could still count scarcely half its 40,000 people. Of the 20,000, at least 19,000 lay sick; and in the end, 5,000 went to the grave.[4] Yet Memphis has more people than ever. The epidemic's last trace has vanished.[5]

3. "The U.S. Surgeon-General referred to Memphis' sanitary conditions as 'shameful and a disgrace'" (Sigafoos, *Cotton Row*, 56). See also Capers, "Yellow Fever," 485–86.

4. Sigafoos confirms these figures (*Cotton Row*, 56).

5. According to Capers, "a second metropolis . . . sprang up like some fungus growth on the ruins of the first" (*The Biography of a River Town: Memphis*, 204). The population had been "diminished by three-fourths . . . but there is life enough there now" and trade "in a flourishing condition" in the "thriving place" (Twain, *Life on the Mississippi*, 248, 249, 250).

A different epidemic proved fatal, not to the people but to the city itself. I mean the epidemic of tax revolt.[6] Two-thirds of taxes could not be collected for years. Meanwhile an unscrupulous clique lined its pockets out of the third that remained. Millions, borrowed to run the city from day to day, also migrated into official pockets. Hospitals and orphanages went unfunded. Essential services such as street cleaning—crucial to municipal health, necessary for well-being, vital to progress—stopped for lack of money. Interest on the municipal debt of $5 million could not be paid. Firemen and policemen worked for months unpaid. In short, conditions seemed imported from Turkey, the mother of such national and municipal misadministration.[7]

No wonder, then, that the city committed suicide. Memphis was dead, as dead as a doornail, without mayor or council. This urban soul had joined that of its Pharaonic sister. Memphis, ceasing to exist as a city, became merely a part of Tennessee, in the same class as a forest or swamp. People everywhere indulged gallows humor when addressing letters. "To X. X. in the southwestern corner of Tennessee," for example. Or to "X. in the place where Memphis used to be." Or to "X., steamboat landing, mouth of Wolf River." Or to "X., Yellow Fever City, formerly Memphis."

The Tennessee legislature passed a law to revoke the city's charter and create a commission to administer the territory and buildings of the former city—whereupon the city's creditors sought help from a federal judge named Baxter.[8] (They stood to lose by the legislature's

---

6. Waste, corruption, deficit financing, the Panic of 1873, the loss of credit, yellow-fever epidemics, and the refusal to pay taxes had bankrupted Memphis. On the eve of Hesse-Wartegg's visit, 31 January 1879, "Memphis surrendered its charter" (Sigafoos, *Cotton Row,* 53–55) to prevent creditors' legal action against city property and thus avoid paying the debt. Upon request, the legislature took the charter, declaring that "the city of Memphis no longer exists" and making it "the taxing district of Shelby County" (U.S. Department of the Interior, *Report on Cities,* 142–43). Rebellion against taxes also took the form of taxpayers' conventions demanding reductions of taxes and expenditures (Eric Foner, *Reconstruction: America's Unfinished Revolution, 1863–1877,* 415–16).

7. Hesse-Wartegg's reference to Turkey was probably an expression of his prejudices and as lost on the American audience of the 1880s as on that of the 1980s. He was nonetheless right about corruption in this region of the United States: If "ubiquitous in American history," corruption "thrived in the Reconstruction South." It "cast a shadow over the conduct of public affairs in nearly every Reconstruction state," thriving because of "the specific circumstances of Republican rule" (Foner, *Reconstruction,* 384–85). See also 385–90; and E. Merton Coulter, *The South During Reconstruction, 1865–1877,* 148–49.

8. "The legislature provided a government composed of a legislative council of eight members: the board of fire and police commissioners, and the board of public works—elected by popular vote" (Work Projects Administration, *Tennessee: A Guide to the State,* 212).

action.) The judge studied what the city and legislature had done. According to a newspaper of another city, he ruled null and void the law to revoke the charter. He summed up the facts and the reasons for the decision as follows. The Tennessee legislature created the municipality of Memphis as a corporation, thus giving it the right to acquire property and incur debts. Memphis did both. The legislature dissolved the corporation, took its property and made it the legislature's and left the city's creditors to wonder how they would get what was owed them. The judge ruled that the obligations of contract had been broken, in violation of the constitutions of Tennessee and the United States. Therefore, he appointed a *"receiver"* to administer the city's property in the interests of the creditors, and to collect taxes.[9]

We shall, for simplicity, continue to use the name Memphis. Though situated at the southern point of a southern state, Memphis should not be called a southern city.[10] To me it looks western, like a city of Missouri, Kansas, or Illinois. The same layout and architecture, the same life in the streets and the inns. It shares with the South only magnolias and bananas in the gardens, the rather sluggish character of the inhabitants, and—*"carpetbaggers."* These transplants, professional politicians from the North, flourish under the southern sun. Botanizing southerners would like to classify them among the parasitical cacti.[11]

The streets follow a regular plan. The wide Main Street of imposing buildings extends two miles: grand public edifices and rows of pretty houses—the most beautiful street between St. Louis and New Orleans. At the midpoint of those two miles, the shady Magnolia Square, or so-called City Park, asserts itself and with it the city's largest buildings: Oddfellows Hall and the Peabody Hotel. The *haut monde* has settled away from the principal streets, away from Main, Front, and Second: in and around Vance Street. Front, perpendicular to Main, follows the riverbank and provides the city its chief emporium for cotton, fruit, and other foodstuffs.

9. "The city's creditors" were Eastern financial institutions. From them "great furor emanated" when the city forfeited its charter and the state began to deal with the problem. Hesse-Wartegg's discussion is neither clear, accurate, nor final because he wrote amid a financial muddle that did not begin to clear until 1881. See Sigafoos, *Cotton Row*, 58–60. For the true story, see also Capers, *River Town*, 200–204.

10. Memphis is "closer in social and economic kinship to the Midwest than to the lower valley" (Carter, *Lower Mississippi*, 188).

11. As elsewhere in the book, Hesse-Wartegg seems to speak of the politics of an earlier time, perhaps recalled from an earlier visit of his. Reconstruction ended nationally in 1877; in Tennessee, in 1870. Carpetbaggers had little influence in Memphis when Hesse-Wartegg visited this time. See Sigafoos, *Cotton Row*, 48–49, 51.

Cotton? Yes. Memphis, latest woes notwithstanding, remains one of the centers of the cotton trade.[12] The trade burgeons. Hub to a big cotton-producing region, Memphis communicates by river with that region, and no city around for hundreds of miles offers any competition. Up to a half-million bales a year arrive, to be bought mostly by New England and to a lesser extent by Germany and Britain.[13] Railroads transport most of it, true, but the river has been taking more and more, making New Orleans the city of cotton export.[14] Besides, Memphis, ideally situated, enjoys not only the central location on the Mississippi, the nation's artery for freight, but also ranks as a rail center, connected by five lines to Charleston, New Orleans, Louisville, St. Louis, and the "great Southwest."

Memphis could blame only itself for the tragedy of last year's malarial epidemic. When I visited the city the condition of the thoroughfares, as well as of many lesser streets and other public spaces, would make you shudder. I had seen many Hungarian, Bulgarian, and Turkish cities. All things considered, they would seem clean and tidy compared to Memphis and its filth upon dirt, mire upon muck, and offal upon excrement. Houses stand in this mess, people sink to the knees in it every day, yet they prefer the shameful condition to the taxes needed to remove it.[15]

Streets from the river into the city suggested at once to us the year-round misery of all these streets: horrible mud, winter and summer, and an endless dust that must prevail in the dry season. The state of all streets—largest to smallest and grandest to meanest—beggars description. You cannot imagine the mountains, ravines, and craters brought about by the so-called Nicholson wooden pavement.[16] Poor mules and miserable horses sink knee-deep in mire and ruts. Cotton wagons would be stuck in a trice, and break wheels and axles. The horse-

12. Founded in 1873, the Cotton Exchange was "the economic heart of the city" (Work Projects Administration, *Tennessee,* 221).

13. Memphis called itself the "Biggest Inland Cotton Market in the World" (Sigafoos, *Cotton Row,* 31). Big Mississippi boats, "piled to the pilothouse with cotton," docked there (Havighurst, *Voices,* 137). Its cotton market would become the biggest in the world.

14. The Memphis & Charleston, the Mississippi Central, the New Orleans & Jackson, the Louisville & Nashville, the Chicago, St. Louis & New Orleans, the Missouri Pacific, and the Southern Pacific provided these connections. See *Encyclopedia of Southern History,* s.v., "railroads."

15. The Memphis *Public Ledger* spoke of "Augean stables with no Alpheus to flow through and cleanse them" (Sigafoos, *Cotton Row,* 56). "The sanitary conditions . . . were perhaps no better than those of the poorest medieval borough," and there was even one instance of a "minnow found swimming" in a pail of milk (Capers, *River Town,* 188). See also Capers, "Yellow Fever," 485–86.

16. Nicholson pavement, "specially treated wooden blocks . . . put down in the business district during the fall of 1867 . . . began to decay in a few years" (Capers, *River Town,* 180).

drawn streetcars accept the rugged terrain, the rails obey it, and their passengers, subjected to jolts and shoves, avoid riding whenever possible. Take that ugly state of affairs, add the mud of the side streets, plus the pools of water on building sites, and pile on the accumulation of months of garbage in the streets. The mess amounts to a picture of civilization in the Bulgaria of America. Yet *white* people live on these streets! They wade through them day in, day out. They know the horrors of filth, miasma and malaria. Yet they will not pay the taxes that must be paid to defray cleaning and paving!

A narrow, marshy arm of the Mississippi empties into the Wolf River to the north, at the same time enclosing Memphis in the backwater of a bayou.[17] A high Mississippi will fill the bayou and the Wolf. At other times, lacking water [out of a low Mississippi], they degenerate to swamps. Into the bayou the sewers of Memphis empty Memphis's dirt, refuse, and junk. The waste lies there the summer, rotting till autumn's higher waters flush it into the Mississippi. Yet it would be simple to ditch and drain the bayou and the Wolf. The model city council rejected such proposals.

Memphis could be made into a city of good health. Malaria stalks in the summer from swamps along the Mississippi to the west, but salubrious conditions could be created to minimize the influx. The streets are already wide, straight, and open to the air; and away from the river there is a large and beautiful park with tall trees, many gardens, and shaded walks. But Memphis also suffered from *moral* rot. A corrupt administration and a sluggish and egotistical populace concerned themselves with nothing but their own fortunes. Too blind they were, and too greedy, to see that spending a few dollars to clean the streets, to ditch for drainage, and to take other sanitary measures would return a thousandfold as well as preserve and extend the lives of inhabitants.[18] History here thus reads like a tale of horror.

These people not only shirked responsibility to themselves and their turf; they also forgot that the United States itself could take them to task. That is, by their infinite neglect, their town became a breeding ground for epidemics in the heart of the nation. Enter Yellow Jack in 1855. People die like flies. New people replace them. In a few weeks every trace of the calamity disappears. In 1867, again, Yellow Jack rages. He ravages. The city does not heed the second lesson. The old ways continue. In 1873, his third visit, the worst yet. He devastates Memphis. About three-fourths of the city, 3,000, die in two months.

17. Probably Bayou Gayso, an "open sewer" (Sigafoos, *Cotton Row,* 56).
18. According to Capers, *River Town,* an ignorant, impecunious underclass prevailed at the polls, electing politicians who would amuse them (200–201).

Memphis becomes a Golgotha. In November at last a frost expels fever's furies. In fourteen days, Memphis counts more residents than ever. Everything is as it has been.

Then the most terrible punishment, the ghastliest of any city's ever, in 1878.[19] Yellow fever walks the streets, invades houses, settles and pullulates in swamps and sinkholes, and wreaks havoc upon the city, savaging it beyond description. Of the 60,000 inhabitants, 40,000 flee. The remainder include 12,000 blacks. Some 19,000 in all, then, and 18,000 fall ill.[20] In other words, nearly the entire populace must suffer. Of the 18,000 sick over 5,000 die in two months.

That despoliation occurred about six months before I arrived in February 1879. Yet I saw a Memphis of nearly 60,000. Three months after I left and following several new outbreaks, 60,000 had shrunk to 20,000 for fear of another epidemic. Again, 40,000 had taken to their heels. Yellow fever did strike, to reprise daily the scenes of the year before.[21]

The status quo has persisted because people in Memphis have not heeded distress but pinned hopes on the future and worked only to *get*. Not responsible burghers but egoistic opportunists have settled Memphis. They have directed every effort to one end: money, personal fortune. Selfishness above all has produced the city's trouble. Community—the commonwealth, the public good, the general welfare—neighborhood and shared space: these have meant nothing. Each person has wanted only to accumulate unto himself. When rich enough, such people would gather up their wealth and leave. Therefore, even after the terrible epidemic of 1873, nobody cared about conditions. Memphis remained as dirty, swampy, and wretched as ever. The consequences could have been predicted.

Only now—after warnings at least once a year and every day of some years, after unthinkable negligence, after terrible punishment inflicted again and again in the form of massacres by yellow fever—Memphis at long last seems to be waking up.[22] The future of human life depends in Memphis upon sanitary measures; they must be enforced *now*. Even the newspapers at last realized that ten times the present taxes would be better than another spectacle of plague running rampant in the streets, leaving 5,000 yellowed bodies to be buried.

---

19. The enormity of this overstatement will emerge from a review of devastated cities, beginning with Vesuvius and Carthage.
20. Hesse-Wartegg gives 19,000 here when it seems it should be 20,000.
21. Epidemics of lessening severity continued until 1897 (Sigafoos, *Cotton Row*, 58).
22. Memphis began to improve its sanitation in 1880 and soon thereafter to solve its financial problems. See ibid., 60–61, 62–63, 65.

In fact, the *Belletristisches Journal* of New York reports that in sanitation "the old harbor of plague has become a new and model town, marshes drained, damp cellars disinfected, and a ventilated, easily cleaned, 20-mile sewerage built.[23] Each cellar has been connected to the system. Bayous are now linked by canals and sluices so that they take and hold the Mississippi's overflow, retain pure water when the river runs low, and do not become a sink of muck and filth in the heat of summer. Costs have totaled about $200,000; but as is well-known, yellow fever has not occurred this year. No fever means a saving, merely in direct costs, of two million dollars. Think of the twenty-two epidemics since the founding of Memphis. What sums could have been saved, had the recent measures been begun fifty years ago?"[24]

On the way south, one meets first in Memphis the Negroes who hold public office in the cities and states. They like best to be policemen.[25] During epidemics in Memphis, the Negroes proved so durable, diligent, and conscientious that the city entrusted public safety to them. A number have continued in law enforcement. But the majority bale cotton and work on the "*levees*" (the waterfront), where employment abounds year-round.

For—besides being the river's leading port, after St. Louis and New Orleans—Memphis constitutes the center and cynosure of Mississippi-valley steamboating. In other words, it is the hub of traffic on the great river and its tributaries. Let me offer as compelling evidence of lively inter-river traffic these examples of ads from a single issue of the leading Memphis daily.[26] Under "*STEAMBOATS*," thirteen announce departures. Destinations include Vicksburg and all "*points*" on the White River. Two are bound for Louisville and Cincinnati; one for Cairo and St. Louis; two for towns on the Arkansas: Little Rock, Pine Bluff, etc., as far as Fort Smith in the Indian Territory; two for Osceola [Arkansas]; and one each for New Orleans, the St. Francis River, the Black River, and Helena [Arkansas]. You can see that steamboats navigate all Arkansas, even to its western boundary, as well as Missis-

---

23. "Sewer construction began in 1880" (ibid., 60).

24. Hesse-Wartegg does not report the location of this quotation beyond the title of the publication, which was at the time the most respected German-American magazine of politics and the arts.

25. "In 1870, at least twelve southern cities employed black policemen, most of them in proportions close to the percentage of blacks in the local population" (Rousey, "Black Policemen," 233). Between 1870 and 1880, only three of the twenty largest southern cities increased the proportion of black policemen in the total force and the ratio to the total population: Galveston, Washington, and Memphis. The largest increase was in Memphis (232).

26. Hesse-Wartegg probably means the *Memphis Avalanche*. The *Appeal* did not use this heading.

sippi, Kentucky, Tennessee, and Louisiana. You can also see that, on countless waterways and bayous, the boats penetrate and traverse regions inaccessible to railroads. All the cotton country, several-hundred-thousand square miles, relies mostly on Memphis as a port. Memphis has its calling, no doubt about it.[27] Memphis shall be one of the major cities, a metropolis of the Mississippi valley.

27. Memphis did solve many of its problems and became a major city of the valley, but never a leader. St. Louis and New Orleans exceeded Memphis in population, commerce, and influence. Hopes in Memphis to outdo St. Louis and Atlanta proved futile despite renaissance and progress in Memphis after 1880. See Sigafoos, *Cotton Row*, 62–63, 65–66.

7. Yellow Jack!

In many a year, two notable guests call at New Orleans, Mobile, Charleston, Savannah, Louisville, and Memphis. The guests, polar opposites, share a characteristic. They are common to each of those important cities of the South. One arrives in summer, the other in winter. The first—malicious, dastardly, lethal: hideousness incarnate—wears the mask of death in yellow. The second reigns as Lord Revelry, Prince Pleasure, King Debauch. The first evokes fear and kindles loathing. People damn the obnoxious intruder. The second arouses joyful expectation. People solicit the welcome caller. Who are the guests who represent pain and joy, signify death and life? Yellow Fever and Carnival.

Carnival has always restricted itself without exception to cities ravaged annually or at least with enough regularity by Yellow Fever. No fact could be more bizarre, no contrast more striking. Automatically it calls up the famous picture of the pair of lovers who, viewed from a distance, become a death's head.[1] Compare New Orleans two years ago. At the start of summer, the proud Queen of the South became the whore of pestilence, the breeder of Yellow Jack.[2]

Who can say where the yellow specter originates? Is Aeolus to blame, collecting pestilence in the swamps of Louisiana and dumping it in the cities? Or does this sluggish Mississippi, the slimy pool, give birth to that dark angel, the death fever? Or have the cities themselves spawned the ghastly, deadly host, in their own swamps and sewers? Who can say? Who, indeed?[3]

    1. In this vague reference, Hesse-Wartegg could mean Hans Balding-Grien's *Death Kisses a Maiden,* Hans Burgkmair the Elder's *Lovers Surprised by Death,* or any number of works by Lucas Cranach, but none of these possibilities exactly fits what he seems to be suggesting.

    2. "New Orleans, principal port of entry, was considered the yellow fever capital of the South. Its epidemic of 1853 was probably the worst ever to strike a major American city" (*Encyclopedia of Southern History,* s.v. "yellow fever"). The Tenth U.S. Census, taken in 1880, found sanitation in New Orleans deplorable. See U.S. Department of the Interior, *Report On Cities,* 287–90.

    3. The disease spread erratically, baffling physicians and laymen. They "debated cause, transmission, and prevention." Some considered it "contagious and imported"; they "favored isolation and quarantine." Others believed that "it originated locally in putrefaction"; they "advocated sanitation" (*Encyclopedia of Southern*

The more mysterious the antecedents, the more shocking the existence, the more horrifying the consequences. A murderous yellow death, origin unknown, daily fells hundreds. Yesterday's happiest and healthiest lie in delirium, wrenched and contorted by cramps. Their shrieks pierce the stale air and hang in the stinking atmosphere, quivering. Hundreds sprawl as twisted corpses orange-yellow in the streets, in the markets, in the houses. Gravediggers ply the trade day and night. Shops are closed, public spaces empty, suggesting a vast field of carnage. How insidious, how malignant, this Evil! It fastens down upon a great city, clings like a leech even to the houses, lurks in the trees, skulks in the sewers, and prepares an ambush in the homes and the beds. People would choke the life out of it. They would kill it before it kills. They pursue it, but only the dead have caught it. No defense prevails because even the powers of nature have foresworn mankind. The evil spirit may hover invisible about the city; a storm could drive it off, but storms disappear. Not a breath stirs. Black clouds sometimes have heaped into mountains on the horizon; their waters would clear the air, but they keep their distance. Not a drop of rain. A day of cold would rout the pest, or kill it. Tropical temperatures remain oppressive, the air persists damp and close. No change, no rain, no wind! Thus the elements join forces against the city, and with them as allies, Dreadful Fever rages among the populace.

Without protection, lacking defenses, what to do but flee? Get away from this pestilential hell, away from these swamps, the breeding ground of this wickedness. In the most fearful excitement, shaking, half mad, not knowing whether the Reaper will cut them down in a minute or two, the runaway thousands crowd the docks and await the steamboat out of this vile place. Negroes in rags, tall planters and their families, merchants, soldiers, beautiful women old and young, children—all crowd the docks. Who knows, has the invisible enemy stalked these ranks? Has he marked this one as prey, that one as victim? With blinding speed he will put the quietus to the strongest person, the most vigorous life. In mortal anguish they study each other, the whites of the eyes, seeking the indelible stamp of Yellow Jack.

Mortal anguish not only reigns in the city and up and down the river's shores. It also seizes the state. It sweeps the South and its millions. An epidemic of fear precedes the epidemic of fever. Every

---

History, s.v. "yellow fever"). Prevailing from 1793 to 1900, these were usually called the contagion and the non-contagion theories. Not until 1900 did Walter Reed confirm that only the bite of the female *Aëdes aegypti* mosquito could transmit the disease. See Howard A. Kelly, *Walter Reed and Yellow Fever*, 84–95. Hesse-Wartegg favors putrefaction and non-contagion practically to the exclusion of contagion.

state, each city, the people one and all, protect themselves as best they can.

Vicksburg, like New Orleans, then Grenada, then Memphis, have fallen to fever. Too late the quarantine of Memphis. Barricades went up after fever slipped in and, beginning softly, claimed its victims. One, two, twenty—a thousand! Raging, it threw half of Memphis onto the worst of sickbeds and into graves scarcely dug. Nothing could prevail against it. Yes, tar pots burned day and night, and rouged the clouds rising skyward.[4] They however did not carry along the miasma, the cause of the disease. True, even the sparse food from a deserted countryside must be disinfected before let past the barricades. But such measures proved futile against malignancy that made itself at home in a filthy city criss-crossed by streams of muck.

In August the frightful epidemic peaked in Memphis. Its victims numbered daily in the hundreds. The city might have been a ghost town—or one big morgue. Two-thirds of the people had left. Only the poor, the old, and the lame stayed: easy prey to the murderous enemy. Houses were locked. A small lamp often burned outside, signifying death inside. Frequently a house might witness multiple deaths. Black cloths would hang from windows. Shops never opened their doors, locked during business hours, proprietors dead or gone.

This hideous disease! Within hours it will pluck the flower of youth, it will choke off young life at its most robust. A slight malaise, fever an hour later, then the worst delirium, then—yellow death.[5] At the street corner, on the square, in the houses: there lie the dead, rushed and overpowered by the fiend. You will find bodies twisted by sickness, stiff in death. Horrible, dreadful shrieks from houses split the air. They are brief; soon it falls silent inside. Noble, self-sacrificing men arrive with caskets, nail them shut, and away they go to burial.

Calm reigns at night. Only hearses speed through the streets, and the doctors, muffled up. Meanwhile, food runs short. Meat darkens and spoils in this stinking, polluted atmosphere. Trains now and then

4. The burning occurred because authorities believed the fever to be caused by an organism in the atmosphere (Capers, *River Town,* 191). Capers notes other measures taken accordingly (197). In New Orleans anti-fever measures included hanging up sheets drenched with carbolic acid to purify the air in homes, while the authorities spread lime, burned tar, and fired cannon in public places (Thomas E. Dabney, *One Hundred Years: The Story of the Times-Picayune,* 268–69).

5. Symptoms of yellow fever are "chills, fever, headache, muscular pain, vomiting, jaundice, and a tendency to hemorrhage." The internal hemorrhaging led to black vomit, the Spanish *vomito negro,* of partially digested blood resembling coffee grounds. In its late stages the disease caused convulsions and perhaps coma, with death usually resulting from liver and kidney damage (*Encyclopedia of Southern History,* s.v. "yellow fever").

can be heard rushing by, far away, racing like the wind, as if pursued by the Furies. No stops at the city of plague.[6]

The wealthy fled north as soon as fever broke out, to St. Louis or Cincinnati or another safe address. The less-well-to-do pitched tents in the hills at a distance and moved their families into them. The poor and the black remain. Only in part does poverty detain blacks; for they have less to fear, as fever strikes fewer blacks, on average. Many high-minded individuals also remain: men and women who could flee the fever cities but stay to nurse the sick and comfort the dying.[7] The heroes bring medicine to the sick and watch over them day and night. Not fearing death, they minister with heroic self-sacrifice. They bury the dead. Tirelessly they work at everything from delivering food to keeping order in cities bereft of officials and services. America may often be called the land without warmth, and of humbug and greed. But America has people so kind and generous as to throw into the shade any Old Country examples.

America has [charitable] institutions the world cannot equal. We should mention the Howard Association first.[8] It has branches in most southern cities. Its doctors, nurses, and agents join with high-minded people of the cities, to advance the association's warmhearted, idealistic purpose: to aid and care for the sick. Without the association's help, Mississippi-valley cities would have felt far more pain and suffered unspeakably increased horror in the days of yellow fever. It is therefore altogether fitting that a memorial be raised wherever possible to the

---

6. "Surrounding towns speedily quarantined Memphis. At Columbus, Kentucky, armed citizens turned back a train on the Mobile & Ohio" (Work Projects Administration, *Tennessee*, 211). Other "shotgun quarantines" isolated towns "everywhere" in the Mississippi valley (Coulter, *South During Reconstruction,* 262–63).

7. As described by the *Memphis Daily Appeal* (18 March 1879), they included pastors who stayed with their congregations, remaining "beside the bed of sickness, soon to be the bed of death." Catholic priests and nuns, notably Father J. A. Kelly, also "took courageous part in the relief work" (Work Projects Administration, *Tennessee,* 212). Twain was sufficiently impressed with the philanthropy of residents during this period to call Memphis "the Good Samaritan City" (*Life on the Mississippi,* 8, 250).

8. Named for British philanthropist and social and penal reformer John Howard (1726–1790), this organization began in New Orleans in 1837. Nonsectarian and not-for-profit, it did social work and gave medical aid gratis and without regard to race or sex. Its chief efforts were for victims of yellow fever and cholera; it did its most notable work during yellow fever epidemics. It consisted of twenty-nine branches in nine states when it ended in 1878, inspiring the public-health movement, the Public Health Service, and the Red Cross (Peggy Bassett Hildreth, "Early Red Cross: The Howard Association of New Orleans," 49–50, 73–74). Provisions worth $417,000 and $500,000 were given to help the Memphis relief effort (Work Projects Administration, *Tennessee,* 212).

association and its members, even if only in words. Let the same be done for the many citizens—postal officials, telegraphers, doctors, journalists, newspaper publishers—who plied their trades amid epidemic and worked during the ghastliest episodes. The publisher of the *Memphis Appeal,* Colonel Keating, produced the paper without fail.[9] Editors, compositors, and printers lay sick or dying, the *Appeal* shrank to a quarter-sheet, but it appeared *daily,* carrying nothing but columns of names of the sick and the dead. Keating fortunately survived even the fifth epidemic.

Epidemics do not occur annually, but yellow fever and the heat arrive together in Mississippi-valley cities nearly every summer. Indeed, the yellow menace stalks so often through the history of these cities and recent epidemics have aroused such alarm across America and in Europe that we would seem obliged to ask: When did they start, when have they occurred, and what is the situation now?

Since 1796, the year of the first on record, thirty-three have afflicted the valley and especially New Orleans. Major ones occurred irregularly (this is a peculiarity) with varying numbers of years between. After the initial one of this century (1817), two years passed before the next, and three before that of 1822. After the one of 1830, they followed in 1837, 1841, 1847, 1853, 1858, 1867, and at last, 1878. Eleven in all that were *major* because they claimed so many victims. Otherwise, only one fact emerges. That is, intervals have lengthened: two years to three, four, five, six, nine, eleven. Consequently, the frequency of major epidemics seems to be decreasing. Minor ones meanwhile remain unchanged: shorter and less deadly, always following the major, and seeming to occur as often as before and to kill as many as ever. Thus we count, in the nine years from 1817 to 1825, three major and six minor—one every year. In the eight years from 1830 to 1837, two major and three minor. (See Dr. Alfred Mercier's essay in *Meschacébé,* 5 September 1878.)[10] After the major of 1830 (one of the worst), three minor followed hard after it. The minor of 1848 nearly equalled the

---

9. John McLeod Keating (1830–1906) published the paper practically single-handedly and served on the municipal government's executive committee besides. His *History of the Yellow Fever* (1879) may have been useful to Hesse-Wartegg. A history in the broadest sense, it not only narrated past events, but also summed up present conditions, discussed theories of the origin and progress of the fever, and considered proposals for control and prevention. See *Dictionary of American Biography,* s.v. "Keating, John McLeod."

10. Mercier (1816–1894) was a physician and author (ibid., s.v. "Mercier, Alfred"). *Le Meschacébé,* a weekly that began publication in 1852, was the journal of the St. John Parish Police, Jury, and School Board (American Library Association, *National Union Catalogue,* 378:72).

major of 1847. Two minor scourges followed the ravager of 1853. The pattern continues: a major in 1878, a minor in 1879.[11]

Selfless, meritorious men have reported what they observed in epidemics.[12] A few of the facts say much about the nature of the fever and suggest abundant measures for prevention. For example, this is a sporadic disease, not one brought into the cities of the valley, for it originates in them. Given the conditions it needs, it becomes epidemic.

New Orleans, historically the principal city of epidemics, has gotten the most attention from federal officials. Yet who shall assert that the next will confine itself to the South? That, aided by atmospheric accidents, it will not cross the Ohio? That it will not erupt in the cities of the West? That it will not spread into the mid-Atlantic states—having appeared there several times already—and bring terror to Philadelphia and New York? In 1879, when each day produced reports of thousands upon thousands sick and hundreds upon hundreds dead, America—all the United States—shuddered at the horror of an impending threat to everyone. A simple turn of luck might bring the fever to the populous states of the North. Quarantines were enforced everywhere, and barriers were erected with equally good reason around fever districts.

Autumn and the onset of cold ended the epidemic for the season. The imminent threat to this vast country thus suspended, people stopped thinking about yellow fever. True, the government appointed commissions and mounted expeditions to the West Indies and Brazil in search of the cause. Quarantines were imposed on ships at New Orleans from points south. Those efforts and others yielded the most barren results: nothing. The cause of yellow fever should have been

11. On the New Orleans epidemic of 1878, see Dabney, *One Hundred Years,* 268–70. This epidemic "led New Orleans to organize its Auxiliary Sanitary Association, induced the movement for a national board of health, and caused practically all southern cities to set up boards of health or strengthen those already in existence" (Coulter, *South During Reconstruction,* 263). The cycle of epidemics broke in the 1880s and 1890s when measures against other "causes" of the fever incidentally destroyed the mosquito's breeding places, ending the menace (Capers, *River Town,* 261, note 9).

12. Hesse-Wartegg's note: "See the annual report of the New Orleans Board of Health for 1878; the report of the Howard Association for 1878; Mercier . . . ; the report of the municipal investigation commission, New Orleans, 1853; Dr. Joseph Holt's report to the Yellow Fever Commission, 1878." Joseph Johnson Holt (1839–1922) was sanitary inspector for the fourth district of New Orleans, physician and author, president of the New Orleans Medical and Surgical association, and authority and frequent speaker on public health, especially yellow fever (American Library Association, *National Union Catalogue* 252:382–83). For a summary of the report by this congressional committee, see Keating, *Yellow Fever,* 303–4. See also Board of Experts on Yellow Fever and Cholera, *Conclusions.*

sought, not far off, but in the valley itself. I have said it before, and not a shadow of doubt remains: Yellow Jack arises in the same places he attacks—the cities of the South. Yet the southern press lacks initiative. With few exceptions the papers are as passive as the majority of the public toward measures against the epidemics. The press neither spearheads movements nor sets a good example, but goes along with the crowd, changing ideas as a chameleon changes color to harmonize with surroundings. I have followed the Mississippi south, entered the land of yellow fever, and found to my astonishment that the last epidemic, barely over, means nothing to a press and a public equally apathetic and infinitely stoical. Do they not know, can they not suspect that a lesser outbreak will ensue upon the major one of 1878? I learned two salient truths from the laudable publications by Dr. Holt of New Orleans:

- "Yellow fever here as elsewhere is and always has been a disease that can be prevented."
- "The origin and spread of the disease occur only in the presence of two conditions generally hygienic in nature. And they must actively coincide, else no fever. That is, as surely as the absence of both, the absence of one precludes fever. One is a condition of the atmosphere; the other, tellurian, or of the earth."

Mr. J. F. Deeves drew up a chart of atmospheric or meteorological conditions prevailing in New Orleans during the last epidemic.[13] The chart is of great interest. The city's *Deutsche Zeitung* refers to four of its points as worth notice:

- *Temperature.* "The average being far lower than in prior years, people on the whole suffered not from heat but from humidity and a lack of storms and fresh breezes to clear the air. This season of fever lasted 102 days but temperatures reached or exceeded 90° on only thirteen: 93° on July 29 (the hottest), 92° on three other days, 91° on four, and 90° on five. On 67 days the temperature ranged from 80° to 89°, including 84° on 13 days and 80° on 10."

13. This paragraph and the long quotation that follows have been inserted here from the end of the chapter, where they are a footnote in the original. Hesse-Wartegg does not specify the source, beyond *Deutsche Zeitung*. A search of its files, which are not complete, has not revealed the chart. Deeves also remains unidentified. Hesse-Wartegg specifies that Deeves charted conditions during the prior year's epidemic, that of 1879, in New Orleans. There is a remote chance that Hesse-Wartegg means an important theorist of yellow fever, Jean Devèse (1743–1829), author of *An Enquiry into the Epidemic in Philadelphia* (1793). Devèse, an early and perhaps the most significant advocate of non-contagion, would have found favor with Hesse-Wartegg and been interested in the data compiled by Deeves. On Devèse, see Powell, *Bring Out Your Dead*, 159–63.

- *Wind direction.* "The wind blew from a different quarter nearly every day in July and August. But between the first and fifteenth of September, in summer's most oppressive period, with fever at its worst, the wind never changed: from the south. Temperatures then stayed between 80° and 86°. Except for a few subsequent shifts, the wind remained there until 31 October. Fever season continued, on and on. Does it not seem that the two months of unchanged atmosphere had something to do with the longest season ever recorded?"
- *Wind speed.* "Many vigorous storms occurred nearly everywhere in the United States that summer, but not in New Orleans and environs. Here winds reached a maximum of twenty miles an hour and only twice.[14] Winds do not approach *storm* until they reach thirty, the speed of a moderate gale, and are not truly at storm until forty, the speed of a fresh gale. Winds here reached nineteen on one day only; eighteen on two; seventeen on one; sixteen on five; fifteen on two; and on more than two-thirds of the remaining eighty-nine, they varied between five and eight. One was calm. Strong, brisk winds could have cleared the stagnant, sultry air. They failed. In addition, in a summer of unusually infrequent thunderstorms, the appropriate clouds—thunderheads—often mounded on the horizon. But thunder and lightning followed merely once, 29 August."
- *Relative humidity.* "Also atypical, it stayed [usually] between fifty-eight and sixty-eight percent. It reached eighty-four once. On that day, 8 September, humidity and fever reached their heights together. When humidity stood at eighty-two on 1 and 8 October, fever deaths increased sharply."

"Summing up," the *Deutsche Zeitung* adds, "we conclude that Mr. Deeves's statistical chart shows last summer's meteorological conditions to be as follows: comparatively low temperatures, seldom over 90°; unusually weak winds; almost no thunderstorms; and relative humidity higher and longer than usual. Exactly those conditions also prevailed during the disastrous year of 1853. It seems that meteorological conditions have more to do with the origin and spread of epidemics than the various investigatory commissions have been ready to admit."

Man enjoys mastery however—nearly perfect control—of tellurian conditions. Therefore man can, if not prohibit the origin of the disease, prevent its spread and end epidemics.

I mean that filth, miserable sanitary regulations, defective paving, inadequate drainage, and the laziness and apathy of most inhabitants

14. Wind speeds have been converted to the Beaufort scale.

of southern cities constitute a cause of yellow fever. Public apathy accordingly deserves to be called *suicidal.* Nevertheless, [Holt's testimony added to] the fact of a significant recrudescence after each major epidemic, ought to have enabled the press easily to shake the public out of its reckless indifference.

Traveling through the center of pestilence, I felt obliged to sound as loud an alarm as I could about the hair-raising neglect of sanitation. (An example, brief but representative of what I said, appears in the prior chapter, in the description of Memphis.) That is, I published an essay in the largest German-American newspaper, the *Staatszeitung* of New York, stressing the likelihood of a new outbreak.[15] The German-American press took up the cry against another epidemic. Many papers reprinted my essay verbatim. It caused agitation and protest, directed at municipal officials responsible for sanitation, with happy results. The *Memphis Appeal* translated and published what I said about Memphis. Through my anything-but-flattering remarks, officials learned what disrepute their city labored under.[16]

Meanwhile, Whitelaw Reid and Bayard Taylor's New York *Tribune* carried in translation my essays on New Orleans and called on public opinion and the government for a change of conditions. One of the few brave and upright journals of the region, the distinguished Dr. Förster's *Deutsche Zeitung* of New Orleans, also reissued my essay verbatim on the front page.[17] The essay backed the *Zeitung*'s appeal to the people to improve the city's sanitation. My essay appeared in Arkansas and Texas. Similar complaints from other quarters struck home with officials and people in fever cities. They realized at last: better to spend to clean the city and the sewers, than spend ten times more to nurse the sick and bury the dead of another epidemic. The necessary work, the following winter, resulted in a merciful absence of fever the subsequent summer.

Statistics seem appropriate at this point. Let me cite some compiled by a newspaper, to illustrate the severity of an epidemic. In 1878, 130,000 sickened; 20,000 died. Survivors took an average twenty-five days to recover. Absenteeism, therefore, with work calculated at only $1.50 a man a day, must be put at $5 million. Business closings, industrial shutdowns, nursing care, and other consequences of sickness

15. A search of the *Staatszeitung*'s files, which are not complete, failed to turn up the essay. It would have been but one entry in the columns of "the leading papers of this country," which carried a full discussion of methods to prevent another epidemic (*Memphis Daily Appeal,* 27 May 1879).

16. The country was "infected with this slander" (ibid., 25 February 1879).

17. Georg Förster, editor 1858–1859, 1866–1896 (Arndt and Olson, *German-American Newspapers,* 177). None of the essays mentioned in this paragraph has been located.

have to be reckoned, too, as well as indirect costs to the people of the regions affected.[18] The grand total for an epidemic the size of the one of 1878 amounts to an estimated $150 to $200 million. Yet people—residents of areas where fever takes a toll—would rather suffer such damage than pay taxes to help prevent it.

18. Hesse-Wartegg refers to "the labor costs of many thousands of nurses and orderlies," but the number seems excessive.

8. Grenada and the Yazoo Country

From Memphis we continued the journey: toward Mississippi, the infamous fever city of Grenada, and the Yazoo River. We soon regretted it—from the bottoms of our hearts. The South may be sunny, but its means and systems of communication and its entire culture still languish in the shade. The truth of this plight does not emerge until the traveler passes Memphis. The northern sun, the orb of civilization, beams on Memphis and the area immediately north. But in Memphis that sun halts and expires. Its last rays still illuminate but do not warm. They touch the surface but do not penetrate. They favor some of good old Memphis but end north of the southern train station.

I mean the terminus of the Mississippi & Tennessee Railroad. The Kansas Pacific, competing with its northern rival, used to post signs, those world-famous warnings against the competitor.[1] I should like to do the same for each of my dear readers, against the Mississippi & Tennessee. BEWARE OF THE M&T. For it is with its own special dignity that our railroad of imposing and vigorous name conveys the traveler to "*the sunny South.*" Trains originate in Memphis and leave a half hour late. They terminate in Grenada three hours late if the end of the line is reached at all. (A train may wheeze its last in some cotton plantation.) I hear that these arrivals three hours late occur always on time. By an exactitude of calculation the extra hours bring passengers into Grenada at the instant the train to New Orleans leaves. They had hoped to catch it; they watch it disappear into the distance. Hence a day's layover in Grenada, the town of yellow fever, what a cozy spot. Hence, too, a crowd of passengers each in the same fix, besieging the station's hotel: a lucrative clientele for an establishment otherwise unoccupied. Hence, finally, the suspicion: boniface and the trainmen may be less than strangers. The M & T itself can only benefit from this tardiness, being without competition between Grenada and Memphis. Competition—what a blessing it would be for the poor traveler here! Improvement through competition would have allowed a happy beginning

---

1. The rival was probably the Union Pacific. The signs were probably posted during their "keen, even bitter rivalry" of 1870–1879 (Charles Edgar Ames, *Pioneering the Union Pacific,* 316).

and a joyous end to our tale of a pleasure-excursion aboard the M & T. The middle, the more difficult part of our tale, must still be told.

We boarded our train [in Memphis]. Everyone brought his baggage and the fond hope of arrival next morning safe and sound in New Orleans, "Queen of the South." Almost everyone would soon lose baggage and hope. Need I say at this point that perforce the luxury of Pullman palace cars had been left in Memphis? We settled as best we could in the two first-class coaches.

Americans in the North plume themselves on the *egalité* of their public transportation. Everyone rides alike: first class in the North, third class in the South. That is, in a northern or a southern train everyone rides in the same cars, but dilapidated, worn-out, northern cars seem to have been shunted to southern stepchildren. I looked for the smoking car. My every glance and sniff proclaimed smoking in both cars. About two dozen ladies and gentlemen of the *"coloured race"* already held places there. Stretched out on the best seats, their dirty laundry and bedrolls piled on the rest, the Negroes—black, ragged, boorish—were masters of the situation. We poor victims of white skins given us by Mother Nature, we crowded into corners. The black race nowadays avenges itself on the white in the way of the white.[2] Once upon a time a black woman would not be permitted to ride in a car with whites, now vice versa. Except that, to be up-to-date, "be permitted" must be changed to "be able." We saw it with our own eyes. A woman, obviously a Northerner, had bought her ticket to New Orleans and headed into our car, only to stop dead on the threshold, with a disappointed *"Oh."*

"Is this . . . is this . . . this . . . the car for New Orleans?"

"Yes, ma'am."

"Are these . . . Nigg— . . . these gentlemen going along?"

"Yes, ma'am."

"In this car?"

We never saw her again. She probably took a steamboat downriver. Best for us too, all around, to have done likewise. Thus the punishment for the curiosity to see and the longing to visit strange lands!

Our train left Memphis and rattled us through cotton plantations. The water of spring rains still stood in most of the furrows. Here and there a lone, leafless bush waved bolls forced open from inside by handsome, snow-white cotton pushing out. Cotton and corn, the only

2. The Civil Rights Act of 1875 legislated equality in public transportation. The act began to lose force at the end of Reconstruction. It would be declared unconstitutional in 1882, but Hesse-Wartegg's anecdote shows that it still had meaning when he was here in 1879. See Foner, *Reconstruction,* 556, 587.

[cash] crops that can be raised here, grow on land cleared for them out of virgin forest. From the shore of the Mississippi the forest stretches far beyond the Yazoo and into the interior.[3] People live along the railroad, people as primitive as the forest is primeval. Moss does not cover nor vines encircle the people as well as the trees, true, but the way of life betrays the state of civilization. Impecunious, forsaken, isolated, out of touch, the people are mostly Negroes tilling morsels of land and raising their potatoes, carrots, and corn. Just enough [of a living] can be scratched out by the man who takes a wife. In addition, now and then, using cash from his annual cotton harvest, he can buy a beautiful necktie and a pair of dress gloves. (That list practically covers the essentials to Negro life in the Mississippi valley.) On Sunday he struts in his new cravat and gloves, lies in the sun on weekdays, and loafs as long as his parade uniform lasts (it consists of the tie and gloves); and then the next season of work begins.

We passed a few stations, each nothing but a log cabin and one or two miserable shacks. Nearly all dwellings seem to be on stilts. (Frequent and severe floods throughout the western part of the state [Mississippi] negate homes in the usual mode, unless the occupants want months of water knee-deep in the living room.) Cellars, of course, are possible only if rock-solid and watertight. Not a cellar but piles—masonry walls or wooden posts several feet high—support a building and constitute the basis for the "ground" floor. Elevation also recommends itself against the several dangerous creatures that begin to occur here as one proceeds south, including rattlesnakes, water moccasins, and alligators.[4]

In late evening we neared the hour of anticipated arrival in Grenada, an hour late so as to preclude our continuing to New Orleans then. That circumstance prompted an inevitable chain of reasoning. Every white passenger accordingly approached the conductor and the fireman to ask, "Is the fever still in Grenada?" To us, even a day's layover would be less than agreeable, amid fever. But it had died in Grenada two months prior, for lack of anything to eat.

About twenty miles out of Grenada the train halted. We thought it must be another of the fifteen-minute "*stops*." They had occurred all along because of hotboxes that set the car on fire. This time the car did not catch fire: we stopped mainly to take on the Negro gentlemen of the

---

3. "This was a land of unbroken forests . . . enormous heights, with vast trunks and limbs, and between them spread a chaos of vines and cane and brush, so that the deer and bear took it for their own, and only by the Indians was it penetrable, and by them only on wraiths of trails" (Percy, *Lanterns,* 4).

4. Hesse-Wartegg seems to intend a list of subtropical reptiles. Of the three, only the alligator would belong on the list.

section gang. They had been laying ties; now they wanted to return to Grenada. What would people say to such a thing in Europe? On the main line an express stops to let on, and into the first-class ladies' car, these black, ragged, besmeared trackmen? And this a *"civilised country"* no less! In such company we crossed the Yalobusha River on the railroad bridge and entered the northernmost city of Mississippi.

Sadness has brought Grenada fame. Before 1878, who of the world's 1.3 billion people knew of the place? Postmasters in the United States, conductors on the Louisville & Great Southern Railroad, residents of Grenada—they and nobody else knew it existed.[5] Even Petermann in Gotha would have been hard put to state exactly the position of the metropolis on the Yalobusha.[6] How different now. The city has shrunk by half, its notoriety swollen by a thousand: "honors" brought by the invasion of Yellow Jack. In the heat of summer last year, not a day passed but the name *Grenada* raced a thousand times over the telegraph. Numbers more or less large would follow the name, and then the daily papers told mankind how many had sickened, how many died in the city of misfortune.

Sorrowful times, those. I have never seen so much sympathy and compassion for another city as for Grenada ravaged by plague. Memories of scenes brought us by the *New York Herald*—of the sickness of thousands and the deaths of hundreds, of a city robbed of law and bereft of morals, of a city indeed of bestiality—these memories vivid, we entered Grenada in late evening, the flesh of many rough with goose pimples. Not exactly comforting, either the prospect of spending the night in a hotel where two dozen had died a short while ago, or the rumor that Yellow Jack still haunted the victimized town. We must submit to circumstances nonetheless. No more trains that day to take us to Jackson and Vicksburg or back to Memphis. Besides, a layover even in Grenada would be preferable to another ride on the M & T. So we must stay.

During our frugal dinner the conversation naturally kept to one topic. Questions about fever bombarded innkeeper and townspeople. We heard hair-raising anecdotes of cruel nurses and orderlies, the helplessness of the sick, and the blessed aid of the Howard Association. In everything they said, however, we could see a listless reluctance to speak of what had been suffered. Meanwhile, they denied with elo-

---

5. The name of the railroad must be a mistake. The L&GSR did not pass through Grenada or anywhere else in Mississippi. See Rowland, *Encyclopedia* 1:804–6, 2: 502–16.

6. August Heinrich Petermann (1822–1878), cartographer and publisher of many maps and atlases in Gotha, Germany (American Library Association, *National Union Catalogue,* 452:498–501).

quence the consequences of fever and contradicted with passion the likelihood that it could happen again. Grenada had suffered *not at all* from fever. The influx of newcomers meant more Grenadans than ever. Business was booming. When we took a walk the next day, we could find no proof for those assertions. The gruesome disease destroyed the bloom of Grenada in the summer of 1878, a few months before we arrived.

Unfortunately, the city has been built on spongy, water-ravaged terrain peculiar to Mississippi. A confusion of rushing streams, dry gulches, and broad waterways crisscrosses the city's gelatinous face. In the spring the face betrays the character of the place. To the north the abundant, vigorous Yalobusha curves past to empty into the Yazoo some twenty miles below Grenada, and in the spring to flood the surroundings far and wide. Several feet of water inundates the streets then. When at last the river recedes to its normal course, stagnant pools remain in the municipal lowlands. Garbage, trash, and filth collect there next, in a city without an inch of sewers. Summer adds the last ingredient to the recipe for the gruesome disease: heat.

Here is a paragraph of a letter from Grenada:

> Most of the houses are built on stilts. Every kind of trash and filth is thrown into the spaces between houses. In the middle of town, plain to be seen, is a slough. It is covered with green slime and it stinks up the whole place. Things are so bad that some people can't stand it anymore. They've gone to the commander of the local army post and asked for help. They wouldn't dream of doing anything themselves. That officer has had some of his men dig a ditch for a drain from the hole to the river. A ton of stuff turned up, from animals, all rotten. Human bodies, too. The city slopes to the river. It would have been the easiest and cheapest thing, all along, to dig drains. Only nobody, of all who live here, thought of it before.

As in New Orleans and Vicksburg, so in Grenada: people know what to but will not budge. The city, they shrug, has no money for such comprehensive and drastic measures. "We're too poor to worry about sanitary measures. The old ways are going to have to be good enough."

Yet this is a town of singular and notable qualities. The hub of a cotton-growing region, it boasts an *"elite"* of planters. Their magnolia gardens surround with perpetual green their handsome houses crowning the hills beyond Grenada proper. The city itself boasts but few streets. They center on the large marketplace. Mostly low, one-story houses of brick and wood occupy the streets, together with businesses that serve the planters: an abundance of agricultural-implement dealers, furniture stores, newsstands, stationers, and of course *"variety stores"* and *"curiosity shops."*

A glance across Grenada reproduces the villages of southern Hungary and the Benat: identical in situation, in the primitive state of the streets, in the horde of pigs in the streets, rooting and grubbing like rats. Many houses are vacant, shops closed, walls tumbled down. Houses once stood in the numerous gaps along the streets. Stubby chimneys at intervals of ten feet or so testify that houses did occupy these vacant lots. The people who lived in them took them down—they were of wood—and reassembled them elsewhere. The chimneys—of brick—were left behind. But the marketplace and its approaches constitute the most significant socio-historical feature. Life throbs on the wooden sidewalks in front of the buildings along the streets to and from there. Every second person was a frayed Negro; but we saw planters, too, on horseback or in carriages. Some of the ancient vehicles must date from the French period. Carriages in the grand style, yes, trimmed in silver and richly appointed, with cushions of silk; but so old that we would have expected them in a museum, not on a street in Mississippi.

Our walk soon brought us to an intersection and the city's most interesting sight: a post about as tall as a man and as broad. Grenada's "iron-clad cudgel" happily gives Grenada perhaps its only thing in common with the venerable capital on the Danube. The authorities nail their announcements to it. So many nails have been driven into it one after another, covering it, that Grenada's (like its worthy ancestor on the Viennese *Graben*) no longer can be recognized as wooden.[7] Nothing can be seen but nail heads.

The next day when I wanted a newspaper, our hotel had none. So I looked for the offices of the local publication. There *must* be such an establishment here. Where in America is the city of a hundred houses and no newspaper? Grenada, too, has its newspaper. His excellency the editor keeps house and his *Grenada Sentinel* in a *"wooden shanty,"* at once editorial office and bedroom, kitchen and library, telegraph station and printing plant. Lest anyone miss the significance of this exalted institution, a sign has been posted on the wall outside:

This is the Sentinel Office
Stop, pilgrim and Subscribe.

And beneath the categorical print, the words in pencil:

Non Subscribers have to advertise.[8]

---

7. The *Graben,* one of Vienna's busiest thoroughfares, contained the fashionable shops and "the *Stock im Eisen* [stump of iron], a tree stump said to be the survivor of a holy grove round which the original settlement of Vindominia sprang up. It is full of nails driven into it by travelling journeymen" (*Encyclopaedia Britannica,* 11th ed., s.v. "Vienna").

8. The meaning of these words, which Hesse-Wartegg gives in English, is not clear.

Unfortunately the editor was out. We bought a *Sentinel.* Let us include an extract from the lead article, on a *"Mississippi hanging"*: ". . . and we would say but one thing in addition: Heed this prophecy, you da—— gunslingers. In our state in the next twelvemonth, more murderers will be convicted and hanged than have swung in the last twelve *years.* Mercy never again for such an outrage." The outrage was the murder by shooting of a Meridian City resident.

Also in the paper: an invitation to immigrate and buy land in the beautiful environs.

Finally, this notice:

Colonel St. Vrain

asks that the *Sentinel* inform all his old friends and the public: tomorrow from 11:00 A.M. to 1:00 P.M., *"chicken salad"* will be served in the Grenada Palace Saloon, free. The colonel and his friendly assistant William F. Barnes will greet guests with their usual cordiality.

(Bear in mind that the colonel is the owner of the saloon.)

The honorable editor-in-chief was away for good reason, having been secretly informed of a *"white washing,"* he ordered his *"city editor"* (i.e., himself) to attend. We happened to be there, too. Walking down the street to the marketplace, we met a Negress somewhat less than clothed. Her face, arms, legs, shoulders, and nape of the neck had been whitewashed; she looked like a female Punchinello. A few street arabs tagged after her, laughing and carrying on. What was the matter here, we asked in bewilderment. Why all this white paint?

"Oh, it's only a white washing."

The answer meant nothing to our virginal minds. We asked a black loafer to explain.

"Oaah," he said, holding the roundest part of his body in laughter, *"oaah, jast dink, dat d——d niggerwoman wanted to marry a vite maan. Dot serves har olright."*[9]

It turned out that a white man and a Negro women intended to marry. The two races, black and white, got wind of the plan. Each considered the union a racial misalliance. They stopped it by whitewashing the Negress. The *Sentinel* remained silent as to whether the blacks had turned the groom into one of their race.

Fact is, everywhere in the South (perhaps with a few exceptions along the Atlantic coast), interracial marriages are as unpopular as anything can be. They rarely occur. We have spoken of a mild reaction,

---

9. Hesse-Wartegg's "English" rendition is quoted verbatim. The transcription is unlikely to correspond to what would have been heard by a native speaker of English.

a mere whitewashing. Had a black man wanted to marry a white woman, he would have been lynched.[10]

I have already mentioned Grenada as a river port. In the winter local steamboats of the Yazoo region ascend the Yalobusha far beyond Grenada to bring out bales of cotton from plantations in the interior of Mississippi.

What of the *Sentinel*'s invitation to come to Grenada to farm? To begin with, the Yalobusha's parent, the Yazoo, drops but 100 feet in 600 miles, or 1 foot per 6 miles. This remarkable fact means the Yazoo cannot accommodate large amounts of water from its powerful tributaries. The slightest rainfall therefore sends the Yazoo promptly over its banks in the upper reaches. And in winter and spring, floods drown a thousand miles of land to a depth of several feet. Always when the floods withdraw, they leave several inches of silt. Looking at those conditions, we cannot urge that the invitation be accepted.

In the Negro cemetery, off by itself here as everywhere in the United States, we saw the fresh, the *mass* graves of fever victims. The graves seemed barely closed: capped but moments before with low mounds of earth and sprinkled with lime, but marked with neither cross nor name. Care of this cemetery had been left to our dear Mother Nature. She abandoned it in utter neglect, downright devastation. Indians and Hottentots look after their burial grounds better than do the black "*gentlemen*." Indeed, this Negro cemetery—ruinous graves, dilapidated picket fences trampled under foot, incredible wretchedness—gives a true picture of the race whose dead lie beneath its greensward. We cannot predict a comfortable future for those who disobey the pious maxim, "Honor thy dead!"

---

10. "Miscegenation, actual or by tendency," would likelier cause whitecapping than whitewashing. Mobs that protected "rural virtue," called whitecappers, would "strike at a Negro who is living with a white woman; at a white man who is stopping with a Negro woman." The violence could go as far as lynching (Ayers, *Vengeance and Justice,* 258–61).

9. Through the State of Mississippi

Either Mississippi or Alabama dwarfs many a European power. Together they compose a domain of colossal proportions. Both, in spite of their miseries, stand on a threshold of magnificence greater than the old slavocratic splendor.

To the foreigner, Mississippi with a million inhabitants seems practically uninhabited and in something of the pristine condition still found in Dakota or West Texas. Giant primeval forests cover it. Tall oaks, cottonwoods, and elms—magnolias among them here and there—still prevail in hundreds of thousands of acres of virgin land where nobody has set foot. Thick vines twist upward and around giant trunks. Heaps of gray-green Spanish moss overload the limbs and branches, droop in long beards, and make the trees look like huge weeping willows. The Mississippi and Yazoo's vast bayous flood the area in spring and summer, rendering them inaccessible.

Mississippi's railroads traverse hundreds of miles that are untouched by the plow. Slaveholders, of course, put their plantations in the best and most accessible places. They prospered. The *"freedman"* lives there now. He struggles with self-government. A problem the white has not solved, it remains a mystery to the black, he being newly emancipated.

Plantations realized worth through slaves bound to them. Slaves were as necessary as sun and rain. Plantations therefore lost their worth the moment they lost their slaves. Perhaps it has been reserved to the present generation to restore by rational agriculture the former glory of this land. A modicum of money and the financial independence that accompanies it would lift the people beyond measure. But the money cannot be found now.

Mississippi, though without important minerals, enjoys splendid soil, expanses ideal for cotton, corn, tobacco, hemp, flax, and in the north, every sort of grain. Fruits of the moderate climates flourish there; in the south, oranges and figs. Since the war, however, as I have said, land values and the state's wealth have disappeared. The worth of real and personal property, over $500 million in 1860, fell to $150 million in 1870. The cotton output, 1.25 million bales in 1860, shriveled to a half million in 1870. It has returned only to 1.25 million.

Perhaps the least developed and most backward of the states, it is scantily populated, having not one city of 10,000 except Vicksburg. It lacks enough railroads and therefore suffers from too little transportation and thus faulty communication. For, in the South (especially the Mississippi valley), navigable rivers and the railroad do not supplement and extend the footpath and the highway; transportation and communication originate on the river and with the railroad. Farmers and planters reach one another and get to town by traveling cross-country or, under the best of circumstances, by following their own *"trails."* Highways and thoroughfares, drained, marked out, and in any other way improved, do not exist in these states. Nor is there familiarity between Mississippi's people and the world outside. Travelers to and from New Orleans, going north or south, speed through at night in sleeping cars. Nobody so much as dreams of pausing in one of the notorious little railroad towns, ill-reputed because precarious; and Mississippi, especially the southern part, barely smacks of civilization.

Fifty to a hundred miles often separate one city or town from another. Nothing passes between them. You can imagine what hardships planters suffer in these remote regions, getting food and other necessities and bringing harvests to market. Yet they persevere, planter and town. Every planter rests assured that the railroad will pass his plantation someday; every town, that it will be selected as terminus for some transcontinental railroad. As not a breath of such success has stirred, patience must equal optimism.

The inclemency, the harshness of this countryside surprised me when I traveled by train through the middle of the state. Sluggish, muddy streams toil through sandy, yellow soil. A stagnant pool or a green pond fills the forest's every depression. No more than a little rain has turned the fields to muck. In the northern part more people occupy a better-cultivated countryside. In the southern an Indian primitiveness still reigns supreme. The railroads themselves are an example. Make a connection? Arrive on time? Not a chance. Trains often stop at will on the open tracks or at plantations and regularly arrive one or more hours late at appointed destinations. Mine stopped frequently because the short-winded locomotive labored on hills. We often stalled two or three times an hour while the locomotive spun its wheels but advanced not an inch. Passengers dismounted. Many helped by pushing or pulling. But the old jade would not go. Repeated retreats and roaring assaults, sand on the rails, other measures: only after all had been taken did the enterprise succeed. Such railway exercises at night in the wilderness do not rank (as you can well imagine) among the joys of travel. Even the otherwise phlegmatic Yankees lost their composure.

I could quote the volcano of curses. It would make interesting reading but expand the book by several chapters. Mississippi is prodigal of curses. So I must limit myself to a short and general discussion. Now, an occasional, brief, pithy curse ought usually to serve the purpose and, like the counterpart in my country, be forgiven in tense moments that provoke them. But such a trifle satisfies neither "*Yankee*" nor "*Southerner*." The high and nasal voice spins a thread of curses instead, but so long and flimsy that the effect crumbles. (A cursing Yankee resembles a miaowing cat.) The curser shoves his hands into his pockets, pulls his soft hat low on this brow, and betrays no agitation. The objective European sees an utterly silly person. Curses among us [on this Mississippi excursion] continued longest when the train would stop in solitary stations where nobody got on or off and our engine struggled its best in vain to move the cars and resume the journey. Meanwhile the villages reminded me of southern Hungary and the Banat: squat shacks and log cabins with pigsties; an expansive square at the station; here and there a few primeval trees, spared the axe; and at the station, bales upon countless bales of cotton everywhere. I got off in Meridian, in the interior [east-central part], at a junction with the train to Vicksburg.[1] I intended to see city and environs in a few days.

The clerk looked at the register, thunderstruck. A flesh-and-blood European, off the train, alive and breathing at *his* desk?

"*You are a fool,* sir, daring to come here!"

I asked the reason. He replied with candor.

"Life and property aren't safe, really, in this part of Mississippi, outside of town. There's no industry at all. Everything depends on cotton and hogs. Farmers haven't got a cent. The niggers are in the hands of bloodsucking Jewish '*storekeepers*' and purveyors.[2] Things are in sad shape around here."

I toured the environs anyway. The land is excellent everywhere. Water, forest, prairie: they lack only settlers, railways, roads. Toughs roam these parts, however, scoundrels not likely to inspire trust. When I had to stop for a night in one of the many taverns in Marion, I spent the evening conversing with a young planter. How charming was his shout to me, "*Stranger, I bet you a hundred-dollar bill you won't see your folks alive again*!" But he had ruined his chances. Not about to let him win so much money, I took the next night train to Jackson, the capital.

1. The Southern Mississippi or Mississippi Southern.
2. Southern anti-Semitism did not amount to much. It usually appeared as reported by Hesse-Wartegg here: resentment against Jewish merchants. They were readily spoken of with "a touch of anti-Semitism" (Taylor, *Louisiana Reconstructed*, 402). See also Woodward, *New South,* 188; Coulter, *South During Reconstruction,* 202–3; and chapter 25, note 16 below. Twain spoke of the "thrifty Israelite, who encourages the thoughtless negro and wife to buy" on credit. The negro's share of the crop then "belongs to the Israelite." Negroes come and go: each "will fatten the Israelite a season" (*Life on the Mississippi,* 290–91).

The Mississippi, the artery of commerce, passes nearby; and the capital of the South [New Orleans] lies but twelve hours away by train. The dual influence manifests itself here. The people you meet, white or black, are well dressed and impress you as prosperous. Pleasant houses and nicely kept gardens confirm the impression. In the valley's prettiest city between Cairo and New Orleans, part of the old planter aristocracy retains its residences. Avenues everywhere; lovely gardens with palms and palmettoes, cacti and orange groves; government buildings open to the public; and on a slight elevation, the elegant and distinguished state capitol, seat of the government. Being the majority in Mississippi, blacks enjoy a big share of government, and hold many important offices, as we have observed: lieutenant-governor, secretary of state, commissioner of education, among others.[3] At the capitol I also noted interesting details about finance and education. The state supports numerous schools. Its two universities are at Oxford, for whites, and on the banks of the Mississippi near Rodney, for blacks (named after a former governor, Alcorn).[4]

By contrast the state's political affairs leave much to be desired. In the rural areas nobody looks after the safety of property or life. The situation, always bad, worsens during elections, when "*rowdies*" often impose a political persuasion on planters and Negroes. Consequently, in the last few years, black landowners have wanted to leave and resettle in Texas or the prairie states.

I stayed overnight in the hotel beside the station. During the night the train brought passengers who, like me, got off here. In the morning after breakfast, they crowded up to the desk, pulled rolls of banknotes out of their pockets, and paid their bills, $3.00 each. They received neither invoice nor receipt. When I saw others pay $2.00, I plunked down $2.00. The clerk looked at me. After a moment he asked with some surprise, "*Are you a drummer, sir?* Another dollar!" I added the third and continued my journey, richer for the knowledge that the common traveler must pay more than drummers pay for lodging. What are drummers? Traveling salesmen: America's "*commercials*." Anyone widely traveled in the United States can tell one by his looks. Drummers share transportation and mingle with regular travelers everywhere: on trains, in hotels, shops and restaurants, on steamboats. Everywhere, that is, except remote, unpopulated places.

3. On black government in Louisiana and other southern states, see chapter 20, note 4 below.
4. Convening in 1870 for the first time after Reconstruction, the legislature reorganized the board of trustees of the state university at Oxford, created Alcorn University for Negroes (named for James Lusk Alcorn [1816–1894]), and voted the same appropriation for both institutions (Henry, *Reconstruction,* 431).

Next I intended some side trips from Vicksburg into the famous "*Mississippi bottom.*" So I returned from Jackson to the Mississippi by train.

Planters are always calling this "*bottomland*" the richest, the most fertile agricultural land in the valley; yet it remains primitive and uninhabitable. It extends some 300 miles, running along the Mississippi's left bank from Memphis to Vicksburg. Thirty to forty miles wide, it amounts to an area that dwarfs the kingdom of Würtemburg.[5] A considerable system of ample rivers, mostly navigable, flows through this wilderness, tributary chiefly to the Yazoo, or River of the Dead, as the Indians call it. At many points the rivers communicate with other tributaries of the Mississippi. But the Yazoo is *the* bottomland river. It joins the Mississippi at Vicksburg. The Mississippi's annual floods inundate most of the bottom to depths of three to six feet. The water recedes in summer, leaving a thick crust of mud that resists cultivation. The bottom nonetheless produces one bumper crop—insects. Oxen and horses, stung by poisonous flies, often die an agonized death in a few hours.[6] In the mostly oak, sassafras, cypress, and silver-poplar forests you will find many deer. Panthers and small black bears dwell in low-lying reed thickets. On numerous crescent-shaped lakes (obviously parts of the old riverbed), pelicans, swans, and countless other birds, and even alligators, disport themselves. In a word, this is a wilderness of a kind described in prior chapters, with the unique features and the advantages and disadvantages of such a wild place. Yet its days are numbered. In time, with the growing incursion of northerners, the land will be cleared and expanses brought under the plow.

No place but Vicksburg, in all the United States, evokes so many sad memories of the terrible anti-slavery war of the last decade. Every hill, every cliff thrusting a sheer face from the river, knows legendary acts of martial heroism. Every square foot of the environs has drunk soldiers' blood. In the river itself, evidence endures of modern history's biggest and bloodiest siege.[7] Indeed, bent by the siege to a different course, the river has kept it.

The city, Mississippi's largest, rises imposingly on steep upthrusts, the "*bluffs*" of the river, which ascend to the plateau at the top. The more distinguished homes of planters join the beautiful courthouse

---

5. Würtemburg had fewer than 1,200 square miles.

6. Hesse-Wartegg's note: "See Somers, *The Southern States*, 255." Somers's words: "Horses and oxen are often worried to death in a few hours by swarms of venomous flies."

7. In his siege of Vicksburg, May–July 1863, Grant "achieved one of the most brilliant military successes in history" (Mark Mayo Boatner, *Civil War Dictionary*, 877). Bombardment, sickness, wounds, and hunger forced the Confederate surrender.

there. And on the heights above them, even now you can see traces of the old fort. From its walls, "Whistling Dick," the Confederates' infamous cannon, hurled hideous death into enemy ranks.[8] Grass flourishes on the ruins but the elevation still commands the river. A long panorama sweeps the Mississippi's twists and bends, the twin cities of DeSoto and Delta on the opposite shore, and the throb of all that riverfront life in the port. Nearer our vantage point, large and handsome hotels and stores line Washington Street, Vicksburg's thoroughfare. The many short, narrow streets seem to plunge from there to the river, to the many massive warehouses and magazines along its banks. People pant and wheeze to the top of the steep streets. Wheeled vehicles cannot use them. To walk is to sink into a foot of debris; the streets are not paved. In every one, fifty Negroes and white vagabonds loaf. Indeed, nothing looks hospitable, nor does the city evoke trust or inspire confidence.

True, nineteen steamboat lines maintain wharves and anchorages, and an impressive traffic bustles on the river and the rails below us. Vicksburg is still one of the cotton country's important commercial centers. True, many of the South's first and oldest planter families live here. But Vicksburg has meant *infamy* since the war. Multifarious riffraff, found in every port city, assert themselves with exceptional energy here. People carry revolvers as a matter of habit, as they might pencils or toothpicks. Lynching, murder, gunplay occurred almost weekly for years. If things have improved in latter days, have the rowdies become as meek as lambs? Not at all!

I see, this time from a boat, a tall flagpole and the Stars and Stripes, marking the national cemetery about two miles off. Many of its occupants died in the siege. The graves extend across fourteen acres of well-cared-for terraces: 18,000 graves, not one empty![9]

In the regions below Vicksburg and even in Natchez (the state's second-largest river port), Negroes constitute the majority and thus hold the most-important county and municipal offices. Much political and social friction has harassed the state since the war. The status of Negroes has been one of the chief causes. In Natchez the races live in peace. But schools, churches, and communities divide along racial lines: all white or all black, no exceptions. Cotton reigns supreme, as everywhere in this part of the country.

---

8. Dick, "perhaps the most famous single gun of the war," was an 18-pounder that had been rifled after being cast a smoothbore. The irregularity put an erratic spin on projectiles and made them whistle (ibid., 912–13). See also Patricia L. Faust, ed., *Historical Times Illustrated Encyclopedia of the Civil War,* 820.

9. See Twain, *Life on the Mississippi,* 302.

10. Ku Klux Klan and Judge Lynch

When the ferocious, gory Civil War ended, a secret society appeared in the cities and states of the conquered South.[1] Applying utmost energy to the task, it brought law and order to districts occupied by the enemy and terrorized by newly freed Negroes. It also punished crimes and constituted a kind of police, clandestine but sovereign.[2] It did its work at night, usually on horseback and with faces muffled or masked. In acts often anything but legal, it would appropriate horses from the nearest convenient farm when night missions also involved distances. But the horses were always returned, punctiliously, a day or two later. Quickly the Klan became a horror to mad, vagabond Negroes, as well as being nemesis to the federal army of occupation and, so the story goes, the avenger of the Confederate dead.

Southerners accordingly believed in the Klan, trusted it, and set store by its ability to protect them.[3] On the other hand, military authorities and the government in Washington hunted it, using many undercover agents.[4] But it so guarded its secrecy that scarcely any

---

1. On the origins of the Klan, see Allen W. Trelease, *White Terror: The Ku Klux Klan Conspiracy and Southern Reconstruction*, 3–110; William G. Brown, *The Lower South in American History*, 199–211; and Susan Lawrence Davis, *Authentic History of the Ku Klux Klan, 1865–1877*, 1–95.

2. The postwar disorder that included marauding gangs and free-roving bandits (see Dabney, *One Hundred Years*, 221) was accompanied by vigilante "justice," administered in part by the Klan. This vigilantism and the Klan's efforts to frighten Negroes and potential agitators may have caused as much of the violence and terror as it prevented. "Terrorism by newly freed Negroes" may also have been more a white fear than a widespread fact. See Trelease, *White Terror*, 101–9; William E. B. Du Bois, *Black Reconstruction*, 670–77; and Foner, *Reconstruction*, 119–23, 425–44, especially 436–37.

3. To white southerners it was the "Ku Klux Klan which during reconstruction days had played so desperate but on the whole so helpful a part in keeping the peace and preventing mob violence" (Percy, *Lanterns*, 231–32). The early Klan was not only supported by "the best element in the South," it was also "given credit for its good intentions by a considerable number of people in the North" (Coulter, *South During Reconstruction*, 171). Articles in the forthcoming *Encyclopedia of Southern Culture* will show that the Klan "was once admired by people across America. Hollywood's 'Birth of a Nation,' a 1915 film glorifying the Klan, helped make moviegoing a major pastime" (s.v. "The South"). Davis expresses admiration to the point of veneration throughout *Authentic History*.

4. State governments also opposed the Klan—with more success, according to

members were discovered. Moreover, if a garrison or a larger unit of occupation in the cities intended anti-Klan measures, the Klan would demonstrate, perhaps parade past the garrison the same night, in such strength that the plan for military action would soon be abandoned.

The Klan wore mummer-like outfits reminiscent of the Inquisition. The black calico gowns, made to order, were called shrouds.[5] Secret couriers distributed the material to certain homes by night. There, southern wives and daughters sewed them into Klan uniforms. Then they were collected.

The Klan originated in terrible times.[6] Political and social agitators arrived from the North, went from plantation to plantation, set themselves up as leaders of the Negroes, and in notorious nocturnal *"meetings,"* inflamed them to annihilate the whites, their former masters. Crime and outrage spread and prevailed. The law meanwhile must remain powerless in these large, thinly populated and devastated states. The Klan's chief objectives therefore were to disarm bands of free Negroes who roamed, robbing and murdering; to punish or hang marauders and notorious criminals; and to restore a general security for life and property, so menaced by anarchy in the conquered South. Especially must the Negroes be subdued. For they considered themselves lords and masters of the land, roved about with empty bellies but armed to the teeth, and garnered livelihood by pillage and theft.[7]

Foner, than Hesse-Wartegg would have us believe (*Reconstruction,* 438–41).

5. The reconstituted, twentieth-century Klan seems to prefer white. Although most common to the Klan of Reconstruction—easily made of bed sheets and producing a ghostly effect—white sometimes gave way to black, as well as yellow, brown, and red. See Trelease, *White Terror,* 53. A picture in *Harper's Weekly,* 19 December 1868, shows Klansmen in black gowns and white hoods. The frontispiece to Davis, *Authentic History,* is of a Klansman and horse both swathed in white.

6. This paragraph takes a kinder view of the Klan than is usually taken today. It also sounds like the Klan "in its earlier and more responsible days" (Henry, *Reconstruction,* 233). It has some evenhandedness, however, when compared to the perspective of Davis, who would justify the Klan and credit it with a role in redeeming the South from Reconstruction (*Authentic History,* v, vi).

7. "It was charged that in North Carolina in 1867 a fourth of the Negro population went armed with guns, pistols, and bowie knives. . . . There was widespread fear in the South in 1865 that the Negroes would engage in a general uprising at Christmas" (Coulter, *South During Reconstruction,* 50). Brown calls the Klan "an outcome of the conditions that prevailed in the southern states after the war. . . . It must be studied against its proper background of a disordered society and a bewildered people" (*Lower South,* 195–96). A century later the threat to life and property, and law and order, seems minimal. Klansmen, especially of the later variety, were not so much vigilantes seeking law and order and justice, as racists out to maintain white supremacy and Anglo-Saxon civilization. See Trelease, *White Terror,* xi, xxii. What can be expected of militant racists when gentle, benevolent ones held such views as the following? "Apparently there is something peculiarly Negroid in the Negro's attitude toward, and aptitude for, crimes of violence. He seems to have resisted,

The Klan soon became the most powerful, the most widespread, and the most feared secret society in any country ever. Unfortunately, in many instances it did not hold to its original good intentions. Acts of savagery and horrible executions, evocative of the Inquisition, spread and multiplied. Thus the Klan gradually lost respect while the government and its officials in time regained power and influence.[8] The fearsome society finally disintegrated. It disappeared primarily in those regions where it wreaked such arbitrary havoc. In some places it has continued to the present day, and acts yet in the office of avenger. The name Ku Klux, little used anymore, appears mostly in the calumniations of the Republican press.[9]

Vigilance committees and Judge Lynch have appeared instead. The committees form sporadically throughout the southern states. In many places they can be called the Klan's legitimate and necessary successor. Judge Lynch—summary punishment of crime, exacted by spontaneous public tribunal—is also warranted in most instances. Murder and rape (the most common capital crimes), as well as manslaughter, maiming, and other atrocities occur unfortunately too often in the Mississippi basin. These southern states are too new, they have too few people, and they lack order and discipline. The law has no teeth, judges are venal, juries frequently decide according to political and personal biases, and lawyers hereabouts are the dregs of society, the lowest sort ever to collect in one occupation. Open any newspaper and find to your horror the long-winded recital of this or that bloody deed. We feel sadly obligated to hesitate and not spell out the details of these unhappy circumstances south of the Ohio and the Arkansas. They exist beyond doubt and are already too well known. To them and them alone can be attributed every last one of the South's horrific crime statistics.[10] We

---

except on the surface, our ethics and to have rejected our standards. Murder, thieving, lying, violence—I sometimes suspect the Negro doesn't regard these as crimes or sins, or even as regrettable occurrences. He commits them casually, with no apparent feeling of guilt. . . . The gentle, devoted creature who is your baby's nurse can carve her boy-friend from ear to ear at midnight and by seven a.m. will be changing the baby's diaper while she sings 'Hear the Lambs a-calling' " (Percy, *Lanterns,* 299).

8. Not public disfavor in the South, but action by the Federal government "broke the back of the Ku Klux Klans." Violence in the South "assumed other forms" (Trelease, *White Terror,* 418). The Enforcement Acts and legislation by various states were harsh against the Klan—so harsh that martial law was declared under the third act, and the acts were declared unconstitutional (Coulter, *South During Reconstruction,* 170–71).

9. That is, the Republican press tried to discredit the Democrats by associating them with the Klan. "The 'southern outrage' story was a standard feature of the Republican press" after 1877, and partisan Congressional investigations "often exaggerated" the amount of southern violence (Woodward, *New South,* 57).

10. The "tradition of violence" of the Old South worsened in the New. It "seems to have been one of the most violent communities of comparable size in all Christen-

cannot, however, state that we approve the sentences carried out by popular, drumhead justice. They are brutish.

Judge Lynch raps his gavel as a rule in the small, country towns of Louisiana, Mississippi, Arkansas, and Kentucky: far from the cities and the occupation forces. Last year's figures show sixty-four executions for murder in the southern states, mostly of Negroes; whereas the rest of the states, with three times the population, counted "only" thirty-seven. All but one were hangings. (In Texas the condemned may choose the rope or the gun. One chose the gun.) In addition to these legal and official executions, Judge Lynch administered thirty-six in the South, including eight in Kentucky and five each in Tennessee, Louisiana, and Texas.[11]

A few examples of the method in the latest lynchings. Mr. Phillips, a young man of universal good name, lived with his uncle on a farm near Tangipahoa, Louisiana. Last December he went to town to sell cotton, then headed back to the farm. Two Negroes, Johnson and Walker, overpowered, strangled, and robbed him. Soon caught and taken to Amité City's parish jail, the murderers sat several months awaiting judgment. Two other murderers had been there three years. George Carroll, a dark mulatto, had strangled his wife and burned the body in a forest in November 1877. Tried, found guilty and sentenced to hang, he followed his attorney's advice and appealed to the supreme court. He had been fed at state expense for nearly three years when Johnson and Walker arrived. His cell mate, Dick Smith, another mulatto, had murdered a beautiful young woman, eighteen years old, three years before in Washington Parish and had been found guilty and sentenced to death. Smith, like Carroll, had won a new trial and a change to life imprisonment. He had appealed the second, too. His case impended at the Supreme Court when the men who killed Mr. Phillips joined him. **Naive people of the parish** had seen to it that the murderers went unpunished.

One Sunday last winter about 10:00 P.M., some 150 local men—in

---

dom" (Woodward, *New South,* 158, 159; see also 158–60).

11. "Foreign visitors to Louisiana were struck by the prevalence of lynch law, especially when the accused persons were black" (Taylor, *Louisiana Reconstructed,* 420). In the mind of the South, "southern individualism" produced among many other things a tendency to violence and a desire for immediate, public, savage expression of anger about crime. Anger would be reduced and the crime punished in a "catharsis for personal passion in the spectacle of a body dancing at the end of a rope or writhing in the fire." Hence the vigilante action of the frontier continued in the South, which became "peculiarly the home of lynching." Probably only a region of endemic lynching could have a Southern Association of Women Against Lynching. As lynching was fundamental to the southern mind, hatred of the Negro did not cause but provided an object for it. Thus, mostly whites were lynched before the war, mostly blacks afterward. See W. J. Cash, *Mind of the South,* 42–43, 113.

disguise, armed, and on horseback—appeared at the parish jail in Amité. "Give us the key." The jailer stalled. After a while they forced it from him, seized the four colored murderers together with two others (accessories to the crimes), and took the six to a woods about two miles from town. (An eyewitness told me what followed.) They dealt with Dick Smith first. Rope around his neck, he confessed his bloody deed. At once they hanged him from a limb. Next, the pair who murdered Phillips. Bullets riddled their bodies while their necks stretched. George Carroll succeeded them on the limb. Then the orders to the accessories. "Get out of this parish, unless you want what happened to your pals." They were let go and in about a half hour, the others' bodies taken down and buried.

The *Deutsche Zeitung* of New Orleans wrote, "Thus the band of avengers freed the community from continued, senseless food bills, meanwhile ridding our torpid Supreme Court of the need to consider another appeal. This grim act of popular justice occurred because regular court procedures give criminals every chance to dodge a well-deserved punishment, as can clearly be seen in the instances here."[12]

Another and more hideous dispensation of popular justice occurred a few months ago in a country town in Tennessee: Hopkinsville. Let us consider it because it not only demonstrates what happens at a lynching, but also illuminates in a properly lurid light the ferocity and the brutality of Negroes in these southern states. Verbatim from the *Staatszeitung* of New York on 16 September 1880:[13]

> Laprade, the murdered man, a wealthy young bachelor, lived near Saddlersville, Tennessee. About a dozen Negroes appeared one evening outside his house and called him to the door. He opened it. They tossed a rope over his head and around his neck, and tightened it about his throat. He could not utter a sound. They dangled him twice, demanding his money. He gave the rascals all he had, a mere fifty cents. When they saw that they could not get what they wanted by hanging, they went for their knives, mutilated his body, and dragged him into the yard by the rope around his neck. They smashed his skull with a hatchet. Finally, they threw the body into a ditch, where it was found a few days later under peculiar circumstances. (A Negro dreamed he had been robbed, hanged,

12. The source of this quotation has not been located.
13. Hesse-Wartegg cites the *Staatszeitung* here and the *Nashville Daily American* later. He combined them in composing this account, which does not agree with both in all details but is more than faithful enough to illustrate his point that the crimes and lynchings were savage. The *American*, 16 September 1880, identifies Lee LaPrade as an eccentric old bachelor with money and gives the place once as Springfield and again as Robertson County. Today's spelling is *Sadlersville* rather than *Saddlersville*.

mutilated, and thrown into a ditch. The dream prompted a search of the ditch, and Laprade's body was found.)

Several of the guilty Negroes had no sooner been arrested than a number of men in masks appeared of a night in the cell of one.[14] (Later he told what they did to him.) They threw a wool blanket over his head so he could not see, bound his arms with rope, and flung him onto a horse. One of the mob climbed up behind him. Two others led the horse to an out-of-the way spot. They dangled him from a limb. They let him down. "Confess. Tell us everything about the murder of Laprade. Otherwise we'll burn you alive." He talked. "I know nothing about it. Only that Bell and Jamison [two of the guilty ones] told me about the plan to rob and kill Laprade, the night before they did it. But I wouldn't join. That's all I know." The masked men forced him to sit on the ground. They shoved his back against a tree, tied him to it, and drove stakes into the ground to either side of his legs. He could not budge. They piled leaves on him, put fire to the soles of his feet, and let it burn until he could no longer bear the infernal pain. He agreed to answer questions. The men set him back on the horse and returned him to the jail. His badly burned feet were rubbed with oil and soda, and bandaged. He was given brandy. But the burning of the feet had disordered his nervous system and damaged even his stomach, lungs, and heart.

Two days after that terrible grilling, the mob moved to punish the murderers [Bell and Jamison]. The *Nashville American,* the state's largest newspaper, gave a thorough and detailed account:[15]

> Tennessee had never seen a more orderly and better-regulated mob than the one at the lynching there in Hopkinsville. Seventy riders, well practiced, entered town in a double column on Port Royal Street, went straight to the jail, arrayed the horses in front of it, and left them in care of eight of the riders. Lookouts had been posted at several points in town. Many townspeople, expecting the lynch party, were awake and burning with curiosity to see what they would do. Some townspeople began chatting with members of the party, though none could be recognized, all being masked. That is, they had pulled hats low and most wore handkerchiefs over the face. When the audience got too near the party or their horses, they were ordered back. The chief of the party sent to the sheriff—he was also the jailer—that he bring the keys. He showed neither hide nor hair. They forced the door and found themselves in his living quarters. In a minute they stopped at a double-locked door to the jail proper. They had equipped themselves with hammers from nearby smithies, and they

14. Jim Higgins was taken out and tortured for the story of the crime. "Two of the guilty ones" were Jack Bell and Arch Jamison (*Nashville American,* 16 September 1880).
15. Ibid., 15, 16, 17 September 1880. It gives Springfield, not Hopkinsville, as the site of the lynching.

applied them. It took three-quarters of an hour nonetheless, before they reached the inmates. Several showed them Bell's and Jamison's cells. Warren Woodard, an inmate who had killed his stepfather, raised such a row as to elicit reassurance:

"We're not after *you*—you can leave—go anywhere you like."

Another masked group had entered with the first. These wanted one Ramsey, a Negro who in an act of treachery had shot a young white woman.[16] When the first party had seized Bell and Jamison, the second would not leave until Ramsey had been given to them. He, however, had remarked in the late afternoon, "I think a mob will be here tonight. My life will cost them plenty—I'll see to *that.*" The prediction came true. He made good the threat.

His cell, the first in the upper tier, must be reached by ladder. There was one in the jail, the party had brought in another, and both were placed to reach the cell. The padlock was soon smashed. Ramsey rained blows on the attackers with a leg broken from a chair. Since only two attackers could approach at a time, the battle raged an hour. The attackers then squirted kerosene into his cell and threw burning paper in after it. In vain. But as flames illuminated him as a target, they fired shot after shot. Every time one connected, he screamed: "You've hit me, damn you!" At the third: "You've shot me three times." One of the party shouted: "You're a liar." Ramsey: "Stop a minute. I'll show you." The attackers paused. Ramsey stretched out his right hand. Thumb and forefinger had been shot off. The battle resumed. From his position behind the wall, he could have stood off a thousand. But a stream of blood ran down his left leg. The loss weakened him. At last he collapsed. An attacker seized the chance and fired from the top rung. Ramsey took the bullet in the chest. Shooting stopped. A ladder served to bring down the body. From their perch only a few feet away, Bell and Jamison watched, trembling, but without a sound. It is unknown whether Ramsey's club hurt any of the attackers.

The body lay on the floor until the coroner's jury had studied it. Bystanders, surging in as soon as the mob left, inspected the damage and resecured the inmates. To penetrate the jail and overpower Ramsey had consumed three hours. Time therefore pressed. Dawn was already breaking. Bell and Jamison having been tied up and lashed to horses, the leader gave the order and the party mounted and gathered into formation and galloped along Port Royal Street and out of town. Perhaps the party intended to collect and bring with them the prisoners in the Springfield jail, then hustle to Saddlersville and lynch near the scene of their crime every last one of the eight-member Negro gang.[17] The stop in Springfield

16. Joe Ramsey "fired two charges of No. 1 shot into" a Miss Holt (*Nashville American,* 16 September 1880) The article does not identify Ramsey as a Negro; in fact, by calling Bell and Jamison "the Negroes," it implies that Ramsey was white.

17. All the prisoners in question seem to have been in the Springfield jail, according to the *Nashville American* (16 September 1880). Hesse-Wartegg is either confused about the place or he means the other prisoners in the Springfield jail. At best he is unclear.

frustrated any such plan. Six miles away, at the point the railway crosses Port Royal Road, the order to halt brought the party to the calm completion of the assignment. The two Negroes, taken from their horses, stood within the circle of armed men. "Have you anything to say, this one last time?" Both confessed. "We're guilty—we will say nothing but the truth." The names of the Saddlersville prisoners were read to them. Were they guilty? Bell and Jamison answered yes. They added the name of another Negro, also supposed to have taken part in the murder. Two large pieces of black crepe appeared and were put over the pair's heads and faces. Jamison was hanged from a limb on the spot, Bell from another a few steps away. The rope, thin but strong, sliced into their necks.

Thus a report of the latest lynching, quoted verbatim. Though not well written, it will represent an aspect of life in the Mississippi valley at this moment. What are we to think but that it offers little to bring immigrants south, or to attract northern capital. Nor does it contribute to the restoration of peace, order, and other normal conditions. Yet this savage justice produces some good results. By administering the code of Judge Lynch, the people have issued by example a warning to the corrupted mass of Negroes, and to the white riffraff. Without such an example, the clemency, bribe-taking, and indifference of the southern courts would have led long ago to more and worse crimes by Negroes and whites alike.

Unfortunately, Judge Lynch tends to be partisan. As a rule only Negroes suffer judgment in his court.[18] Whites, while committing perhaps as many murders, rarely pay such penalties. The *"freedman"* seems independent and self-reliant. But he remains what he used to be—stepchild to whites in the South!

---

18. The Negro, as the object of white hatred after the Civil War, became the appointed victim of lynching (Cash, *Mind of the South,* 113–18). See also Du Bois, *Black Reconstruction,* 699–701. But whites too "were victims of illegal summary justice" (Taylor, *Louisiana Reconstructed,* 420). See also 267, 285–86; and Woodward, *New South,* 351–52.

11. Days on the River

Traffic on the Father of Waters is insignificant in comparison to the size and importance [physical presence] of the river itself.[1] Now and then we meet a steamboat headed upstream. Or at least we hear the shrill, long-drawn blast of its whistle through the trees of an island that divides its course from ours.[2] In a day we see one or two *"flatboats"* going slowly downstream, the craft about which Gerstäcker has told us so much.[3]

These flatboats, unique to the Mississippi and its tributaries, are essential to planters, lumbermen, hunters, squatters, and the like, who live near rivers and far from railroads. Flatboats are often their only means of communication with the rest of the world, year in and year

---

1. The Mississippi, in the Algonquin tongue *missi-sepi,* signifying variously The Great River or The Father of Waters, is barely second to the Missouri as the longest in the United States (2,348 miles) and, with the Missouri, the longest in North America (3,710 miles); thirteenth in length in the world, or third when combined with the Missouri; often a mile and a half wide; the main stream of the world's largest drainage area, draining all or part of thirty-one states and two Canadian provinces (almost 1.25 million square miles); the eighth greatest river flow in the world, discharging 350 billion gallons a day. Hesse-Wartegg's "insignificant" traffic was indeed by comparison only, for the Mississippi was and remains, regardless of losses to other forms of transportation, one of the busiest waterways in the world. See *Columbia Lippincott Gazetteer of the World,* s.v. "Mississippi River"; and *Encyclopaedia Britannica* (11th ed.), s.v. "Mississippi River."

2. The meandering lower Mississippi, Twain's "long, pliant apple-paring" thrown over the shoulder, has surrounded lands of various sizes and flows in channels among these islands (*Life on the Mississippi,* 153).

3. Friedrich Gerstäcker (1816–1872), German novelist and travel writer, wrote novels and travel books about America, and the Mississippi figures in several. See *Oxford Companion to German Literature* (2d ed.), s.v. "Gerstäcker, Friedrich." Hesse-Wartegg's reference is probably to the three-volume, 1848 novel *Die Flusspiraten des Mississippi* (Pirates of the Mississippi), in which flatboats are depicted. Flatboats, which are rafts elaborated with sides, cabins, and steering sweeps, should not be confused with simple rafts made of logs fastened onto nothing more than free-floating platforms. Flatboats succeeded rafts as the Mississippi's most common conveyance of people and freight of all kinds. In 1846 over 2,000 flatboats reached New Orleans; in 1855 there were 718. By 1860 raft and flatboat had given way to the steamboat as the most significant means of carrying people and cargo on the river. But in 1881 flatboats were still used, primarily to float craftsmen and merchants along the river, as Hesse-Wartegg points out. See Havighurst, *Voices,* 20–42; and Carter, *Lower Mississippi,* 215.

out. The good business done by these floating "*stores*" proves that more people occupy the Mississippi's wooded banks than one might first think. Indeed, the majority of riparian dwellers depend on flatboatmen for all their money, their annual income. But don't think these poor river folk are blessed with earthly treasures!

Truly original types dwell along these desolate shores. The white people include nomads who move yearly or even oftener from one isolated home to another, scrupulously avoiding towns. So-called "*poor white trash*," whose way of life resembles that of ancient Celts, these people inhabit mainly the interior of Tennessee and Alabama, as well as the course of the Mississippi and its tributaries; they are degenerate generations, detritus pushed aside by civilization's mad rush forward.[4] They subsist in crude log cabins by hunting, fishing, and theft. In presidential elections they still vote for Lincoln.

Backwoods whites' counterparts are blacks or "*nigger trash*."[5] The ways of life are much alike; only dispositions contrast. Whites avoid their own kind and are, if anything at all, pessimists and cynics. On the other hand, "Sammy" and his smiling, happy family are the purest of epicureans. They enjoy themselves and give banquets and feast on potatoes, corn, and fish, as delighted as a virgin with her first love. They care solely for today and are miserable in winter, joyous in summer. Working only as much as necessary to keep from starving, Sammy and Aunty divide the rest of their time between sleeping and *dolce far niente* [sweet idleness].[6]

A third class of riparian dwellers are the lumbermen. They spend the year searching for trees in Missouri, Arkansas, and Tennessee. Rifles across their backs, game bags at their sides, revolvers in their

---

4. In use since at least 1833, the phrase *poor white trash* to describe the poor whites of the South was coined by slaves, who spoke contemptuously of white servants (Mathews, *Dictionary* 2:1283, 1868). See also Theodore Saloutos, "Southern Agriculture and the Problems of Readjustment, 1865–1877," 58–60. Hesse-Wartegg may be referring to "river rats": white Anglo-Saxons who spoke an English of Queen Anne's day and were known for squatting "on bars and bits of mainland," raising vegetables and corn, selling stolen timber to the mills, and relying on fishing for food. "Illiterate, suspicious, intensely clannish, blond, and usually ugly, river-rats . . . lead a life apart, uncouth, unclean, lawless, vaguely alluring. Their contact with the land world around them consists largely in being haled into court, generally for murder. No Negro is ever a river-rat" (Percy, *Lanterns,* 16–17; see also 19–21).

5. *Poor colored trash,* a rare corollary to *poor white trash,* came into use about the time Hesse-Wartegg wrote this book (Mathews, *Dictionary* 2:1284). Mathews does not record *nigger trash.*

6. The stereotype of the happy, carefree black may have begun with the depiction of Sambo the slave, an image that several generations of eminent historians helped perpetuate. See, for example, Samuel Eliot Morison and Henry Steele Commager, *The Growth of the American Republic,* 1:537; and Robert E. Riegel, *America Moves West,* 230.

belts, and axes on their shoulders, they cruise the primeval forest, find the tallest, strongest and most attractive trees, fell them with axe and fire, cut them into logs, and note their positions. With the coming of spring and high water, when the river overflows its banks for hundreds of miles around, they gather their logs, now afloat, make "*rafts*" of them, and head them into the river's main course. In a few days the strong current carries them to Memphis and even New Orleans. There the rafts are sold for logs. The lumbermen return to the forest in summer and fall when the floods have receded.

With these people—white trash, nigger trash, and lumbermen—flatboats do business, as well as with small plantations here and there in tiny clearings in the forest or near countless bayous and inlets. Flatboats, built upriver in such big cities as St. Louis or Cincinnati, are broad and low and have little wooden houses on them. The boats are loaded with all kinds of household goods, tools, clothing, coffee, sugar, ammunition, etc. A flag is fastened to the roof and a bell fixed in the prow. The miniature Noah's ark pushes off downstream to trade in every small settlement and bring wares to customers. Thus the flatboatmen live all summer and fall on the river. Finally reaching New Orleans, they sell their boats, return to St. Louis, have another boat built next year, and again take the trip downstream.

Other flatboats are used only by fishermen who stay on the water summer and winter, catching huge "*catfish*" that often weigh 200 to 300 pounds, as well as "*buffalofish*" and other varieties, which are marketed directly or processed for oil.

But among the craft that ply the Father of Waters, the most peculiar are the floating museums and theaters.

In Memphis I bought newspapers to help pass the time on this long, boring steamboat journey downriver. You can get little reading there but the daily press. In it, as a rule, Americans find everything that could interest them, every subject from the Orient to theater and art. In the four-page, five-foot-square Memphis *Avalanche,* theater and art are relegated to a microscopically small space of notices about opera troupes performing locally. In that category this notice interested me most:

> Dan Rice's opera boat sails slowly south. Like all Dan Rice's enterprises, this boat is "the world's greatest."[7]

7. Dan Rice (1823–1900), showman and circus clown, was better known for riverboat circuses than floating opera houses. Beginning annual trips on the river in 1842, his showboats were one of the river's features and the cause of at least a minor sensation wherever they docked. Hesse-Wartegg must have visited one of the last: Rice completed his final tour in 1886 and retired. See *Dictionary of American Biography,* s.v. "Rice, Dan." The last tour, "another gigantic enterprise . . . a floating opera

I did not understand it. Had American opera impresarios' spirit of enterprise gone astray on the Mississippi? Thespians on tour in land conveyances, yes, but Thespians afloat, Thespian steamboats? Who had ever heard of such a thing?[8]

"It's nothing new, sir—not at all unusual for us," said a fellow passenger. "We are *a wonderful race, sir*."

"But why opera on a boat? Why doesn't the troupe go from place to place by train, like all the rest?"

"*Well, sir*" my Yankee friend answered, "I'll explain it to you. People in this country must always have something cute and different. Dan Rice is a smart fellow. He always has what's wanted and makes money hand over fist. On this river, these thousand miles to New Orleans, you'll see hundreds of plantations, settlements, and towns; but damn few theaters. People here don't even know what 'opera' means. Dan Rice built himself an opera house and sails it downstream from place to place. Look, stranger, the best thing for you to do is look at it for yourself. Dan Rice's boat is anchored off Helena."

That night we arrived in Helena, Arkansas. Our boat had to stay until morning to take on cotton. I wasn't sure I should believe that Yankee; his tales of a "floating opera house" sounded too tall. So I got up early and went to see for myself. There was the proof in big letters! Six giant posters, side by side on the wharf, featured the flashy portrait of Dan Rice, the famous impresario.[9] A slight importunity, true, but effective. The advertisement framed the portrait. Above and below the smooth-shaven, roguish face, I read: "*Dan Rice's Floating Opera House and Museum*"; and on the sides: "Playing here for three days, the 25th, 26th, and 27th."

Admission to the floating opera house	50 cents.
Reserved seats	75 cents.
Children	25 cents.
Admission to the museum	25 cents.

house with which he made a circuit of the South . . . was not a financial success" (Brown, *Life of Dan Rice,* 164). Brown suggests that the 1886 tour was the first floating opera for Rice—years too late for Hesse-Wartegg to have seen it (164).

8. Many kinds of entertainment plied the rivers by 1850, and held on into the twentieth century—"simple, grass-roots entertainment" at first, changing to "burlesqued melodrama." The "biggest of the circus boats, the white and gold *Floating Circus Palace,* could seat a thousand" (*Reader's Encyclopedia of the American West,* s.v. "transportation on the Mississippi River system"). See Percy's description in *Lanterns,* 41–42: "Showboat! I never heard of such a name in my time. Everybody knew it was the *Floating Palace* and worthy, a thousand times, of its title" (42).

9. By 1879, Hesse-Wartegg's year on the river, Rice "himself had become the most attractive exhibit in his circus" and perhaps "the most colorful figure in the Middle West" (Graham, *Showboats,* 39).

No doubt about it now! It was over there, that wonder rivaling the Hanging Gardens of Babylon, Dan Rice's floating opera house. Its outward appearance would best be compared to Noah's ark as depicted in children's illustrated Bibles. The keel of this operatic ark was a large flatboat or, better, a raft of long logs bound together; and the weather deck, a small wooden playhouse of the kind we meet so often (but, of course, only on dry land!) at European fairs.[10] Pictures of all kinds of monsters covered the four walls, probably the cast of the museum rather than the opera. Big portraits of Dan Rice, placards, slogans, etc., gave this strange opera house the look of an American street corner. Above it flew the Stars and Stripes and below them a large white flag that asserted: *Grand Opera House.*

The craft was anchored at the riverbank but the gangplank was up. I shouted: "Hello! Opera!" Dan Rice himself appeared, Yankee hat pushed back on his head, quid in cheek, hands in pockets.

He roared at me: "What the hell do you want here at seven in the morning?"

"Sir, my boat sails in a quarter of an hour. Before it does, I want to visit your famous opera house."

"Come aboard, sir," he answered obligingly and pushed the gangplank to shore.

I paid my fifty cents.

"I'm afraid you're early for the opera. My troupe is still asleep inside."

"At least show me where they perform!"

"Can't do that, either. Occupied."

"And just how big is your troupe?"

"*Well, you see,* the women sleep on the stage, the men in the auditorium, with the curtain down between. But you can look at my museum, the greatest, most beautiful, most inter——."

I interrupted him. The museum contained the usual curiosities to be found in roving European shows, plus an Indian, also asleep. My time short, I couldn't wait for the first performance. (There were two a day.) But Dan Rice did tell me why and how he runs this enterprise.

"*Well, sir,* you see, people along the Mississippi and near bayous and on adjoining rivers in Arkansas and Louisiana could never watch such a show if I didn't bring it to them. I've tried to tour the region

---

10. When Rice expanded the show in 1870, he used the *Will S. Hays* to carry the show proper and the *Dan Rice, Jr.* for "the advertising contingents and the tons of illuminated and gorgeous circus posters, to herald the coming of the largest show on earth or water" (Brown, *Life of Dan Rice,* 154). Brown seems to say that, contrary to Hesse-Wartegg's anecdote, Rice in 1879 was running a circus with permanent river craft to carry it, not an opera house on temporary flatboats.

with only my troupe, but it costs a lot of money and these towns have no theater or hall for my performances. Here I had to make do in a cotton shed, there in an old warehouse. The show didn't pay until I used a flatboat. I live on it with my people, have my opera house always with me, and sail downriver from place to place. In two months I'll be in New Orleans and the trip won't have cost me a cent."

"But then what? How do you get the boat back upriver?"

"I don't. In New Orleans, you see, I pack my museum, costumes, and sets, sell the boat for wood, and my troupe "*busts*" and scatters to other theaters. I buy a ticket on the first steamboat for St. Louis and there have another flatboat and opera house built. Then I announce new artists in "*star engagements*" and head downriver with a fresh troupe."

"And your repertory? What do you perform, Colonel?"[11]

"Well, stranger, whatever the people down here want. We try everything. They like singing best. I have a prima donna now, sir, the greatest in the world. Too bad you can't hear her. Voices crack a little when we approach New Orleans. You know how it is, two months or more on the river—think of it! *It's hard work, sir.*"

"I can imagine, Colonel. God be with you. You are a great man, Colonel. Until we meet again, downriver!"

"Thanks, stranger! So long!"

Dan Rice's picture stayed with us the whole trip. At every wharf, in every newspaper, there was the sly, smooth-shaven face of the impresario. He had sent a "*drummer*" ahead, an advance man who pasted it on each post and every wall. Dan Rice is surely the Mississippi's Barnum.

Another notable feature of life on the river is the giant barges of coal that float 1,200 to 2,000 miles from St. Louis or Pittsburgh to New Orleans, where it is to be sold to transatlantic steamships. The barges' size shows, better than anything else, how big the Mississippi is and how much North America's greatest river can transport. From a distance the barges look like huge, floating islands of five to ten acres. As the barges draw near, coasting freely on the current, you can see they are composed of sixteen to thirty immense flatboats joined together and guided by a steam-powered towboat.[12] Each flatboat is 200 feet long and 34 wide, with a draft of 6. Hence a barge of twenty of these flatboats does indeed cover five acres.[13] Its load, 30,000 to 50,000 tons, is more coal than a dozen of the biggest transatlantic steamers can

---

11. Rice was no ordinary southern "colonel." Hesse-Wartegg uses the title bestowed on Rice *honoris causa* for service to the nation and to entertainment.

12. The craft that propelled and steered was often called a towboat, though it usually pushed.

13. Hesse-Wartegg's calculation of five acres is somewhat high.

carry! The flatboats are fastened together and to a triangle, base headed downstream. At the pointed, upstream end, the large tug serves as rudder, keeping the barge in navigable water as it is carried by the current. Naturally such loads—perhaps the biggest ever moved at one time—go very slowly, taking several months to reach their destination. Many barges have sunk, usually after hitting the riverbank. Still, this mode of shipping coal is so cheap that traffic in coal keeps exclusively to the Mississippi.

At the moment the river is losing a substantial part of its other traffic to railroads.[14] I say "at the moment" because, without doubt, the utility of the river as an avenue of commerce will be recognized and shipment of freight return to it. Experience has long shown that railroads cannot compete effectively with the river. Rather, they add their freight to the increase of the river's.[15] Take the Hudson as a telling example. Two railroads, with twin and even quadruple tracks, run nearly the Hudson's length. Yet river traffic grew after they were built and continues to grow. Let the West be as populated as the East. Let the 100,000 square miles of wilderness, primeval forest, and virgin land of the Mississippi valley be settled. Both will require many decades. But then today's 1,200 steamboats will have swelled to 12,000. Then the mighty Mississippi's broad back will be as trafficked as the Thames is now. Only then will the valley's one million inhabitants see how much they have the Mississippi to thank for their prominence, their wealth!

One feature of life on the Mississippi seems gone forever. Faster movement of goods by rail has stopped the notorious steamboat "*races*."[16]

14. Early railroads were built to provide access to waterborne traffic. After 1860 railroads became a mode of transportation in their own right, ignoring waterways and hauling as the market dictated. By 1900 railroads had driven out steamboats. See Thomas D. Clark, *Frontier America,* 360–61; and Frederic L. Paxson, *History of the American Frontier, 1763–1893,* 572. Twain observed that "these railroads have made havoc with the steamboat commerce" (*Life on the Mississippi,* 476).

15. This forecast came only partly true. In time boats returned, and railroads and the river traffic cooperated. But railroads claimed greater general importance because they could be extended almost anywhere; rivers had to have passengers and freight brought to them. Despite the declining use of the steamboat, however, barge traffic expanded to carry heavy, bulky cargo uneconomical for railroads. See Havighurst, *Voices,* 154, 247–248; Hunter, *Steamboats,* 588–89; and Carter, *Lower Mississippi,* 229–30.

16. Though racing was neither as frequent nor as colorful as fiction and romance would have it, plenty occurred and it was exciting and dangerous (Hunter, *Steamboats,* 405–8). In June and July of 1870, the *Robert E. Lee* and the *Natchez* ran the most famous race; no other "excited so much interest throughout the civilized world" (Morrison, *Steam Navigation,* 250; see also 250–52). The victorious *Lee* gained St. Louis three days, eighteen hours, and thirty minutes out of New Orleans. Preparations and progress had been telegraphed and cabled around the globe (Keir, *March of*

People still shudder to remember those hair-raising contests and how often boilers burst or a boat rammed an island or hit a *"snag"* and sank with every soul on board. Today, races are rare. When they do occur, two boats do not run side by side, machinery overheated. Victory goes to the skillful pilot who knows how to shave banks and find the fastest currents. The trip from St. Louis or Cincinnati to New Orleans takes seven to ten days nonetheless. The many stops are to blame.

The infamous piracy of former years has also ended. Before the war, when people had to travel by river, when rich planters with fat purses went to slave markets in St. Louis and Memphis, piracy paid and paid well. Backwoodsmen soon mastered this Tunisian art.[17] The war increased the number of pirates, and many steamers and flatboats came to grief. Gone are the planters, however, the noble prey; and with them the pirates, the river corsairs. The pirates have quit their boats and forest hideouts for the decks of passenger steamers. Instead of demanding passengers' money with a six-shooter, they take it gently with cards.[18]

"*Poker*" remains the most widespread game of chance on Mississippi steamboats.[19] Once-ragged bandits have made themselves over into "honorable gentlemen" who look respectable and travel in threes and fours on a boat. One poses as a *"judge,"* a *"colonel,"* a *"governor,"* or other titled personage; and the rest pass themselves off as planters, steamboat captains, or the like. On one of my trips to a city in Arkansas, I saw a *"gang"* of that kind take a backwoods planter for his every cent. *"Mister Judge"*—the ringleader, I believe—was a respectable-

---

Commerce, 92). As for danger: on 25 April 1838, the *Moselle,* out of Cincinnati and racing against time, burst all four boilers at once and hurled debris and bodies a quarter of a mile. At least eighty people were killed (Riegel, *America West,* 228).

17. Hesse-Wartegg's allusion is to the "Barbary pirates," the piratical rulers in North Africa whose demands for tribute provoked a war with the United States at the start of the century. Infamous Mississippi pirates included the outlaws of Cave-in-Rock near the mouth of the Ohio. Samuel Mason, alias "Wilson," lured many an unwary captain and passenger to his Liquor Vault and House of Entertainment, where they were separated from money and possessions (B. A. Botkin, *A Treasury of Mississippi River Folklore,* 196).

18. Among the steamboats' multifarious crowds moved sharpers and other quick-witted, deft-fingered rapscallions who gambled and played confidence games with gullible passengers. See Clark, *Frontier America,* 350–51; and Keir, *March of Commerce,* 86. Such were "the elegant tricksters who preyed upon the river traveler" (Herbert Asbury, *The French Quarter: An Informal History of the New Orleans Underworld,* 201; see also 197–212). The king and the duke in *Huckleberry Finn* represent an assortment of rascals who lived by their wits.

19. The passenger not content "merely with eating . . . could sit in on the interminable poker games. Usually he was fleeced, for the river gamblers were adroit and frequently dishonest" (Carter, *Lower Mississippi,* 228). See also Hunter, *Steamboats,* 408–10.

looking, elderly man, calm and dignified. An accomplice, a fat, squat fellow whose chubby, smooth-shaven face shone with oil, smiled constantly and cracked bad jokes. A *"bon vivant,"* his task was probably to use his open, cheerful manner to strike up an acquaintance with the victim. The third member was the second's opposite. Small, lean, shifty-eyed, black-bearded, and unkempt, he played the loser. He talked to onlookers, grew frantic, placed large bets, and thus aroused passengers' interest in the game. If a victim had been found, he was fleeced.[20] If nobody took the fourth seat, another of the gang had to take it; and then an onlooker was selected as victim.

Almost all day long, cards are played at one end of the long salon. The gaming table is a fixture of every Mississippi steamboat.

Otherwise, life aboard is pretty monotonous. Bad coffee is served in the morning, along with "bread" baked on board. Popular American *"buckwheat cakes"* and *"flannel cakes"* arrive searing hot, with honey, and always have their takers. The "gong" announces the noon meal. Women and family men sit at one end of the long table, single men at the other. Negroes bring food that disappears astonishingly fast. Each diner gets the meal from small bowls and usually all courses at once; sometimes there is a row of twenty to thirty bowls in front of me. Americans like to put a half-dozen or even more foods on the plate at once and enjoy unusual mixes. To Europeans this way of eating is repugnant, especially because food is cold before it reaches the table. After the meal everyone repairs to the *"saloon"* and then each sex to the end assigned it. Conversation as a rule is sparse.[21] The American, uncommunicative with friends or fellow citizens, thaws out in conversations with strangers and foreigners, and praises the United States. Not even exciting events like running aground, collisions, dockings, etc., disturb his indifference.

The left, or west bank, of the Mississippi resembles the banks of the Yazoo previously described: primeval forest, bottomland and in the lowest parts, swamps. Americans call it *"virgin soil,"* inhospitable and uninhabited today but with potential for a productive and populated

---

20. This sort of swindler took as a rule for success, "Let the sucker think he's going to beat you" (Riegel, *America West,* 230). Canada Bill, greatest of the three-card-monte men, lured victims by impersonating a jake of the greenest kind. Chicken-headed, simpering, shuffling, squeaky-voiced, awkward: he looked like the rankest of suckers, but he did the taking, often for the victim's every cent (Botkin, *Treasury,* 196–97). For what appears to be the same gang described by Hesse-Wartegg, see Nichols, "Down the Mississippi," 841–42.

21. Hesse-Wartegg's description may highlight the contrast between the golden age of steamboating, 1830 to 1860, and its decline by 1879. Life aboard the earlier vessels was said to be exciting, and the table sumptuously supplied. See Keir, *March of Commerce,* 90, 92; and Clark, *Frontier America,* 351.

agricultural district. Today, however, immigrants still find millions of acres of prairie in other states. Not until those are taken will farmers' attention turn to the Arkansas side of the Mississippi. Speculation has not arrived yet, although farther north, along the Missouri, it raged twenty years ago. Speculators ahead of the times conjured up an urban dreamland, issued stocks and bonds, and sold building sites in dreamland to people in the East. True, there was only open space where a city was to be founded. But a detailed map showed universities, monuments, water mains, and railway stations; every buyer of a town lot could select the location of his future house. How disappointed the poor devils were! Cities, stock companies, and deeds vanished in the wind.[22] The land is as virgin today as before the dream-city swindle.

The one town of size on the 200 miles of the Arkansas shore from Memphis to the mouth of the Arkansas River is Helena, a lively commercial center of 6,000 people.[23] Even the mouth of the mighty Arkansas is forsaken. Years ago a fairly big town was there, ominously named Napoleon.[24] The Napoleonic dynasty and Napoleon, Arkansas, disappeared together. During the Civil War, Napoleon was an important rendezvous for gunboats and other warships. Its repute was like that of Cayenne [French Guiana] or Denver. Not a day passed but a man "died with his boots on"—shot, stabbed, or beaten to death. When a steamboat docked, passengers scarcely dared venture on deck for fear somebody in town would enjoy firing a six-shooter at them. Pilots told me horrifying tales. Then Napoleon's fortune sank; the Sodom of the Mississippi got its punishment. The river itself, in one of its evil tempers, steadily undercut its bank at Napoleon. Every day a

22. Hesse-Wartegg refers to "paper towns," a feature of "town-booming": "one of the favorite forms of speculation throughout the West." Land in the wilderness, on prairies and in forests, would be platted with proposed features such as lots, streets and public buildings, and the lots sold to absentee buyers. Often the towns never existed except on the paper that advertised them and the deeds that signified ownership. See Dan Elbert Clark, *The West in American History,* 250, 331.

23. "Helena occupies one of the prettiest situations on the Mississippi" (Twain, *Life on the Mississippi,* 260). Though ravaged by floods, Helena was prosperous in manufacturing and trade, and the surrounding countryside produced lumber, cotton, and grain.

24. Frederick Notrebe, once a general on Napoleon Bonaparte's staff, founded Napoleon, Arkansas, in the 1820s. The site of a federal hospital built in 1855, Napoleon was captured by Union forces and nearly destroyed by fire in the Civil War. It regained importance after the war as a point of transshipment between the Mississippi and Arkansas Rivers, becoming a roaring town as wide open as any in the "wild West." But while the French throne tottered under Napoleon III, both rivers were inexorably undercutting Napoleon, Arkansas; the last resident fled in 1874. Twain was astonished to watch the Mississippi roll where he had known a substantial town. "Behold," he wrote, "Napoleon is gone to the catfishes" (*Life on the Mississippi,* 288; see also 286).

foot of land washed away; every day the masses of water surged inexorably nearer. Seeing that Napoleon was not to be saved, people left. Only the riffraff remained, seeming to want to cling like rats to the nest until Napoleon would be afloat on its own deluge.

We tied up for a short time at Napoleon during the night. Next day we gained Vicksburg. Will it remain one of the most important cities and ports in the Mississippi valley? It lies, unfortunately, on the outer side of a large bend. Years ago the river began to ignore the bend and has broken a new channel. Old Vicksburg has already silted up so much that deep-draft boats can no longer reach the docks. In a few years, Vicksburg will be a quarter-hour from the river and have lost trade, wealth, and perhaps life itself.[25] On the other side of the river a new plot will rise. Nothing is there but a miserable little town named after the Mississippi's discoverer, DeSoto. Will it grow in a few years to a big city with thousands of people? A start has been made. A railroad, from Texas and Louisiana east to the seaports of Savannah and Brunswick, crosses the Mississippi at DeSoto. Because the wide river cannot be bridged, railroad cars must be ferried and people of DeSoto get enough work and income. Who knows? Maybe DeSoto will prove worthy of the appellation the few shacks and huts have chosen for themselves.

During several days in DeSoto, which is in Louisiana, I saw many Negro families with bag and baggage.[26] Having arrived from Louisiana's interior, they planned to emigrate to Kansas and were waiting for a boat upriver. Most were sad cases, lacking money and clothing, having barely the minimum of household goods and blankets. Of the land of their dreams they knew nothing but the lies they had been told: Blackville, Kansas was a paradise, a Canaan for blacks, where neither labor nor poverty existed. So they wanted to go there. They camped near DeSoto on the riverbanks. When the desired steamboat came by at last, they hailed it and negotiated with the purser the passage to Kansas. The black leader offered seventy-five cents a head. The purser assumed the sum signified that they meant the place upstream thirty

---

25. After suffering almost as much from carpetbaggers and Reconstruction as from the Civil War, and heavy with debts caused by graft and mismanagement, Vicksburg saw the Mississippi break through the tongue to the north and create a new channel in 1876, leaving the city high and dry, apparently doomed as a port. But Hesse-Wartegg's prophecy did not come true. Thanks to the revival of commerce on the river and especially to the diversion of the Yazoo into the Mississippi's old bed in 1902, Vicksburg was restored to prominence as the chief river port of the state of Mississippi (Work Projects Administration, *Mississippi: A Guide to the Magnolia State*, 275).

26. Recognizing the significance of their movement west, Hesse-Wartegg devotes the next chapter to these "Exodusters." See chapter 12, note 1 below.

miles or so, Kansas Landing. The blacks jumped for joy when, a few hours later, they were put ashore at Kansas Landing. Thinking they had reached their destination, the state of Kansas, the miserable creatures were appalled as it dawned on them that they were still in "*Losana*" and several hundred miles from Kansas. One small example of the black exodus and how the poor devils are treated on the way to the promised land.

12. The Negro Exodus

Time after time last spring (1880) the news came from St. Louis as well as other cities of the "Great West." Negro families, in their mass migration from the South, were reaching the prairie states, especially Kansas.[1] The number amounted to nearly 5,000 in St. Louis alone.[2] After that trek they arrived hungry, exhausted, and destitute—and became a public responsibility. True, their fellow blacks, together with the municipal government and private charities, provided food and temporary shelter in the hospitals and churches. But the flood of these immigrants continued into the summer. In a matter of weeks the exodus so swelled that it seemed less a voluntary migration than a stampede. Of course, the government could not afford to pay their way to their destination, nor even to keep them for a while. The mayor therefore felt compelled to make a public proclamation. It warned black emigrants not to abandon one home without the means to travel elsewhere and establish another.[3]

The proclamation drew America's attention again to the exodus of the Negro from the South. For it had begun in 1874, principally in western Mississippi, with the departure of several thousand "*freedmen.*"[4] The stream dried up, however, after many returned disap-

---

1. These were the 20,000 to 40,000 "Exodusters," southern blacks who sought homesteads in Kansas (where John Brown had drawn blood for black freedom) during the "black migration" or "Negro exodus" of 1879. Word had spread that they would be welcomed to a life better than they had in the South. They set off in a "pell-mell landrush," a "unique mass movement" (Robert G. Athearn, *In Search of Canaan: Black Migration to Kansas, 1879–1880,* 4, 7). The migration began in earnest in the spring of 1879 and continued, though diminished, in 1880. Kansas was a northern state, had free land, could be reached with comparative ease and relatively little expense, and Kansans seemed ready to accept blacks as full citizens (6–7, 259–60). See also Painter, *Exodusters,* for a history of the movement.

2. Not 5,000 but over 20,000 passed through St. Louis in 1879 (Athearn, *Canaan,* 33). Therefore, Hesse-Wartegg may be referring to the spring of 1879, when about 5,000 may have reached St. Louis, rather than 1880, when the number had reached 20,000. His remarks later in this chapter seem to describe 1879.

3. Probably Mayor Henry Overstolz's proclamation of 15 March 1879. See ibid., 16.

4. Blacks had been trickling into Kansas since the war, and some founded the town of Nicodemus (ibid., 4).

pointed and worse off than when they left. True, many still moved from one southern state to another or shifted their nomadic existence to the North. But these random wanderings lacked purpose and a destination, their cause being only the Ethiopian migratory instinct.[5]

Then, last year, the swelling to a flood: an exodus of incredible size. Within a few weeks some 15,000 left their plantations and headed north by every possible means. On my way south I met so many of these wretched, ignorant emigrants. They walked along the tracks or rode in open freight cars. Riders paid a small fee to go north or rode free because someone pitied them. I passed many river landings with camps: families and their bundles and bedding. They would go by boat, at a dollar or two apiece, to "*Se Lui.*"[6] All northerners on our boat felt sorry for them. Often we took up a modest collection, sometimes to benefit aged, white-haired ones. Southerners among us, however, especially planters, showed not the slightest compassion.

Emigration began in Mississippi and Louisiana. Those modest origins grew and grew until they included the entire South.[7] Planters and the conservative element of the former slave states therefore took a stand against emigration. They kept Negroes on the plantations, sometimes by promises, sometimes by threats. The situation made a stir: the causes of emigration, long known to persons familiar with the South, have come to general awareness at last.

And what are these causes that have set Negroes on the move? Poverty and distress in the South since the war and bad treatment from planters and officials.[8]

Changed conditions and bad harvests lately brought misery to the Mississippi valley in particular, a misery the outsider can scarcely imagine. Huge plantations, with fabulous revenues years ago, have fallen into neglect: fields unworked, dwellings of owners and tenants in ruins, owners and tenants with nothing to eat.[9] If this is the plight of

   5. The *St. Louis Globe-Democrat* believed "they were not by nature a migratory race"; hence the "stories of political terror and economic injustice . . . must be true" (ibid., 21). In general (the exodus to Kansas being an exception), "the Negro population showed little inclination to emigrate" (Cohn, *Life and Times of King Cotton,* 155). Twain, however, thought "they only want to be moving" (*Life on the Mississippi*).
   6. This is Hesse-Wartegg's phonetic transcription, no doubt adapted to the German ear.
   7. According to Painter, "Afro-Americans migrating to Kansas in the Exodus of 1879 came from four states, Mississippi, Louisiana, Texas, and Tennessee" (*Exodusters,* ix).
   8. For a detailed discussion of this plight of southern blacks after the war and especially after Reconstruction, see ibid., 3–68.
   9. "Planters and plantations" and "thousands of small farmers" had been

whites in the valley, what must it be of blacks? Of a hundred former slaves in Mississippi and northern Louisiana, do five have the mules, the wagons, and the implements to succeed at farming? The other ninety-five? Degradation: wrapped in rags, without bread, without roof over head, a problem for the authorities and a burden on their fellow man. Meanwhile they dodge work that could earn at least subsistence. They loaf everywhere in the South's country towns, steal food, sleep in the open, and wait to see what will happen. Events have dealt still harsher with those who became a black laboring class. Some had even been employed by planters for wages. When harvests failed, financially straitened employers let go by hundreds the Negroes on their plantations.[10] Other Negroes had leased a piece of land and farmed it. Of course, harvests failed for them, too. They could neither pay rent nor buy food. Hope gone, they gave up that work and lived at another's expense or looked for a better way to make a living.

No wonder, then, that appeals for immigration emanating from Kansas, Arkansas, and other regions found the warmest reception among these people. Everywhere they heard those states described as a farmer's paradise, especially Kansas. A true description. Everywhere they heard of sudden prosperity in the prairie states, of rich harvests, and of racial equality and equal protection before the law. Then they heard from agents of those states the tidings that on the golden mountain there would be added unto them, by the government of the United States, forty acres and a mule.[11] How understandable therefore that they used every last cent, exhausted every resource, and followed the call to the "promised land."

Most of the five million Negroes stayed with the soil after emancipation. They had been fed and cared for as slaves, they had rarely if ever seen money, and they had lived without regard for the future because planters provided for them even in old age. But slaves could not at once be set free and inculcated with thrift and love of work as well as a desire for domesticity and family life.[12] Slave liberation, especially in Loui-

---

"ruined by the war" (Cohn, *Life and Times of King Cotton,* 146). "No other ruling group in America had ever found itself in such bleak circumstances as the cotton planters a decade after Appomattox" (160).

10. Neither Athearn, *Canaan,* nor Painter, *Exodusters,* considers crop failure a factor in the black exodus.

11. The golden mountain (*auf den goldenen Berg*) alludes to the promise of mountains of gold in Terence's *Phormio* (1.2.18) and suggests enticement by promising everything, perhaps the impossible. "Forty acres and a mule," widespread in English and given by Hesse-Wartegg in German, may have originated in 1865 when General William T. Sherman proposed to reserve land in South Carolina for blacks and to loan them mules. See Foner, *Reconstruction,* 70–71.

12. This view of paternalistic slave-owners and physically comfortable slaves even carried into historical scholarship of the next century. Its leading academic

siana and Mississippi, turned into a curse. Many came to grief. Others lapsed into savagery: vagabonds today in cities and the countryside. A relatively small number, an energetic few, went north and bettered themselves. But the mass stayed on the plantations, as employees or as small lessees who tilled a few acres of cotton and corn. The leases on the little farms cost so much, however, and the lessee must pay the planter or the Jewish storekeeper such prices for food and other necessities that a former slave's annual debt amounted to a figure the hardest work and the best harvests could not equal. Negro farmers remained in arrears with the planter and the storekeeper, year in, year out.[13]

The fortunate thousands, telling their stories after reaching St. Louis or the towns of Kansas, have provided detailed information about life among the South's emancipated Negroes. The information has made its way into the American press [and from there into German publications]. Let me give an example from the excellent geographical magazine *Aus allen Welttheilen*.[14]

> Negroes have come by the thousands to St. Louis. Impoverished, they await God's mercy to go from there. One of them, a mulatto named Orange Pucket, fled Tensas Parish in Louisiana, bringing wife and two children. His experiences exemplify what has happened to blacks in the South. "With heavy hearts we tore ourselves away from our home on twenty-five acres I had leased from *"Mas'r"* Jones. I had farmed it as my own for fourteen years, worked hard, yet had not got out of debt." The contract stipulated that Orange Pucket was to plant cotton and corn on said twenty-five; i.e., twenty-two of cotton and three of corn. His wife and children were to share with him the work of the field. In return for the lease he was to deliver:
>
>   5 bales of cotton for the 25 acres,
>   2   "   "   "   "   " use of two mules,
>   2   "   "   "   "   " feed for two mules,
>   1 bale "   "   "   " use of tools.

proponent was Ulrich Bonnell Phillips. See *American Negro Slavery*, 261–330, especially 293–96. See also Morison and Commager, *American Republic*, 537; and W. E. B. Du Bois, *Black Reconstruction*, 9–10. With the end of slavery, provisions by planters for slaves' clothing, shelter, garden plots, and care in old age became "commodities for which payment was due" (Foner, *Reconstruction*, 131). The rules of a cash nexus meant that he who could not pay must suffer. On the Negro's ability to organize his life, manage his money, and plan for his future and his children's, cf. Foner, 107–10. Though at the mercy of planters and other employers as well as storekeepers, Foner says, Negroes succeeded well enough as freedmen, one way or another.

13. On "the economics of oppression," see Painter, *Exodusters*, 54–68.

14. This was the nineteenth-century German *National Geographic*. Painter attributes the Orange Pucket example to the *Chicago Daily Tribune*, 17 May 1879 (*Exodusters*, 57). Hesse-Wartegg's source for it and for the George Holiday story is Julius H. Stackemann, who cites no sources in "Ein Negerexodus" (1880).

In addition, $5.00 would be charged for every bale of [his own] cotton processed at the planter's gin.

A harvest of ten bales will thus bring the planter about $400 in cotton. He will therefore get $400 a year from twenty-five acres that would sell for less than $300. And then a mill, set up and ready to run, costs at most $300 and daily does eight to ten bales. Fifty cents a bale consequently being a handsome fee, the charge for "*ginning*" is ten times too high.

Now how much will twenty-two "*acres*" yield? In a good year, bottomland averages half a bale an acre; higher ground a third. One per acre would be the extreme. Few farmers can boast having enjoyed such bounty even once. In a good year, on average, Orange Pucket would produce eleven. Only one of them was finally his, of course. The planter paid him $27 for it, after subtracting $5.00 for ginning. On this $27, Orange Pucket, lessee, must support self and family for a year! Orange Pucket, however, knew how to grow cotton—he had been at it for forty years—and by tireless diligence and the nastiest labor he wrested more than the average from his acres. The autumn of the year he left he got all of fifteen bales. Yet even this abundance would not pay for necessities. Look at the balance sheet. Provisions— salt pork, flour, molasses, sugar, tobacco, a hat, three pairs of shoes, a portion of rough unbleached cloth, or "*domestic*," and twenty yards of calico—$159.50 (true retail value, at most, $45).[15] Yet the wretch received only $110 for the additional five bales of an exceptionally fine harvest. So, in this blessed year, our wretch had nothing to show for twelve months of work and self-denial: nothing but almost $50 of debt.

Yet we have seen only one aspect of the vicious circumstances that ask everything of the Negro, that demand life itself (hence the exodus). Our short history of Orange Pucket provides a true and representative example of the situation in the regions depopulated by migration. Orange Pucket can also tell us about the freedman's political "rights" there. In substance this is his bizarre-sounding but true account:

> Moreover we Negroes must fear for our lives. The planters required that we attend the rallies of their political party and vote for their candidates. In turn they should guard us against mistreatment. I decided with my two brothers not to vote, worked hard, minded my own business, and caused no trouble. Soon after election day, whites from New Hill rode up

---

15. These figures would vary from place to place and owner to owner. See Painter, *Exodusters,* 55–56. Domestic, a plain, cotton cloth, was so called to distinguish it from imported fabric (Mathews, *Dictionary,* 1:503).

to my cabin, called us "*damned Yankee niggers*" because we had not voted, and though we were unarmed, blazed away. My brothers fell dead. I escaped into the nearby woods and hid for fourteen days. By then the need grew urgent; my fields must be worked. I went to them during the day and kept an eye on the road, and slept in the brush at night. It was yellow-fever season. Mas'r John and the rest of the planters had fled north. I tarried a good while—I did not want to leave the old home—but my wife pleaded and I gave in. She thought I might be killed anytime. So, with my family, I got away as quietly as I could.[16]

Negro emigration naturally hurt planters and landowners. Nothing could have hurt them more. They knew without doubt they must have the Negro on the plantation; they could not forgo his labor. Whites could not replace blacks in the cotton fields, on the sugar plantations, or in the rice paddies.[17] Consequently, and perhaps also for political reasons, planters and landowners opposed the exodus in every way possible. They leveled threat upon threat at steamboat captains: *Do not take black passengers.* Planters with guns appeared at landings and drove away blacks, and at stations kept them off trains.[18]

One of those who told of it, a certain George Holiday, escaped like Orange Pucket from Tensas Parish, Louisiana. We have the story from *Aus allen Welttheilen,* No. 5 (1880).[19] Whites in the parish had vowed to "shoot on the spot any '*nigger*' about to leave." Armed, they occupied every steamboat landing nearby, allowing no Negro aboard. Holiday, to get himself and his brother and sister on a boat, must send them at night to the landing two miles upstream, while he went a mile downstream. He took two mules. He had raised them and they were his, but whites robbed him of them when he got aboard. He meanwhile escaped death by hiding among bales of cotton. Negroes, camping everywhere in droves along the shore, begged and pleaded: "Take us along." The captain put in at Greenville, but a horde of whites in a rage forced him with drawn revolvers to lift his plank and move on.

Questions now arise. Will the migration benefit the Negro? What of settlers in the prairie states? Is it to their advantage to receive a colossal influx of this sort? Finally, what consequences will the migration produce in the South?

16. On "bulldozing" and terrorism for political purposes, see Painter, *Exodusters,* 19-21; and Athearn, *Canaan,* 203-5.
17. Efforts had failed to bring Europeans and Chinese laborers in numbers to southern agriculture. See chapter 27, note 5 below.
18. Methods usually "were not as gentle as verbal persuasion"; the most common were brute force and imprisonment for debt. "In the end, only the refusal of riverboats to stop for Exodusters," and the starvation of migrating blacks, "broke the movement's momentum" (Painter, *Exodusters,* 196).
19. That is, Stackemann, "Ein Negerexodus."

Weighed and considered, these questions compel one conclusion: migration can be of no good for blacks or whites. Blacks would do better—far better—to stay home.[20] Granted, it sounds *so* nice when northern newspapers speak of "the promise of liberty achieved at last among free people," and "emancipation from the ancient yoke of slavery," and so forth. But let such phraseologists see with their own eyes the conditions in the Gulf states. They will change their tune.

"Conditions in the Gulf states" reveal what emigration means to the region. It means everything. Should the flight increase, who will replace the Negro in the cotton field, on the sugar plantation, in the rice paddy? True, things being what they are, the South suffers anyway. But let black labor vanish and the misery of the South shall multiply. Today's wretchedness, transitory, will pass; no doubt about it. Unfortunate circumstances (such as recent years' bad harvests) and a lack of investment capital: each has been a cause. Two or three good harvests could restart the stalled machine. Work and money would again suffice for blacks and whites. The improved social and economic conditions in turn would draw a continual flow of northern capital and northern influence. Yes, this rehabilitation will take years. But when it occurs, Gulf-state blacks, laborers and tenants alike, will be better off than ever. Had the exodus continued instead, the South, by losing this significant and indispensable part of its people, should have been ineluctably hurt for a long time. As matters stand now, one lesson must be learned: the exodus admonishes the South's whites and cautions the planters: Treat black workers and tenants with greater concern and more justice *from now on!*

Still, Negroes have migrated. Will they better themselves in the new habitat? I answer after months of travel in the prairie states and after having seen the first of them at work there. *I doubt it.* Imagine them on the trek to Kansas. They depart with not a penny more than the minimum. They either fall by the wayside or arrive without a cent, having spent everything on travel. Worse, they neither want to work nor understand the work they must do. They have picked cotton all their lives; now they are to be experts at agriculture? They take up their own plot, beyond the edge of civilization; they start farming the remote prairie; and—alone, ignorant, without neighbors, lacking wherewithal of any sort—they are to bring bread from this primitive, this stubborn soil! Such procedures, as anybody can see, can only lead the poor devils to sure and rapid ruin. The fortunate ought to muddle

---

20. "Kansas was a doubtful Canaan, and the hegira was a general failure" (Athearn, *Canaan*, 255).

through to some success and make a living as farmers.[21] Nothing realistic remains for the rest but wage work and day labor. But the thousands upon thousands of white workers already there, do they not constitute a labor force? What of the thousands of other immigrants who must seek day labor on arrival? Let there be no mistake: farmers in Kansas and Arkansas will prefer, not black, but intelligent and industrious white hands. Still, supposing a part of the blacks *can* be accommodated, what of the rest? A *"poor colored trash"* will emerge in the prairie states, similar to the poor colored trash ubiquitous in the South now. In the prairie states the black race will be dispersed and, little by little, disappear. Let those states not cast too wide their nets for immigrants! Let them mind what classes of immigrant will do them good! And not forget what could result from the agglomeration of impoverished masses in the young states of this country! Last year alone, Texas got over 200,000 new residents; Kansas, 140,000; Nebraska, 100,000; and Arkansas, 60,000. To swallow is easy; to digest, hard.

In the eastern states and Europe, people entertain notions and cherish hopes about Negro migration—all false. These people make everything sound so easy, so neat. Conditions in the South have become unbearable? Away from there! (So they say.) Ah, but whither? On the prairies, and in the much-sung agricultural states, the situation is not so bright and shining as the immigration agents portray it. Where capable white enterprise again and again fails of even a green twig, there must ill-equipped, badly prepared, impoverished, apathetic, feckless blacks go straight to wrack and ruin.

Blacks in the South have not lacked voices of council and caution. All reasonable and intelligent colored people, Senator Pinchback among them, tried their best to keep their fellows in the old homeland, to stop the wild flight to Kansas.[22] Meanwhile, the government took measures to prevent the systematic exploitation of blacks in the South and to rearrange labor conditions so that "plantation hands" not lease for a portion of the harvest but work for planters and get a cash wage. At the same time, harvests have improved, capital flows steadily from the North, and the blacks have seen at last that to earn a living they must work, if not harder, at least as hard in Kansas as here. Therefore,

---

21. Cf. ibid., 255–58, which generally confirms Hesse-Wartegg's prediction that, by and large, blacks would not prosper in Kansas.

22. Pinckney Benton Stewart Pinchback (1837–1921), state senator and interim governor, son of a white male planter and a slave, was important in Louisiana public life and a political leader from 1867 to 1882. See *Dictionary of American Biography,* s.v. "Pinchback, Pinckney Benton Stewart."

the exodus, looked upon with great expectations in Europe, is drawing to a halt.[23] This year has seen the fewest emigrants since the exodus to the "promised land" began. Planters and Negroes seem to have learned from the experience of recent years, suggesting a future of greater harmony between the races living side by side.

---

23. The expectation that the 1879 outpouring would swell in 1880 was not fulfilled. The flow continued; but, slowing, it soon became a trickle, then dried up. Public interest evaporated about as fast. See Athearn, *Canaan,* 243–44, 259–60, 275.

13. King Cotton!

South of Memphis [at about 35° north] you enter the so-called *"cottonbelt."* You will leave this, the cotton-growing region of the United States, at 31°, or around the mouth of the Red River. Cotton culture resists precise boundaries, but climate and weather limit it to the area stated, a transcontinental zone reaching all the way to the high plateau at the foot of the Rocky Mountains.[1] North of 35° 30' shortened summers and occasional frosts may mean the bolls will not ripen. At the lower boundary cotton enters competition with the crop second to it in the South, sugarcane. Cotton continues to the West Indies nevertheless, stops there, and resumes with equal flourish in the corresponding zone of the Southern Hemisphere.

Mississippi, *par excellence* among the so-called *"cotton states,"* produces over a half-million bales a year. The Gulf states of Alabama and Louisiana come next. Texas may soon pass Louisiana.

As a rule the tourist sees some of the specimen plantations of the "good old days" of slavery: planters' grand dwellings, romantically situated, spruce in aspect, near the towns and with roads to them, and—on either hand—thriving tropical gardens and a spacious, comfortable way of life. Plenty of such estates still exist, especially in the Atlantic states. Many of these rural seats resemble in size and layout the famous chateaux of France or the celebrated country houses of England. The ignorant accordingly amuse themselves with dreams of life on the plantation. However eventful they are, even exciting, conditions in the typical agricultural enterprise contradict such fantasies. Every last one of the examples of antique grandeur obtrudes from a time lost and gone forever.[2]

---

1. The cotton belt later crossed the Rockies and extended to California (Cohn, *Life and Times of King Cotton,* 171).

2. Despite his skepticism about these "fantasies," Hesse-Wartegg seems to agree that grandeur, romance, and a supposed glorious old order did exist in some measure in a few places—enough to foster a tradition and a legend, sometimes called the "plantation legend." "Cotton's halcyon days on the river" occurred between 1830 and 1860. King Cotton established "his richest baronies on the Lower Mississippi" and nowhere has cotton "exercised a stronger directive force upon the people producing it" (Carter, *Lower Mississippi,* 200.) Although by the time of Hesse-Wartegg's visit the "epoch is closed and the system has passed, it stands as a kind of American

Today's cotton grower rarely commands the resources to build a mansion.[3] He lives in a log house with wide wooden verandahs. Usually an enclosed yard is attached. In the yard, jerry-built roofs without walls shelter stables and pens for the more important animals, and cover granary, smokehouse, and bales of cotton. Log cabins or, "*quarters*," for field hands and domestic help, stand near the main house on one side. On the other are small orchards, little vegetable gardens, and sometimes orange groves. The arrangement puts the house at the center of an extensive establishment.

The planter lives on his plantation in splendid isolation. Having conferred with his "*overseer*" morning and evening, and visited his neighbor, he has exhausted his sources of entertainment. The Negroes remain alien, what with their precious humor and droll ideas. Marriage, offering him "a field of domestic bliss amid life in an isolated wilderness," makes this existence bearable and agreeable.[4] At these distances from civilization, where contact so often fails with the outside, a wife twice blesses her planter-husband. Fortunate is he who has a wife!

"Fortunate" is the word, because planters do not have wives. Luxury, high living, and the love of finery have penetrated, with railroads and travel, into even the tiniest town. The planter no longer finds easy the taking of a wife. She will not give up the new amenities and follow him to where cotton grows in loneliness and isolation.[5] In these small, venerable towns, the pleasures of the rural life and of tilling the soil have nearly disappeared. Young men as much as young women prefer the ease of urban life; all gravitate to it but the few who by some force of circumstance remain behind on the land. Many rally to the slogan, "Better a chambermaid in a city than the wife of a man with a plantation." Consequently, planters usually return from the bridal hunt empty-handed. To their blessed good fortune, the work of the plantation demands most of their time.

In their fields you will see mainly cotton and corn. Sometimes there is rye or barley, sown in September, usually grazed by horses and mules in December, to shoot forth again with the original flourish in spring.

---

embodiment of the golden age" (Francis Pendelton Gaines, *The Southern Plantation: A Study in the Development and the Accuracy of a Tradition,* 4, 143–46). See also Woodward, *New South,* 157.

3. Two movements in southern architecture—the grandeur of Greek Revival and the Gothic on one hand, and the autochthonous double-log house on the other—did not survive the war. Typical architecture remained bad, without character (Bonner, "Plantation Architecture," 370–88).

4. Hesse-Wartegg does not identify the source of the quotation.

5. On the loneliness of rural life, the migration to towns, and the significance thereof, see Cash, *Mind of the South,* 189–90.

You meet clover, too. But cotton and corn dominate. They alternate on a field—corn one year, cotton the next—in the sole *"rotation"* practiced here.⁶

Negro hands have recently stopped living as a group near the main house. They build shacks near fields allotted them.⁷ They have become somewhat independent, happy to have their own homes and gardens, and perhaps to be able to ride their mules to town on Sundays. Money comes either as cash by the month or through the so-called *"share system"* of half the crop in return for the labor.⁸ The system's difficulties cannot be denied, but the Negro stands to lose far less than does the planter. In the first place, the system does not bind the Negro to a *meum et teum* of the harvest. During cotton picking the planter cannot oversee Negroes often numbering in the hundreds. How can he know what they spirit from the fields?⁹ He gets half of what they put before him. The other half they keep as their wage for the year. Furthermore, even in the worst of all possible harvests, the Negro cannot lose much. As he usually never has a cent anyway, the planter or the *"storekeeper"* must have outfitted him in the spring with everything he needs—clothing, shoes, food, tobacco, tools, etc.—*on credit* against the anticipated har-

---

6. Rotation between cotton and corn, sometimes including peas and oats, had been practiced for years (Swearingen, "Thirty Years," 205). After the war "the fertilizer craze" and its humbuggery deadened interest in rotation and other methods of improving the soil (Coulter, *South During Reconstruction,* 216). Some planters did continue with fertilizers, rotation, and other modern practices. See Chester M. Destler, "David Dickson's 'System of Farming' and the Agricultural Revolution in the Deep South, 1850–1885," 30–39.

7. "In slavery days the darkies lived in 'quarters,' a group of cabins not far from the 'big house' of the owner. Today each family on a large plantation lives in a two- or three-room house on the fifteen- or twenty-acre tract it is renting and working" (Percy, *Lanterns,* 23).

8. Hesse-Wartegg has arrived near the end of the wage system and the start of sharecropping. His interpretation follows Somers, *Southern States,* 128–29. See also Cohn, *Life and Times of King Cotton,* 158. On the rise of sharecropping and the nature of the system, see Saloutos, "Southern Agriculture," 70–73. Cf. Foner, *Reconstruction,* 106–8, 173–75. Foner discusses the position and condition of owner and tenant under sharecropping and sums up the necessity for it even though planters would have preferred the wage system (405–11). The wage system folded because laborers wanted to stop work and spend when paid. Holding part of the wage until year's end meant a longer period of spending before the return to work—if planters could pay the larger sum in a year of smaller harvest (Coulter, *South During Reconstruction,* 77). Hesse-Wartegg's interpretation favors the landowner. Percy's explanation also favors the owner, though he admits that bad owners abused the system (*Lanterns,* 275–76, 282).

9. "In the aftermath of abolition, as under slavery, planters complained of widespread theft by blacks" (Foner, *Reconstruction,* 202). The southern-white view of the Negro as lazy and thieving was "often absorbed by Northern visitors" (Fred A. Shannon, *Farmer's Last Frontier: Agriculture 1860–1897,* 96).

vest at year's end.¹⁰ The Negro's livelihood has thus been assured, crop or no crop. Is it any wonder that the losers when the crop fails, the planter and the storekeeper, plan ahead for generous profit? Little of the Negro's half remains for him even in the best of years.

Besides half the crop, the "*darkey*" (another name for the Negro) enjoys privileges enough to provoke envy by many an intelligent white laborer.¹¹ First and foremost he gets his little house (and boards up its windows when he moves in, leaving only the door for passage). The planter's forests provide plenty of wood to build barns and other outbuildings, as well as fuel for fires. The Negro can graze swine, cattle, and mules on the planter's meadows, gratis. He can hunt at will and shoot game for the table. Come harvest, he reaps half for himself after putting not a penny into the sowing. He is subject to no taxes but the "*poll tax*." A school levy, it would be expressly for the education of Negro children, were it ever paid.¹²

The Negro enjoys all those considerable privileges and one more. His crop harvested, he can pick cotton on other plantations and earn $1.50 to $2.00 a day in wages.¹³ The planter meanwhile must care for

10. Hesse-Wartegg states in a sentence the essence of the postbellum southern lien system, "one of the strangest contractual relationships in the history of finance" (Woodward, *New South,* 180). The lender, usually the local storekeeper (called the furnishing merchant or supply merchant), who might also be a landowner and, indirectly, a planter, usually advanced credit in goods and commodities to the borrower in return for legal rights to the crop to be produced. "The country merchant became the most important economic power in the Southern countryside" (Harold D. Woodman, *King Cotton & His Retainers,* 296). The system was "the new evil" that "may have worked more permanent injury to the South than the ancient evil" of slavery (Woodward, *New South,* 180). The furnishing merchant and the planter, initially distinct, tended "to become one" in the lien system of southern agricultural credit (184). Tenants and small farmers, the new slaves, produced up to seventy percent profits for these economic masters. See 180–185; and Woodman's chapter "The Furnishing Merchant," in *King Cotton & His Retainers,* 295–314. On stores and storekeepers, what they sold and how they did business, see Bull, "The General Merchant," 37–59.

11. Nathaniel Davis of Beaver Bend Plantation, Alabama, 1876: "Hands work four days for me for which I feed them 4 days in the week & give them 6 acres of land to be worked by my team & implements" (Weymouth T. Jordan, *Hugh Davis and His Alabama Plantation,* 165).

12. The tax, usually $1.00, was for Negro schools, if collected. It was also to control Negro voting: no tax, no vote. Hesse-Wartegg implies that Negroes did not pay the tax. According to Foner, Negroes favored taxes that would benefit them, including the poll tax, though it may have done more for whites. The poll tax thus seems to have usually been paid (Foner, *Reconstruction,* 205–7, 327–30). According to the counterargument, Negroes usually could not or would not pay to vote, Negro schools went unbuilt or unsupported for lack of funds, Negroes avoided schooling for lack of schools or lack of interest, and no effort was made to collect the tax, which went unpaid—to everyone's satisfaction (Coulter, *South During Reconstruction,* 86, 358).

13. Wages in cotton production actually averaged about fifty cents a day (Wood-

him, haul the crop to market, and do all sorts of other work as much to the Negro's benefit as to his own. Yet the Negro realizes no pecuniary success. Rarely is he able *"to square accounts"*—that is, to pay the storekeeper in full—let alone put aside a few dollars! The rare savings go straightaway for a holiday, as swiftly squandered as they have been slowly earned.[14]

In many ways the planter gains more on the share system than by paying a monthly wage. Defects riddle the system nonetheless. The Negro on shares does nothing but the work essential to the crop. He worships his field or *"squad."*[15] If the livestock graze on it, he drives them onto his neighbor's field, though that one really belongs to the planter too. The Negro cares nothing for buildings, fences, tools, and the rest of the plantation's equipment. Let them fall to pieces around him, so long as his squad goes unharmed! The planter must therefore pay for all repairs.

In recent times, employer and employee seem to prefer the monthly wage over shares.[16] White overseers help the planter direct the work when the planter pays wages. Moreover, a white labor force seems essential to the plantation, not only to oversee the Negroes, but also as repairmen, blacksmiths, carpenters, and the like. White immigrants thereby find much well-paid employment in southern agriculture.[17] These occupations meanwhile offer the best opportunity to learn the running of a plantation. Immigrant workers can thus become planters

---

ward, *New South,* 207). Perhaps Hesse-Wartegg refers to wages when demand for pickers was high.

14. On the widely held white view of black thriftlessness, see Painter, *Exodusters,* 65–66. Hesse-Wartegg was also not alone in his negative view of the Negro attitude toward work. In Percy's words, whereas the white man "feels that work is good, and idleness, being agreeable, must be evil," the Negro "feels that work *per se* is good; it is only a means to idleness ('leisure' is the word in white circles)" (*Lanterns,* 23). As a slave the Negro "had associated the idea of freedom with idleness, and the ease with which a bare subsistence could be obtained in the South made it difficult to divest the freedman's mind of this idea" (Cohn, *Life and Times of King Cotton,* 157). See also M. B. Hammond, *The Cotton Industry: An Essay in American Economic History,*, 125–26).

15. In point of fact, *squad* refers to a group of freedmen who replaced the slave gang as plantation labor, not a plot of ground. See Edward King, *The Great South: A Record of Journeys,* 1:273; and Foner, *Reconstruction,* 173. For Hesse-Wartegg this is a rare misuse of an English word, unless his *squad* is a shortening of *squadron* in the obsolete sense of a division of land. See Mathews, *Dictionary* 2:1623; and Craigie and Hulbert, *Dictionary* 4:2206.

16. Sharecropping and the share-wage system are often confused because of overlapping characteristics. Sharecropping came last "in the decentralization of plantation agriculture" (Foner, *Reconstruction,* 173).

17. Blacks also plied such trades and received higher pay than field hands (ibid., 172).

in their own right in time. It is perhaps the most remunerative agricultural pursuit in America.[18]

Plantations cannot do without Negroes or mules. No other domesticated animal possesses the strength and endurance of the mule in summer's stifling heat. Large plantations keep horses only for riding. As for cattle, milking cows are kept by few; sheep and goats, none at all. Sugar as well as cotton plantations keep instead another that thrives and pullulates: the pig. You meet this useful and tasty fellow in plump and multitudinous families everywhere on the plantation: in the field, on the meadow, under the trees. Pigs scramble about the Negroes' quarters, play with the black children, and squeal and grunt—a scene jollier than the circus. In the afternoon, some small Negro boy and his whip drive the pigs from the plantation's far corners to the yard for a feed of corn. Then, satiated, they retire for the night. Therefore well-rested, they awake at the crack of dawn. Their squeals roust out the plantation, every last person and animal.

Planter and Negro alike prefer pork to any other food. In winter, after the first few cold days, the endearing little creatures meet their bitter end. Old Negresses, each stout beyond 200 pounds, gather round the dissecting table, little pipes between thick lips, butcher knives in hand. "*Hog killing*" for the winter's meat begins.

So much for the plantation's inhabitants. Now to the plantation itself. It demands work the whole year, except a few weeks after Christmas. The weather, ultra-mild even in winter, encourages work outdoors. The planter and a few old, trusted "*hands*" spend days mending fences, clearing ditches, and cutting brush. Plowing starts in March and is followed by thorough tilling and manuring, then furrowing for the new crop. Guano and the more-common manures so favor cotton cultivation that many planters shun large acreage to concentrate on smaller: spreading manure soon after Christmas, covering with a few inches of soil, then planting carefully in the spring. Result: as much as one and a half bales per acre, not the average one-half to three-fourths. At the beginning of April, Negroes sow the seed (which has been soaked in water a few hours), usually planting about 1,000 pounds to four acres.

After planting, quiet prevails again on the plantation for a while until tiny green shoots appear. Hard fieldwork begins. Cotton, more demanding than any other crop, succeeds only with supreme care. Furrows around young plants must be cleared and weeded. Blooming begins in June, turning the plantation into the loveliest of sights, more

---

18. Earlier, however, many northerners came south and to grief trying to be cotton planters (Henry, *Reconstruction*, 146).

like manicured flower beds than fields of crops. Reaching an average height of three or four feet, weak and sensitive cotton plants stand row upon arrow-straight row, demarcated by deep furrows. Snowy-white flowers with open calyx appear among large, hand-shaped, dark-green leaves. The flowers, so white, so fresh on the first day, will never be white and fresh again. Yellowish in the morning, blinding-white at noon, touched with pink in the afternoon, and next morning, red. The sight of broad fields, in these colors of profound contrast, boggles the mind. In time the blooms yield to small, green capsules, or bolls, that become the size of a walnut and contain the cotton. The bolls ripen, turn yellow, and burst into a snowy-white tuft.[19] At that moment the plantation's mortal enemy attacks.

The cotton worm wants nothing but the encapsuled cotton and, multiplying fast, can devour the crop in a week. Fortunately, the first hatch appears at a time when, with torches and other fire at night, the planter can hunt down the moths of the adult stage and thereby preclude the second and third hatches. The ally of the cotton worm, the bollworm, can be seen [in the adult stage] flitting about the fields in the summer. Swarms of small and delicate moths hasten from bloom to bloom, laying an egg in each. Larvae appear in three or four days and gobble their way through the boll and into the stem, destroying it.[20]

With luck those perils will have been averted, the bolls will have opened their small white beards, and the harvest can begin. Each plant bears an average of twelve to fifteen bolls, sometimes as many as sixty. The planter hires a number of itinerant Negroes, male and female. Like European migrant reapers, they stay for the duration of work on one plantation, then move to another. A pair of linen trousers or a petticoat and, of course, a big straw hat: these constitute the one and only uniform. At work each adds a linen sack, suspended from the hips, to hold the picked cotton.[21] They pluck the white tufts from bolls with astonishing ease that never interrupts their "*plantation songs*," simple melodies, joyous or sorrowful and of great charm. Pickers average 100

---

19. "The poet would want to put into words" the "cycle of the river and cotton: the thrusting seeds bursting into sunlight in the lush, green spring when the river itself throbs and swells," and the "autumnal birth of the fibered bolls, when a tired river flows in unthreatening majesty between the fields it has created" (Carter, *Lower Mississippi*, 203).

20. Neither of the insects of this paragraph is the famous boll weevil, which did not enter the United States from Mexico until 1892. These are the budworm and the bollworm, the chief enemies of cotton before the weevil left farmers no recourse but to pray for salvation. See Vietmeyer, "War with the Boll Weevil," 64, 65.

21. Although Hesse-Wartegg has *Leinenhose* and *Leinensack,* he may not have meant the cloth of flax, but linen in the sense of any cloth—as likely cotton homespun as anything else.

to 150 pounds a day each. The adroit may gather twice that much. They are not paid fixed wages, but for what they pick, thirty cents a hundred pounds, as a rule. Always the Negro must be impelled to this tedious and time-consuming work and supervised closely besides. Not infrequently anywhere in the South, as late as February you will see white bolls of last year's crop still on the plant awaiting harvest. Bolls do not mature together and ought be picked as soon as they open, so fields must be crossed four or five times at intervals during autumn.

The plantations' *"gin houses"* receive cotton that has been emptied at once from full sacks into big round baskets or onto carts. (Negroes coined *"gin"* by shortening *"engine,"* the word for the machinery that sorts fiber from seed.)[22] The houses—or, better, large sheds—contain the gins. Fiber departs from fast-clinging seed there. In 1797 Eli Whitney invented the *"saw gin,"* one of three types and the oldest used in the South. Its tiny saw blades rip seeds from fiber. This gin, however, proves less effective than the *"roller gin."* Its dual cylinders grip the cotton, pull the fiber through between them as they roll against each other, and leave the seeds behind. The third type is *"MacCarthy's gin."*[23] Mules or water usually powers a gin. Steam has been applied recently on the largest plantations.

The seed, or the part of it not kept for planting, will yield a tasty oil when pressed; hulls become excellent fodder.

Ginned fiber goes into large bales compressed as small as possible before shipping. In the seaports or such major cotton emporiums as Memphis and St. Louis, hydraulic presses give bales a final squeeze, reducing volume by as much as three times. A bale of 500 to 600 pounds occupies about twelve cubic feet then. Planters would multiply profits, could they but do the last baling and, better still, clean the cotton on the plantation. They would, as part of the baling, also wrap the bales in sacking. Two costly operations, now done in the ports or at last resort at the spinning mill itself, would be eliminated there; and the planter might get twice what he gets now. Opening bales, rebaling,

---

22. *Gin* did originate from *engine,* but in the twelfth century as a variation of the old French *engin* for *engine* (*Random House Dictionary of the English Language,* 2d. ed., s.v. "gin"). For a description of the cotton gin and its workings, see *Dictionary of Southern History,* s.v., "cotton ginning."

23. In these terms, there were only two kinds, and the roller gin was M'Carthy's roller gin (Hammond, *Cotton Industry,* 112). Cf. *Dictionary of Southern History:* Whitney departed from the "roller method" to a cylinder with wire teeth. Hodgen Holmes improved on Whitney with the "saw gin," which had sawlike teeth "cut into iron disks" (s.v., "cotton ginning"). Classification is unclear; other types include "the barrel gin; Eve's gin; and Whitney's saw gin" of 1820 (Watkins, *King Cotton,* 75–76). Hesse-Wartegg's claim for the roller gin as more effective was true only for long-staple or sea-island cotton. See 75–76, 83–84, 95–96, 128.

transporting to and from presses, and other procedures would be done away with. Above all, the cost of rail shipment would be cut in half. True, a few machines would be needed; but cheap ones, quickly paid for. Immigrants, were they to take these things to heart, could thereby easily make their fortunes on the plantations. For, though cotton has flourished over a hundred years in the South, its technology has progressed little.

In conclusion, a few remarks on the size of harvests. The one that began in 1879 and ended in 1880, America's largest, amounted to 5,757,000 bales. (That of 1878 has been reckoned at 1,561,873 bales, but the figure may not be reliable.)[24] It is interesting to note the increase over the years. The harvest of 1821 totaled 430,000 bales at most. The amount grew annually, exceeding a million bales in 1831. With annual increases most years, the number passed 2 million in 1840, 3 million in 1852, and 4 million in 1860 (4,669,770, to be exact). After 1862 (and the 4.8 million of that year) the war reduced the number of bales to 300,000 in 1865. But increase began as early as 1866: 2,154,476. Again increases almost every year: over 5 million in 1878, and 5.75 million in 1879! Furthermore, the average weight of bales (varying from year to year and, last year, larger than ever) exceeded by 8 pounds those of the year before.[25]

Prices reached 13.75 cents a pound on the New York market in 1879, with a low of a little less than 9 cents. In 1874, 25.5 cents and 13.5 cents were the high and low.[26] The greatest differences occurred during the war: $1.90 and 72 cents in 1864; $1.22 and 33 cents in 1865. Cotton brought its worst in 1848: a high of 8 cents and a low of 5 cents.

---

24. The number 1,561,873 must be a misprint: 5,561,873 would be closer to the official figure of 5,074,000 (U.S. Bureau of Census, *Historical Statistics* 1:518). Note that a few lines later Hesse-Wartegg refers to "over 5 million in 1878."
25. Remarkable increases continued into the nineties. Woodward, *New South,* 185. Weights of bales varied between 300 and 500 pounds, until 500 became unofficially standard after the 1860s (Phillips, *Life and Labor,* 104).
26. The decline continued long after 1874, down to 4.6 cents a pound in 1894 (Woodward, *New South,* 185). The socioeconomic significance of the prices and production of cotton was that a decade of harvests and generous returns helped recovery after the war. How much they helped would be seen when the trend turned "fatally downward" after 1878, depressing sectors of the southern economy into the twentieth century. See Cash, *Mind of the South,* 149.

14. Arkansas

Until 1812 the 52,000 square miles of Arkansas belonged to Louisiana Territory. Arkansas organized itself as a territory seven years after the Louisiana Purchase. It became a state in 1836. In 1870 it counted 482,000 souls (including 122,000 Negroes) and nearly twice as many in 1880: 751,000. Arkansas nonetheless has been, except for Mississippi, the southern state least settled and least favored by immigration, no doubt about it.

The two states, at similar latitudes on the east and west banks of the Mississippi, resemble one another in many other ways. With respect especially to the land and the people, what can be said of one state can be said of the other. They produce the same agricultural commodities. Each partakes, along the Mississippi, of what is called the "*bottomland*": those notorious thousands of square miles comprising some of the richest and most fertile acreage in the United States but also the most sparsely settled because at present it cannot be drained. No other states enjoy such navigable streams as criss-cross these. Unfortunately, their people are the coarsest and least educated; their social conditions, except in a few larger cities, deserve nothing more than suspicion; and the immigrant, here because he listened to the land agent's claptrap and the railroad representative's ballyhoo, will have his problems among a populace singularly provincial. (Newspapers have reported such things; they are well known in America.) Law and justice may suffer accordingly in the remoter regions. The authorities serve the people who put them into office and forget their obligations to law and freedom. They think rather of how, by looking the other way or by favoring "*wirepullers*" and political vagabonds, they can assure reelection. (In America, people apply to influential politicians the word for the person who pulls wires and moves the puppets in a puppet show.)

The Massere Mountains run across the west of Arkansas, and join the more extensive Park Mountains in the northwest.[1] No state of the United States and scarcely any country in the world knows so many navigable streams. They touch fifty-one of the seventy-three counties.

---

1. Hesse-Wartegg must mean the Ouachitas in west-central Arkansas and the Ozarks or Bostons in the west and northwest.

The Arkansas River, a superb waterway, bisects the state diagonally from northwest to southeast. Its large tributary, the White, and *its* tributaries (likewise navigable), drain the state's northern half; and the Ouachita and the Red, the southern. Add to them the St. Francis, cutting through the "*Mississippi bottom*" from north to south. Steamboats from New Orleans, Memphis, St. Louis, and other river ports navigate these rivers. Therefore the remotest parts communicate by boat with the great seaports, industrial centers, and coal regions of the United States. Only in years to come, when Arkansas prospers, will this advantage be appreciated. A glorious future beyond doubt awaits Arkansas. I would go so far as to say that it and Missouri, measured against their relative position today, will in a few decades outdo the others of the South and "the great West" as well.[2] No such prospects await Arkansas now, however, nor for the next several years.

Edward King, in *The Great South,* tells of times when a journey up the Arkansas would likely mean risky adventures.[3] Debarking at the capital of Little Rock, passengers routinely set a Bowie and a Colt beside the knife and fork of the hotel's dinner table.[4] In days gone by, criminals and fugitives came in numbers and liked the majestic mountain landscape so well that they stayed. Yes, some became upright. But others kept their criminal ways and continued to rob and murder until they met death out of the muzzle of a revolver or a rifle. A large part of the populace remain almost as bad. Complaints from every quarter bewail slipshod farming, drunkenness, coarse living, quarrelsomeness, and so on through the catalogue of vices, which include an obtuseness about influences of the edifying and ennobling sort, such as schools, churches, and family life. Meanwhile the government does nothing to remedy the sad state of affairs.

Until a few years ago, blame could be laid to the insufficiency of steamboat transportation and the lack of railroads. Things have changed for the better. The great iron cultivator, the railroad, has begun to till Arkansas, shoving to the fringes of the state the wild lawlessness of bush life. The first and most important railroad, the St. Louis Southern & Iron Mountain, went from St. Louis through the Black and the White River valleys and south to the capital, Little Rock, and diagonally southeast and across the Red River in the southeastern corner of the state. At Texarkana the Southern & Iron Mountain joined the immense Texas rail net, thereby connecting the Atlantic states with Texas and creating the first transportation line of continental signifi-

---

2. This assertion, carefully qualified by *verhältnissmässig*—meaning relatively, proportionately, comparatively—is as vague in the original as in the translation.
3. See King, *Great South* 1:280.
4. Dueling abounded (Davis, *The Arkansas,* 263).

cance. To it Arkansas owes much of the thanks for prosperity. Farms and plantations have appeared along the railroad; also towns and cities. (Arkadelphia and Fulton, to name two.) Plantations and farms, for all their excellence, remain uncommonly cheap. The mountains [west and north] hold pine forests beyond measure. Oak, ash, and walnut spread in masses along the Red River valley [west and south]. Lands ideal for cotton lie in between. Another railway runs now from Memphis west past Little Rock and straight across to the Indian Territory at Fort Smith.[5] Smaller lines link the Mississippi with cotton-growing regions of the bottomland. Their fertility can be seen in harvests, especially along the White: a bale and a half of cotton, seventy-five bushels of corn, or twenty-five bushels of wheat per acre!

Elsewhere I have shown comprehensively and conclusively that the United States pursues a railroad policy—the best possible—to promote settlement of the nation's open lands.[6] The concession by Congress of two million acres adjacent to the railroads, has eased the railroads' immense outlay [for construction].[7] But the railroads must pay taxes on it, be it settled and farmed or not. Therefore, the railroad, as a matter of vital interest, will sell land to good farmers and proficient husbandmen, and thereby populate the countryside. The faster the railroad does it, the sooner the railroad's taxes ease, while profits rise from passengers and freight. Thus here in Arkansas, too, the railroads have helped the quick settlement so remarkable in the United States in the last years. Railroads unfortunately do not go everywhere yet.

Meanwhile, also unfortunately, evil flourishes to the west, particularly along the Indian Territory, where "*border ruffians*" dwell. Whiskey, revolver and Bowie knife are their bread and butter. The state can do nothing about the ruffians at present; they shall hold sway there unless they exterminate one another. True, a famous frontier post, Fort Smith, has been there for years. Law-abiding merchants and "*traders*" have settled under the cannon. Short work has been made of criminals who could be caught; they have been strung up.[8] But this lone fort will not suffice. The populace must endure amid semibarbarism, as long as the adjacent Indian Territory—an independent dominion and an outlaws' roost—remains the traditional haven for criminals and beyond the

5. The Chicago, Rock Island & Pacific.
6. Hesse-Wartegg's note: "See my *Prairiefahrten* [Journeys on the Prairies], Leipzig: Gustav Weigel, 1878, 3 marks."
7. It is unclear what two million acres Hesse-Wartegg means. Between 1850 and 1871, federal and state grants for railways totaled 176 million. See *Dictionary of American History,* s.v. "land grants for railways."
8. "Federal Judge Issac C. Parker, the 'Hanging Judge'. . . sent to Fort Smith in 1875 to establish order . . . sentenced 151 men to the gallows during his 21-year tenure" (*Encyclopedia of Southern History,* s.v. "Ft. Smith, Arkansas").

jurisdiction of the United States. In this border district and in all the mountainous area, saloons and boardinghouses outnumber the few schools and churches.

On the other hand, along the lower Arkansas the traveler meets his first rock only after a considerable journey upstream from where the Arkansas empties into the Mississippi. The rock, a small one in the currents of the river's western side, dramatizes by contrast the flat, alluvial nature of the Mississippi valley. Somewhat upstream the rocks increase in size, up to the "*big rock*," counterpart to the small rock. The city in question does not extend to the big one, however, but remains along the lower shores of the broad, imposing river, beside the small one. Hence Little Rock, the capital. A city of 25,000 to 30,000, it swelled after the coming of the railroad and the construction of the giant bridge across the Arkansas.

The business district occupies a high plateau along the river. The attractive capitol, shaded by tall trees, the state medical college, and the schools—the handsomest buildings—are also here.[9] Shaded walks border some streets. In many a garden the visitor sees japonica, azalea, magnolia, and the orange. Outside the city: a federal arsenal and an army post, and on a rocky elevation, the prison, immense and ponderous. The Negro community, strongly represented in Arkansas, has been making more progress here than in other southern states. (That is if Arkansas can be called a southern state, what with its crossing the northern boundary of the cotton belt.) Negroes occupy many leadership positions in state government; witness the superintendent of schools and secretary of education (no less), as well as numerous judges. Many own homes in Little Rock and have amassed assets of $10,000 to $15,000. "*Back country*" Negroes have not done so well; whites do not allow them to join the feast at the public trough. Segregation still prevails in education—black and white children each to their own schools—and the separation continues into the colleges and universities.

An excellent spa has grown up around the famous "*hot springs*" in the center of the state. A destination for the railroad now, too, the Teplitz of America attracts thousands from all parts of the Union.[10] It will equal the elegant Saratoga before long in wealth and "*fashion*."

For the time being, European immigrants need not worry that land

9. The college (*Kranken-Institute*) and the schools are probably the University of Arkansas School of Medicine and the Arkansas Schools for the Blind and the Deaf, although the medical school lies at a distance from the other two. See Work Projects Administration, *Arkansas*, 181, 183–84.

10. Teplitz, called Teplice today, was a renowned spa in northwest Czechoslovakia, with hot mineral springs known even in pre-Roman times.

for settlement will run out. Yes, the best for farms has been taken. Think, however, of the 25,000 square miles of public land passed to settlers in one year, 1879–1880. An expanse one-third smaller than the Kingdom of Bavaria but one-third larger than the Kingdom of Hanover! Note especially that these 25,000 square miles, divided now into countless individual farms, *scarcely dent* the empty domains awaiting purchase.[11] In other words, a torrent of immigration and settlement notwithstanding, the United States has thousands upon millions of acres empty and awaiting occupants. The whole, though a significant part cannot be used, amounts nevertheless to some *seven times* the area of the German Empire!

---

11. Hesse-Wartegg seems to be considering a larger area than Arkansas, perhaps the entire United States.

II. Louisiana

15. Louisiana

The farther south we go, the more the riverscape changes. No more the virgin forests on either hand. The southern sun shines warmer on broad waters of deep yellow. Along these low shores, willows, tall magnolias, and oaks draped in long gray moss dominate here and there in an otherwise open countryside. The mill or sugar refinery among them has been in ruins since the war. Or a few small planters' houses, fetching and dreamlike, stand amid splendid shady gardens asserting full-bloomed splendor in the face of mid-February. Back from the river and among the trees, perhaps we see the white buildings of sugar refineries and a *"quarter,"* the name for Negro homes on cotton and sugar plantations. Then another small rice or sugarcane field.

Thick smoke billows to heaven and shuts out the horizon all around. The dense cloud surges skyward—here like steam, here black or yellow—in a circle four miles across. Plantation owners have set afire not only their fields, but also the alligator's bailiwick and the cottonmouth's playground: the infamous Mississippi *"swamps."* The swamps burn to prepare them for drainage; the fields to rid them of sugarcane waste, the so-called bagasse. What are moor fires in the Baltic countries or prairie fires in the American West compared to wilderness conflagrations in these tropics? Thousands of giant trees on fire! Millions of such mammoths, dead of age or felled by storms, float in the shallows; and another generation of trees and other growth has long since covered them and died, to fertilize the third generation growing on top of *them*. Thus the primeval swamp: organic and nothing but organic, easily ignited, quickly consumed, like tinder. Moss—old, gray, dry—drapes every tree; it burns first. Fire moves like a dragon from limb to limb and trunk to trunk. But it touches neither limb nor trunk. It precedes the holocaust that consumes the swamp from ground up. Dense smoke chokes flames on the ground but combustion continues. It eats its way across a wide front, slowly, sinking its teeth into every trunk. Little by little it devours root and branch, even green saplings, and spreads in its wake a wasteland of grayish-black ash a foot deep on the water. At night the scene is of Hell. Fire—as flame, as coals—dominates the horizon full circle. Flames lick the sky with tongues six feet [above the treetops]. They color blood-red the clouds of smoke.

On the river and safe, we register an uncanny impression nonetheless. What an interplay, what a contest! On one side, Civilization. On the other, Nature, vicious Nature! Each contestant armed with fire and sword! Wild, savage tribes once annihilated Civilization, burned its towns, and devastated the countryside. Today, Civilization attacks a savage Nature with fire and axe, exterminates its ferocious offspring, burns the virgin forest, incinerates the swamps, and brings agriculture and abundance to the land.

When we have descended Louisiana by half, the other bank is still Mississippi far below Vicksburg. South of the Red River, Louisiana swallows us: Louisiana on either hand now.

Here we come into the part of the South devoted to sugar. Louisiana [not only produces it but also] helps lead the world in consuming it. Compare annual amounts: Russia a mere seven, Germany nineteen, and America thirty-eight pounds per person. How fortunate that sugar melts when eaten, transforms chemically, and leaves the body in other forms. Think of the alternative! In two years an American would contain seventy-six pounds; in four, a hundred and fifty-two; and in the end nothing but sugar. America uses so much that Louisiana's plantations can supply but thirteen percent. [Most of] the rest comes from the West Indies and [the refineries of] Europe.

Sugar nevertheless has meant, will mean, and does mean prosperity for Louisiana. The census of 1870—that long ago—shows 87,000 "*hogsheads*" produced in the United States, 80,000 in Louisiana alone. South Carolina and Texas divided the insignificant remainder. (The hogshead, a measure of capacity, equals about 1,300 pounds.)[1] Every subsequent year the output increased about 10,000 hogsheads. Now—in a Louisiana flourishing after the ravages of war, epidemics, and political turmoil—sugarcane culture shall soon increase to undreamed-of dimensions.

No soil could be better for it than the moist, fertile earth of southern Louisiana. The principal region of production occupies extensive river shores fifty miles north and fifty south of New Orleans, and a mile or two inland along that hundred. Baton Rouge marks the northern limit at present. This sugar-producing area amounts to some 12,000 square miles of mostly Mississippi delta, divided among eighteen "*parishes*." (In Louisiana, parish means county.) More than half the state's people live here. Before the war this small space contained an astonishing number of slaves: 150,000! Taxable property, slaves included, was

---

1. This weight is probably too much. The hogshead, a large cask varying in size from 63 to 140 gallons and in weight from 504 to 1,120 pounds, was usually 63 gallons and 504 pounds (*Random House Dictionary of the English Language,* 2d ed., s.v. "hogshead"; and Craigie, *Dictionary* 2:1258.

worth $271 million. Reduced to scarcely $100 million after the war (emancipation wiped out $150 million) taxable property cannot have rebounded to more than $150 million now. Sugar refineries, so-called "*sugar houses*," number about 1,200, with about 900 powered by steam.

During my journey south I visited several of the old Creole plantations. The house and its verandahs, piazzas, and green jalousies would be secluded and private in the shade and show of magnolias, with flowering gardens around—of aloe, palmetto and palm, and green lawns and groves of oranges—an idyllic residence. Among trees in the distance, the little white houses of the so-called quarter, home to the Negroes. Over there, in low-lying fields, Negroes and mules at work and an overseer on horseback, the air above them quivering with heat. Away on the horizon, the Mississippi's bright surface would seem to extend to infinity, an ocean of a river! Big three-masters and European steamers would be passing to and fro. Now and then the whistle of one or another local steamboat might add a shrill note to the songs of the Negroes. And—in between—a dike to shield the plantation from the monstrous currents of the Father of Waters. The flimsy barrier has often broken, putting the plantation's every inch at the mercy of the elements.

Yankees and their northern capital and northern energy have taken over many old plantations.[2] Smokestacks in one place, machinery in another, sully the idyllic aspect. On the shores of bayous and estuaries, along Bayou Lafourche and Bayou Sarah, around Baton Rouge and Uatshita—only there do hereditary planters hold their ancestral seats.

The Red River (aside from the Father of Waters) bids fair for honor as the chief river of beautiful Louisiana. The Red arises in the frightful wilderness of Llano Estacado in northern Texas, enters Louisiana's northwestern corner at the thriving commercial center of Shreveport, diagonals across, and joins the Mississippi between Natchez and Bayou Sarah. No city, not even a village, marks the confluence. Too many floods by the two giants, over too wide an area, prohibit settlement there. Few people indeed occupy the rest of northern and northwestern Louisiana, and for the same reason. It is a region without cities except the one I just mentioned, Shreveport. Water, the much-desired blessing on the prairies, has cursed this part of Louisiana! I devote the following chapter to the oceans that gather here in the spring. Their malevolence besets even the steamboats on the Red between New Orleans and

---

2. "The movement of northerners into the South after the Civil War" saw more than 5,000 former Union soldiers settle "in Louisiana alone." Industrialists and investors came, too, bringing industry and capital, building railroads and factories, and buying "farm land and other properties" (John Hope Franklin, *Reconstruction: After the Civil War,* 92).

Shreveport. Wood and more wood floating annually out of the forests of the Indian Territory sometimes blocks the river from shore to shore. Trunks piled one upon the other in confusion, and crowns woven in chaos: on such rafts, and from soil and vegetation heaped upon them, new vegetation springs and flourishes. So the Red figures in American stories as home to the celebrated floating islands.

River craft must nonetheless ply the Red, the only direct route between Arkansas, northern Texas, and the Indian Territory on one hand, and the port of New Orleans on the other.[3] Therefore, even the big steamboats travel the river regularly, though they can succeed only as far up as Shreveport. It remains to the small sternwheelers to continue to the places in question. Danger stalks the sternwheelers as they twist through the bayous, where they often get stuck. Of the rivers of the Mississippi basin, the upper Red poses the worst dangers and demands the annual sacrifice of several steamboats.

Still, except around the mouths of rivers (where floods often inundate everything), Louisiana boasts excellent areas for agriculture in every part of the state.[4] Inland, the soil could be turned into the best fields of wheat. The six parishes on the Red offer excellent sites for sugar and cotton. Yet the parishes' 8,500 square miles lie idle, waiting for immigrant settlement. In the southwestern part of the state, three million acres of this inexhaustible terrain remain innocent of agriculture. Vast forests teem with the finest commercial wood of every sort. Along the shores of lakes and rivers, giant cypresses await the woodman and his axe, offering centuries of raw material for sawmills and shipyards.[5] In Iberia and St. Mary parishes, an immense swamp stretches to the Gulf. In a belt around the swamp the densest of virgin forests averages a width of *two miles*. The Attakapa Indians once occupied the two parishes and three others, Vermilion, St. Martin, and

---

3. Traffic diminished on the Red after "the construction of the Texas and Pacific Railroad, running nearly parallel with the river, and touching it at Alexandria, Shreveport, and other points [and diverting] a large quantity of cotton." In addition, a bar at the mouth and low water to Shreveport kept boats off the lower Red. In 1886 only one line ran regular service (U.S. Treasury Department, *Report on Commerce*, 149).

4. "The rich earth of Louisiana" earned praise from outside the state (Edwin Adams Davis, *Louisiana: A Narrative History*, 294).

5. Hesse-Wartegg, like many Americans of the time, was ambivalent about conservation. Elsewhere he speaks of forests as threatened and to be conserved; here, as if they are limitless. Until the late nineteenth century, forests and other resources were thought inexhaustible in America, even as something to be moved out of the way of progress. Conservation as a movement was just beginning and would not realize success until Theodore Roosevelt endorsed it. Scientific forestry had been practiced in Europe, particularly Germany, but did not appear in the United States until the founding of the American Forestry Congress in 1882.

Lafayette. Nothing of the Indians remains, only their name. But their land has found no other masters.

What has deflected the immigrant influx from Louisiana then? Political unrest and uncertain and often venal law enforcement, as well as lynchings and assassinations.[6]

We gain, farther north of the Gulf, the equally large region of Opelousas, Grand Choiseaul, Prairie Mamon, Calcasieu, and Aubine, and their savannah and prairie. Seldom do we recognize a name and then only from old Indian sagas. No road, no rail penetrates here. French and Spanish shepherd folk tend flocks and herds in idyllic seclusion.[7] These people know nothing of the feverish hustle and bustle of the world outside. At the beginning of the century, the French paid these grasslands much attention. Up to the Civil War, some of America's biggest "*vacheries*" were here.[8] (The war ended that sort of thing.) If we assume that one animal needs five acres, a quarter of a million cattle could be fed on the prairie of Opelousas alone! Huge territories in every part of the continent and almost nobody knows they exist! How immense is this America!

A hundred years ago the Acadians, deported [from Canada] by the British, settled in beautiful Louisiana's matchless part. They had made their way through the alligator swamps and primeval forests of Atshafalaya, a region lovely and pristine. Here, west of the Mississippi at Bayou Teche, the grandest natural largesse has been bestowed upon a pearl of the South. Here the Acadians created a new homeland amid an incredibly opulent Nature. They tamed some of the wilderness. Creating plantations, they uprooted virgin forests, cleared pastures and fields, built idyllic dwellings, surrounded them with pretty gardens, where they put flowers and other decorative plants, the grandest and most glorious they could bring from neighboring places.

Small local steamboats come to the bayou from New Orleans. On this ride you soon find yourself in a strange landscape, a mixture of lake, swamp, and primeval forest, of garden and plantation, a panorama of the most delightful vegetation. The little steamboat takes you past venerable country seats and charming modern villas secluded in sylvan isolation. You pass Negro villages; you go under giant cypresses and magnolias overhanging the bayou; and having come through all

6. Carpetbag government created "governmental, economic, and social disorder" (Davis, *Louisiana,* 284), probably enough to discourage immigration. Causality remains hard to prove, however.

7. A large ranch in this area was "like those of a later-day west," on "open prairie, dotted with patches of trees along the water courses . . . 'one of the meadows of America'" (ibid., 205).

8. Vacheries were the "French equivalent of the cattle ranch, and many could claim several thousand head" (Kane, *Bayous,* 279–80).

this scenery, you arrive at the town of New Iberia. From here you need not travel far to reach the wild and primitive locale of Lac Peigneur and to a place so well known in America, Orange Island, the summer home of the actor Jefferson.[9] The old French and Acadian planters of this region know well the two most famous thespians of America: Jefferson, now living here in his declining years; and Minnie Hauk, who spent several summers of her romantic early youth in the seclusion of these forests.[10]

Of all the subtropical areas of the United States, this part of Louisiana belongs among the most beautiful and most fertile. We can only marvel that Bayou Teche remains even today so unchanged and undisturbed by outside influences, especially after Yankees have penetrated everywhere else.

---

9. Playing with renown on the American stage for seventy years, Joseph Jefferson (1829–1905) took comic roles chiefly and in *Rip Van Winkle* especially, from 1865 until the end of his career.

10. Hauk (1854–1924), Mrs. Ernst von Hesse-Wartegg, a diva of international acclaim, lived a while in New Orleans as child. She made a debut of sorts in the Grand Opera House there, singing "some of the most difficult operatic airs" at the age of nine "rather as would a girl double my age." It "was the turning-point of my young life" (Hauk, *Memories,* 24–25).

16. Controlling the Mississippi

The Mississippi originally emptied into the Gulf 500 miles north of where it does now. Not only has it been extending itself, it has also been changing its course ever since. Countless lakes, lagoons, swamps, and ravines, ten to fifty miles from today's Mississippi, offer proof positive of their former status as riverbed: they run parallel to the river from north to south, and each is shaped like a *C* or an *S*. The river flows fairly straight as long as rock determines the course; in other words, down approximately to the southern border of Illinois. But as soon as it enters upon alluvium, it cuts its way in horseshoe bends, sometimes so severe that it advances one mile via forty to fifty miles. The remarkable fact is, people can try—planters far from the river and wanting to bring it to their plantations have tried—to straighten it by piercing the intervening peninsulas at the bends.[1] The straightened river begins the next spring to make a new, crooked bed. All in all, however, it has gotten shorter and shorter by hewing through peninsulas. In 1722 it abbreviated itself some thirty-five miles by slicing across the curve at Port Hudson, Louisiana. Another reduction occurred at the start of this century when the Raccourci "*cut off*" eliminated twenty-eight miles. Let a simple statistic show the length the river gains by taking different directions and making new beds. In 1721 the river measured 1,215 miles from Cairo to New Orleans; today, 975! So it has shortened itself about 240 miles in 160 years! The fact depends upon last century's measurements, of course. Were they right? The purported size of reductions would prompt doubt, but sections of old bed, far from today's river, verify the reduction.

Yet people cannot straighten the capricious river. Each effort has been in vain. True, they have cut through curves and shortened the channel. But along with its own continual alterations, the river asserts another peculiar feature. It transfers acres (yes, I can say it removes a half-square-mile) at a time from one shore and deposits it along the opposite.[2] So as early as a year after shortening, the river has piled a

---

1. Some farmers and planters cut ditches to bring the river to their land, "quadrupling its value" (Twain, *Life on the Mississippi*, 154).
2. The river built "islands one year to eat them the next; gnawing the bank on one shore till the levee caves in and another must be built farther back, then veering

bar in the channel, directing itself into a breakout, and has taken a new, crooked route. Hurdles, fascia, anchored inclined planes [as banks], and other devices successful in Holland and elsewhere have been proposed for the Mississippi several times in Congress. On the Mississippi they have proved ridiculous. In smaller rivers and for short distances, yes, these things might work. But effort spent thinking about them for the Mississippi would not be rewarded with a way to regulate the giant waters.[3] With respect to transportation and safety, let Nature direct the course and flow.

The Father of Waters asserts yet another peculiarity. He refuses to be satisfied. After making his bed, he often finds it inadequate. And his tributaries, though smaller and subservient, can overwhelm him. Then he rises and pours right and left, leaving hundreds of miles flooded. Let me cite official data laid before the Congress of the United States, lest my last sentence be deemed exaggerated. Along its lower length the Mississippi annually floods to a width of forty-seven and a half miles, and to a depth of *twelve feet*! This lake of twelve billion cubic feet would require forty-eight days to drain via the normal river if not another drop arrived from the upper Mississippi and the tributaries below Cairo. Furthermore, Mississippi valley rainfall amounts [annually] to another lake 400 miles long, 49 wide, and 160 deep. In other words, enough to turn Louisiana into a sea eighty feet deep. The time the Mississippi alone would need to drain this mass of water? Three years![4]

You can therefore see what immensities of water must be reckoned with. Evaporation and absorption do remove plenty. But in the spring the regular river cannot suffice to carry away even the water gathered by normal drainage in the Ohio and Missouri valleys. Furthermore, as if that tide were not enough, swollen tributaries of the lower river—the Arkansas, for one, and the Red and the Ouachita—vent their deluges into the turgid Mississippi's flanks. Moreover, these torrents not only displace the Mississippi's, they also form a kind of barrier, a dam to the Mississippi that contributes to its flooding of the states along its shores.

And so the land swims for hundreds of miles: several feet of water over plantations, fields, gardens, virgin forests, cities, and villages.

---

wantonly and attacking with equal savagery the opposite bank . . ." (Percy, *Lanterns*, 14). But "the Mississippi is a just and equitable river; it never tumbles one man's farm overboard without building a new farm just like it for that man's neighbor. This keeps down hard feelings" (Twain, *Life on the Mississippi*, 214).

3. It would be to make "the Mississippi over again—a job transcended in size by only the original job of creating it" (Twain, *Life on the Mississippi*, 234).

4. Exact measurements of Mississippi floods cannot be taken, making statistics speculative and therefore inconsistent from statistician to statistician. All agree, however, with Hesse-Wartegg that Mississippi floods are huge.

The river's environs look a desperate wilderness of water, nothing showing but trees. Naturally such a situation repels settlement. This land could become some of the most fertile and remunerative in American agriculture. But unless properly drained, it must be left to additional centuries of the river's powerful caprices.

Meanwhile, what has been done about the floods? Up to now, nothing but the construction of dikes, the so-called "*levees*" or, to their enemies, "*mud embankments*." They have been erected everywhere along low shorelines on both sides of the river. They date from 1818 when riverside owners each at his own expense began to build them.[5] Of course, a levee protected the owner's land but increased the flooding of the neighbor's that still lay exposed. When one landowner paid for a levee, his neighbor paid for lack of a levee. Therefore, most low-lying plantations gradually acquired them. Congress helped defray expenses by indemnifying the planter with marshes and other wetlands adjoining his plantation.[6] In Louisiana, Mississippi, and Arkansas, these subsidies have grown to exceed $100 million [worth of land]! Unfortunately, thirty million valuable acres have been given away in the name of reparations and then sold to finance levees. Additional millions, coaxed from taxpayers' pockets under the pretense of levee building, have migrated into the pockets of a "*ring*" of officials and contractors.

Have the levees served their purpose? No, they have done the opposite. The Mississippi shares the experience of the Po. That is, dikes have been built in Italy, too, and the river forced between them. But it carries sediment, the bottom silts up, and the river rises and overflows the dikes, flooding the land again.[7] Dikes are built higher—and on and on the game goes to and fro, and for so long that the Po now flows atop an extended ridge far above the land that once enclosed it.

---

5. In point of fact, the levee at New Orleans "was almost a mile long" by 1727, and levee-building was de rigueur on plantations of the 1790s (Carter, *Lower Mississippi*, 350–51).

6. "After reconstruction [and after landowners failed to control the river], no more vital problem perplexed Delta statesmen than how to convince the Federal government of the propriety of contributing to the cost of building levees" (Percy, *Lanterns*, 13). The 1890 Mississippi constitution "spoke at length of the maintenance of a levee system along the Mississippi River—which really has no place in a constitution" but reflected "the economic interests of those who drafted it" (William Winter, former governor of Mississippi, quoted in V. S. Naipaul, "A Reporter at Large: The Old South," pt. 2, p. 62). Congress passed the Swamp Acts of 1850 in response to the problem (Carter, *Lower Mississippi*, 353). Hesse-Wartegg gives the figure in the next sentence as 400 million German marks, about $100 million. He must have misread it: Carter gives $1 million (354).

7. This is one of three common misconceptions about the Mississippi. "During the past 1,500 to 2,000 years the river has not measurably built up its bed" (Gerard H. Matthes, "Paradoxes of the Mississippi," 20). See note 12 below.

The Mississippi has suffered something of the same misfortune. Levees, the unhappiest idea that could have been implemented, not only cost hundreds of millions to build, but also have done more harm than good.[8] Though nothing wrong could be seen above the waterline of the levees, the river was driving uprooted trees and other driftwood against them while a species of river life peculiar to the Mississippi bored at them.[9] The river breached levees thus undermined, broke through as if through paper, and ripped the levees in countless places. The openings or *"crevasses"* let the land flood as it has always flooded, but enough levee remained to keep the land from draining as it used to drain. Plenty had been spent to build the levees, and again to inspect and maintain them, yet floods had to be suffered anyway. Those floods over, a second levee must be built behind the first. Later—the second being subject like the first to ravages of water—a third must be built behind the second.

Let me stress again: no artifice can restrain, nothing artificial control such a waterway—nothing! Only natural measures can save land flooded by the world's largest river.[10] In one measure the shores and alluvial areas have to be raised *naturally*. By a second measure, water so excessive as to produce floods has to be eliminated, also naturally.

The first method would be surefire but its time has passed. To begin with, ordinary Mississippi water contains particles of earth. Pour it into a glass; they will soon cover the bottom with as much as a finger of sediment.[11] It covers flooded land likewise; for the flood, after standing for weeks, departs with the retreating river, clear, having deposited its sediment. Deposits amount annually to several inches.[12] Now, what if nothing had interfered with the river inside well-defined boundaries, and the river been left as always to build its own banks? Floods then

8. Hesse-Wartegg has missed the fact that state, local, and individual measures, largely the building of levees, controlled the river well enough before the war. Levees deteriorated or went unbuilt during the war, and the lower valley suffered floods after the war, including one of the greatest, the rampage of 1874 (Coulter, *Reconstruction,* 250–51).

9. Hesse-Wartegg perhaps means crawfish, which bored through levees. See Percy, *Lanterns,* 246. Muskrats also bored through, and alligators undermined levees, with fatal results (Phillips, *Life and Labor,* 117).

10. It is not the world's largest in length, but in area drained: nearly 1.25 million square miles of watershed that comprises six basins and occupies the center of North America.

11. A tumblerful "holds nearly an acre of land in solution" (Twain, *Life on the Mississippi,* 190).

12. This is another false assumption about the Mississippi as an alluvial river, Twain and his tumbler notwithstanding. In truth, the river is relatively clear, it scours as it goes, and it has not built up its alluvial plain (Matthes, "Paradoxes of the Mississippi," 20).

would not occur in today's magnitude—that's for sure.¹³ But, as I have said, time has run out on this measure. Revert now, with riversides so thickly settled, to the ways of pristine Nature? Wait for such a snail-paced lifting of the land in the Age of Mechanization in speed-crazy America? Never!

The second and only feasible measure would rid flooded land of water.¹⁴ The old Mississippi traveler, Captain Cowden of Memphis, passionately champions what I mean: an elaboration of man-made drains: the so-called *"outlet system."*¹⁵ I have already noted that the lower river is too shallow to contain the torrents of spring. Rising water, forced between levees, overflows them. Were they pierced for exit at appropriate spots, not only would the river be freed of excess (a kind of blood-letting for plethora), but the "drawing off" (so to speak) at these cuts would also accelerate the flow. The measure has proved excellent where it occurs naturally, and application of it has been satisfactory.

A turgid river has twice broken through and created its own *"outlets,"* at Point Coupé and at Bonnet Carré near New Orleans, the most important of the natural outlets. At Point Coupé a part of the spring flood, rather than follow the river to its multi-mouthed terminus, goes straight across the peninsula and into the Gulf 100 miles sooner. Of course the gradient increases in proportion to the decrease of distance, producing a correspondingly stronger discharge from the river's main flow.¹⁶

A few years ago, about thirty-five miles above New Orleans, seeking

---

13. Hesse-Wartegg's argument is specious. The river had been taking its natural course for millennia upon millennia before man began to interfere. If it could not lift its shores and stop flooding in that time, how could it have done so in the few years of man's presence?

14. In fact, four measures had been proposed and disputed: new and renewed forests to reduce runoff; reservoirs to hold excess water; levees or other confinement to keep the river in its course; and diversion channels (also called cutoffs and outlets), chiefly below the mouth of the Arkansas, to drain excess and prevent flooding. A comprehensive plan would have used all the measures. See Arthur DeWitt Frank, *The Development of the Federal Program of Flood Control on the Mississippi River,* 113–14, 130–33; and John A. Fox, *Mississippi River Flood Problem: How the Floods Can Be Prevented,* 20–23.

15. James A. Cowden and John Cowdon seem to have been the same, an "outletter," who "for years appeared before all possible Congressional Committees with elaborate plans for constructing spillways and diversion channels and with severe criticisms for the supporters of levees" (Frank, *Flood Control,* 113). See also American Library Association, *National Union Catalogue* 125:454–55. Hesse-Wartegg thus takes his stand in this old and heated controversy, as an "outletter," against the supporters of levees.

16. This sentence is too vague in the original to be anything else in translation.

release, the river broke a crevasse through a strong levee at Bonnet Carré, and took the shortcut of only eight miles to Lake Pontchartrain, the most salient of the natural vents. The lake, part of the Gulf, stands at the same level as the Gulf. Therefore, water of the outlet at Bonnet Carré achieves in eight miles a gradient equal to that of the rest of the Mississippi in 150 miles. Again the drawing-off accelerates the flow, and the unusual speed not only keeps the channel free of bars and snags, but also drains the river to an extent noticeable as far as Vicksburg and Memphis. Indeed, the acceleration reduces depth at Vicksburg eight or nine, and at New Orleans *five feet*.

So, having looked at the two, levees and outlets, we see which excels. Whereas levees prove themselves harmful rather than useful, outlets speed the flow and discharge of excess. Cowden's proposal will therefore almost surely pass Congress and be implemented as soon as possible.[17] A new, man-made outlet below New Orleans will carry to Lac Borgne, a Gulf inlet, another measure of excess, lowering levels another five feet and accelerating the present speed by about ten percent.

Should the lower Mississippi still lack a sufficient safety valve for excess (such an eventuality exists), Cowden's plan calls for further action. The Red, the worst troublemaker, will be diverted. A canal, from near Alexandria and ahead of the mouth of the Red, will do the simple and relatively easy trick of keeping the Red out of the Mississippi by joining the Red to the Calcasieu, a river that runs (as everyone knows) straight to the Gulf. The Red would thus get a new mouth. Instead of joining the Mississippi for 500 miles (today's route) and flooding large areas, the Red's annual excesses would flow away with the Calcasieu a mere 80 miles to the Gulf. Of course, diverting the Red by canal thus would dry up the Red below the canal. True, the ever-abundant and dangerous Ouachita (Washita) now terminates there. But, rather than let the Ouachita take its natural course in the dry bed, a cut of only a few miles would connect it to the nearby Atchafalaya, which goes as straight as the Calcasieu to the Gulf. The

---

17. Cowden's plan did not pass Congress. The controversy continued before Congressional committees and in other parts of the Federal government and has not stopped. In 1879 Congress created the Mississippi River Commission, a seven-member panel appointed by the president to protect the shores, prevent floods, aid navigation, and promote commerce and communication (Fox, *Flood Problem,* 18). The commission kept exclusively to levees until the 1930s. Levees had always been the method of the U.S. Corps of Engineers, who dominated the commission. See Frank, *Flood Control,* 97–133; Fox, *Flood Problem,* 19–25. In the 1930s the commission added "artificial cutoffs" to its policy (Matthes, "Paradoxes of the Mississippi," 19, 22; Carter, *Lower Mississippi,* 367). Matthes' article, it should be noted, is by an engineer formerly with the commission, and thus as much a statement in favor of commission policy as a study of Mississippi flood control.

Ouachita now joins the Mississippi; the new route, through the Atchafalaya would shorten by 300 miles the Ouachita's way to the Gulf. Furthermore, by this simple procedure the Mississippi [below this point] will lose a ninth of its water, thereby gaining space for the glut from the north. Moreover, the acceleration of the Ouachita and the Red will soon free from floods the whole of Louisiana and Arkansas.

To sum up: the Mississippi can be regulated and the valley kept free from floods by either of two measures. One would raise levees between Cairo and the mouth to a height of seven feet for 2,000 miles at a cost of $100 million. Or the water can be lowered seven feet at a cost of $250,000. The decision is up to Congress.[18]

---

18. "Ten thousand River Commissions, with the mines of the world at their back, cannot tame that lawless stream." (Twain, *Life on the Mississippi,* 234). Twain says this is the view of "one who knows the Mississippi," but "a discreet man" would be quiet and wait and see. The commission and their West Point engineers might succeed in "making the river over again" (234). See also the remainder of Twain's chapter (235–41) and his Appendix B (507–10).

17. Arrival at the Port of New Orleans

At last, after almost two months in states along the immense Mississippi, I was approaching the capital of the South, also called the Crescent City because it bends to the shape of the river. The captain, the night before, trusted he could anchor at the "*levee*" early next morning. Therefore I dressed and betook myself up to the pilothouse at 4:00 A.M. I wanted at the earliest what I had so long awaited: a look at New Orleans.

The pilot would have it otherwise. We must make way during the night for lumber rafts and coal barges. So we anchored a long time at the Mississippi River city and former capital, Baton Rouge. We did not see the steeples and chimneys of the metropolis until nearly noon, far away on the horizon. And we saw nothing but steeples and chimneys! Looking at a city amid a land so flat for 100 miles around, in a countryside far below river level in many places, the viewer might fancy a city beneath the river; houses, streets, churches *submerged*. A second, an American Stavoren?[1] I could not help thinking of the famous Munchhausen tale.[2] On a winter journey he tied his horse to the top of a steeple. What if our pilot lacked the skill to avoid the steeples? Or ran aground on the ridge of a roof of an underwater cotton mill? If the bank sank, what then? Well, we passengers would be on the streets of New Orleans, exactly where we wanted to be!

On the shores all around we see more and more signs of our approach to a big city: plantation houses of pleasant aspect, expansive but usually low to the ground, painted white except jalousies and verandahs of green, with ivy and other vines twining about the pillars; the workers' cabins grouped like cubes around the main house; all overpowered by the immense "*sugarhouse*," home to machines and vats

---

1. A Dutch port situated below water level and protected by dikes. New Orleans at flood time is fourteen to eighteen feet below the river. See Price, "Lower Mississippi," 682.
2. The original Baron Munchhausen (1720–1797) was supposed to have served in the Russian army against the Turks and to have recounted his experiences with gross exaggeration. Rudolph Erich Raspe published a version of these tales in 1785: *Narrative of His Marvelous Travels*. Hesse-Wartegg refers to one in which the Baron, in a Russian blizzard, ties his horse to a post, later to discover that it was not a post but the top of a steeple, so deep was the snow.

for extracting and processing the juice of sugarcane; and here and there the squares where rice flourishes.[3] But seldom a road, almost never a wagon. To what purpose a wagon? Local steamboats provide communication and transportation upstream and down from New Orleans into every bay, canal, and bayou, and bring to the hub, New Orleans, the harvests of autumn: barrels of sugar, bales of cotton.

Now in February, however, stillness reigns—desolation! Harvests done, planters are resting from the profound rigors of winter's labor and gathering strength for those of spring. The southern sun has turned warm already, beaming out of a sky clear and blue like Italy's. The air is fresh, invigorating. We are in the deep South, nearly on a parallel with the West Indies, in the Italy of America. But if we do not dream ourselves into the blue sky, if we look at the land around us, nothing reminds us of Italy, nothing at all! Louisiana indeed, like its principal city, expresses a character so original and so unique that I cannot compare it to any other in either hemisphere.

River life quickens: ever more and faster. Small local steamboats churn the deep, coffee-yellow river or lie at shabby wharves of landings. Over there, among chimneys and steeples, roofs appear—or, if you will, peaks of waves on the sea of houses—as well as tall masts that fly pennants. Straight over the side, scarcely a mile from us: New Orleans. Only, at this moment, the Mississippi describes a wide curve. We unfortunately must obey. We have been aiming for the city, now we turn our backs and leave it for an hour. Let me end here the suspicions about Moslem connotations that attach to New Orleans. Despite any Turkish conditions that used to prevail, "Crescent City" refers to topography alone, the shape of a half moon. At last we steam again toward the levee dead ahead. We have reached our destination!

Whether coming in by land or water, at practically any time of year, the newcomer will never forget what he sees, it looks so overpowering, so magnificent.[4] American views too often prompt superlatives, but nothing else will suffice here. After several years of touring North America from end to end, I certainly cannot recall anything to rival

---

3. In this "homelike" and happy-looking region between Baton Rouge and New Orleans, Twain described "great sugar-plantations" crowding the sides of the river. War had left its blight, however: mansions were decayed and neglected, Negro cabins lacking their former whitewash (*Life on the Mississippi*, 335–37).

4. Hesse-Wartegg arrived "when the miles-long rows of docks did not altogether hide city and river from each other. The docks lay above and below the foot of Canal Street, with a long stretch of broad, open levee in between; and the levee was one of the city's most popular promenades. There was always the kaleidoscopic view of moored and moving shipping, water-borne sights and sounds and smells from the near and far places of the earth, and New Orleans liked to look at its river" (Harold Sinclair, *Port of New Orleans*, 11).

this river port, no other scene that, in such little space so grips the ear and fixes the eye.[5] The levees—that is, the wharves and anchorages of the Mississippi here—belong, no less than New York's Broadway and San Francisco's Chinatown, to the wonders of the New World.

Not London, not New York, not St. Petersburg, but New Orleans is the world's largest river port. Those three, despite riverside locations, receive mostly seagoing vessels. Here the world's oceans extend in one direction, the world's greatest river and its tributaries in the other, making New Orleans a seaport and a river port. In addition, the river system carries traffic inland for a million square miles far and wide.[6] No other port can boast anything like it.

New Orleans had to become one of the most important commercial centers on this continent.[7] If such circumstances as the war and political unrest, in addition to competition from transportation lines based elsewhere, have diverted part of the trade to other ports, New Orleans by virtue of location cannot but return as the valley's chief port, once normal conditions have been restored. The latest years show a sure and steady improvement. Last year, 1879–1880, a third of America's cotton passed through here, only a fifth through New York. As for imports, New Orleans has taken first place in the cotton South.

The imposing life of the river in and near New Orleans proclaims a commercial eminence. Though not nearly so wide as in places halfway up [to St. Louis], the river remains nearly three-quarters of a mile wide here. It reaches depths of 150 to 200 feet (no more the danger of running aground). Almost everything of the harbor, including anchorage for steamboats and oceangoing ships, occupies the left bank. On the right, nothing but the station of the first railroad to Texas, newly completed, as well as the Morgan Line's steamboats and platterlike, steam-powered, cross-river shuttles or "*ferryboats*." The Line plays an increasingly important role in the development of commerce here. In midstream a few oceangoing vessels—steamships, three-masters, brigantines—lie anchored. At the harbor's upper end, a heavy American warship, a monitor, rides at rest on the waves. The Crescent City's gatekeeper, so to speak.

Though waves run high here, these craft scarcely stir: a quiet side-

---

5. "One of the truly great riverfronts of the world" (ibid., 12). The extent of Hesse-Wartegg's travels makes this compliment especially significant.

6. Hesse-Wartegg may have rounded the figure. At that time it should have been around 1.25 million (U.S. Treasury Department, *Report on Commerce,* 7).

7. Despite the logic of this statement, New Orleans has never achieved such importance. "The Civil War may be responsible for this failure" as "a natural magnet," and New Orleans has not lived up to its potential as "the metropolis of the South." See Sinclair, *Port of New Orleans,* 266–67. Hesse-Wartegg takes up the topic again at the outset of the next chapter.

show to the grandiose main event: river life along miles of levees on the left bank. Nothing less than an encyclopedic description can represent a harbor so unique, so different from any other in America or Europe. Dry docks, wet docks, stone piers, stereotypical and inevitable in other harbors, do not occur here. A parquet of beams and planks replaces them along the entire front, part fixed to the shore and part floating in the river.[8] At a glance I estimate this giant raft to be about fifty feet wide. Behind it a broader strip, extending unpaved along the river for several miles, admits to the harbor no fewer than 150 streets. Railroad rails crisscross the shores. Warehouses, railway stations, roofs without walls [shelters] of giant proportions, and of course the mountains of boards and beams, baled cotton, barrels of sugar, and barrels of petroleum—each occupies occasional portions of this vast space; none comes at all near filling it anywhere. Railroad cars, dozens of horse-drawn wagons, and hundreds of heavy-duty carts, full and empty, go to and fro in unbroken lines. Thousands of people—officials, merchants, sailors, policemen, passengers, fruit and vegetable handlers, and inevitably dockworkers—hurry among baled cotton, agricultural implements, and every other product imaginable. To me in the pilothouse it looks like an anthill, this tumult spreading beyond visible distance, an anthill my febrile imagination expands to fantastic dimensions![9] Dark and dirty rows of buildings, far away, enclose the port with a background to complete the picture. The buildings give way in their solid line only to narrow streets that pierce it. The streets exude and reabsorb floods of people, wagons, and trains.

Not only an emporium, this is also a harbor and we are verging on it! Broad wooden piers for oceangoing ships extend into the river from shore, each at the end of a street. The municipal map puts the number at about 100 above the custom house, 60 below it. In earlier chapters I have described steam-powered riverboats. Here they assert their three and four levels of cabin, thrust up their pairs of black, dragon-mouthed stacks, and extend their gallowslike cranes. Every last one of the cranes works at full speed; cargoes must be hoisted from holds and put ashore *now.* Our boat approaches at last. Passing an unbroken mile-long line of white, colossal Mississippi steamers, we puff to our place at a landing.

Two huge ones, like ours, have left a slit between them. At noon our pilot brings his steam-powered giant about in a deft turn and heads into that squeeze. Ropes of course must help, and heavers, anchors, even pickaxes, to pry the boat into what we might call its "étui." Many

---

8. Twain describes such a "vast reach of plank wharves" (*Life on the Mississippi,* 340).
9. On the tumult of the riverfront, see Joy J. Jackson, *New Orleans in the Gilded Age,* 9–12.

a plank pulverized, many a rope shredded, but we have docked. The whistle, that unhappiest of instruments invented for the torture of mankind, shrieks us a farewell serenade. In the saloon the dreadful Negro band does its best in, thank goodness, its last piece for us. We prepare to get off. The plank drops to shore at last. The pilot having done his duty, the captain reassumes command. He girds for his hardest and most time-consuming duty: unloading. That toil, those tons upon tons of cargo, concern us not at all. One leap puts us on solid ground. In New Orleans.

18. International Port

New Orleans ought always to have been the chief commercial center of the Mississippi valley at least, if not of the United States. So it would seem by virtue of location. Consider however the colossal growth of Atlantic seaboard cities, and of agricultural states between the Mississippi and the Rockies, as well as of great cities of the West. Compare them with New Orleans. You will soon conclude that New Orleans has been left behind. All the nation's major cities exceed New Orleans. Yet the clear and unfailing laws of world commerce assert that where New Orleans is, there must arise a leading, if not the foremost, emporium in the United States. So you wonder, how could New York, Boston, Baltimore, Philadelphia, and even Chicago and St. Louis have passed the metropolis of the Mississippi? None of them can boast a geographical situation as favorable as that of New Orleans, where two continents join hands.[1] South America and the West Indies lie to the south, with their enormous [tropical and] subtropical produce, large population, and immense needs; to the [south]west, Mexico and Central America; and north, the United States. Remember also that Nature herself has equipped these parts of both continents with magnificent potential for transportation: the Gulf and rivers that empty into it. The rivers offer navigation to oceangoing vessels deep into the continents' heartlands. Everything points to New Orleans as the center of commerce in the Western Hemisphere.[2]

Despite everything in her favor, New Orleans has not lived up to potential. Other cities have outdone New Orleans even in trade with countries that for the best of reasons ought to have continued it with New Orleans. In fact such a pass has been reached that coffee, sugar, tobacco, and the like—the most important goods of the Western trade—do not use the inexpensive route by water via New Orleans and up the

1. "Ties with Latin America," strong then, "are still strong" but "prosaically commercial," especially notable for the trade in bananas and coffee (Sarah Searight, *New Orleans,* 70).

2. Hesse-Wartegg omits population patterns in this analysis. Settlement, however, ignored geography in the sense that he means it here. Among other factors, water routes would be bypassed if the railroad best served a market or other need. See Emory R. Johnson et al., *History of Domestic and Foreign Commerce of the United States,* 270–71.

Mississippi to St. Louis. They go at least 1,000 miles roundabout, via New York and then on railroads inland, at the expense of a Western populace numbering millions, many of them Germans, to the enrichment of New York and the railroad coterie.[3] Strong reasons must produce such unnatural results.[4] Let us examine the reasons.

Undoubtedly first and foremost New Orleans trails because of the war. Nowhere does the pulse of the southern states, especially of those in the western South, beat stronger than at New Orleans. She is their chief city, for sure. When they win, she wins double. When they lose, she loses double. The South, ergo New Orleans, lost the war and suffered the consequences. Political uproar and intrigue, and sickness and epidemics, arrived with the distress of defeat, likewise exerting baneful influences upon trade and credit. Yellow-fever quarantines included the port of New Orleans for six and seven months annually, thereby closing it to South America and the West Indies. With them New Orleans would have had its most profitable trade. Yet strangely enough the government did not close to West Indian and South American trade the ports of Baltimore, New York, Boston, or even the southern ports of Norfolk and Savannah, though all had suffered fever and proved themselves susceptible to it. Trade understandably must turn more and more from a New Orleans treated like a stepchild.

Quarantine would have been easily justified, even unavoidable,

3. According to the U.S. Treasury Department, on the other hand, if "the railroad lines have greatly extended their business in the last few years," they have in part brought business to the river in goods for "river points in the interior." Besides, the river continues "to be above all competition in certain lines, such as grain, coal, cotton-seed, etc." (*Report on Commerce,* 144).

4. To a degree, history bears out this statement. New Orleans has prospered when transportation and trade have been allowed to go their natural ways; other cities have prospered at the expense of New Orleans when transportation and trade have been forced into unnatural ways. The closing of the Mississippi in 1784 produced hardship for the valley until Americans gained the right of deposit at New Orleans in 1795. The city at once began to stir economically, proving its "natural" role in transportation and trade. Waterborne traffic, canal and river, declined after 1860 in North America; but steamboating prospered for a time on the Mississippi system. Steamboat trade made New Orleans the nation's leading export outlet until the Civil War closed the river. Though the federal government spent millions to improve the river, its commerce decayed nonetheless. Railroads meanwhile handled traffic on either side of the river, putting Mississippi-valley commerce on an east-west axis. Indeed, links of New Orleans firms to those in the East brought goods east on the Erie Canal in the 1830s and 1840s, and later on the railroads to Baltimore, Philadelphia, New York, and Boston. Railroads were already capitalizing on the advantage they would hold over the river: speed. The blocking of the river's mouth by silt further hindered traffic and aided the railroads. When Eads and his jetties reopened the river in 1879, New Orleans prospered again. See Sinclair, *Port of New Orleans,* 175–76; *Reader's Encyclopedia of the American West,* s.v. "New Orleans"; and Johnson, *Domestic and Foreign Commerce,* 269.

only the facts speak otherwise. Yellow fever appears in New Orleans as it appears in Havana and other ports: more or less spontaneously. But etiology aside, the unilateral closing of one port, the largest, while keeping others open, seems not only an injustice to New Orleans but a blow to the great West. To quarantine New Orleans, thus closing the Mississippi, in turn cutting the West's main line of transportation, could be said to amount to going for the jugular. Quarantine hurt the vital economic interests of both New Orleans and the West, hurt them as seriously as they could be hurt. It forced the West in its own interest to turn from the nearest, shortest, cheapest, natural route and turn to the railroads and a gigantic detour via the Atlantic ports! Twenty million, or half the people of the United States, live in the Mississippi valley and consume their half of the subtropical commodities produced around New Orleans. But those people do not get their half by way of New Orleans. About ten percent comes through New Orleans to St. Louis and the West. The rest takes the route via New York and Boston. Annually the United States pays $15 million for imports from Mexico. But only one-fifth enters at New Orleans. Yet entry at New Orleans means at least 1,500 miles less than entry at New York!

New Orleans has also trailed as a port because of difficult access to the Mississippi's mouth. Transatlantic steamships usually had to struggle to enter at Southwest Pass. Often they must wait along the mud banks, stalled for weeks before a higher tide or a rise in the river lets them in.[5] This obstacle has fortunately been removed, as we shall see in another chapter. The biggest steamships can reach New Orleans safely and without trouble now.

A lack of railroads between New Orleans and newly settled areas hurt the city's development, too.[6] In fact, New Orleans ought to have been the point of control for industry and commerce in those places— for its own state as well as for Arkansas and Texas.[7] Nor was there ade-

---

5. "It is impossible even to estimate how many millions of dollars were lost on that pile of Mississippi mud" (Sinclair, *Port of New Orleans,* 174).

6. New Orleans had always believed in its own natural superiority by geography: commercial success was inevitable. Overconfident, it failed to develop the railroads needed to compete with rivals in the North. New Orleans also held to tradition and custom, indulged "the good life" too much, felt secure in its plantation trade, and lacked manufacturing and other industries to promote railroads and commercial development (Clark, "New Orleans," 134–35).

7. Railroads as competitors to the river were therefore not as unnatural as Hesse-Wartegg claims. See Dabney, *One Hundred Years,* 88–90. Competition was a stage in the progress toward cooperation. Water dominated before the 1870s; the railroads' challenge led to the deterioration of waterborne rivals; then rails and water began to combine and accommodate one another; and eventually some transportation firms employed both. See James P. Baughman, "The Evolution of Rail-Water Systems of Transportation in the Gulf Southwest, 1836–1890," 357–81, especially 362, 363, 381.

quate communication with the large region that grows cotton. This hurdle also has been cleared. Until now, defective communication [with New Orleans] forced Texas into an unnatural commercial relationship with St. Louis, and St. Louis has been spreading its tentacles leisurely around that market. Now the line to Texas, universally deemed essential, has been completed after years of waiting. Today the iron horse roars straight from New Orleans deep into the heart of Texas.[8] At Houston it connects with the Texas rail net. A large part of the business of the giant state will therefore resume a natural course. It rests with the merchants of New Orleans to remove obstacles that may block their control of the Texas market. Already the railroad's beneficial effects can be seen. According to the *Deutsche Zeitung* of New Orleans, orders from Texas, especially for agricultural machinery, have exceeded every expectation. Soon there will be more railroads to Texas. The Morgan Railroad Company has been building a branch line from Vermillionville [Louisiana] to the Louisiana cities of Opelousas and Washington. This line in turn will be extended before the end of 1881 to the Red River near Shreveport, on the Texas border. Then the most beautiful and most productive part of Louisiana will be in direct communication with New Orleans.

Transportation and communication have advanced. Witness an open Mississippi and new territories reached by rail. Public health and sanitation have improved. Indeed, to put New Orleans into the race with cities of the Atlantic seaboard, one obstacle remains. A monopoly must be broken. Those cities and the eastern railroads wield influence, not only on trade between Europe and the United States, but also, as we have seen, on trade between the western states and South America and the West Indies. The monopoly's coterie of rich railroad directors, importers, merchants, and big industrialists—the rulers de facto of this country—affect Congress and its legislation. They also buy branch and competing lines, and maintain in every legal and illegal way their contrived hegemony; theirs is the power of capital amounting to billions. Meanwhile they know full well the consequences should they relax their machinations and stop their crafty railroad politics. Trade and commerce [to and from the West] would no longer move as they have been forced to move. They would return to their natural routes, which certainly do not go through New York and Boston.[9]

8. A combination of the Louisiana & Texas; Texas & New Orleans; Galveston, Harrisburg & San Antonio; and Houston & Texas Central took New Orleans deep into the heart of Texas in the 1870s. New Orleans became a rail center and led in the export of cotton until 1899. Galveston then took the lead because it got the enormous output of Texas, much of which had gone to New Orleans via rail. See Baughman, "Evolution of Rail-Water Systems," 368, 374–75; and Johnson, *Domestic and Foreign Commerce,* 280.

9. Whether or not by "natural routes," railroads "headed directly toward Eastern shipping points and centers of manufacturing" (Shannon, *Farmer's Last Frontier,* 105).

That is, the West lies outside the empire of New England's financial and industrial barons. As population grows in the huge states west of the Mississippi, so shall needs increase and output expand. The costly railroad lines, now running 2,000 miles to ports on the Atlantic, shall no longer suffice. The natural order of things compels the West instead to the grand avenue: the Mississippi. What is at stake? Mutual interests of two regions: those of the prairie states, north to the Canadian border and west to the Rockies, and those of the Mississippi valley and New Orleans. If only the West and South would realize that their interests ought to unite them to break the New England monopoly!

Still, according to newspapers and reports I have received, a significant improvement has occurred despite perverse transportation.[10] Unfortunately, I base this conclusion on scanty evidence.[11] By letter I queried governments and agencies of western cities and states, and got information, statistical data, and the like—abundantly. But every one of my letters to southern states and city governments, and to southern newspapers, has gone unanswered. I stress my queries to Louisiana. If this is the way the authorities act, they will not get the immigration they want so much. At any rate, in 1878 New Orleans received 11.25 million bushels of grain for export [an improvement].[12] Still, New York ranks first among American ports: 124.5 million!

Here is a table of grain received by the seven leading ports:

	1876	1877	1878
New York	71,820,000	81,202,000	124,661,000
Baltimore	29,552,000	23,537,000	39,672,000
Philadelphia	31,272,000	21,502,000	38,203,000
Boston	13,244,000	13,491,000	18,234,000
Montreal	13,207,000	13,428,000	12,858,000
New Orleans	5,450,000	8,226,000	11,189,000
Portland	2,569,000	1,212,000	2,607,000
Total	167,114,000	162,598,000	247,424,000

Directness would seem as natural as any other reason for a transportation line.

10. Improvement did occur, but not despite railroads and other "perverse conditions in transportation." It occurred because of better railroad transportation, in addition to the elimination of yellow fever, removal of obstacles to river navigation, and alleviation of the effects of war, all reasons discussed earlier in this chapter. See ibid., 109–10.

11. Probably because "the statistics of the river traffic of New Orleans are very defective" (U.S. Treasury Department, *Report on Commerce,* 143).

12. "In grain, accurate statistics are preserved, but in most articles there are no statistics at all as to the river business" (ibid.).

New Orleans notably (as observed by the *Anzeiger des Westens*), though still in sixth place, has made the most significant progress.[13] In spite of yellow fever, grain exports from New Orleans have more than doubled since 1876. It can be fairly assumed that without the horrific plague—enough to stop shipping on the lower river a full four months—New Orleans would have passed Montreal and perhaps Boston last year. If fever stays away this year, New Orleans will be fourth. Friends of the jetty system [to aid Mississippi navigation] had predicted and still hope New Orleans can compete with Philadelphia, Baltimore, and New York, cities that handle four-fifths of the grain from the Atlantic coast. Time will tell whether these people are right. At least the latest reports confirm what the *Anzeiger* expected. Grain from New Orleans has risen in 1880, last year, to 15.25 million bushels.

It would seem that more and more of America's grain will arrive at New Orleans to be sent abroad. For not only has the time come when the greater part of this export originates on the western shores of the Mississippi, but it can move downriver to New Orleans for as little as half as much as it would cost by rail to the East Coast.[14] Of course, jetties must prove themselves over the long term. People used to give several reasons against New Orleans as a city of grain export. Above all (they said) heat would spoil grain. That objection and the others have long since been laid to rest. California grain crosses the equator twice before it reaches the European market. East Indian grain passes through the Red Sea, quite the hottest place on Earth. Therefore, we can surely expect a bright future for the grain trade in New Orleans and in St. Louis as well.[15]

Even the foreigner can appreciate the extent and significance of waterborne commerce in New Orleans.[16] Let us but take up a newspaper at random and look at the four or five columns devoted to this reportage. American newspapers excel at organization. Here, accordingly, the reader sees at a glance the shipping at New Orleans. Three

13. The *Anzeiger des Westens,* important in the large and vigorous German-language press of nineteenth-century St. Louis, ran from 1835 to 1912 (becoming the *Abend-Anzeiger* in 1898) and "was widely known as a great newspaper" (Arndt and Olson, *German-American Newspapers,* 250).

14. The commercial convention in St. Louis in 1867 showed, in its memorial to Congress on "bettering Mississippi transportation," that a ton of average freight cost five to six times as much by rail as on the river (U.S. Treasury Department, *Report on Commerce,* 100).

15. With this prediction, Hesse-Wartegg's accurate discussion of the grain trade ends. Even the marked increase of 1896 brought the Gulf only twenty-nine percent of the nation's exports of wheat and less than four percent of the flour (Johnson, *Domestic and Foreign Commerce,* 271–74).

16. The river remained "one of the most important avenues of the city's commerce" (U.S. Treasury Department, *Report on Commerce,* 144).

rubrics head the divisions: river news, maritime news, and steamers.[17] Under river news: boats arriving, expected, and departing; and dispatches on water levels in ports upriver, telegraphed every day at 3:00 P.M. (To steamboat pilots the levels are of utmost importance.) Here is an example. Bear in mind that such intelligence usually includes many other ports on the Mississippi's tributaries.

Port	Above normal levels		Change since yesterday	
	Feet	Inches	Feet	Inches
Cairo	24	1	−1	2
Cincinnati	0	0	0	0
Louisville	8	10	−0	2
Memphis	22	0	0	0
Nashville	8	3	−1	0
New Orleans	4	4	−0	2
Pittsburgh	0	0	0	0
Shreveport	6	8	0	4
St. Louis	12	9	−0	2
Vicksburg	34	11	−0	1

General news follows: the latest about shipping along thousands of miles in the valley. Finally, what has been so important until now: "*From the Passes,*" or news of the Mississippi's mouths, including levels at the "*bar*" and the arrivals of oceangoing vessels from domestic and foreign ports.

Such reports [of arrivals] usually occur in any port, under "*Marine News.*" Departures are likewise announced. The extent of waterborne commerce can thus be calculated. New Orleans papers announce twenty to twenty-five [arrivals and departures] per *day*.

Naturally the recent turn of events has disturbed the moneybags of northeastern ports, notably Boston and New York.[18] Said bags have been doing everything to keep trade and commerce on the old, unnatural routes. The Erie Canal, hitherto the main life for freight between

17. In the *New Orleans Daily Picayune* the heads were "The River" and "Marine News." There was also a section of steamboat advertisements: passengers are solicited, and routes, stops and times announced.
18. "The recent turn of events" probably refers to what Hesse-Wartegg has been saying about the improved position of New Orleans with respect to trade and commerce. That is, the city is now able to compete with the East because of better public health and sanitation, a newly opened Mississippi, and recent rail connections with new territories.

New York and the West, is to be extended and deepened at government expense, and tolls are to end for crystal-clear reasons. Mississippi River shipping has hurt New York's export business, and these measures are to counter the competition. The big railroads between New York and the West, for all their strength, face the threat of losing the most profitable part of their freight. Chicago, Detroit, Cleveland, and Buffalo share with New York a vested interest that grain from the Northwest not turn to the Mississippi but be kept on its present routes.

Mississippi freight has recently multiplied nonetheless. Everywhere on the upper river—St. Paul, Winona, La Crosse, Dubuque, Keokuk, Davenport, etc.—newspapers and the business community discuss *the* topic more than any other: proof of interest the river and its southern metropolis can spark as far away as the valley's northernmost points. Even the rich Illinois Central Railroad, owned and run largely by Chicagoans and New Yorkers, intends to get into the shipping of grain down the Mississippi, and in a big way, from Cairo, by building large elevators at the mouth of the Ohio there. One of the St. Louis riverboat firms, the Mississippi Valley Transportation Company, recently sent downriver a flotilla of fifteen big barges, loaded with over 11,000 tons of grain (nearly 400,000 bushels), escorted by two large steam-powered tugs. Another firm, the American River Transportation Company, has been assembling a similar flotilla. Railroads cannot match shipping of this magnitude.[19] Thirty locomotives and five hundred cars could not have moved such a mass of grain.

In addition, the Mississippi enjoys an advantage in being popular all over the Northwest. The region's "*Grangers*," who hate the railroad combine, not only see in the new route an excellent way to reduce freight below its cost on the New York route, but they also welcome an ally against the hated railroads.[20] Furthermore—and this is what mat-

---

19. By 1887 railroads had gone everywhere in the lower valley, rendering the steamboat obsolete by virtue of speed. But barges competed successfully against railroads with heavy, bulky cargoes of the sort that Hesse-Wartegg describes here. See Carter, *Lower Mississippi,* 229–30. Hesse-Wartegg might also have mentioned the acres of log rafts, some as big as small truck farms, being moved efficiently and at minimum cost. For the river's superiority for this sort of cargo, see Havighurst, *Voices,* 247–48. See also Shannon, *Farmer's Last Frontier,* 105. Indeed, steamboats proved too capable with heavy, bulky cargoes. In 1881 they carried rails, locomotives, and railroad cars: materials for the very railroads that would do them in (Havighurst, *Voices,* 154). The decline of steamboating came slowly and at various times on different parts of the river (Hunter, *Steamboats,* 588–89).

20. The National Grange of the Patrons of Husbandry, the farmers' association that led a proagrarian movement, favored regulation of railroad rates as an aid to farmers. Regulation and other profarmer legislation constituted the "Granger laws" (*Reader's Encyclopedia of the American West,* s.v. "Granger laws"). See Woodward, *New South,* 32, 34, 94. It should not be inferred from this discussion that Hesse-Wartegg

ters—to ship on the southern route costs so much less than on the eastern, that the eastern interests will be hard put to make up the difference. The calculation is simple, the result obvious. Mississippi barges and their steam-powered tugs move wheat and corn to New Orleans from St. Louis for five cents a bushel, and from St. Paul for fifteen cents.[21] True, the cost is lower from New York to Liverpool: only about two and a half cents as compared to twelve cents. On the other hand, it is twenty cents from St. Louis or thirty-three from St. Paul to New York. Riverboats and steamships move a bushel from St. Louis to Liverpool for seventeen cents, whereas it is twenty-nine and a half via New York. A difference of twelve and a half cents in favor of the southern route from St. Louis, and all of fifteen and a half from St. Paul! (These figures are from the *Belletristisches Journal* of New York.)

Cotton, however, remains the commodity for New Orleans.[22] Forty-four percent of American cotton passes through here. The cotton exchange opened with 100 members in 1871; now 300 belong and the budget includes an annual $30,000 for rapid delivery of news of the trade in all parts and every city of the world! Easily half the enormous American crop goes to Liverpool, about a fifth to Le Havre and New York, and the rest to other cities spread as wide as St. Petersburg, Marseilles, and Vera Cruz.

In 1872 more than 2,500 steamships arrived in New Orleans with 3.5 million tons worth $160 million. Of that, $90 million went up the Mississippi. Trade in New Orleans can be estimated at about $400 million a year. Imports from foreign countries account for about $19 million; exports to them, $90 million. Five steamship lines connect New Orleans and Europe directly: one, the North German Lloyd, to Bremen and Havre; three—the Liverpool Southern, the Mississippi and Dominion, and the State—to Liverpool.

What New Orleans lacks would magnify the city's increased prosperity: a direct line to South America, especially Brazil.[23] The West's

---

believed in Forty-Eighter liberalism or entertained anything like populism. He was aristocratic and royalist to the end, favoring any policy that would produce efficiency and prosperity.

21. Hesse-Wartegg's analysis was right: barges would give the Mississippi and New Orleans leading roles in valley commerce. But a lack of barges prevented it for a while. The 120 barges and 16 towboats of 1887 "could not handle more than a tiny fraction" of the potential traffic (Sinclair, *Port of New Orleans,* 266).

22. In 1880 over $75 million worth of raw cotton left New Orleans; of corn, the second-largest export, less than $4.25 million (U.S. Treasury Department, *Report on Commerce,* 382).

23. Statistics confirm that New Orleans sent most exports to Europe rather than Latin America; whereas imports from Brazil to New Orleans were nearly twice those from Britain and Ireland in 1878, and those from Cuba only slightly less than from Britain and Ireland (ibid., 379, 381).

big industrial centers and the agricultural states must use New York in the Brazil trade. Grain headed there on the New York route costs seventy-five cents a barrel to ship; on the New Orleans, thirty to thirty-five! Brazilian coffee in America finds (no doubt about it) most of its consumers in the West, the Mississippi valley, and certainly beyond the Alleghenies. The cargo (1,834 million sacks, 238.5 million pounds) would follow the cheapest and straightest route to its markets. But all that coffee goes to New York so the city and the railroads can take their profit before the consumer gets the product.

These things are temporary. The West and its chief port, New Orleans, will and must grow equally and together. Trade will take its natural course. Of North American ports, the future can and will do the most for New Orleans.

19. The Metropolis of the South

New Orleans, city of surprises, offers the visitor the greatest contrasts imaginable in people, streets, and views. His first half-hour walk takes him along streets that could belong to Paris, New York, Palermo, or Madrid.[1] He will be able to observe the nervous, fast, businesslike life of Yankees and next to it the *dolce far niente* [pleasant idleness] of the Latin races, as well as scenes of the semibarbarous life of Negroes and the miserable existence of the last Indians. He will see a gathering of the most heterogeneous peoples on Earth, he will hear many languages, and he will realize what this city requires of one who would know her: long residence and hard study. Some tourist from Europe has sniffed, "See one American city and you've seen 'em all." Obviously he never saw San Francisco or New Orleans, else he would not have laid down such a dictum.

New Orleans, once capital to Louisiana, shared the destiny of the vast, old, Latin colony, until the colony became a commonwealth of American states. No longer the political capital of Louisiana, New Orleans has become the cultural and commercial capital of a region: the South.[2]

Louisiana, for 150 years the dream of every European monarch and occupied by [European] military forces, therefore cannot be separated from the history of Europe for those years. A worthwhile prize, Louisiana reached out to touch 500 miles of the Pacific, 700 miles of British possessions, and 1,400 miles of the Maschaschébé (the name for the Father of Waters then), closing the circle with 700 miles along the Gulf—a colony of nearly 1.5 million square miles! French and Spanish, Canadians [British colonists] and Yankees, all eyed this magnifi-

1. "He can easily fancy himself in the older streets of Bordeaux" (Chambers, *Mississippi River,* 198).
2. New Orleans was the political capital of the French and Spanish colonies of Louisiana. After Louisiana became part of the United States, New Orleans was its political capital from 1812 to 1825, 1831 to 1849, and during Reconstruction. It has always been the cultural and commercial capital of the lower Mississippi valley, if not the South. It was the "good-time town of the Mississippi," the "playground for the Americans of the upriver plantations, a racing mecca of the nation" as well as "the business heart of the valley and the cultural metropolis where the opera thrived and the drama was honored" (Carter, *Lower Mississippi,* 253).

cent yet monstrous jewel that for a while graced the crown of the French king.[3] Military campaigns, armed conquest, battles against Indians, diplomatic negotiation with the provincial governor, expeditions of exploration into unknown lands: thus the history of that 150 years. Historic names tower yet from Louisiana's past, including Bienville, DeSoto, Don André Almonaster, and Carondelet.[4]

In order to understand the New Orleans and Louisiana of today, let us be somewhat versed in the events of those times.[5] Today's capital of half a continent did not exactly glitter 150 years ago. Think of a low-lying swamp, partly covered by dense virgin forest and crisscrossed by pools and ditches that divided one terrain into many islands. A small area on the banks of the river, a little higher than the rest, had been cleared of primeval growth and parceled into small, regular squares. The area remained exposed to the river's floods, true, but was the best available far and wide. Deep ditches usually ran along the sides of a square, for drainage. They surrounded it, collected stagnant water and muck of the swamp, and in the heat of the sun, returned the foulest vapors. Palisades and a moat surrounded the "city" in turn, leaving it to be reached only from the river. A few houses occupied each square. Reeds and marsh grasses flourished around the houses, even crowding the doors. Hoarse croaking of myriad frogs mingled with vesper hymns of pious colonists in the evenings. Introduced from Africa, Negroes had been brought in the slave-ships of the Parisian Rothschild, Antoine Crozat.[6] They moved about on the banks of the Mississippi, these Negroes, with their old strut, heads high, obstinate. (Years of slavery produced today's bent and humbled figure.) Some of the colonists were daredevil cavaliers and aristocratic ladies—they lived in the new capital's shacks—and what a contrast it made, their elegant man-

3. By Canadians Hesse-Wartegg may also mean, not the displaced Acadians of *Evangeline* fame, but the French and French-Canadians under Pierre Le Moyne d'Iberville. They came in an expedition to realize LaSalle's claim to the region as the property of France. See Kane, *Deep Delta Country,* 6–7.

4. Jean Baptiste Le Moyne, Sieur de Bienville (1680–1768), French-Canadian explorer, founder of New Orleans; Hernando de Soto (1496?–1542), explorer who reached the Mississippi in 1541; Don Andres Almonaster y Roxas (1725–1798), Spanish grandee, several times benefactor to New Orleans; Francisco Luis Hector, Baron de Carondelet (1748–1807), Spanish governor of Louisiana, 1791–1797.

5. Hesse-Wartegg's sketch of Louisiana's beginnings—short on facts and dates, longer on impressions, especially portrayal of hardship, and accurate enough as far as it goes—seems intended to show what grand things grew from meager prospects.

6. A few slaves came earlier, but "the slave agriculture system was launched in Louisiana" about 1720 when two ships from West Africa landed 500 slaves (Sinclair, *Port of New Orleans,* 28). Crozat (1674–1738), merchant and entrepreneur, became one of Europe's richest men. He held Louisiana and a monopoly on its trade under a proprietary status from 1712 to 1717 (*Dictionnaire de Biographie Française,* s.v. "Crozat, Antoine").

ners and stylish clothes with these wretched, muddy surroundings. The governor's entourage, together with officials and other colonists, assembled around large, rough-hewn crosses and said their prayers; churches did not exist here then. Negroes in the city outnumbered whites two to one.[7] Horses and other domestic animals were so rare that it became a capital crime to kill or injure one. Jesuit priests and Ursuline nuns had arrived in "Nouvelle Orleans" to found their missions.[8] Thoroughfares of a municipality wrested from swamps received names of princes: Maine, Conde, Conti, Toulouse, Bourbon. Charles Street took the name of the regent's son. Even the colony's governor, Bienville, gave his name to one of the new avenues.[9]

Along the Mississippi for miles above and below the city, sons of noble French families founded plantations and lived exciting, voluptuous lives while slaves tilled the fields under overseers' whips. Slaves, objects of control and supervision, wore unmistakable signs of their status. The colony excluded Jews, permitted no religion but Catholicism, and forbade men to marry slaves or make them concubines.[10] Strict observance of Sundays and holidays included a ban on work.

Meanwhile, the colonists had enough trouble and work to render arable the forests and swamps, and build levees against Mississippi floods. From time to time the rage of hurricanes destroyed homes, plantations, and villages. Wild tribes nearby—Choctaw and Chickasaw, for example—never stopped feuding with one another.[11] Ships from France with colonists and troops seldom arrived; the colony had to mobilize its own forces. Long-drawn-out, wearisome battles with the Natchez and the Chickasaw put them to the test.

Yet the colony grew, gradually, until the middle of the last century, when the king of France made a gift of it to his cousin in Spain.[12] Under Spanish rule, the character of the place transformed. Nothing but French names continued. New houses—flat-roofed, low, with wrought-iron balconies, smacking here and there of antique Moorish architecture—appeared along the streets of New Orleans.[13] To ensure control,

---

7. Hesse-Wartegg does not mention the chiefly German "redemptioners" or bond servants, an important class of "slaves" (Work Projects Administration, *New Orleans City Guide*, 10).

8. Capuchins as well as Jesuits worked here (ibid., 11).

9. That is, the colony's founder, Bienville. See note 4 above.

10. The exclusion of Jews seems to have been less due to anti-Semitism than to the proscription of all religions and denominations except Catholicism (Sinclair, *Port of New Orleans*, 36).

11. "The Indians were in a continuous state of war somewhere" (ibid., 19).

12. Louisiana passed to Spain by the Treaty of Fontainebleau in 1762.

13. The original French city, today's French Quarter, boasts not French but Spanish architecture: in "general style" and most features and many details "as Spanish as the mantilla and fandango" (Sinclair, *Port of New Orleans*, 96–97).

troops were brought from Spain, and posts and forts built. No more the elegant, easygoing French garrison; the serious, rigid Spaniard ruled with an iron hand. The number of monks and nuns grew while the populace remained at a few thousand. Louisiana did not remain in Spanish hands, however, but early in this century went back to the French.[14] America's General Jackson sealed Louisiana's fate by trouncing the invading British below New Orleans.

One immense, unoccupied colony has become a dozen of North America's most prosperous and heaviest populated states.[15] The name *Louisiana* specifies but a vestige of the old colony, about a thirtieth of what Louisiana used to be, a scrap of the former 40,000 square miles. Louisiana has thus diminished. Meanwhile, the chief city has swollen fifty times its colonial size. Buildings cover the miles between the Mississippi and Lake Pontchartrain; the population is almost a quarter million souls. Frenchmen and Spaniards laid the foundation, yes, and left their mark on people and appearance. But American rule produced today's prosperity and size—and Americans shall guide the city into a grand future.[16]

One characteristic alone may prove French origins. The streets of New Orleans do not follow the checkerboard of most American cities. Streets may be straight; each quarter may obey a plan. But their relation to one another conforms in part to the bends of the Mississippi, in part to the shape of large areas once privately owned. The oldest and busiest quarter occupies a bend of the river; newer ones fill the space from there to Lake Pontchartrain. A number of bayous and ship canals cross the city in various directions. The Father of Waters prevails as ever: not only the main artery but also the bearer of prosperity and the agent of destiny, the alpha and omega of New Orleans. Business, concentrated in streets nearest the port, radiates from the hub and penetrates many another street in the inner city, to expire at last in residential ones and their gardens and walks. A number of straight avenues, miles long, crisscross the residential districts, converge and diverge, and lead at last to some destination on the river or lake, without so much as having touched an important place. Of hundreds of streets, not a dozen go in the same direction.

Streets in American cities typically have been numbered in se-

14. By the Treaty of San Ildefonso in 1800.
15. Hesse-Wartegg, nearly right about the number of states (though all were not yet states), is clearly wrong about population.
16. Except for the chapter 22 below on the cockfight and some references to gambling, one topic is conspicuous for its absence in Hesse-Wartegg's pages: New Orleans was "notorious throughout the world" as a "cesspool of sin" and rife with prostitution (Asbury, *French Quarter,* 350).

quence. Here, because streets lie at random and run without purpose, the practice would be impractical, pointless. Streets go by name instead, names drawn as for streets of European cities, from every source imaginable. I have already mentioned how names in the old quarters recall the French monarchy; and in the newer, the Republic and Empire—Marengo and Austerlitz, for example. To help designate modern streets of the American period, the muses have been used, and demigods, fairies, titans; in short, mythology has been plundered. Felicity accordingly intersects Dryades, Elysian Fields and Magnolia, and let us not forget Melpomene's Avenue. Columbus appears in the beautiful company of demigoddessess while the Olympian gods and goddesses surround the French kings. Nowhere else can you so disport among such an exaltation of royalism! American heroes and presidents have been settled near a catalogue of virtues such as genius, strength, wisdom, and benevolence. Finally, across the river are the suburbs: Algiers, Tunis, Belleville.[17] With such honeyed words and proud names and poetic titles, the map of New Orleans strikes a handsomer pose than that of America's other cities and their cold numbers 1, 2, 3, 4.[18]

A lack of elevation also distinguishes New Orleans. Height nowhere favors city or environs, which extend for miles, rise not an inch, and remain as flat as a pancake and several feet *below* the Mississippi at high water. A break in a levee would inundate all. Fortunately, Old Man River has rested content that his young metropolis respects the power of his waters. Over the centuries he has let a beautiful city expand to its present extent, undamaged. True, the ancient and crotchety fellow has indulged in a prank here and there, a thumb through one of the giant levees and an advance upon the land for a glance around. But he has been pushed back fast to his own bailiwick and blocked by a second levee from further encroachment.

In a city so low, where land for construction has had to be gradually wrested from swamps, there can be no digging of cellars, no building underground. The sewer system remains unsatisfactory. Happily, the large lake to the east, Pontchartrain, lies a little lower. Sewers can be made to empty far out in it. Even where land is relatively high, water must be dealt with always and everyplace. In the drainage canals and at lower points of the old, sleepy, tall-tree-shaded city park, water stagnates in ponds. In cemeteries, swamp muck makes burial a conundrum. Street pavement finds no satisfactory foundation. With few places excepted, holes riddle it. In a downpour, when the city goes under water from end

17. Algiers has become part of the city but with a notable identity of its own. See Work Projects Administration, *New Orleans City Guide,* xxii, 358–62.

18. Hesse-Wartegg skips some categories of names (authors, for one) but conveys the variety of nomenclature. See Sinclair, *Port of New Orleans,* 290–91.

to end, nothing but lower-lying Pontchartrain and its communication with the Gulf permit a measure of drainage. What a blessing for New Orleans, this lake with its seawater ever renewed by tides, its beautiful beaches, and the fresh sea breezes that sweep across it from Gulf to city![19]

So much for the bird's-eye view. Let us take to the streets. In from the levees we come unwittingly upon a street less than beautiful in name but in fact the most beautiful here if not in all America: the magnificent Canal Street.[20] This Mississippi of streets opens onto the Mississippi itself, the street the perfect counterpart to the river. In New York, Europe lies at one end of Broadway, America at the other. In a few miles Broadway unrolls a continent for us to see. A step on Canal Street and we recognize the Broadway of New Orleans: just as important, equally imposing and, if anything, *more* characteristic.[21] Here the South lies at one end of an international thoroughfare, the tropical West Indies at the other. The contrasts collide in one city, it seems, and in *this* street. Situation, prospect, traffic, the splendor of shops, all of life as lived in a street—in a word, *everything*—says we stand on the boundary between two great but distinct cultures. Anglo-Saxon and Latin meet *here*. Everything says we tread the contiguous edges of geographical zones. Tropical and temperate intersect *here*.[22]

Canal Street runs the city's length, dead straight and more than seventy paces wide, dividing the city almost exactly in half. Businesses and residences line this imposing thoroughfare.[23] Size, multiple stories, and commercial inventory speak for the United States. Architec-

---

19. "The prevailing breezes in summer-time being from that quarter" (New Orleans Progressive Union, *New Orleans—What to See . . . A Standard Guide*, 7).

20. One of the widest streets in the United States (171 feet), Canal is the center of the city, from which all activities "radiate and the goal to which all return" (Work Projects Administration, *New Orleans City Guide*, 286). It extends from the Mississippi to Greenwood Cemetery and is the baseline for numbering all north-south streets. Nearly every street between the river and Rampart Street changes name when it intersects Canal. Probably "every visitor" late in the nineteenth century "made an appearance" on this street, becoming "part of the colorful panorama which caught the eye of every chronicler of the period" (Jackson, *New Orleans in the Gilded Age,* 12).

21. "Canal Street is as indelibly associated with the 'Crescent City' as Broadway is with 'Gotham' " (Chambers, *Mississippi River,* 197).

22. "Only the 'neutral ground' running down the center of Canal Street preserves its impartiality, on lamp posts bearing plaques that refer with equal disdain to French domination, Spanish domination, and American domination" (Searight, *New Orleans,* 209). Hesse-Wartegg's paragraph must be admired as perceptive. However, "two great but distinct cultures" is overstated. The old Creole "way of life was only a museum piece which would pass out of general existence within thirty years" (Jackson, *New Orleans in the Gilded Age,* 14).

23. "During the 1840s Canal Street became the city's main shopping street" (Searight, *New Orleans,* 210). Hesse-Wartegg's description implies more beauty than is usually seen in the street (210–11). See also Jackson, *New Orleans in the Gilded Age,* 12–13.

ture—beautiful balconies and picturesque verandahs circling a building at every story—represents Spanish culture.[24] The verandahs project far out over the sidewalks from many buildings, amounting to an arcade where crowds pass to and fro in shelter from rain and excessive sun. Flowers at windows, tropical vines and ornamentals on balconies portray the South. Signs in garish colors, messages over a building's front from top to bottom (gross advertisements screaming Buy! Buy!) evoke the North. The names we read there and the language give us a fresh example of where we are: a city of polyglot, a Franco-Hispanic-American Babel.[25] Tall flagpoles lift the Stars and Stripes above every building. Green jalousies and awnings jut from facades. One window features an advertisement; another, the mug of a smart, tobacco-chewing Yankee; another, the piquant-brown face of a Creole lovely.

Miles of big stores, shops of splendid elegance under the arcades, large restaurants, French cafes, oyster bars, billiard halls, and nothing to interrupt them but the many narrower but equally flamboyant, equally vivacious side streets that enter upon Canal. Wide sidewalks, laid with big, beautiful slabs of stone, edge the fronts of buildings. Streets partake of a thicker version of this excellent pavement. In their centers long double rows of trees shade grassy boulevards and well-sanded footpaths, creating two passages for wheeled traffic.[26] Between a sidewalk and the shaded central path, a narrow, open drainage ditch divides each lane yet again. Stone slabs cover the ditches at intersections. Each traffic lane maintains its integrity of width, twenty paces everywhere, but yields to dozens of rails. These carry the streetcars, horse-drawn and steam-powered, a phenomenal traffic, especially at the junction with Charles Street. Here we learn beyond doubt that we are in a commercial city of the first magnitude. For, despite the incredible number of cars, each is full and sidewalk traffic and private vehicles undiminished. The network of streetcars, probably covering more than 100 miles, serves every part of the city with Canal Street as the hub.[27] Truly a blessing, what with these distances. Mules pull the

24. The architecture amounts to a unique French-Spanish combination (Work Projects Administration, *New Orleans City Guide,* 147). Cf. Twain: "In broad, general terms, there is no architecture in New Orleans, except in the cemeteries" (*Life on the Mississippi,* 340).

25. "The clashing of a dozen tongues could be heard." The language and culture of French rivaled the English language and American culture because "the French tradition so gripped the Creole mind" (Sinclair, *Port of New Orleans,* 188).

26. New Orleans boasted "an abundance of trees and flower gardens" (Jackson, *New Orleans in the Gilded Age,* 21). The paths were called "neutral ground" (Work Projects Administration, *New Orleans City Guide,* 286).

27. The extensive streetcar system, "the most vital means of transportation" in New Orleans, provided the readiest and most interesting but not always the most pleasant way to get from place to place. See Jackson, *New Orleans in the Gilded Age,* 162–64.

"horsecars"; mules can stand the heat better than horses.

We soon learn the chief sources of wealth in New Orleans: commerce and plantations. Most of the commercial streets lead into the half of Canal along the river. Each specializes in its own item. For example, cotton is the chief commodity in Carondelet, site of the Cotton Exchange.[28] Hubbub rules the exchange in the mornings. Two million bales, bought and sold here, leave for every corner of the world. To the exchange, from the plantations, the seaports, the factory centers of Europe and America—from wherever cotton matters—comes news to be posted hour by hour on great black display boards; and demand for cotton and the price follow accordingly. A little farther and we come to the seat of trade in staples of *"the great West"*: bacon, ham, salted meats, corn, and other grain; then the warehouses of sugar, molasses, leather, hats, tobacco, etc.

Plantations will not be found on Canal Street, of course. To approach the [plantation owners' homes and the evidence of plantation wealth] we must leave the commercial district and penetrate deeper into this expansive city's confusion of traffic. Many streets and many a district pose riddles to us as we negotiate them. Differences multiply in contrast [to what we have just seen]: rows of houses, lifeless, empty as if deserted like those of Philadelphia. Narrow streets. Miserable shacks. Storerooms and warehouses mean and locked. Grass and weeds sprout from cracks in defective pavement. Dirt and trash in the gutters. Many a home empty, uninhabited. Damp walls. A cool, sultry atmosphere. Street lamps broken. Where is that clear and sunny sky that arches over the smiling prospect of the city yet sends not a ray upon this desolation?[29]

A few steps and we debouch into a broad avenue of superb gardens and majestic villas.[30] The old, conservative planter class lives in this exclusive district much infiltrated lately by Yankee newcomers.[31] The

28. The Exchange, founded in 1871 as a clearinghouse dedicated to the cotton trade, became the leading commercial association in the South within a decade. See L. Tuffly Ellis, "The New Orleans Cotton Exchange: The Formative Years, 1871–1880," 545–64; and James E. Boyle, *Cotton and the New Orleans Cotton Exchange: A Century of Commercial Evolution*. The "hubbub" in Hesse-Wartegg's next sentence is certainly not portrayed in Degas' painting *The Cotton Exchange* (1872). The Exchange had just begun then, and perhaps the painting is set in the more tranquil afternoon.

29. "New Orleans, with a long start over her sisters, easily achieved pre-eminence among unsanitary cities by the filth and squalor of her slums" (Woodward, *New South,* 227).

30. This is the domestic, private architecture that, in contrast to his opinion of the public architecture, Twain called "reproachless" (*Life on the Mississippi,* 343).

31. The urban planters probably included landowners who had left their rural seats to overseers, fled the loneliness of the countryside, and become absentee landlords. See Cash, *Mind of the South,* 189–90.

Civil War laid heavy toll upon planters, but they have recovered somewhat. By dint of what remained, they created new wealth.[32] Accordingly, opulent wrought-iron [fences] and splendid gates, shady magnolias and graceful palms, banana and cypress groves, flower beds and manicured lawns insulate houses from the street. At a door several Negresses flirt with the Negro doorkeeper, they in costumes of droll color, he white-haired and bent. We see magnificent carriages in the carriage houses. Everything speaks prosperity, *wealth.* Gardens sometimes embrace city blocks. A fragrance of balsam wafts from orange groves in bloom. Intoxicating!

Turning from planters' majesty around us, we look at the street itself. Instead of opulence we see filth.[33] These beautiful homes and divine gardens enclose routes that, observed in bad weather, remain enigmatic of purpose. Are they for wagons, sleighs, or boats? Piles of rock alternate with sinkholes and heaps of filth. Rocks occupy the ditches, water takes to the streets. Nobody cares. Let it all go to Hell![34]

Proceeding, we reach the poor quarter of narrow streets, tall, overcrowded *"tenements"* and boardinghouses—much dirt, many children at the doors: home to the Negro, the semiskilled, and the laborer. Pestilence has visited and revisited the Beautiful City of the South. This is its focus, the breeding ground of yellow fever! Here are cemeteries in low-lying, waterlogged parts of the city, where the dead go into ground too wet for a latrine. The crassest example, the graveyard of the impoverished, *"Potters Field,"* occupies a square in the city's center. In houses around it people live who have complained for years about its shocking situation, about having to look at mud-mounded graves crawling with flies, about odor (the stench of corpses) that permeates homes in summer, and about the horrible, the repulsive state of affairs during epidemics, when corpses awaiting burial pile up under the broiling sun. They complain to no avail. Epidemics strike, carry off lives by the

---

32. Wealth had been mostly invested in land and slaves, the rest in the Confederate and state governments. War reduced the bonds to souvenirs, emancipation took away the slaves, and the land lost value because there was neither capital to apply to it nor labor to work it. Using free labor, machinery, and new methods and techniques, planters gradually prospered again. See Jordan, *Hugh Davis,* 167. On renewed prosperity, see chapter 27 below.

33. New Orleans "had the dirtiest and most unkempt thoroughfares in America, and yet every householder cared meticulously for his own small plot of earth" (Sinclair, *Port of New Orleans,* 276).

34. "A certain prevalence of the 'tomorrow-we-may-die' feeling" led to various sorts of neglect—besides causing vice and yellow fever (Sinclair, *Port of New Orleans,* 186). The city was a "pest hole" of dirt and disease: bad garbage collection; "innumerable smelly, refuse-cluttered ditches and canals; yellow fever in season, and typhoid, malaria, smallpox, and diphtheria year-round" (Jackson, *New Orleans in the Gilded Age,* 21).

thousands and thousands, disappear, and nothing changes afterward. Under such conditions, yellow fever has been and remains ineluctable. We pity the Beautiful City, so demoralized and neglected because of a corrupt administration, apathetic civic leaders, and a mercenary, "*city ring*" system of plundering politicians and stupid Negroes![35]

Lest there be doubt of the truth of what I say in the last two paragraphs, let it be noted that I published them in the *Staatszeitung* of New York and the *New York Tribune* last year. Mark especially that the *Deutsche Zeitung* of New Orleans reprinted them with prefatory comments that included: "His estimate of sanitation in New Orleans, though stern, is nonetheless true and apt. It follows weeks of careful observations."[36]

We resume our stroll. Gross contrasts continue everywhere. Plush palaces and newly built homes beside old Spanish churches and cloisters. Broad canals versus stagnant water unused by any boat. Squares of small, intimate gardens opposed to the strange, polyglot life of bustling market halls and tropical products for sale. Streets without end are home to the petite bourgeoisie in little one-story houses with the obligatory balcony and flower pots at the windows. Streetcars roll and bump along, amid chime and clank of rolling stock on bad rails. A car comes by every five or ten minutes; gates open and let passengers in or out. It rolls away—one of the cars that absorb the pedestrians—and stillness returns, the silence of the grave. A few boys may be fishing in the canals. Ragged Negroes loiter before houses in bright sunlight. Over and above everything, a steamboat's whistle sends weak tones from the river in the distance. Otherwise peace and tranquility reign: no clang of hammers, no rumble of rolling mills, no puff of steam engines. New Orleans is not industrial.[37]

At Rampart, a street beautifully sunny and lined with fine buildings, we make a slow turn, come back to parts better known to us, and find ourselves again in Canal and its grand, imposing traffic. It seems to us as if we have emerged from a remote and forgotten town in Provence and into a capital—from Tarascon, for instance, to Mar-

---

35. New Orleans, for years the "dirtiest and most unhealthful city in North America," owed the distinction "not a little" to "corrupt government": politicians who "didn't believe in giving the city *anything* for its money" (Sinclair, *Port of New Orleans,* 206–7). Hesse-Wartegg refers to the carpetbag-scalawag government of Reconstruction. In 1880 reformer Joseph Shakespeare would be elected and begin the first chapter of a new era (Jackson, *New Orleans in the Gilded Age,* 4).

36. The files of these newspapers reveal nothing by Hesse-Wartegg.

37. Commercial rather than industrial, New Orleans did have rice mills and cotton presses; hundreds of small shops that made beer, soap, bricks, and other consumer goods; and foundries, machine shops, cottonseed-oil mills, laundries, cotton gins, and small food-processing plants (Taylor, *Louisiana,* 357).

seilles—so profound is the change. In Canal we see beautiful churches, huge cotton balers, theaters; in the middle, at the intersection with Charles, the monument to statesman and orator Henry Clay; from the foot of his pedestal, in the appropriate direction, the levees and the steamboats (giants among giants); and near them, to the east, a massive four-story granite pile in bastille style: the Custom House. In its broad spaciousness it could accommodate other branches of government, the post office, for example. It has already cost about $13 million and remains to be finished, a sad example of mismanagement by southern cities and states.[38] West from our vantage we see the noble majesty of a colonnaded facade: the St. Charles Hotel, the South's finest caravansary, where rich planters stop, along with the rest of high society. What life in these streets! What a mingling of peoples! Americans and Brazilians; West Indians, Spanish and French; Germans, Creoles, quadroons, mulattoes, Chinese, and Negroes surge past us. We hold fast, sharing place only with a few newspaper and shoeshine boys, and flower and fruit sellers. A shawled feminine form huddles on the steps, offering small bouquets for sale. As if oblivious to that mad roar of life, she stares with vacant gloom at nothing. We speak to her, she barely understands. A remnant of another world, a nation that used to live here: she is one of the last Chickasaws.

This manifold population includes some 70,000 French and Creoles, 30,000 Germans, 60,000 Negroes and mulattoes, and 10,000 Mexicans, Spanish and Italians.[39] Therefore, the Anglo-Americans cannot number more than 80,000 or 90,000. They are the Crescent City's most enterprising, prosperous, and promising element. Each nationality moves in its own circles and mingles little with the others.[40] Each has its daily press: the Americans, the *N. O. Times* and *Picayune;* the Germans, their excellently edited *Deutsche Zeitung;* and the French, their *Abeille de la Nouvelle Orleans.* But the South's splendidly warm climate and everlasting sunshine do nothing for intellectual life. It approaches stagnation. People want little from bookshops except cheap French novels, American magazines, and German weeklies. Booksellers are indigent in the Gulf states. Recent Yankee immigrants, far

---

38. Hesse-Wartegg's figure is 50 million marks, worth about four to the dollar.

39. In 1880 there were 17,475 Germans in Louisiana and 13,944 in New Orleans (John Fredrick Nau, *The German People of New Orleans, 1850–1900,* 12). It is strange that Hesse-Wartegg says so little about this large, influential community and about the famous and important "German coast" west of New Orleans, where Germans had begun settlement in 1719. See Taylor, *Louisiana,* 165, 183, 227; and J. Hanno Deiler, *The Settlement of the German Coast . . . and the Creoles of German Descent.*

40. "Life went on in a series of orbits within orbits . . . racial factions [that] formed their own social pools . . . [while overlapping] in many ways [such as] municipal affairs and the Catholic Church" (Sinclair, *Port of New Orleans,* 286–87).

too concerned with *"money making"* and *"politics,"* have little taste for belles lettres. On the other hand, the long-resident Creoles dwell far too much in *dolce far niente*. Their lives revolve around love and hedonism. They spend winters in their pleasant, spacious plantation homes on the river or quiet bayou and in the summer go to cooler places, to the spas of Virginia or New York. In New Orleans, churches and casinos enjoy a more passionate clientele than do schools. Theaters, shunned after the war because of mourning and a lack of money, have been seeing better attendance. Indeed, this year the French opera returned to its Creole Land metropolis. Despite the most brilliant antebellum troupe in America, it had to shut down for lack of attendance after the war.

This enthusiastic increase in theater-going in recent years evidences most surely the economic recovery of New Orleans. Wretched postwar conditions have so improved that in a few years the city will have better times than the best of the slave region. War wounds have largely closed and healed. Except one. Emancipation seems to have dispossessed one Louisiana class, the French and Spanish Creoles. Sovereign princes on their plantations, used to being masters, they answered to nobody; they counted incomes in the hundreds of thousands; and their lives passed in luxury, pleasure, and amusement. Of work they knew nothing. War came, devastated and burned their plantations, and carried off the most valuable part of their fortunes, slaves. Nothing remained but empty, ravaged land. Because owners lacked money, the land passed to rich capitalists from the North. The Creole caste, the old Marquises and Chevaliers, rulers for years upon years, found themselves on the rocks and in an alien environment fresh with revivified life. They were antiques in the robust vitality sprung from ruins. We must therefore visit their quarter.

Canal Street divides New Orleans as the Straits of Dover do England from France. Indeed, English culture and French—better called Anglo-Germanic and Latin—could not be more precisely and more surely set at intervals than here, on either side of our broad Canal Street. From the Mississippi inland [along Canal], everything to the left is Anglo-Saxon [or Anglo-Germanic], and to the right it is Spanish, Italian, and French. Canal, Rampart, and Esplanade Streets (names confirm function) enclose the old city once ruled by the French. Today they mark off the French quarter, what could be called the bastion of Creole culture.[41] West of Canal, then, we hear *street, cents,* and *mister* without exception; east, *rue, centimes,* and *monsieur* also with-

---

41. "There were ancient Creoles and their ladies who, a decade after the Civil War, could boast they had never so much as visited the bustling American city above Canal Street" (ibid., 315).

out exception. Ask directions in public and get the answer in English to the left, in French to the right. Each nation dwells as a separate society, isolated from one another, not mingling. The segregation shows no sign of ending. Enter the old city and your first glance will provide proof positive. You are in Nouvelle Orleans, not New Orleans. Public inscriptions, names of establishments, newspapers: French. Individual shops and certain homes look French, like those of southern France. Buildings in general and the streets, however, hail from the Spanish. Wide balconies, beautiful convex balustrades, grated windows, forbidding doors, stillness and emptiness in the streets—these incite memories of old cities in Sicily and Spain. Yes, wandering in these streets, I felt in the former capital of the Spanish Bourbons [in America] the same atmosphere, same pulse as in Palermo. Yet what a difference, the way the old Hispanic-Moorish civilization relates to the strong, free, youthful American civilization and its brilliant future! That is, in the struggle of new with old, the old has surrendered its outposts, the plantations, and renounced open warfare and retreated here, where it barricades itself into the last bastion of old Orleans. But it cannot stand the test of time. It will be routed. It will drown in the rush of American culture.

An equestrian statue of General Jackson stands at the hub of a garden in Jackson Square.[42] The square, in the middle of the French quarter, was *place d'armes* in French and Spanish times. The three-towered Cathedral of New Orleans rises here. Its two old annexes serve as courthouses. The garden, with Jackson's statue as its focal point, flourishes in tropical luxury shielded from the river by tall orange trees and magnolias along the edge of the quiet square. But step between the trees and onto the levees: quiet ends with a *bang*. We are near the French market, considered by Americans a sight typical of New Orleans.[43] To me it brought memories, vivid recollections, of bazaars in Constantinople and Tunis; only the people animating them belonged to a different race. Here, as there, under low, outspread roofs without walls, everything that can be sold can be bought, anything a person could need. Hundreds of small counters and stalls, row upon row, and clothing, knitted goods, furniture, silverware, and especially food: meat, fruits, vegetables. To each category its own little street or aisle, or as Arabs say, "souks." Everything about this place—the organization, the appearance—so recalls the Orient that we need only dress the sellers in burnooses and put turbans on their heads to see ourselves in

---

42. For the sights in this paragraph, see Work Projects Administration, *New Orleans City Guide,* 255–57.

43. "Always one of the first stops for tourists" (Jackson, *New Orleans in the Gilded Age,* 12).

an Arab bazaar. Women, of course, make it hard to complete the illusion. In the Oriental market, women circulate under wraps, veiled, silent. Here—without such covers, more than open, more than talkative—women brighten and vivify the market.

Before I end this chapter, let me show you one more thing, also for the most part in the center of town, unfortunately. I mean the French cemeteries.[44] Poorer people in New Orleans go where people usually go after death, into the ground. But the ground of New Orleans being swamp, people with money prefer to inter above.[45] The majority of cemeteries, therefore, feature spacious, compartmented sarcophagi of brick or marble and often several stories high. Walls, also high, ring expanses of these severe white monuments. A slab of marble, properly inscribed, seals a compartment after a coffin has been slid in. Many congregations, societies, guilds, and other organizations own "burial houses" for their dead. The houses, therefore, often hold hundreds of compartments, inscriptions accordingly cover houses, and houses array themselves row upon row, presenting an alien, hostile appearance. Yet we should prefer to ours this manner of burial, practiced here and in all low-lying places of Louisiana. The sites remind me of the new Camposanto of Genoa and the small pyramids of the Egyptian desert.[46] In these graves—hermetically sealed but exposed, year in, year out, to a tropical sun—corpses do not rot but undergo natural cremation.[47] A cemetery is a city of the dead in the midst of a New Orleans feverishly alive, telephoning, telegraphing, pursuing the dollar![48]

44. See Work Projects Administration, *New Orleans City Guide,* 186–98.
45. A funeral for someone going into the ground might include "the bailing out of the grave, the floating of the coffin," a problem solved by "above-ground tombs" (Joseph Judge, "New Orleans and Her River," 163).
46. Cemeteries in Genoa and Pisa are named Campo Santo.
47. "The vaults are used time and again as older burials are pushed to the rear. The bones spill down a shaft and the tomb is ready for the next generation" (Judge, "New Orleans and Her River," 163).
48. Twain in 1882 saw "a 'boom' in everything" except architecture. "The telephone is everywhere" (*Life on the Mississippi,* 341, 342).

20. A Black Government

I have mentioned the St. Charles Hotel. In the good old days of slavery, Louisiana had another, a larger and more distinguished caravansary, in the French quarter of New Orleans. Year after year the richest of Creole planters from the oldest families stopped at the St. Louis.[1] The *haute volée* [upper crust] of city and country threaded its corridors, crowded its parlors and smoking rooms, and ensconced themselves in the luxurious French furniture. In the evenings the joyous and elegant company assembled at dinners where champagne flowed. The ball or concert that followed in the tall and spacious rotunda yielded little in sartorial splendor, in feminine pulchritude, in elegance itself, to the aristocratic reunions of the Faubourg St. Germain. Life then in the St. Louis resembled life in the three famous grand hotels of Saratoga now.[2] Even the streets around the palace would admit only millionaire plantation owners. Negroes, the black rabble, shied from the seat of their lords and masters, not even so much as lifting an eye to the stately edifice.

Things have changed a little. Today the visitor to the rotunda might think he would find on the polished floor the evidence of terpsichorean excesses, such as wilted flowers and scraps of silk. But today's rotunda serves a purpose perhaps more amusing: state government.[3] Numbers have disappeared from rooms, furniture from salons, and the hotel has passed into yesteryear. The kitchens have become the state archives.

---

1. "The $1,000,000 St. Louis hotel, a massive, four-story structure" on "St. Louis street between Royal and Chartres" (Dabney, *One Hundred Years,* 229).
2. Around the St. Louis "all social activities of the Franco-American city revolved during the first half of the nineteenth century. . . . Duels were arranged" there, and "the great ball of each winter" given. It was the Creole favorite (Chambers, *Mississippi River,* 198). Saratoga Springs boasted more than three famous Victorian hotels. Hesse-Wartegg probably refers to the Grand Union and the United States. The third may have been any of a number. See Work Projects Administration, *New York: A Guide to the Empire State,* 306–7.
3. Baton Rouge is usually called the capital after 1849, but the carpetbag government of Reconstruction sat in the St. Louis in New Orleans. If the hotel's decline from a salon and cynosure of high society to the decaying seat of government distressed Hesse-Wartegg, its deterioration would have appalled him in the 1930s: corridors abandoned to bats and pigeons, the rotunda to mules (Searight, *New Orleans,* 195–96).

Junoesque beauties, the bloom of Creole society, dwelt and slept in rooms that accommodate whiskey drinking, tobacco chewing—and statecraft. Blacks, former slaves, have taken up some of the reins of government.[4] The bottom has risen to the top while many of the top have sunk unfortunately to the pits. Sambo from Africa—Sambo the sweaty, black, thick-lipped, simpering slave—Sambo on whose back the whip has so often cracked—Sambo, *Senator* Sambo, the representative of the people, sits in the venerable leather of the easy chair that belonged to the Marquis "Questcequ'ildit" [Lord Has Been], his former master.

The St. Louis, once so bright and beautiful, has become a casualty of modern culture, a symbol of the state of Louisiana. Hotel and state, both formerly rich and radiant, have fallen to the disgraceful gang that has ruled Louisiana and New Orleans—the gang that has cadged and sponged off city and state, ruined the public credit, made a fraud of revenues, and would turn the old slave state into a new Haiti.[5] War brought Yankee adventurers, politicians, and hangers-on. In league with blacks and elected by them, they have taken over the state as surely as they have seized the hotel. In a few years the hotel became a dingy, unkempt, ruinous pile—and so it looks to the astonished tourist. At the last moment the state escaped a similar fate.[6] Louisiana's inher-

---

4. By inaccurately describing Louisiana as "A Black Government," Hesse-Wartegg succumbs to a Reconstruction "myth that has survived by oral tradition and has been perpetuated in print" (Charles Vincent, *Black Legislators in Louisiana During Reconstruction,* 219). Still, the label is more accurate for Louisiana than any other state: "Only in Louisiana did blacks hold more than one major position from the beginning of Republican rule" (Foner, *Reconstruction,* 352). Though forty-two blacks sat in the first legislature, they "were in the minority," as were those "in succeeding legislatures." Three served as lieutenant governor and others in lesser but important offices (Franklin, *Reconstruction,* 134–35). The best-known black in Louisiana, P. B. S. Pinchback, served briefly as governor (1872–1873), the only black governor in American history. Hesse-Wartegg must be discussing a black government that held office before his visit, since the governor from 1877 to 1880 was Francis T. Nicholls, a white Confederate veteran who had lost an arm and a foot in the war. "After the withdrawal of the Federal troops in 1877, native whites quickly gained control of parish and local governments," and the 1879 constitutional convention wrote a document that ended benefits granted to carpetbaggers, scalawags, and Negroes by the constitution of 1867 (Davis, *Louisiana,* 286, 288). Blacks thus continued in office in decreasing numbers and fading influence (Jackson, *New Orleans in the Gilded Age,* 20). Cf. Perry H. Howard, *Political Tendencies in Louisiana,* 149–50. Some blacks held office until "the 1890 constitution of Mississippi became a model for other southern states—in its resourceful provisions for the discouragement of black voting" (William Winter, former governor of Mississippi, quoted in Naipaul, "Reporter," pt. 2, p. 62).

5. The Reconstruction government of carpetbaggers, scalawags, and blacks committed excesses, plunged the state into debt, and caused "governmental, economic, and social disorder" (Davis, *Louisiana,* 284).

6. Hesse-Wartegg probably means better times brought by the end of Reconstruction and the promulgation of a new constitution.

ent strength, natural wealth, and advantageous location have recently restored it to its old eminence.

Meanwhile the capitol teems with dirt and dust. This building—doors sprung, banisters wrecked, many windows broken—houses the offices of governor, cabinet (including the secretary of state), and the chambers of the senate and the house of representatives! The higher we climb, the greater the toll of neglect. The fourth floor, where signs on doors said *Engineer* and *Architect*, had not seen a broom for months.[7] We learned we ought not be surprised if the decision on repairs had been made several times and the repairs several times paid for. The money went astray.

How droll some of the moments when one of the many black gentlemen in dirty underwear, soiled coat, and the defective English of his race, would rise to join debate in the halls of legislation.[8] Empty bombastic phrases, repeated at every opportunity. Stumbles. Tangles. Again. Again. At last the honorable orator would extricate himself by blurting out his proposal, his "*moshun*," and sink back into soft leather: the easy chair behind him. We must remember of course that these "*gentlemen of the house*" used to be slaves. They learned to read and write only after emancipation, if at all. These black "*gentlemen*" ("*nigger*" is taboo with them), though big and robust in the way that served them well as field hands, cut a sad figure in the representative assembly of a state with a million residents and a world-class capital.[9] I have justifiable concerns about the next generation.

Though by now translated somewhat from white to black, parliamentary procedures of northern states were adopted here. Smoking therefore abounds during debate. Chewing, too. And sleeping. And

---

7. When Twain visited a little later, the St. Louis housed city government and still lacked evidence that "a broom or a shovel has ever been used in it" (*Life on the Mississippi*, 355).

8. Hesse-Wartegg's image is similar to "Colored Rule in a Reconstructed (?) State," a picture in *Harper's Weekly*, 14 March 1874, in which Thomas Nast ridiculed blacks speaking in a legislature.

9. "The question of the Negro's fitness for self-government is pertinent, for without education and no previous political experience, the undignified and frivolous behavior of Negro representatives in the General Assembly was predictable" (Howard, *Political Tendencies*, 128–29). Cf. Foner: "A considerable number of black officials" were uneducated and even illiterate. Many others were literate and educated. Some had studied law. On the whole, blacks seemed capable of self-government. (*Reconstruction*, 359; see also 346–64, 610). Indeed, the "frequently voiced opinion" is false. Blacks were not "ignorant former field hands." They could lead and they worked for modern legislation (Vincent, *Black Legislators*, 222–23). Some had been freemen before the war and were of the professional classes, fluent in French, even wealthy (David C. Rankin, "The Origins of Black Leadership in New Orleans During Reconstruction," 417–40).

eating. And why not? Don't these black lawmakers live in a free country?

I shall not mention theft and deceit done with the aid of blacks, or election campaigns, or political unrest and the consequent moral and financial discredit to the state. Neither shall I speak of "*carpetbagger rule.*" True, these sad conditions have been remedied somewhat in recent years. But Yankees and Negroes continue in power. Louisiana's honest and upright folk have not rid themselves of apathy and turned the rascals out. Meanwhile, after running the state deep into debt, the rascals refuse to pay interest, or they pay one percent. Furthermore, they squander revenues or make off with them. These little adventures in government are occurring this year!

Fortunately, the worst times are over. Louisiana's wealth, together with good harvests, have shoved such grievances into the background. Louisiana approaches a calmer, a better epoch.

21. Carnival

Carnival did not begin here until this century, when young Creoles brought it from Paris. Few people participated at first. In time, more and more partook of the joys served up by Prince Carnival. Today at last, though Carnival in New Orleans differs from Carnival in Europe, it belongs as much to life in New Orleans as in Italy or on the Rhine.[1] Indeed, here the prince has been crowned king. He comes to his loyal New Orleans for only two days a year, then disappears as if by magic. He rules a mere two days as absolute monarch of this and every other city of the South.[2] No sovereign has enjoyed the love and the celebration this supreme ruler enjoys. He can do no wrong. Had he a parliament, it would present no opposition. The committee of the exchequer would not deny him a cent, especially since his court, bodyguard and army pay their own expenses. No conspiracies seek the life of Rex, the divine king. His crown sits as securely on his head as he on his throne. His kingdom embraces the wide, wide world; his palace located nobody knows where.

So far I could be speaking as much for Carnival in Europe as in New Orleans. In Europe the prince remains mysterious, loved but unknown, the object of homage but unseen. In the New World—in the cities of Louisiana, under the warm sun of Alabama, Carolina, and

---

1. Carnival, in its strict and original sense, signifies communal celebrations of a religious or otherwise supernatural nature, usually ritualistic and following the calendar or the seasons. In Catholic countries it is the period of merrymaking before the solemnity of Lent. From Epiphany to Shrove Tuesday in New Orleans, it dominates the city with parades, balls, and madcap revelry. By 1766, "though sketchy and crude," it "was an established custom" (Robert Tallant, *Mardi Gras,* 97). It was suspended in 1806 and resumed in 1823, the balls "soon more numerous and more brilliant than they had ever been" (100). "After the Civil War, the celebration of the carnival season culminating in Mardi Gras had become increasingly elaborate, with more parades, carnival balls, and visitors flocking into the city to share in the frivolity" (Jackson, *New Orleans in the Gilded Age,* 21).

2. "There are many carnival kings, but there is only one King of Carnival. He is Rex, who leads his parade through the streets of New Orleans on Mardi Gras" (Robert Tallant, *Mardi Gras,* 48–49). For a description of preliminaries that confirms Hesse-Wartegg's, see 47–51. Rex as a fixture originated with the visit of the Grand Duke Alexis of Russia in 1872 (Jackson, *New Orleans in the Gilded Age,* 304). For pictures of parades not much different from those he observed, see Carolyn Bennett Patterson, "Mardi Gras in New Orleans," 726–32.

Tennessee—the fantasy grew and grew, the more the people celebrated Carnival. Hearts of hot-blooded Creoles and quadroons throbbed for Prince Carnival. These people yearned to see him with their own eyes. He—prototype playboy, conqueror of so many female hearts, the old roué—could not escape similar feelings. He longed for the lovelies of Creole Land no less than they for him. Behold, he landed on the coast of America one fine day and appeared in person for a short stay in New Orleans. He liked it so very much, and Louisiana's handsome women accepted his advances so very willingly, that he has honored the faithful Crescent City with a visit every year since.

This year once again, King Rex made his triumphal entry into New Orleans. Carnival's two days passed with such transport, was it all a dream? The facts confirm that Carnival occurred; the experience was real. King Rex appeared! Again in his omnipotence he turned everything upside down and changed paragons of rationality into lunatics. For two days they tumbled head over heels in the whirlpool of madness that floods New Orleans. After he worked all this mischief—after he took the money out of fool's pockets, stole the ladies' hearts, and pulled the bottles' corks—he disappeared presto, leaving his loyal city to its tumult, its ecstasy, and its folly.

The degree of self-deception seems incredible at first glance. Weeks before the appearance of His Majesty, his top officials grace the city with their presence, to prepare for the reception. Everybody from the general who commands the United States Army in New Orleans, to the governor of Louisiana, to the mayor of New Orleans, and down to the lowliest dockworker, puts himself willingly and without reservation at the beck and call of His Majesty's officials. At present, Bathurst is Lord High Chamberlain; and Warwick, Sovereign Lord Marshall.

The people behind these exalted titles, behind the king himself, make their identity so secret that the public knows nothing about them. They are locals who get the positions the way that prevailed in France and as prevails in Turkey: with money. The greater the contribution to the municipal Carnival fund, the higher the contributor's title, from mere baronet, and up and up, to Duke of Louisiana.[3]

Weeks before Carnival the king's proclamations flood the United States. Big, bright-colored posters, decorated with all sorts of coats of arms and other designs, carry a kind of speech from the throne, announcing *Mardi Gras in New Orleans* and requesting *come one, come all*.[4]

---

3. "There is such a tradition [that people who play the roles and hold the offices are heavy contributors to the organization] but it is never recognized at carnival time, and seldom believed by the ones most interested" (Grace King, *New Orleans: The Place and the People,* 394).

4. There is a difference between Carnival and Mardi Gras: "Carnival is the

Bathurst, lord high chamberlain, soon follows with the first official directive. It goes as a letter to functionaries concerned and to every newspaper for publication. To illustrate the style I take one from the *Deutsche Zeitung* of New Orleans.[5]

> Department of the Lord High Chamberlain
> New Orleans
> 19 February 1879
>
> The Honorable W. O. Rogers
> Superintendent of the Public Schools
>
> Greetings:
>   Our Most Noble Majesty, desiring that young and old be made happy by his presence, hereby directs that the public schools of New Orleans be closed on Monday and Tuesday, the 24th and 25th of February.
>   You shall therefore, in conformance with His Majesty's wishes, order the schools closed on the days specified.
>
> By order of Bathurst
> Lord High Chamberlain
>
> Espy
> Secretary

A similar one went to the mayor on cleaning the streets. He replied:

> Office of the Mayor
> New Orleans
> City Hall
> 19 February 1879
>
> The Right Honorable Lord Bathurst
> Lord High Chamberlain
>
> My Lord:
>   City Engineer H. C. Brown, inspired by the commendable desire to remove from the streets anything that could hinder the procession of His Majesty at Mardi Gras, has presented himself to His Honor the Mayor, to learn the route of march.
>   Unfortunately, owing to the condition of the streets of His Majesty's

---

entire program of balls and parades; Mardi Gras is but one day—Shrove Tuesday [the last day of Carnival before Lent]. The terms, however, are used indiscriminately, even by Orleanians" (Tallant, *Mardi Gras,* 9).

5. For another example of them, see *New Orleans Daily Picayune,* 19 February 1879. On these letters and the news releases that precede Rex's arrival, see Tallant, *Mardi Gras,* 47–48, 49–51. In 1871 a society was formed to organize Rex's communications. In 1872 he issued his last request and his first edict (Perry Young, *The Mystick Krew: Chronicles of Comus and His Kin,* 98–99).

capital, time will be required to insure that they present nothing to hinder the procession.

I have the honor to be Your Lordship's most humble servant.

Chas. Macmurdo
Private Secretary

Bathurst likewise decreed "by order of the king" that on Carnival Day, 25 February, places of business and public offices, including custom house and post office, be closed. Bathurst wields unlimited power in these matters. Woe unto him who does not obey, because the people back Bathurst in full sympathy; they would of their own volition see his will be done, by force if need be.

About a week before Mardi Gras the papers carry the first news of the fleet that is to bring king and court to New Orleans. Stories go something like this:

> The royal fleet called yesterday at the Azores. We can accordingly expect His Majesty to arrive on time for Carnival. Accompanying the king are the beautiful Berengaria and the noble and witty Edith Plantagenet, the brave Saladin, the gallant Keneth, and a host of history's other heroes, celebrated in song and story. Rumors that the mouth of the Mississippi has silted up and that the heavy-laden ship cannot negotiate the river are fantasy, sheer fantasy.

Another report, this from the *New Orleans Times,* says that His Majesty's ship "draws beyond measure. New equipment must therefore be built to dredge the mouth of the Mississippi to the needed depth. We beg the governor and all the government to take every measure to aid His Majesty's passage into the harbor."

Among "Bulletins from Abroad" in the daily press, one always appears on the progress of *the* voyage. At last we read: "His Majesty has safely cleared the sandbars at the mouth of the Mississippi—the royal fleet may arrive tomorrow afternoon."

Tomorrow afternoon! Anticipation boils. Self-deception swells to such extremes that the arrival of the king, his appearance in person, becomes synonymous with Carnival. Cockfights and dogfights, always magnets to the public, have been held in the French and Spanish quarters of this cosmopolitan city as a celebration preliminary to Carnival. From every city in the country—St. Louis, Memphis, Louisville, Galveston; yes, even New York, 1,500 miles away—the grand pleasure steamers have departed for New Orleans. Their loads of passengers will live on them during Carnival. The city has been decorated in an American magnificence of banners, festoons, and flags. The royal colors stand out, conspicuous, salient.

The longed-for afternoon is here. To the many tourists on the quay, it seems like a warm afternoon in late summer. New Orleans, on a day in the second half of February, flourishes no less green and in full bloom. The crowd awaits the arrival of the king.

On ordinary days the quay—Louisianans say *"levee"*—offers a fascinating sight. Today it is magnificent. Hundreds of steamships and steamboats extend one after another in rows without end. The black, sea-going vessels with masts; the snow-white, grand, imposing palaces of Mississippi steamboats with tall pairs of black smokestacks; the countless flags and streamers that decorate masts and rigging everywhere; and then the stir on the quay, where, among thousands of massive bales of cotton and barrels of sugar, the municipal honor guard and the militia have drawn up to receive the king: the scene amounts to a special sight, a bonus attraction for any tourist.[6]

At last the splendid steamboat, king and retinue aboard, comes into view. *Now* Carnival has begun. Other steamboats ring bells, fire guns, and blow steam-powered blasts on screeching whistles. Add to this din the shouts of thousands. A dozen bands strike up. From the city at a distance, church bells peal *hail to the king*. His boat docks and the triumphal entrance begins.

The city militia, heading the procession, seems to represent most of the world's armies, judging by the uniforms. People of German, French, and American origin live here, as well as thousands of Spaniards, Italians, Mexicans, Swedes, Japanese, and more. Since each mounts a battalion of militia, this royal guard is formed not only of United States regulars, but also of Spanish infantry, Mexican artillery, German home guards, Zouaves, Bersaglieri, Cazadores, etc., all in uniforms of the homeland and each with its musical corps. Then the "Centennial Guards" in the uniforms of last century's soldiers. Finally, the king's own troupe. Heralds first, then ministers and top officials on prize horses and in gold-braided uniforms, then the marshalls. And the king himself, of course. His mounted guard, in fine costumes, follows him. Baggage wagons bring up the rear.

This pageant makes its way along majestic Canal Street to City Hall.[7] The mayor presents the king the key of the city and gives himself up as a prisoner. Rex takes leave of the troops as they pass in review. He goes to his lodgings in the St. Charles. In the evening, top government officials will be welcomed at a grand reception there.

The Carnival parade, this year as every year, took place on the day

---

6. The greeting and the parade, as well as "the general pattern for Rex's entire carnival behavior," began in 1873. See Tallant, *Mardi Gras,* 140–42. The year's "annual pageant" of Carnival is described in several columns of the *Picayune,* 26 February 1879.

7. Carnival centers upon Canal Street (Tallant, *Mardi Gras,* 10–11).

of Mardi Gras. Rather more at home in the French quarter, Carnival appeared in the Anglo-American section as something of an exotic of circus riders, to be watched by the public at a distance. The splendor and opulence would throw many European cities' celebrations into the shade. Half a hundred four-in-hands carried costumes and scenes of mythology and history, each a Parisian creation and probably years old. This masquerade preceded troops and the royal party, already described. Paraders wear masks, whereas we saw few masks among spectators thronging the streets. Rex now appeared as Richard the Lion-Hearted at the head of his Crusaders.[8] Everybody admired the costumes, arms, and armor.

Yet, though the parade lasted an hour, the fact must be noted that the public took little part in Carnival this year. True, people surged in the streets and enjoyed themselves and welcomed the parade. But this year passion failed. One organization, the star of Carnivals past, did not take part at all. Though hundreds of masques and masqueraders usually participate, this one lifts the celebration to the heights it reaches in Rome and Venice. The "Mystik Krewe of Comus" puts its peculiar name on the locus of foolishness.[9] Its members, who number about 100, are unknown to the public. At every Carnival, with a nocturnal parade in masks behind King Momus, the Krewe stages its masquerade apart from Rex and his followers.[10] As a rule, in the French opera house afterward, the Krewe throws the brightest ball of Carnival. This year, Carnival was held in the aftermath of the yellow-fever epidemic of 1879, which ravaged the city a few months before. The breach of etiquette hurt the thousands of families in mourning. This pain, together with the absence of the Krewe, dulled Carnival's luster.[11]

Beautiful women constituted the chief attraction. Splendid verandahs and balconies in the style of Spain and the American South (the pride of every floor of nearly every house here), displayed the finest in beautiful young women. These Creoles have not only retained their beauty despite the Civil War, but the war has enhanced it. Once rich,

8. "Themes and titles of the balls are of infinite variety" from "history, legend, and literature" (ibid., 20).

9. This Carnival organization began in 1857, "found itself famous" after its "first spectacular performance," and continued as the standard by which others were measured (ibid., 115; see also 116–28). The Krewe and "all Carnival organizations are secret societies" (13). They "vary a great deal" in membership "and almost every social layer is represented" (26).

10. Each ball has its king and queen (ibid., 15). For the Krewe's ball, see Young, *Mystick Krewe,* 68–78. Momus was the god of censure and mockery; Comus, of sensual pleasure. The Krewe probably proceeded behind both of them (Young, 70).

11. The Krewe distributed relief during the epidemic: thousands of bottles of beef soup and beef tea (Young, *Mystick Krewe,* 153–54). Young mentions the abbreviated Carnival of 1879 without reference to the Krewe (154).

now poor because of the war, old families of the sugar and cotton plantation no longer dress so sumptuously, nor wear jewelry of the former brilliance. But the soul of each woman expresses earnestness and pride called up by the grisly event and its aftermath. In wide Canal Street, the Corso of New Orleans and the only Corso of the New World, you see more beautiful women in an hour than in the whole of Carnival in Rome or Naples.[12]

Carnival in Rome means madness and folly above all, along with individual pranks and personal foolishness. Much the same can be said for Carnival in Flanders. Nothing of the sort in New Orleans. Here Carnival means only the rule of King Rex, two extravagantly colossal parades, and the climax of Mardi Gras, the balls.[13] The king comes with his throne to [this year's] grandest and most entertaining, the Rex Ball. The kingdom's dukes and dignitaries, and state and municipal officials from all over Louisiana, attend it. The pride of the city's wealth, beauty, elegance, and distinction are here, too. City belles have assembled. Rex selects one to be his queen.[14] He crowns her. Ladies-in-waiting and the royal court have gathered around the throne. He leads her to it. There, King-for-a-Day accepts homage, bestows medals, distributes awards, and confers a host of knighthoods. Now begins the fete that will last till morning. Masked balls also take place in the city's many theaters, on every dance floor, and at each of the concert halls. Nobody could wish for more madness. Rex and court enjoy themselves. Today—today only—they hold power. City and state belong to them.[15]

At the first ray of dawn, revelers steal away one by one. When the last dancers tire and leave the ball, king and court have long been "back on the high seas." As if by a stroke of magic, the city has become its old self. It wears its usual look. Carnival is over.

Carne vale!

---

12. The Corso is the grand avenue in Rome.
13. The many and various balls begin on Twelfth Night and continue with increasing frequency until Mardi Gras. See Tallant, *Mardi Gras,* 8, 14, 16.
14. King and queen in 1879 were James I. Day and Jessie May (ibid., 261).
15. "Carnival is, in fact, the keystone of social structure [in high society]. To be chosen king or queen of one of the older societies is a stupendous social compliment . . . an honor . . . remembered for a lifetime" (ibid., 185).

22. A Cockfight

Beautiful Louisiana cannot deny proximity to the [former] Spanish colonies. Spain's New World possessions, Texas and Mexico among them, inherited from the mother country the bullfight, the dogfight, and the cockfight.[1] As one people usually learn from another the vices before the virtues, so did these amusements (these brutal, grisly sports) cross the Rio Grande and establish themselves all over America, way up to the Canadian border. Bullfighting might have become the national pastime had states not enacted laws and were they not too hard to flout. Dogfights and cockfights, also banned in most northern states, continue because laws are not enforced.[2] Major cockfights, held under cover of darkness in city and countryside, often draw thousands of spectators. Twenty or thirty cocks may be sacrificed in barbaric matches, to indulge savagery and satisfy the gaming lust of some "*sportsmen.*"

America's southern states—Louisiana, the Carolinas, Alabama, and others—have not outlawed cockfights. They occur in broad daylight and so often that thousands of cocks may die every year. Worse are the crueler and bloodier contests that set dog against dog or man against dog.[3] When dog battles dog, combatants as a rule perish in the

---

1. Hesse-Wartegg says *Stiergefechte,* or bullfighting; but he could mean bullbaiting, which pitted dogs against bulls and was more popular than bullfighting outside the Latin countries. In New Orleans in 1817 the "Amphitheatre featured fights between an Atakapas bull and six dogs, six bulldogs against a Canadian bear, a tiger against a black bear, and an Apelousas bull against twelve dogs" (Davis, *Louisiana,* 238). There were also matches between asses and dogs in New Orleans (Dabney, *One Hundred Years,* 35). See *Dictionary of Southern History,* s.v. "recreation."

2. In New Orleans before the local SPCA was organized in 1888, dogfights and cockfights were frequently and regularly held in their own arenas in the city and environs. On Sundays men carried gamecocks in bags on the streetcars to the fights (Jackson, *New Orleans in the Gilded Age,* 24). According to the sportsmen, who call themselves cockers, cockfighting is one of mankind's oldest and noblest pursuits. They claim the cock "asks for no better death than with his steels on" (Pridgen, *Courage,* caption facing 173). See also 77–78; and "The Humanity of Cockfighting" in Lawrence Fitz-Barnard, *Fighting Sports,* 10–13. Cf. Don Atyeo, *Blood and Guts: Violence in Sports,* 85–88, 95–100.

3. Although fights between men and animals were popular amphitheater events in ancient Rome, it cannot have been anything but bizarre in modern times. No history of modern blood sports mentions it. Prizefighting was popular but illegal until 1890 in New Orleans (Searight, *New Orleans,* 138). Blood sports involving ani-

arena, laying down life for victory as well as defeat. Man versus dog? Yes, and frequently enough. (In England, too, by the way.) Let us not forget fights between young bulls, staged more than seldom in states of the lower Mississippi and in Texas.

New Orleans, metropolis to Louisiana and all the South, serves as center and cynosure of these monstrous popular amusements.[4] Life naturally beats faster in this huge port. People entertain the demon of gambling much more here than elsewhere and indulge the pleasures enumerated above. Still, those contests of animals cannot rightly be called "popular" amusements. Unlike Spaniards, the best and by far the largest part of this populace avoids them, moreover opposes them with every means available. Such cruelties seem pointless anyway, except to gratify the gaming urge of the politicians and the elegant urban nomads who have descended in droves upon New Orleans and most other southern cities since the war.

In the old Spanish regions, in Mexico and Texas, holiday celebrations include animal fights. In New Orleans they join cards and roulette as nothing more than vices of society's dregs. Therefore, they cannot be easily got rid of. The legislature, the people's representatives, ought to bring them to terms. But the opportunists, the political bloodsuckers who use Louisiana to achieve their own selfish ends and to advance their parties, need the votes of the urban nomads—so much that the politicians would never go so far as to make enemies of them.

During the famous Carnival I saw in the papers the announcement of an interstate cockfight to be held on several successive days at the big Spanish "*cockpit*" at the corner of Dumaine and Roman Streets in the French quarter. Georgia on the one hand, Kentucky and Tennessee on the other, had sent many of their best fighting cocks. In addition, thousands of people had streamed in from southern and western states to attend Carnival. They so filled the city to overflowing that you could count on crowds at the fights.

The way to the arena led through a chaos of narrow, dirty, abandoned alleys in the quarter, once the center of Louisiana's Creoles. Mean, dilapidated, empty houses. Unpaved streets, or at best with potholed and torn-up surfaces. No lights.

A circuslike, brightly lit pile took impressive shape at the corner of

---

mals were made illegal about this time. Cockfighting, though illegal in most states, persists in the South, California, and elsewhere. It remains legal in Louisiana.

4. Cockfights were "good box office" in New Orleans "in the eighties and nineties" (Sinclair, *Port of New Orleans,* 284). However, public opinion forced denial of a permit for a bulldog show in February 1879 and a bullfight in 1880. The "twenty-one bulldogs were to demonstrate how living flesh could be torn and living bones crunched" (Dabney, *One Hundred Years,* 311–12).

Dumaine: the cockpit. About a dozen people loitered about the door. Two dollars, cash, at the window. No ticket in return. I went into a spacious and bare outer hall. Big cages for the cocks lined the walls to the ceiling. On one side, the Georgians; on the other, the Kentuckians. A narrow passage went at last into the amphitheater.

Initially I could think of nothing but a seat at a window, so stupefying was the tobacco smoke, the reek of every sort of liquor, and the crush of people. I climbed the benches one by one to the highest and the only one not taken. From there I could survey with utter clarity the whole wild scene. A thinly sanded track circled a ring at the center. Benches provided seats for about 500. Perhaps another 500 filled the entranceway, the gallery, and the rest of the place. Still they poured in. A few gas jets barely lighted these broad spaces. Fighting had not begun.

Spectators—not a woman among them—consisted, in the lesser half, of curious tourists; in the greater, of vagabonds of the saloon, the casino, and the streets. Unemployed, without steady income, often unsure even of a place to sleep, the vagabonds live from hand to mouth by gambling during the day and spending nights at cards, roulette, or the "*cockfights*." They are the curse of normal society and the enemy of the law, the rowdiest and most dangerous of the Crescent City's diverse elements. Though uniform of character, they vary in appearance. Here: Negroes and Yankees from poorer neighborhoods along the river, unkempt, in threadbare clothes. There: mulattoes in urban finery, with monocle, patent-leather shoes, and walking stick. Here: shipping-company agents. There: rich planters in suits of cool linen and broad-brimmed hats. Finally: French Creoles. *They* look *so* stylish, presences fit for the boulevards of Paris, descendants of the old French-planter aristocracy, as good as destroyed as a class now. These last scions, knowledgeable as masters but ignorant of work, spend their lives (so the example of the majority would lead us to believe) doing nothing during the day and gambling at night. Seeming to enjoy a privileged position at the fights, they join none less than the owners and promoters in the best seats in the house, and disport themselves like rich English lords on Derby Day. On benches opposite them a few Mexican and Texas caballeros lie stretched out. They wear traditional dress: wide-brimmed hat, jacket with intricate trim, leather chaps, and in the belt the inevitable and only-too-often-used revolver. Below them the likes of Cubans, West Indians, and other Latin Americans mingle and contrast with stocky, red-cheeked farmers from Tennessee or Kansas.[5] Farmers have come to New Orleans to deliver grain or cotton, and

---

5. For undetermined reasons Hesse-Wartegg has "Peruvians" (*Peruaner*), which has been rendered "other Latin Americans."

to the fights to sample a bit of the city's exotic life. A motley crowd, colorful yet placid.[6] That is, its multitudinous members converse with the calm reserve so characteristic of Americans. Not the unfailing shouts, not the commotion of such events in other countries, but quiet prevails: what might be called an *eerie* quiet.

At about 8:00 P.M., two men appeared from the outer hall. They entered the ring. Each carried a big bird in his hands. In Europe we have been accustomed to the presence of authorities such as referees and policemen, and ushers to clear the ring. Nothing of the sort here. Yet the event unfolded with order and in calm. Tourists and insiders alike left the ring of their own accord. The ring no sooner emptied than the two "*backers*" put the antagonists on the ground. Each wore another set of spurs attached by small leather straps to its own: a pair of three-inch steel bayonets. These "*gaffs*" do resemble the bayonet in form, except the upward curve that ends in a honed needlepoint.[7] The Georgian, black and of the best breeding, also weighed the most: a five-and-a-half-pound, so-called "*shawl neck*." The Kentuckian, red, weighed a little less.

No sooner had they come into view than the Kentucky side asked odds at seven to five. Georgians responded for theirs at eight to five.[8] As a rule the American carries his banknotes in a roll in his vest pocket. Rolls changed hands now, sometimes passed to a third party, always as if not a word ought be lost in the process.

The antagonists took one another's measure for a few seconds, Georgia Black versus Kentucky Red, then each hurled himself at the other. The first round or "*pass*" had begun. Black struck for Red's comb, neck, and head. Red ducked and attacked Black's wings and legs. In a moment their gaffs tangled. The backers must disentangle and separate the birds, both unhurt. No sooner back on their feet than they flung themselves at each other in a rage. This time Red gave Black a stab in the thigh that floored him. Red pecked and hacked like mad at him for a while, then stood beside his bloody foe and regarded him lying there as if dead. Red's head sank after this quiet moment. He turned to the ground and began to peck about [as if in search of food]. Black sprang up at the instant, seized Red's comb, and jerked him down. The onlooker could not see what hold each had on the other as

6. Unlike Twain's cockfight audience, Hesse-Wartegg's does not look like one at a prayer meeting. But Hesse-Wartegg also seems to witness no "traditional brutal faces" (*Life on the Mississippi*, 366).

7. On *gaff* and other terminology, see Pridgen, "Glossary," in *Courage*, 259–64. Scott, *History of Cockfighting*, 188–93.

8. The fighting and the betting at southern cockfights did not change much between 1879 and 1939. See E. Jerome Vogeler, "Cock Doom Makes Everybody Equal," 274–82; and Pridgen, *Courage*, 243–58. These activities also resemble those in England at an earlier time (Christina Hole, *English Sports and Pastimes*, 106–8).

they rolled like two balls of feathers on the ground. Red got the better of it at last, pinning Black between his legs.

So ended the second pass. The backers picked up their birds, smoothed their feathers, and again put them on the ground about three feet apart. Georgia Black, unable to stand, collapsed. He did not get up. At each of the enemy's thrusts he struck back with his beak. If Kentucky were a *"fighter,"* the sportsmen were saying, he would exploit the advantage and finish off that Georgian. But Kentucky hesitated, wavered, shilly-shallied, obviously badly hurt himself. After a few minutes the backers returned their birds to the position of attack.

Thus, no fewer than twenty passes, with alternating luck for the pair. Bettors at ringside accordingly preferred one, then the other. "Ten to five for the red!"—"A hundred to ten for the black!"—"A hundred to fifty." Back and forth, back and forth, one bets and the other accepts by extending his hand to seal it. Neither thinks of welshing. It astonishes newcomers that bettors can remember so many different bets.

Battle had lasted over thirty minutes yet not been decided. At first they tore into one another as soon as put down. Engagements shortened, pauses for rest lengthened, until at last each round consisted of two or three rushes and a bit of a tussle. Everybody could see it plain. The end was near. The backers could still pull and pat their birds erect, but the birds could scarcely stand when put down. They staggered about like drunks or they collapsed. So proud, so handsome only a half hour ago, miserable looking now: disheveled, spurs and legs bloody, combs practically gone, heads and necks plucked clean. Yet the outcome remained uncertain. Kentucky, the early favorite, had lost the advantage. Odds about fifty-fifty now.

In the twenty-sixth pass, he sank again. Georgia Black reeled on splayed legs for a while; then, ignoring his own bloody head, attacked and seized the comb. It was Black's last effort. He collapsed in front of Red, a bit of Red's comb in his beak. Red, sitting, stabbed Black with enough force that his gaffs had to be pulled out. Red had delivered the *coup de grace.* For, put down for the twenty-seventh pass, Black staggered forward a few steps and fell dead. Red outlived him—by a few seconds.

During the last pass, excitement swelled among the spectators. Betting quickened. The nearer the end, the more the Creole heart pounded behind a cool Yankee facade. The original, feigned indifference gave way to a paroxysm of gesticulation, shrieks, cheers, and curses.[9] Only genuine Yankees stayed calm and put winnings into vest pockets without turning a hair, or met losses with equal indifference.

9. Twain "never saw people enjoy anything more than this gathering enjoyed this fight." He could not stand it, and left before the end of the first bout (*Life on the Mississippi,* 367).

The Kentucky/Georgia bout, the only *"main"* this evening, would thus be the only one to count in the interstate competition.[10] Twenty-six had been announced for the following evening and fourteen for the day after. Tonight a number of *"hackfights"* followed the main: wild bouts that did not count in the competition: random matches staged by individuals hoping to win large bets. Pairs fought until one died. Each bout lasted anywhere from five to thirty-five minutes.

All wagering, as I have noted, took place bettor to bettor orally—not, as at the races, through *"bookmakers."* A rough estimate put the total at $14,000. Tonight, after the first three or four matches, tourists left in a huff, abandoning the turf to true sportsmen. *They* stayed until dawn and spent their winnings on whiskey or champagne.

There was gambling also at a rouge-et-noir table in the outer hall.[11] The person who wanted to bet could lose his money more "legitimately" and more comfortably there than at a gruesome, bloody, disgusting ringside. Stakes and emotions ran high out there, too, with bets (usually indicated by small ivory discs) often $20 to $50. There, Creole cavaliers tried to recoup cockfight losses. Grain, rice, and cotton merchants constituted most of the victims.

In New Orleans and many other cities, the English-language papers carried columns on the fights. Nothing about the fights amazed me more than the length and content of the columns. Among all those words, not one, not a hint of regret at such vulgar amusements. Here in the South, too, the American reporter restricts himself to what happened, as true an account as possible. He allows himself neither to add anything nor to reflect on what he has seen. A few days later in the same arena, English and Boston dogs engaged in a series of fights, uncommonly bloody, before equally big crowds.[12] The paper likewise reported these "events" down to the last detail. But nobody thought it worth the trouble to speak against the abomination of making animals fight. It seems in a distant future that the Anglo-American press will wake up to its responsibilities and do what it ought to do.

---

10. In England any match was called a main (Hole, *English Sports,* 107).

11. "Gambling could be found almost everywhere" in New Orleans (Jackson, *New Orleans in the Gilded Age,* 63).

12. It is unclear whether Hesse-Wartegg means dogs of unspecified breed from England and Boston or breeds such as English bulldogs and Boston terriers.

23. My Steamboat Excursion to the Sugar Plantations

The United States is a country of small maps. A European at home looking at one would never suspect that beyond New Orleans a *region* not only exists but also merits touring and describing. The map would not tell him; he would be deceived.

This one small space along the Mississippi for about 100 miles between New Orleans and the Gulf holds so many interesting things that it is scarcely to be believed.[1] Sights strike the tourist's eye, sights he has not seen before. In one sense the area consists of nothing but two of Big River's levees, a pair of peninsulas hardly two miles wide and in places only one. Thus, you cannot walk far on either side without falling into the river or into the Gulf. Levees, manmade embankments, protect the riverside half; the other extends unbounded to the Gulf. Freshwater swamps mingle with saltwater tides on the gulf side. Search there in vain for the rendezvous between the rim of the American continent and the beaches of the Mexican Gulf. Look and you will see through cypress groves the broad, level surface of the land. You will see expanses of water stretching to the horizon. But where they join, that juncture you will not see. Along the river on both sides, civilization and refinement; toward the Gulf, wilderness and virgin forest. Along the river: life, action, and splendid homes everywhere, in the old Spanish style, amid gardens of roses, in the shade of magnolias, where people of pride continue to dwell. Scarcely a few stones' throws away toward the Gulf, alligators inhabit the swamps, alligators and turtles, horned toads, cottonmouths, and rattlesnakes. Between these contradictions, between high civilization and the wildest of wilderness, the plantations abide in tranquility, and their owners grow sugar, oranges, and rice.

A few small steamboats carry the traffic between the South's metropolis and her satellites on the Mississippi below her. Daily from the levee, this boat or that boat departs as the day's one and only conveyance to the parishes of Plaquemine and St. Charles—the sole and

---

1. "It is a land weird, sinister, and unfriendly to the sympathetic stranger, but to the initiated it has a rare and exotic quality all its own, a quality unmatched by any other place in the United States" (Sinclair, *Port of New Orleans,* 4).

solitary postal service, the single and exclusive milk run. Tiny, fragile thingamabobs, these steamboats: pocket editions, let us say, of the Mississippi titans that depart Cincinnati and St. Louis and go all the way to New Orleans.

At another place on the levee, the *Great Eastern*s of riverborne commerce lie anchored: palaces, seats of government to His Majesty, King Cotton.[2] Here at the lower end of the levee, our little local tubs await their turn at negotiating the river to its mouth, at running up into bayous and adjoining waterways, and at serving southern Louisiana's *petit commerce*.

Our little tubs await their turn. As a matter of fact we have been waiting the last five hours. We? I mean the passengers, not the boat.

Yes, the notice in the *Deutsche Zeitung* of New Orleans said

> Steamboat *Jenny Lawrence*
> will depart this morning at
> 11:00 *sharp*, for Quarantine
> Station and all "*way landings*."
> Apply, etc. etc.

Only the captain forgot to add that he probably meant Fiji Island time. This adjustment would put the hour at no earlier than 6:00 P.M. in New Orleans. And I hustled sweat-soaked toward the boat at five minutes before 11:00 so as not to miss it. I arrived exhausted, waited at least an hour on deck, and saw not a sign of departure. I mean not even fire in the boilers. The clock struck noon. *Now* the boat seemed to stir. An old, fat, French Negress crossed from Canal Street. "Arretez, arretez, je pars avec vous! Arretez!" [Stop, stop, I'm going with you! Stop!] she shouted while making every possible sign with the green parasol in her hand. With true Creole gallantry the captain returned his boat to the dock and took the black lady on. Once more we set out. Only, from the same Canal Street, a Negro cart approached with a barrel of whiskey. The driver had no green umbrella, did not signal, but the boat returned anyway, to take on this spirited freight. Would we be away now at last? (At 12:30 here, it must be 11:00 in Mexico—so this logic goes.) Another loaded wagon, lumber this time. It, too, went into the bowels of the boat. Meanwhile (11:00 in the Sandwich Islands?), other wagons arrived with loads of all sorts. Of course the boat waited.

I spoke to my companion about this indifference to passengers. I asked him to intervene with the captain. My companion—the once and it seemed the probable future governor, one of Louisiana's men of

---

2. The British *Great Eastern*, 693 feet long and 82 wide, was the largest ship in the world for nearly fifty years after completion in 1857.

influence—smiled and shrugged.³ I understood. Here as in every state of the union (and every empire of the ballot), His Excellency the Governor depends more on the simplest steamboat captain than the captain depends on his Excellency the Governor.

Back to our boat! The clock in the Fijis says 11:00 now. We stick fast. What did the captain mean, "depart . . . at 11:00"? Black and ragged Negroes continue to load our little steamer. We stand on the hurricane deck (roof to the passengers' cabins) and watch the guys work. They could easily do eight or ten hours and earn as much as $2.00 a day. They are too lazy for such strain. Two hours gets forty cents, and forty cents does them for the day—for two if need be. They sleep under the large roofs-without-walls on the levees or in one of the abandoned houses so plentiful in New Orleans. Bananas and oranges are inexpensive. There are leftovers from meals served on boats. They drink out of the Mississippi. How amusing, how comical to see these guys scoop up water—such water!—in their hats—such hats!—and drink the cloudy, muddy stuff. A practical farmer could put the hats to use on his fields, as manure. Yet what king has sipped the finest vintage from a golden goblet with more relish than these stout and sturdy Ethiopians imbibe Mississippi Yellow? Has nectar tasted better to gods than this nectar to those who dip it for themselves out of the river?

At last, after we wait long hours in the heat of a March day (don't forget, we are near the tropics), we depart in our sternwheeler down the wide river. A sternwheeler, by the way (literally "wheel at the back"), is a steamboat that, instead of paddle wheels on the sides, has one big one at the rear, beyond the rudder. Cincinnati and Pittsburgh build mostly sternwheelers.

Soon we have left the cityscape behind. Low shores rise barely two or three feet above powerful currents. As far as the eye can see, charming little houses dot the shores. Plantation fields sprawl behind them. Truly tropical vegetation begins here. We notice tall magnolias reaching for the sky everywhere, and shady orange groves interrupted by the most beautiful flower gardens. In their midst, plantation houses, so deserving of their fame: small, low, and of wood; ringed by arcades and broad verandahs; each house painted the brightest white; so well cared-for; so clean you would think yourself in southern Holland. How nice it must be to live here! The big river and its action before you, the city so near,

3. Henry Clay Warmoth (1842–1931), governor 1867–1872 and owner of Magnolia Plantation. Continuing to be important in Louisiana politics, he ran again for governor in 1888 but lost. See *Dictionary of American Biography,* s.v. "Warmoth, Henry Clay." What transpired between him and the beautiful black lady Calypso, described below, must remain a matter of conjecture.

yet you dwell in a tropical paradise. Greater beauty cannot be found on the island glorified by Saint-Pierre in *Paul et Virginie*.[4]

An apt comparison to southern Holland. The river deposited alluvium as soil and now flows at a level above the land it created. Nothing but low, weak, earthen embankments, the levees hold masses of water within a wide, yet often too narrow bed. The immaculate, white-scrubbed settlements; the flat, low-lying land; the pure, clear air!

But instead of Holland's paltry canals, the world's greatest river flows through here. Instead of slow, phlegmatic, clumsy *Trekschuiten* [tugs and barges], the mightiest Indiamen and the grandest transatlantic ships steam past on the river. Their masts can be seen towering above every tree.[5] Sometimes at sharp bends you can see the tips of masts describing the circle of the horizon above and beyond the land and its forests.

Our boat calls at plantations and country houses, for neither city nor village exists below New Orleans.[6] With at least 100 such stops on the 100 miles between there and Quarantine Station at the mouth, you can imagine how long it took to go the distance.

Yet, for the person not in a hurry, such a journey offers charm without end. In this part of the South and from these decks, the traveler will become acquainted with the old romantic life of the plantation, albeit the ruins of that life. Throbbing northern ways have not reached here. Yes, grand enterprises in world commerce, bound for the port city, pierce the region's heart, but they share nothing with localities on either side along the way.

The long, narrow saloon of our fragile steamboat holds an amazing potpourri of passengers. At the lower end, reserved for ladies, only white ladies relax in the armchairs—mostly young ladies of attractive figure, dark hair, and pale complexion. Black women, in the saloon but at the opposite end, have nested amid their bundles, baskets, and

---

4. "The best introduction [to the region] is by the river, from a steamer in the spring" (Kane, *Deep Delta Country*, xi). Jacques Henri Bernardin de Saint-Pierre (1737–1814) wrote a "nostalgic evocation of a lost paradise" (Mauritius), including "sumptuous descriptions of nature and landscapes." *Reader's Encyclopedia* (2d ed.), s.v. "*Paul et Virginie*." Among Delta dwellers it "was a favorite, but who can now recall that title, though no book ever had more warm and innocuous tears shed over it?" (Percy, *Lanterns*, 7).

5. Steamships kept masts and sails for a long while. For example, the *Princeton* of the Perry expedition (1854) was a clipper but also steam powered (Stuart, *Naval and Mail Steamers*, 50, 108).

6. "Every boat as a rule would stop anywhere to deposit freight or passengers . . . or to take traffic on signal" (Phillips, *Life and Labor*, 150).

boxes. Capital presences, shapes of grand magnitude, these women have to be seen to be believed. They can no more be separated from corpulence than from blackness. Corpulence forces them to comic ways of walking and sitting; you cannot help laughing at them. They have learned enough of the white race's cosmetological mysteries to coat their cheeks with white powder, to wear kid gloves in light colors, and to carry green parasols. Would they but learn someday how much prettier they look in cheeks the black of printer's ink, their natural color!

Among the younger ones we saw a few to call Junoesque. Lovely of face, slim in form, sensuously feminine, voluptuous to the last inch, they provide the most plausible explanation for the horde of female mulattoes playing the role of half-ruler, half-slave on today's plantations. Older hearts than of extinct planters would catch fire at something like *that*![7]

Outside in the boat's gallery, several old, weather-beaten Negresses sit, pipe in mouth and bottle at the ready, smoking, drinking, chattering. What language? The gabble sounds like a flock of black geese in a coffee klatsch. Here and there we can understand a word or at least divine a meaning. Yet the language eludes our strain at identification. I asked the captain.

"French."

Amazed, I replied, "But I don't understand any of it!"

"No wonder. It takes a black ear to understand plantation French."

Perhaps half the Negroes in this part of Louisiana understand scarcely a word of English, and speak only this "French."[8] On this bizarre linguistic island, speech has lost similarity with the mother tongue because it has been sealed off from the rest of the world.

Let us see if we can talk to these people and make ourselves understood. Our linguistic research leads us to choose—surely there is nothing wrong in it!—the most beautiful of the black beauties: eyes aglow with southern fire; full lips and half-open mouth of singular charm; bright-green turban over the hair; long, glass earrings dangling at each side; scarlet, close-fitting bodice enclosing ample bosom; arms bare of sleeve but thick with cheap bands and glass beads. Her name is Calypso. So much we learn and nothing more. Our dozen questions in

---

7. Carter agrees and approves, endorsing the racism and chauvinism of many white males, European and American, then and since. Planters, he says, desired among other things "a comely slave woman or two. Earthy longings, but not without merit" (*Lower Mississippi,* 205).

8. The language is gumbo (or gombo) French: the Gallic transmogrified to a patois peculiar to Creoles and blacks of Louisiana (Sinclair, *Port of New Orleans,* 276–77).

Parisian French each bring a smile and a shrug. Soon I give up my wish; I stop trying to unravel the mysteries of Negro dialect. My friend persists. He has an obviously greater talent for making himself understood, though he speaks not a word of French. He must have discovered a language he and his black and passionate Calypso both savvy better than this French. They stand together in the dark shadow out there. Both look black, of course. What is it they speak? Parisian perhaps, but not French!

Landings crowded one after another on both sides. Our boat must therefore go, not straight downriver, but from shore to shore. A zig-zag like the lace of a shoe. Jogs and jags of a mile or two from stop to stop. We persist in staggering hither and yon—and twisting—and turning—and stopping—and steaming full ahead. Carpetbaggers have been confounding people in the worst way, but this crookedness must have been enough to confound *them*. Still, all in all, we should not have resented the vagaries, had something of significance been loaded or unloaded. Significant cargoes, however, obtain only in early winter, the sugar-shipping season. During our journey we would put off at a stop, at most, one big demijohn of whiskey (we had an infinity of them), then a few sacks of Indian corn; finally, fresh meat and canned goods.

Fortunately, a landing took but a moment. With a blast of the whistle, the boat would announce itself at plantations enough in advance that people would be on the levee to receive. The plank teetered and wobbled in the bow. When the boat neared shore the Negroes would ready our few things at the far end, completed with astonishing deftness by the black tightrope artists. But their risk was minimal, wasn't it? As dirty as a potato field, they could only have felt good after a bath in the river.

The boat approaches as near as depths permit. A steam crane, called a "*Nigger*," lets down the plank. Demijohn and other things go to the levee. Away the boat steams, as fast as it approached, even in the absence of anyone to receive what has been left. At postal stations the exchange of pouches takes place, too. Letters arrive; letters depart. The United States assigns for this purpose a postman to every mail steamer. The Mercury on ours, a comical duck full of laughs and jests, knew every last person, each tree, and every house hereabouts. We never saw him but in his shirtsleeves—no wonder, of course, in the warm weather of February [days]. But he also wore no coat after dark.

"Hallo, postmaster, aren't you cold?"

"O no, sir. I haven't put on a coat the last five days."

The big leather pouches exchanged at postal stations hung as limp as collapsed balloons, holding perhaps a letter or two and one newspaper or another: the *Louisiana Country Visitor,* the *Deutsche Zeitung* of New Orleans, or the *Abeille.* Let us call it proof positive of this climate's mildness that he did not sweat because of honest toil.

So we crept along for hours, zigzagging down the Mississippi, through driftwood and the wreckage of ships. The powerful river, over 150 feet deep, sweeps away both forms of debris or collects them in dents in the shore. Now and then a planter would wave a handkerchief or a little flag of crude assembly, and our accommodating captain would steer to the spot. Only two docks exist (boats stop wherever they please) on the Mississippi below New Orleans. We sailed a river so high the levees exceeded it by a scant foot. Pray no crevasse open! Pray one of the many clumps of roots, whirling past, not rip into the levee and break through! (The consequences boggle the mind.) Often we noted evidence of such rifts. There the original had been closed by another of U-shape, forming a bulge in the original about twenty paces deep. Heaps of driftwood fill these bulges. In places where land diminishes, we would observe a third levee behind a crevasse in the second. In but the rarest instances can a crevasse be simply plugged. Another levee must go behind it, if the land be spared devastation. On one occasion New Orleans missed a catastrophe like Szeged's only because the military commander had a large ship sunk in the crevasse.[9]

The action of water and a journey along perhaps 3,000 miles of river have transformed the driftwood heaped in backwaters at points of levee repair. In one example of the singular metamorphosis, soil carried by the Mississippi impregnates the porous roots of the cypress, and when planed and polished in New Orleans, they become razor strops. Again, the river rounds small pieces of wood to the shape of river-bottom pebbles. They look like sponge balls and can be squeezed to mush in the hand. Dried, they weigh less than sponges.

The river's wood dumps usually provide anchorages and points of origin for land-in-the-making. The Mississippi never stops pulling acres from a shore and depositing them at another, such as in the eddies that collect wood. Magnolia Plantation gained about twelve acres in ten years. When enough soil collects to resemble a swamp, fascines and struts and rocks are implanted to shut out the river. In the swamp a lush tropical vegetation soon develops. Roots secure the soil.

The landing of steamboats, but most of all the colossal traffic up river and down, agitate the placid river and chiefly cause the washing-out of levees. Perhaps it would therefore be only right that the United States and not impoverished planters maintain levees.

---

9. Szeged, a city in southern Hungary at the confluence of the Tisza and Maros rivers, was partly destroyed by flood in 1879.

My Steamboat Excursion to the Sugar Plantations • 189

Landing proved hard for us at some places where new swamps had accumulated. How droll the procedure for putting passengers ashore there. The *"nigger"* would lower the plank to touch the water at the plank's far end; then a few *"roustabouts"* would go with boards to the end. With the boards they begin to bridge the gap, using tree trunks, brush, and anything to hand that might provide a base. Boards half-secure, our Ethiopians do a balancing act with more lumber out over the river. So the bridge takes shape between boat and land. The roustabouts carry ashore the demijohn of whiskey, full, and the mail pouch, empty. How beautiful, were the opposite true! Slipping cannot be avoided, of course, but the roustabouts regain their balance with catlike deftness. They have done well enough. What of passengers who follow?

Namely two fat old Negresses, including she who detained us in New Orleans. Revenge is sweet, we thought, especially on sugar plantations. In a moment, her just deserts. Fearful, she scolded the captain to bring the boat closer. (Easier to bring the shore to us. We could not budge.) Gingerly the tonnage walked to the end of the plank. It creaked and bent—the second beauty had entered upon it. Sammy stood beside the "nigger," hand on the controls. He smiled at the fatties. Even as Mrs. Black began a stride to reach the plank, something like a diabolical grin twitched on his face. With a push of the finger, the "nigger" lifted the plank, and showing the grace of a cotton bale, the heavyweights took the plunge.

Black people's laughter cannot be described. Convulsions and fits seemed to seize the roustabouts. They twisted and bent double and ignored the captain's command. In a moment laughter infected everyone on board. Laughter rocked the saloon. Laughter moistened every eye. Meanwhile Sammy had gently returned the plank to the water. The hippos labored out of muddy but mercifully shallow water and gripped the plank, snorting. They tried, they failed, to snatch the pipe and the green parasol bobbing away on the current. Their clothes stuck wet to their bodies, bringing to view a voluptuousness verging on the terrifying. Louisiana's tropical excess set itself forth plain. Mrs. Black found her tongue. She, who had only discoursed in a French jargon, poured a flood of [English] invective on the roustabouts.

"O you d——d niggers! O you dirty niggers! Oh! Oh! Oh!"

The pair in the water would have climbed moaning and groaning back. We had no time for it. At a wave from the baggage master, two roustabouts sprang to them, grabbed their hands and feet despite resistance, and balancing while shaking with laughter, carried the pair ashore. A few leaps brought the roustabouts back. The plank lifted. A jerk parted the boat from land, and the journey continued with no further concern over the black daughters of Louisiana.

Not long afterward, we noticed young blacks new to boat work. They snickered among themselves and would roar with laughter when a white favored them with a smile. One of them approached my companion the governor—he also owned one of Louisiana's largest plantations—and asked for a job.

"I want to go to your plantation in the summer, Massa. I'll earn more there than on a steamboat. I'm fed up with being a roustabout." He said "*lansabut*" for roustabout.

Another nudged him in the ribs. "*You d———d nigger! Do's do Govana Lana!*" (That's the governor of Louisiana.)

"*Dat's all de same to me. Ah doan kayuh if he's govana or no, is money ah want—ah doan kayuh!*"

He shrugged, turned on his heel and strode away with such royal nonchalance, such aristocratic impudence, we must stand agape. These sovereign "*Negroes,*" these "*coloured gentlemen of the South*"—they are all like this!

Here and there we met big three-masters and transatlantic steamers headed up to New Orleans. They represented all manner of ships and every flag. The largest and most-imposing one flew the German flag. This steamer of the North-German Lloyd represented the company with the only direct passenger service between Europe and the South, specifically New Orleans. No other line serving the South, English included, can match Lloyd's ships in size, safety, and comfort.

Aided by tiny, powerful tugs, the ships of sail passed us double-quick. Did we resent their speed? I believe not. On the Hudson or Long Island Sound, we should have lost patience the first hour, perhaps have left the boat and taken the train. Here on a subtropical river in the South's tranquility and warmth, the traveler catches *dolce far niente*. It puts us in such good spirits. On this boat nothing interrupts peace and quiet but the scuffling of roustabouts in the engine room. We relax in the outermost gallery, in cool shade, and smoke Partagas, a gift of the captain.[10]

We were headed for Magnolia Plantation, the governor and I. At last, toward midnight, we neared it. About twelve miles remained when we left the boat. To avoid a huge bend in the river, he had arranged for a carriage to call for us at a plantation above Magnolia's landing and carry us to Magnolia, straight there overland, sparing us a leg of the voyage. Hercules, the governor's personal coachman, waited with the carriage at the ready, and sped us over the rough country road perforated with potholes and wet with puddles, to Magnolia, Louisiana's biggest sugar plantation.[11] In moonlight we passed small homes

10. Partagas is probably a brand of cigar.
11. Henry Clay Warmoth, Hesse-Wartegg's traveling companion, expanded the famous Magnolia to 5,000 acres, provided access to it via a sixty-mile railroad, and

of planters, Negro quarters, and a small, frame church and its miniature cemetery with graves like graves in New Orleans: above ground because of soft, wet soil; brick-faced mausoleums that looked like ovens. The moon did its part to heighten the romance of this remote corner of the world, wrapping some graves in its ghostly veil of blinding white, leaving others in the dark. (Grand oaks threw shadows across graves.) The oaks, draped in tresses of Spanish moss, looked like weeping willows. We could hear magnolia and orange trees whispering overhead. To the side the river kept rolling along, only an earthen embankment separating it from us. The surface lay at eye level; a glance would run along the top of the water to the opposite shore. Let someone scrape for a half-hour with a walking stick: the river would be out of its bed, onto the land, and rushing at us. Influx would begin as a little purling brook. Before dawn it would become a lake, thousands of people and millions of things inundated. Each resident can answer for the region: "To be or not to be?"

Finally our carriage spun along the packed gravel of the garden lane toward the house.[12] Without a sound the black watchman let us pass. Dogs leaped about the carriage, tails wagging. We saw the house, shadowed by towering magnolias. No light from shuttered windows except where it beamed from the main kitchen: we were expected.[13] Soon we sat before logs ablaze in the tall, ancient fireplace.

---

brought important people there to observe the latest in sugar production. When he eventually had to sell, a massive debt testified to the plantation's magnitude (Kane, *Deep Delta Country,* 72–74).

12. Rather than Greek Revival columns, the house boasted "unusually thick walls" of "plaster-covered brick," which gave it stability and comfort, if not style (Work Projects Administration, *New Orleans City Guide,* 388).

13. This, "the Warmoth plantation, covers a vast deal of ground, and the hospitality of the Warmoth mansion is graduated to the same large scale" (Twain, *Life on the Mississippi,* 383).

24. Plantation Life in Southern Louisiana

Until now in our journey on the Father of Waters, we observed nothing but life along the river as seen from the river. Now, crossing the delta, we found solid ground and orange groves, large gardens and fields of sugarcane, and marshy areas and rice, amid the crisscross of swamps, creeks, and bayous of the same river. But square mile after square mile offered neither city nor town nor inn. Any traveler in this countryside must take lodging in plantation houses because there are no other buildings except Negro shacks and a few small churches.

At any rate, to experience the plantation in its own right, we must have recourse to Creole hospitality on one of these many plantations. For, self-contained, this way of life revolves about itself in a world unto itself.[1] Its boundaries, its fences, become its Pillars of Hercules. Its tiny populace lives an independent and self-sustaining life unlike any other, cut off from everything in the world outside. Political events, new ideas of consequence, wars, revolutions: little of them gets this far. These people devote every effort and all aspiration to the few hundred acres of sugarcane between their homes and the Mississippi's "*swamps*." Doors are by and large open to the tourist. Planters welcome visitors, especially Europeans.[2] After all, these plantations doze in a quiet, remote corner of the world, so peaceful, so removed from life elsewhere, so seldom visited by travelers, that the resident family considers a visit an occasion almost to celebrate. The longer the visit, the more their happiness. They look upon the guest as a member of the family; only with heavy hearts do they let him go.

Blissful peace reigns, winter and summer. The planter's lovely, spacious home rises not far behind the levee that shields the land from the mighty Mississippi's floods. A road follows the levee, but through the garden's trees, dense with subtropical foliage, the house can scarcely be seen from it. We walk toward the house across a soft lawn replete with flowers. The house beckons from its distance, like an idyll incarnate.

---

1. For a complementary discussion of plantation life in southern Louisiana, see Henry C. Castellanos, *New Orleans as It Was*, 177–81.
2. One planter, introduced to "a party of Philadelphians" in town, "invited them for the whole of the next day," showed them around, and answered their questions: "rather an interesting interlude in our quiet life" (Ripley, *Social Life*, 207–8).

Old, thick walls, tall windows with green jalousies closed, and broad verandahs running all the way around: it seems rather like a chateau out of the French Middle Ages. Skyscraper magnolias throw it into deep shade. Stately palms thrust slim trunks out of a thicket of mandarin oranges. Aloes enclose with ponderous leaves the wide, sanded terrace in front of the house. Rosebushes cover the fences with a riot of blooms. The garden continues to the right in a forest of orange trees a mile long. At the peak of blossom now, in February, they exude an intoxicating fragrance. Peacocks and turkeys strut back and forth on the greensward in bright sunlight. Now and then the cries of these birds shatter the peace and quiet of a perfect pastoral scene.

The women of the house do us the most cordial of honors in the absence of the planter at work with his overseers and Negroes in the fields. Elegance and refinement remain with the aristocratic and once-proud Creole race. Stripped of power, bereft of wealth, they remain well bred nonetheless.[3]

Something more than a stone's throw from the house, a few dozen tiny houses duplicate one another. Frequent floods and wet soil forbid cellars and walled foundations. Therefore, these houses, like many buildings on the delta, seem built on stilts.[4] Though they form a group, they obey no pattern; nor do they touch—to deter the spread of fire. A larger one serves as infirmary, another as church. This is the so-called "*quarter*," home to the Negroes, former slaves. Here they live in families, and the children romp outside the houses and in the fields.[5] Negroes take a certain pride in their houses, "*home*" to them. They appoint them with all sorts of little pictures, colored paper, old furniture, and rags of curtain and carpet. Nothing could be funnier than these decorations. Women at this moment are with their men in the fields, so we see at an occasional doorway only an old Negress in bright dress and turban. Here one such "*mammy*" feeds her small, naked grandchildren. She holds on her knees a bowl of some kind of pap. The urchins crowd around and let her stuff their mouths until they threaten

---

3. Not only Creoles but all planters had lost power and wealth. They controlled the South once. At the time of Hesse-Wartegg's journey, they barely controlled their workers, they had lost most of their political influence, and they struggled to remain solvent (Foner, *Reconstruction*, 399–401).

4. "Every man-made thing stands on stilts or piling, not even excepting the oil storage tanks, though in fact you can't *see* the piling on which the latter rest" (Sinclair, *Port of New Orleans*, 3).

5. This plantation design, with the Negro quarters grouped at the main house, may be either atypical or dated. "In 1860, the plantation's entire black population lived in the communal slave quarters [clustered at "The House"]. Two decades later, the families of sharecroppers and cash renters were scattered on individual plots of land" (Foner, *Reconstruction*, 407).

to choke. Piglets as black as the people also bunch around her. Now and then they snap away a morsel intended for their human playmates. Old pigs risk but a rare sortie from nests under the house, to snatch a dribble from her spoon. What an idyllic scene!

Meanwhile, a few charming, coal-black youths sit beside a ditch and fish for crabs. Having never worn a stitch since birth, they relax congenially at ditch-side as free and easy as the original man. Tackle consists of a piece of thread with a bit of meat tied to the far end. A crab bites and they pull it out of the murk as fast as they can. So these rascals spend their youth. To the fields they go when big enough to cut sugarcane, leaving juvenile pursuits to younger brothers.

Sleepy now, the quarter throbs mornings and evenings. The big bell on the roof of the kitchen no sooner sounds a second time than the broad, shady square in front of the little houses begins to fill with Negroes. Overseers line them up as they did in the days of slavery, count them, and lead them to the fields. They have more pep, more zest, nowadays. Singing, laughing, prancing, the crew goes out to the plantation. Baskets on heads and tools on shoulders, they frisk in the highest of spirits across the wide yard, past the main house, to the fields. Even at the most ordinary humdrum, the Negro displays a certain panache and flourishes a burlesque of elegance that set him off to advantage against his white counterpart. (White plantation hands look uncouth and sullen.) The Negro does his work—smiling, singing, chattering—and returns to his quarter as happy as when he left.[6] The gang is never more comical than when it meets a few young Negresses. All the energy and every effort to be found in such a monotonous life bursts forth in a priceless scene. Such amusement! Everybody flirts with everybody else. They shoot amorous glances at one another, make signs of love, and shimmy and shake as if they would dance a cotillion in a ballroom.

These lively young Negresses of the plantations—what splendid creatures! Nature and the warm southern sun have endowed them with a voluptuousness that would look depraved in white women. In black it might set fire even to one of these poor Creole planters. But they share a vice with white sisters: compulsive talk. They *must* chatter, be it with children, the so-called pickaninnies who play at the side of the road or with little pigs that sniff at their feet. Failing anybody or anything else, they chatter with themselves in a mirror!

6. Hence the preference for Negroes over whites as tenants and workers, Negroes being cheerful and content with what whites would consider poverty and hardship: "four pounds of meat and a peck of meal a week, in a little log cabin 14 x 16 feet, with cracks in it" big enough to let in a large-sized cat (Woodward, *New South,* 208). Whites would not be farmhands if they could help it (Foner, *Reconstruction,* 393).

An hour later [after morning call on the bell], work in the fields proceeds apace. Blacks work with blacks, whites with whites, as segregated as in housing. People and their many mules, under a sun that blazes down in a broil, suffer in the oppressive fire of February. Horses cannot stand [hard work in] such heat. None are used except those the overseers ride about the fields while supervising. The overseer plies no longer the fearsome lash. Former slaves look up at him freely without fear when he remarks on their work and urges them to more. Backs no longer bend in fright at the sound of discipline and punishment galloping toward them. The curse and the crack of the whip have stilled—song, joke, mirth, serenity instead.[7]

What a difference between then and now, slavery and freedom! The black man's work has been lightened, too. Pairs of steam engines, pulling plows of twenty and more bottoms, turn the soil and relieve the former slave of the hardest labor.[8] Steam and the machine do all [of the worst work]. Dredges clear the mucky, alligator-infested ditches on the edge of the forest. Steam and the machine have made the Negro a human being.

The huge bell sounds noon. It can be heard for miles. Men toss work aside, a hundred mules bray for joy, and every able fellow leaps onto the best at hand. They gallop—bounce, bounce—to the quarter. We must wonder—*ouch!*—how these guys can sit such gross beasts, without saddle, without bridle, astride those bony backs. The beasts know the way for sure. Into the yard they thunder like troops of cavalry. In a trice the yard resembles a military camp in a rage of hustle and hustle.

Horses and mules line up and get fed. Long tables groan under steaming soups and platters of meat and vegetables. White field-hands and white sugar-mill workers eat apart from blacks. For a while not a sound [from people] except the rattle of knives and forks. Dozens of big, black porkers grunt around the tables. Dogs, chickens, little pigs, pigeons, and the rest of the animals have rendezvoused, too. Only the proud peacocks and aristocratic turkeys keep their dignified distance, removed in the garden like Spanish grandees. People take meals alfresco, year in, year out [whatever the month or season], under this warm and cloudless Italian sky, never risking that the soup get cold.

---

7. Cf. Cash: The planter "must stand over [his Negroes] all day, lashing them with his tongue (and sometimes with the whip itself; for, especially in the deeper South, [slavery had been abolished but the whip's] use on the Negro was far from having disappeared)" (*Mind of the South*, 151).

8. These steam engines, the "great hope of the immediate postwar years," were expensive, hard to operate, and unsuccessful in the long run (Taylor, *Louisiana*, 371). Twain describes "the thing" at work: it "looks like a fore-and-aft brace of a Hudson River steamer inverted," pitches "like a ship at sea," and "not every circus-rider . . . could stay on it" (*Life on the Mississippi*, 383–84).

Back to the field, everybody, an hour later, back to pulling weeds.

Much calmer at the house. Boring, if you will. The day consists of reading and a few strolls. What of the hammocks swaying in the breeze between limbs of splendid magnolias? On the river do not a few small, slim boats dance on currents beside the dock? Are there several hunting rifles leaning near the door in the house? Is that not a target among the fat, bushy, thorny aloes? Are there various riding horses pawing the ground in the stable? The carriages, the games—tennis and cricket—everything, *everything* is here! But the proud, placid, pale women vegetate in easy chairs among grandly elegant furniture in the great hall. They stare into space. They press their foreheads against the glass of windows and . . . ? This is no joyous, delighted *dolce far niente,* not at all. *Far niente*—idleness, yes. As for *dolce,* of the sweetness the women know nothing. There used to be a plantation way of life. It is dead.[9]

Things change when foreign guests arrive! The planter's wife, a Creole daughter, knows what she must do then. With what grace she greets them, such kindness![10] New life seems to have come to her. Callers, society, companionship are what she needs. She has them now. She enjoys them. Each day holds a new delight when guests are here, every day its own surprise, because the program changes daily.

Today several horses wait saddled at the verandah outside the glass of the tall, wide door. To morning coffee the women come dressed for riding. A tour on horseback awaits us: out to the cypress forests along the bayou on the other side of the plantation. There (on the edge of the narrow land between here and the Mississippi) lie the famous swamps, the subtropical, half-submerged, primeval forests and their bewitching vegetation and rare animal life.

On our own we had tried to penetrate that jungle. Every try failed.

---

9. Hesse-Wartegg seems to be saying that plantation women have changed since the war. The literary and popular tradition described "fairly true to facts" an upper-class southern woman as attractive, sympathetic, poised, vivacious, energetic, graceful, and hospitable. The plantation mistress was a busy, unselfish, capable factotum, who taught, nursed, and fed the people of the plantation, black and white. She was the "executive of the complicated system of plantation domestic economy" (Gaines, *Southern Plantation,* 177). The few antebellum visitors who "observed a languor in Southern women" were exceptions, their comments "unimportant fragments" (179; see also 174–81). Here and elsewhere in the book, Hesse-Wartegg reports that these women exhibit boredom, ennui, languor, and probably unhappiness; but he does not account for the change. Was it because, on a plantation altered by emancipation and mechanization, the plantation mistress was no longer the center and cynosure of a realm that needed her and that she governed?

10. At the Le Beau plantation below New Orleans, "a guest was always brought ceremoniously to the great hallway clock; as he looked, it was stopped on the moment of his arrival. Time, sir, would have a halt during the glad days of this stay!" (Kane, "Land of Louisiana Sugar Kings," 536).

We had reached the border of the plantation and entered the swamp soon enough. We spied among reeds the enormous alligator and the ugly cottonmouth. Now and again what looked like solid ground had given way beneath the hooves of horses that sank without warning to the haunches in muck without bottom, to be freed only by supreme struggle. Even if we reached the edge of the forest, we could not advance. We could not pierce on horseback or afoot those thickets of palmetto and cactus, and that forest of dense vines and ruins of fallen trees.

But now the women who rule this region are to guide us. Like Amazons of another world, leading a mounted Negro escort, they gallop among orange groves and around fields of sugarcane and into the forest.[11] Over ditches and pools, and amid banks of dry reeds often more than twenty feet high, they take the way known only to them. Soon we find ourselves at the center of the shady, rustling forest. We reach in a few hundred feet the shore of a lake as clear as glass. At a narrow bay we tie the horses to old cypresses. Several Negroes leap into the two boats and row us silently and at a measured tempo through the swamp. But few of a burning sun's rays pierce the foliage of oak, ash, maple, palm, laurel, magnolia, and especially the gigantic cypress draped in long, thick moss, a heavy veil of mourning. Rarely do we see a speck of brightness through a thick primeval canopy.

A warm, fragrant, blissful atmosphere spreads over all. Life seems everywhere. Now and again we hear the bark of the alligator or the scream of the bird of prey but do not see the creatures themselves. We glimpse neither bird nor beast. But an eternal, a universal whirring, flapping, chirping, buzzing, rushing, crackling, rattling, and splashing—now near, now far; stronger here, weaker there—tell us that life teems in this humongous swamp. Meanwhile the magnificence of an enchanting scenery so engages us in the first hours that we have little eye for animal detail.

Reeds and water lilies half-hide the swamp, blue and white flowers cover it, and we luxuriate in a broad compass. Now we move in restricted channels on clear currents; now on unshaded expanses that glitter in the sun; now under cypresses with dirty-white trunks or magnolias heavy with vines that bend low to us; and often past low and shadowy arbors where everlasting twilight must prevail. At other points, where the forest thins, we can glimpse a fantasy of sun-swept pools, greenswards thick with flowers, and mournful ruins of trees, once giant, now crumpled and rotting. Every pull of the oar changes the

---

11. A literal version of what has been translated "of another world" would be "of the southern continent."

scene, until a final turn puts us into the bayou's open waters. Even these spaces brim with variety when we look through calm, crystalline depths to growth thick and green at the bottom. The water here would seem immobile for millennia, not ruffled by rain, not troubled by storm. A few strokes of the oars and we meet a current surging through these still waters. Masses of lilies and other broad-leaved plants bend to its power. Whence this flow? Whither? Our study produces no answer.

Sometimes we seem lost in a labyrinth of swamp, water, and forest. Not a sign of a way out. But our black boatmen, trusty and skillful, know where to go. In a wink they steer hard into what looks like a wall of reeds. A thrust—a shove—and we cross to a brisk flowage. Slim, stately palms, sometimes alone, sometimes grouped, relieve the view. Magnolias assert themselves on the opposite shore, dark and lush and thick. We see the forest a second time, mirrored in all its colors, on a smooth and shiny surface, so calm is the water. We in turn seem aboard a boat on the wing, plying the air, with forest and sky above, forest and sky below.

Only now, gradually, do we grow accustomed enough to the scenery that our eyes distinguish the fauna so immense in variety here. Insects everywhere, sumptuous in every color. Hundreds of large turtles sun themselves on a dry ridge. A watchful heron perches on a fallen tree, ready to pluck its prey from the water. Proud kingfishers dive into the depths. Small birds balance easily on broad leaves of *Nymphaeaceae*. Cranes huddle into balls of feathers in the thicket. From the thicket we hear the wild turkey call. Cardinals and other birds—scarlet here, blue there—flit beyond number in the oaks and maples, like sparks flashing from branch to branch. Now and then a few giant alligators surface, massive jaws open, or dive from the bank into their second element as soon as they sense the boat. Nobody could have been here before, we think. But people lived here, centuries past. Now and again out in the forest, Indian "*mounds*" appear: mysterious burial sites of a long-gone race.

Big Muddy passes the plantation on his way to the Gulf. To him each and every one of these swamps and bayous pays tribute. Yet how different the views here on his shores from those in nearby swamps! It would be most risky to dare with our small boats this fast, muddy, coffee-yellow flood. Even to gain the other side, a mile and a half away, bigger and stronger must be used: ones that can resist choppy waves and negotiate whirlpools and other turbulences of a river 150 feet deep. We need all of two hours to cross, and our old Negro boatmen toil to defy powerful currents that intensify on a diurnal rhythm with the rise and fall of tides in the Gulf. A broad levee rises a little above the water, to shield low-lying plantations. A road on the levee follows the river to its mouth. On the road we see of a Sunday the planters' handsome victorias and landaus, pulled by fiery steeds, going to the little church the local Creoles have built amid their plantations. We see a life so refined, so aristocratic, so elegant that we believe we have entered an avenue of a wealthy metropolis. On these occasions and when they visit one another, planters rally again the old grandeur that suffered a mortal wound in the war.

Our own plantation we can barely descry, being on the opposite shore. Trees and low-set white houses seem almost to stand in the river. On this bright day the yellow water reflects their image. Occasionally a forcible transatlantic steamship passes upriver to New Orleans, or a brace of sailing craft, in a tug's tow, glide downriver to the mouth.

So much for the river in summer. It changes profoundly in winter and spring, of course.[12] It receives much more attention then. In the hot months it flows peaceful and powerless to the Gulf. In the spring, if high waters of the Ohio and Missouri recede, the Mississippi poses no further threat. On plantations work in the fields can begin. But as long as dispatches from the north report rising tributaries, travail of a different sort continues in the owner's mansion and his Negroes' huts. Women and old men watch with younger people around the clock until danger passes.[13] Planters and their men frequent levees day and night, regarding anxiously the mounting currents nearly topping them. The river has risen far above the land behind the levee. Let not creatures of the deep or the water itself undermine the levee and it give way, God forbid! Should but a slit open and the leak begin even as a trickle and not be plugged by the plantation's workers—and the river not be kept in—woe unto all! Homes of planters, plantations, every human habitation—in short, every man-made creation—will be under water soon, ravaged and destroyed. Plantation Negroes all fill sandbags to be piled at critical points and to be thrown into breaks the moment they occur.[14] When the river recedes months afterward and the water returns to its bed, mud (often a foot of it) covers the once-beautiful land and buries agriculture. Water control therefore spells weal and woe to Louisiana as it does to planters' counterparts in Hungary and Holland. Here, as there, millions have been spent for it.

12. "In spring, high and loud against the tops of quaking levees; in summer, deep and silent in its own tawny bed" (Percy, *Lanterns,* 14).
13. Keeping watch had changed little a generation later. See ibid., 242–48.
14. "In the absence of my husband one time I was awakened, in the dead hour of the night, by a touch on my shoulder. 'It's me, mistis; de levee's broke.' A crevasse! Without taking time to put on an extra gown, I was an hour giving orders and dispatching men. . . . For a week . . . I fairly lived on horseback at the levee, superintending the repair work [of] driving piles and heaping sand bags" (Ripley, *Social Life,* 196–97).

Thus the scene shifts on the river from season to season: cheerful, calm, carefree in the summer; dark and depressing in the spring.

Much, so much remains to be told about lives of former slaves and erstwhile masters, and about families, "*meetings*," parades, and celebrations. There is no life like that of this Deep South, unknown to the rest of the world, fascinating to the person seeing it the first time!

25. A Sugar Plantation

In Georgia, Alabama, and Mississippi, King Cotton rules. He waves the scepter and brings forth his product in quantity to exceed any other in those states—by far. But in Louisiana, sugarcane surpasses even cotton. Sugarcane has become an abiding source of wealth everywhere in the southern part.[1] There the rich, moist soil proves excellent. As long ago as 1870, Louisiana produced not fewer than 80,000 of the nation's 87,000 hogsheads. Texas, Tennessee, and South Carolina shared the paltry 7,000. (*Hogshead* means nothing like the head of a pig but a unit of weight, 1,300 pounds.)[2] In the most recent years the output of Louisiana's plantations has soared above even that of 1870. As for the future, a state lately racked by political struggles will thrive. Part of the abundance will be sugarcane in amounts never dreamed of before.[3]

Sugarcane culture occurs mostly in the aqueous area on the shores of the Mississippi and a mile or more inland, fifty miles north and fifty south of New Orleans. Baton Rouge remains the northernmost point.[4] From there, as from New Orleans, small local railroads run to various destinations in the sugar area. The trains serve as "steam buses," stopping where you want to get on or off. Does a planter want to go from plantation to town? He takes post track-side at an apt time and flags the train with his handkerchief. Or he flies a flag on his roof. The train stops, he boards, and they continue to the next stop and the same procedure.

Our destination: a plantation near Baton Rouge. The owners have invited me to spend a few days as their guest. They cultivate only about 800 of their 2,500 acres. The plantation's value plummeted after the

---

1. "Cane sugar was the basis of economic life in south Louisiana and in a restricted area of Texas," and "at no time prior to the twentieth century did Louisiana produce less than 95 percent of the total southern sugar crop" (J. Carlyle Sitterson, *Sugar Country: The Cane Sugar Industry in the South, 1753–1850,* vii).

2. Cf. chapter 15, note 1 above.

3. Planters had to start almost from scratch after wartime destruction. The rebuilt industry would not equal the 1861 crop until 1893 (Walter Prichard, "The Effects of the Civil War on the Louisiana Sugar Industry," 332; see also 313–32).

4. The distance from New Orleans to Baton Rouge is closer to 100 miles than 50, depending on the route.

war and cannot be more than $100,000. The main house is one story, square, dazzling white, and ringed by the wide, ivy-covered verandah so characteristic of southern houses.[5] Here, as usual, a garden surrounds the house. Negro quarters and the "sugar house" adjoin the garden. Then the fields. Finally, the aboriginal swamp, home to countless alligators, rattlesnakes, turtles, and let us not forget the strong and poisonous cottonmouth. Man does not welcome them as guests. They do not expect his hospitality; they fear him. They attack him only when he attacks them. How much happier planters would be could they say the same for *"mosquitoes"* and *"jiggers."*[6] They make life miserable in the summer in these swampy lowlands. (God, it is said, wrought Creation for the benefit of man. False when it comes to mosquitoes. Man has been created for them!)

Sugarcane, a reed-like plant two to four meters tall, has a stout, tough stalk and thick leaves of beautiful green. Nodes take shape eight to ten centimeters apart on the stalk and ripen gradually upward from the ground, turning a lovely red like that of the stalk.[7] Plants form a dense stand in the field.

To thrive, sugarcane must have careful attention but demands less than cotton. For the typical farmer used to farming European-style, a sugar plantation might seem too demanding, especially in May's oppressive temperatures.[8] But he can quickly adapt to it. First there must be a system of ditches to drain the fields. It means work merely to keep them clear. After planting in January and February (even as late as March) and then months of painstaking cultivation, at last in June the crop can be left to itself. In October it has ripened to the cutting. Sugar extraction begins then. This procedure has been followed on individual plantations until the most recent times. As a rule it lasts two or two and a half months, therefore into December.[9]

Extraction begins with cane brought to the boiler and conveyed mechanically between rollers and pressed. Mules once drove this machinery, mostly given over to steam now. The rollers separate juice

---

5. This, not the Louisiana Classic style of modified Greek Revival, was probably representative of planters' houses. See Sitterson, *Sugar Country,* 73–75.

6. By jiggers Hesse-Wartegg probably means chiggers.

7. This seems to be a variety of ribbon cane, all-important to southern sugar development. See Sitterson, *Sugar Country,* 120.

8. No doubt Hesse-Wartegg is applying the climatic standards of his European audience.

9. For more on this agricultural rhythm, see Sitterson, *Sugar Country,* 112–19; and Phillips, *Life and Labor,* 119–23, 125–26. Thomas Spalding, "Observations on . . . Sugar-Cane," 230–63, gives a detailed description of growing and processing cane in Georgia, including use of a mill-house constructed on a plan imported from Louisiana.

from "*bagasse*," or pressed cane. The juice goes to a reservoir. It passes next through a system of vats, where it cooks. It has reached a certain degree of refinement. After cooling, it proceeds to tanks with bottoms like sieves. Molasses separates from crystals there. The molasses moves to another container and undergoes a second separation by centrifugal action. Sugar goes into barrels and to New Orleans or New York and the big commercial plants for one last refining before market.[10]

To work a plantation, the planter needs one Negro per seven acres. The Negro, paid no more than $18 a month and housing, receives two-thirds of each month's pay at the end of the month and the rest in a lump at the end of the year. The workday, usually twelve hours, reduces to eight and a half during severe labor in the processing plant. More work at night adds another fifty cents. Negresses work in the fields, too, at the same tasks as men (except digging ditches) but at a daily wage of fifty cents.[11] In addition, the Negro often enjoys a garden and a portion of field, put at his disposal to grow vegetables and corn.

Wage and perquisites would be plenty if the Negro knew anything of organization and thrift. But he indulges "noble passions," whiskey chief among them. Plantations usually being far from town, every Negro "*camp*" has its "*store*" to supply the plantation's laborers whiskey and brandy as well as tools, clothing, sardines, and other foods. Stores belong to whites, of course, and not seldom to the planter himself. He keeps a store and runs the plantation, both to a handsome profit.[12] In many places the practice has been to pay the Negro, not cash, but with a "*ticket*." It states the number of days worked and the wages to be paid. He exchanges it for coupons worth various sums: a dollar perhaps, or parts of a dollar—fifty, twenty-five, or as little as ten cents. Coupons serve as currency to buy food at the store during the week. Those not spent will, as I have said, be swapped for cash, part at the end of the month, the rest at the end of the year. Savings as a rule do not amount to much. More than two-thirds of wages make their way into the storekeeper's till.[13]

---

10. For a fuller description of sugar-making, see Sitterson, *Sugar Country*, 140–44. See also Twain, *Life on the Mississippi*, 384–85.

11. Hesse-Wartegg's discussion of wages, though accurate enough, is oversimplified. See Sitterson, *Sugar Country*, 243–47.

12. On this wage labor, which gave way to tenancy and sharecropping, and on the role of the store and its keeper, see Woodman, *King Cotton*, 308–13. On the failure of the wage system and the shift to sharecropping, see Oscar Zeichner, "The Transition from Slave to Free Agricultural Labor in the Southern United States," 26–32.

13. "More than two-thirds" sometimes meant every cent of a person's wages. See Sitterson, *Sugar Country*, 244.

In England they call this the "*truck system*."[14] Here it prevails less on sugar, more on cotton and rice plantations. It minimizes planters' operating capital and often helps make them rich.[15] The system does gouge the Negro, but where planters' stores do not exist, his situation goes from bad to worse. He falls into the hands of the Jews. How wrong it would be to believe *they* have become more high-minded and merciful in the American South than they were in Russia or Poland.[16]

Louisiana in its present circumstances offers notable advantages to the European settler. The immigrant who commands several thousand dollars can be rich in a few years. On a sugar plantation he need not wait year after year for profits. They come immediately and in amounts as must seem fabulous to the European farmer. An acre of fertile land yields in an average year a hogshead (1,300 pounds) of sugar and two barrels of molasses, but much more in a year of abundant harvest. Large plantations, larger say than 1,000 acres, return [annually] in sugar and molasses $100,000. Practically half can be considered clear.[17] The cost of such a place being about $200,000, you see that the investment repays itself in full in three or four years, given good harvests.[18]

---

14. The term, which occurs in American as well as British English, means to pay in goods instead of cash. Hesse-Wartegg, amid changes from one to another, could not know that four "systems" of labor and ownership would appear in the decades after the war: wage labor, tenancy, sharecropping, and the crop-lien system. Worse for the observer, the systems were neither uniform, regular, nor systematic in operation or appearance. They were less systems than makeshift arrangements. See Shannon, *Farmer's Last Frontier*, 80–97.

15. "The opportunity for abuse [by the planter-storekeeper] was not always resisted" (Sitterson, *Sugar Country*, 244).

16. In 1871 Robert Somers also criticized Jewish businessmen in the South, claiming to see "sharp, active young men of Jewish aspect" doing lucrative business as agents of New York firms: advancing "money on cotton at the approach of the picking season at as much interest as they can extort" (*Southern States Since the War, 1870–1871,* 151). They were part of the "invasion of Jews to reap a harvest in trade" after the war. According to Coulter, though Jews engaged in "sharp practices," foreclosed when borrowers did not pay up, and even "cheated the Negroes out of their lands," southerners "never developed anti-Semitism" (*Reconstruction,* 202–3). Percy thought that "every American community has its leaven of Jews. Ours arrived shortly after the Civil War with packs on their backs, peddlers from Russia, Poland, Germany, a few from Alsace. They sold trinkets to Negroes and saved. Today they are plantation-owners, bankers, lawyers, doctors, merchants; their children attend the great American universities, win prizes, become connoisseurs in the arts and radicals in politics. . . . Why shouldn't such a people inherit the earth, not, surely, because of their meekness, but because of a steadier fire, a tension and tenacity that make all other whites seem stodgy and unintellectual" (*Lanterns,* 17). Woodman has pointed out that Jews did not "dominate the furnishing merchant business. Most storekeepers were indigenous" (*King Cotton,* 304). See also chapter 9, note 2 above.

17. In the 1880s, 1,000 acres would gross more than $100,000, but probably no more than a third would be clear. See Sitterson, *Sugar Country,* 303, 305–6.

18. Although plantations worth $200 to $400 an acre in the 1850s "were valued at

Besides, often a mere tenth of the price need be paid on date of purchase.

Plantations could be had for a song in the decade after the war. Prices have risen, especially in the last few years. Everyone accordingly got rich who bought one in that first decade. New York and St. Louis capitalists buying then invested in what has amounted to a gold mine.[19] They winter with their families in Louisiana now. Their presence brings no small benefit to the former slave state.

Hitherto a plantation must have been of at least 200 acres in order to maintain its own mill. Recently the attempt has been made to divide large plantations and to separate the growing of cane from the extraction of sugar; a change for the profound good of every aspect of production.[20] In this beneficial division of labor, planters can devote everything to the plantation.

Furthermore, when a plantation has been subdivided, the less-than-affluent settler can buy fifty acres or more of excellent land for $500 to $800.[21] He will spend a few thousand on equipment, mules, and the rest of the essentials. In but a few years he will earn it back in abundance.[22]

Meanwhile, refineries incorporate. Larger than the old plantation mills and equipped with the best machinery and the latest technology, they do a better job and bring to market a superior product.

---

succession sales in 1869 and 1870 at $35 to $75 an acre" (Sitterson, *Sugar Country,* 296), prices were rising. Hesse-Wartegg's $200,000 purchase was possible but probably not typical by 1880. He also does not state whether his prices include equipment and improvements. See 295–96.

19. Northern businessman Daniel Thompson, for example, bought Calumet, a plantation in St. Mary's parish, and made it prosper. See C. L. Marquette, "Letters of a Yankee Sugar Planter," 521–23.

20. Central factories would separate cane culture from sugar manufacture. Both "would profit from their separation" by concentration of "energies and resources to the end of maximum production" (Sitterson, *Sugar Country,* 259). On land ownership and the size of plantations, Hesse-Wartegg in general is right, but the situation was more complicated than it appears here. See Shannon, *Farmer's Last Frontier,* 80–82. It should be borne in mind that Hesse-Wartegg observed a situation in transition; subdivision had just begun in earnest. See Shugg, "Survival," 314–15.

21. These figures agree neither with the records of the time nor Hesse-Wartegg's figures above.

22. Hesse-Wartegg is affirming "the celebrated breakup of the old plantation into democratic small farms." Though praised by others of the time, this movement may not have been what it appeared to be. See Woodward, *New South,* 178.

26. A Rice Plantation

On our many excursions from Magnolia Plantation I noticed another on Big River's opposite shore: a small, low-built house at the mainland's southernmost edge. Looking across the river with a telescope, I could descry nothing better than a small garden. Even the "*quarter*" seemed half deserted. The area beyond the levee showed not a trace of cultivation: not a tree, not a bush. The land stretched away to an indeterminate end where the horizon deliquesced into the sultry quiver of heat above it. I was looking at a rice plantation.

Thick columns rise daily behind the levee over there: stubble burned on fields gives off smoke that scatters every which way on the wind. The day came when fires ceased. Weather being clear and beautiful, Hercules (the expert black navigator) and his able-bodied seamen got orders: *Row us in the big boat, across to Plaquemine Parish.* (Louisiana does not divide itself like the rest of the states into counties but observes the old English system of "*parishes*." Originally a parish meant an ecclesiastical district centering upon a church.)

Not easy, such a voyage, and seldom tried across a torrent churned into peaks by three-masters and huge transatlantic steamers. We must avoid ships, dodge tree trunks sweeping at us with treacherous malignancy beneath the surface, miss whirlpools, and parry waves, while the oarsmen pull obliquely upstream lest the current drive us downstream. In addition, we could at any moment capsize. Our ebony boatmen, wearing nothing but scanty loincloths, were ready for such a plunge. The bath would probably do the grubby fellows good. It would make us miserable. Meanwhile, having quarreled with the overseer, Hercules burned with the worst desires. Bobbing in a skiff on a dirty-yellow wave, unable to see plantations on either shore because levees blocked the view, only then did we learn the Mississippi's width and appreciate its enormity. I cooled Hercules with the gift of a red-silk handkerchief.

The crossing took far more than an hour. It took all his love for the handkerchief. In the end, nothing but his adoration for that scarlet cloth brought us from shore to shore. We arrived exhausted. The current had driven us far below our destination.

Drainage ditches crisscrossed low-lying fields of wet, soft, peaty soil. People and mules cleared weeds from ditches and plowed fields. The mules wore big, leather shoes to keep hooves from sinking into muck. Nothing deserved study except the drainage system, a most clever arrangement. So I asked the planter to explain rice culture.

First, let me say that from the beginning rice has been a chief source of revenue in the South, especially Georgia, Louisiana, and South Carolina. Before the war, South Carolina boasted no fewer than a million acres of it. Only 250,000 remain, of course. In 1850 the South produced 108 million kilos, which declined, but only to 95 million by 1860. South Carolina exported 60 million. Then came the war. And for 1870: South Carolina, 16 million; Georgia, 11 million; Louisiana, 8 million.[1] But every sign points to a resurgence of this once-lucrative crop.

Plowing, the planter said, will continue until February or March, followed by harrowing necessary to pulverize the soil. A man and a mule harrow about eight to ten acres a day. Next the soil must be furrowed to receive seed. Then the picturesque processions of Negresses across the fields. Thick-lipped, plump-limbed, stupid-faced black daughters of Guinea—in little more than a loose and scanty skirt draped from hip to knee—carry seed in aprons or little baskets and plant it by hand in the furrows. About 2.5 bushels to the acre. "*Coverers*" follow them, burying the seed by smoothing the soil until it is approximately level. They use a crude tool, a short board with a handle stuck into it. Some planters leave seed uncovered.[2]

Planting done, sluices or "*trunks*" are opened and fields flooded. Trunks, unique in design, consist of an oblong wooden box set horizontally in the levee that separates river from field. Gates, one on each face of the box, can be raised and lowered from the levee but opened and shut sideways [by the pressure of the water] as well. To flood a field, raise the gate on the river side. Water flows into the box. The pressure opens the gate near the field and keeps it open until water inundates the field. Lower the river gate to stop influx and the field gate shuts itself. Reverse the procedure to drain excess from the field.

You can imagine the difficulty of installing and maintaining trunks. Each costs between $100 and $120. Once begun, installation cannot

---

1. After 1880 Louisiana and the other Gulf states, using the agribusiness efficiency noted elsewhere by Hesse-Wartegg, took a larger and larger share of American rice production. See Edward Hake Phillips, "The Gulf Coast Rice Industry," 91–93.

2. For an account of rice culture that complements this one, see Phillips, *Life and Labor*, 115–18.

pause. Tides must be obeyed. Should the cut into the levee start too late, for example, the tide will have been out for its six hours, return before the box is in place, fill ditches, flood fields, and ruin the crop. (Rice must have fresh water; salt kills it.) Planters higher on the river enjoy a better situation than those near the mouth, where salt tides often penetrate. Planters near the mouth must build reservoirs for fresh water. These, at 100 to 500 acres, require water piped as much as twenty miles. Constant and serious attention must also be paid them because levees often break after rains. Daily inspections must be made, therefore, and every hole plugged no matter how small. Tiny though it may seem, neglect of a hole frequently means not only fields destroyed, but also the home and the Negroes' quarters. A levee may burst at a length of thirty to sixty meters, as if shaken by an earthquake, and torrents rush with horrific force over plantations.

Water brought into the field after planting, the *"sprout flow,"* remains about four days: until the seed has germinated. The field must be drained at once, else the sprouts die. If by chance the river has risen higher than the fields, the seed shall be lost, crop ruined. Pump out those masses of water? Impossible! Let the threat be averted and the sprouts see daylight. New enemies appear. Birds and worms, especially the ugly, black, rice worm, sometimes savage the crop. Water must be laid on again, the only defense against them. A saline river, a dry reservoir, each means a lost crop. These catastrophes often occur.

After the sprout flow, fields remain dry until the rice spreads its green carpet of thin, erect, needle-shaped shoots. Time now for the *"stretch flow,"* the second inundation, lasting thirty to forty days. When the grasslike leaves have lengthened enough and float like seaweed, fields are drained again.

The next task, weeding, fills the time until May. Then comes heat; then miasmas that rise from wet expanses of rice culture. Planter and family must retreat to higher ground or risk fevers that claim many a victim. What of Negroes? In days gone by, he owned them. Partly for humane but mostly for expedient reasons, he fed and cared for them exceptionally well. They suffered far less than whites from fever. Now, with the poor creatures left to their own devices, it ravages them much more than it does their lords and masters. The future looks worse to them than it did when they were slaves. Over and over I heard them wish for the *"old slavery times."* The poor devils want the "good old days of slavery"!

After the stretch flow, five or six weeks of dry growth, until heads show. *"Harvest flow"* is at hand, six more weeks of water, until the grain starts to ripen. Again the grand plantations bustle with people and animals. The ricebird [bobolink] arrives in the second half of September, regularity unfailing. Dainty, chubby little beasts in swarms from the North, they invade the rice-growing regions and wreak havoc. The grain, underripe, contains a milky substance. With sharp, pointed beaks the pests open hulls and suck it out, ruining the grain. Planter and overseers spend the days from morning till night in the fields, trying to shoot the pests or at least scare them off. Hundreds appear on his table. Though fat and delicious, they pay a minimum of reparations, having destroyed as much as forty to sixty percent of the crop.

Come harvest, Negroes cut rice with a tool for the purpose: a large sickle, the so-called *"rice hook."* Upon cutting, they sheave it. The planter might be happy, except August's downpours often ruin his joy. Given good weather, everyone hastens to the field. Negro women and children busy themselves in skillfully sheaving the beautiful golden-yellow stalks. Negro men move sheaves to cover, distance permitting. Otherwise they load them on rafts and pole them along canals to the plantation's buildings. Truly what a charmingly lovely scene ensues! Plantations reminded us of southern Egypt: clear, blue sky; broad, golden fields crisscrossed by canals; in from the river, a dark grove; the house to be seen among the tall shady trees, along with the quarter, or village of white huts; river beyond, contained by levees; imposing steamers and stately ships of sail passing back and forth; Negresses in fields with short skirts gathered up; and Negroes in scanty breeches. In the open near the buildings, a dozen or two of the Ethiopians thresh. Or we hear the clatter of the machine that has replaced the flail on many plantations.

Straw often becomes fodder, baled like hay. Grain goes by ship, like tobacco or wheat, to a common feature of the American landscape—the *"elevator,"* or giant granary. There the planter's harvest awaits his pleasure, his order for *"milling"* and *"pounding."*

In sacks loosely packed, the rice moves to the mill for a profound cleaning. The *"sandscreen,"* a system of sieves of various gauges, removes foreign substances such as grass seeds and sand. The millstone grinds off the hulls. In the *"shaker"* a blast of air separates hulls from kernels by blowing away hulls while kernels drop into the *"ground rice bin."* They proceed under pestles. Pounding frees kernels of the dark crust of bran always found under the hull. Pounding takes an hour or two. A second series of sieves separates kernels from bran and sizes them. A kind of rotating drum takes kernels (still segregated by size) and "brushes" or "polishes" them. They drop through tubes into barrels for shipping. Away they go to market. Charleston (the South Carolina metropolis) joins New Orleans as an emporium for the rice trade. Annually 200,000 or 300,000 barrels reach Charleston for export.

When all is said and done, rice culture poses difficulties, demands work, yet returns profit but seldom.[3] We can only marvel at the courage and tenacity of these planters.

3. In the prior chapter, Hesse-Wartegg recommended sugar planting as a profitable endeavor for the immigrant; unprofitable rice gets no such endorsement.

27. Progress and Prosperity in Agriculture and the Basic Industries

The prior chapters have emphasized the lower Mississippi valley's society and commerce [and have considered its agriculture]. Let us turn to the industry of that complex of states. During the slave era a mention of "southern industry" would produce laughter. Not one important factory existed in the million square miles of superb real estate. Steam power had strayed in, but sporadically, in riverboats and locomotives, and no further than the sugar plantations' *"sugar houses."* The miner's pick had only scratched the enormous deposits of coal and ore of the western slope of the Alleghenies. Life and work centered upon the rearing of slaves and the production of sugar and cotton. The South did not grow even its essential food, nor make the necessary clothing, but imported everything from the North: the plow and the steam engine to begin with; linens and knitted goods, too; and even flour and salted meat.[1]

There were rich masters and poor servants, planters and laborers, but no true middle class in that society. Planters scorned work. To qualify as a gentleman, one must own grand plantations, many slaves, a home in the city, and horses and carriages, and live recklessly and frivolously on one's income. The minute this fellow went to work he lost his prestige.

In the last half-generation, that state of affairs has experienced an unexpected revolution. The majority of planters have become not just poorer, but also wiser. If they have given up their carriages and perhaps condescend to work, they do it for an additional reason than the loss of huge sums. They have realized that nothing but work and thrift will restore their former status. Indeed, Yankees having come from the North and settled in plantation country, the old planters must practice the two virtues to keep themselves independent amid the industrious, ambitious interlopers.[2] Furthermore, the South's indigent whites never

---

1. Less than perfect self-sufficiency must be granted, but the South was not so dependent that it "imported everything."

2. Many "Yankees coming from the North" were carpetbaggers who became planters or merchants as well as politicians. Some had been in the South before, often in the Union army, liked what they saw, learned something of the region, and

could have been in the same class as the planters, who called them "*poor white trash*" and avoided them. But the new arrangements have opened to the poor the way to prosperity and respect. They can compete at will with the old slave barons. When people in large numbers and capital in significant amounts arrived from the North, they completed the revolution.[3] Fundamental change followed in industry as well as agriculture.[4]

People no longer look askance even at the European immigrant. In fact, they greet him with pleasure in most states, and help him as best they can. In the southern states the road to affluence is open to the immigrant who arrives with adequate means. It follows that [European] emigration is already turning south.[5]

---

returned as informed civilians and energetic opportunists. They brought a different way of life and enjoyed the influence to assert their way upon southerners. Foner offers as an example the Vermont carpetbagger Marshall H. Twitchell (*Reconstruction*, 356–57). There were also the notable examples of Henry Clay Warmoth (1842–1931) of Illinois, Hesse-Wartegg's friend, planter, and governor of Louisiana; and William Pitt Kellogg (1830–1918) of Vermont, federal official, senator, and another governor of Louisiana.

3. The arrival, especially of capital, was only beginning as Hesse-Wartegg wrote these words. Investors had feared political uncertainty in the Reconstruction South and "preferred the lure of the North and West. The flood of capital anticipated by Republicans . . . would not come until after the end of Reconstruction" (Foner, *Reconstruction*, 391).

4. "Toward the end of this decade of despair," 1870–1880, a "sudden quickening of life in commerce and investment" has "sometimes been taken to mark the opening of a completely new era in the region's history" (Woodward, *New South,* 112). Woodward prefers to call it "The Industrial Evolution," and his chapter by that title (107–41), may be read as a corollary to this chapter by Hesse-Wartegg. Woodward discusses coal, lumber, iron, and other constituents and aspects, as well as causes and effects. Hesse-Wartegg himself uses the word *revolution* in referring to this change. He realized its antecedents and some of its causes. He was probably too close to appreciate the complexity that later scholarship would establish. See 112–15.

5. White southerners, not wanting the New South to be the Black South, desired white immigration, either to take over the farms made of subdivided plantations or to take the Negro's place as plantation labor. "The region sought immigrants by chartering immigration companies and sending agents to Europe." Planters also tried to bring Chinese coolies to southern cotton fields (Cohn, *King Cotton,* 153–54). See note 9 below. The effort to recruit immigrants probably began at the end of the war and continued to 1900. See Bert James Loewenberg, "Efforts of the South to Encourage Immigration, 1865–1900," 363–85, especially 364, 376. Fleming says the effort did not begin until the early 1880s ("Immigration," 276). Some planters thought they could exploit immigrants to create a new wage slavery that would not only be profitable, but would also keep the Negro in his place (Foner, *Reconstruction,* 213–14, 418–20).

Few immigrants, however, came to the South between the war and 1900. Europeans feared heat, malaria, bad water, lazy and proud whites in control, no crop to grow but cotton, bad schools and churches, and hordes of lawless Negroes (Fleming, "Immigration," 276). They also avoided the impecunious lot of the southern agricultural laborer, and sought the brighter economic conditions of the North and West (Taylor, *Louisiana,* 390). See also Woodward, *New South,* 297, 299; Coulter, *Recon-*

Immediately after the publication of my prior book on America, German emigration societies put to me many questions about how to get to the United States.[6] What was the best route? Which steamship line? They can be answered in a few words. The German going to America should choose the ships of the two large German lines, the North German Lloyd of Bremen and the Hamburg America Line of Hamburg. Theirs, the biggest and most comfortable, also serve the best food. The ships of the Stettin Lloyd have also proved excellent in the emigration service. The emigrant who does not mind the journey to England, Liverpool to be exact, can secure the shortest ocean voyage. He should choose the steamships of the Inman Line, the National Line, the White Star Line, the Cunard Line, or the American Line. Theirs number among the biggest and fastest of the Atlantic fleet. The emigration ports of Antwerp and Rotterdam lie nearest the emigrants from Westphalia and the Rhineland. Each city offers a line, the Red Star of Antwerp and the Holland America of Rotterdam. The Anchor Line with offices in Hamburg, has also been much sought after and widely used in recent years.[7]

In earlier chapters I mentioned the increase in machinery and steam on plantations. In the slave era the blacks did everything. A planter needed neither machines nor intelligent white labor. At any rate, it never occurred to anyone to replace blacks with machines and skilled whites.[8] Only now the new freedom of blacks to give or withhold labor and competition from skillful planters from the North have forced the southerner to think of organizing the plantation along rational lines. He has learned two things fast. (1) Steam and the machine have largely freed him from the expensive and doubtful use of free blacks. (2) Any human labor, grown expensive, cannot begin to match machines. Thus, commercial fertilizers along with steam-drawn plows, cultivators, and other agricultural machinery of all sorts (unknown in the earlier South) find the widest application now. In fact, on my southern journey I rarely saw a steamboat or a freight train from the North that

---

struction, 102–5; and Saloutos, "Southern Agriculture," 69–70.

6. The prior book was probably *Prairie-Fahrten* (1878).

7. Hesse-Wartegg here refers the reader to the back of the book, where advertisements for the shipping lines were included. They have been omitted from this edition.

8. The machine and the changes it would bring did not occur to the southern mind until forced upon it by the war. Altered agriculture would be part of the passage of Old into New South (Cash, *Mind of the South,* 180–82). Scientific agriculture and diversified farming, as well as a modernized and expanded industry, began but did not receive wide support until the end of Reconstruction (Foner, *Reconstruction,* 210–11). Hesse-Wartegg is observing evidence of a different way of life even as it takes shape around him. He reports the details but misses the main point.

did not have such machines among the principal cargo. Bumper crops beyond expectation prove the effectiveness of the new devices, which greatly increase, if not double, the South's capacity to produce. Planters in addition have begun to turn to crops other than cotton. Corn, wheat, vegetables, tobacco, and potatoes have been grown and processed. Gradually the region emancipates itself from the North, at least with respect to food.

The attempt to employ Chinese on plantations in many parts of the South—will it succeed and spread? I rather doubt it. The Chinese, though more intelligent, quicker, and more industrious than the Negro, proves unreliable as plantation labor. Southerners, black and white, hate the Chinese besides. Furthermore, there are not enough in the United States to constitute a labor force. Moreover, Americans in general oppose Chinese immigration. The South has so many black and white workers that it does not need the Oriental. Never mind, then, that a half-dozen plantations have employed Orientals.[9]

For all the advances in agriculture, the South has progressed industrially even further.[10] Southern states, at least those on the Atlantic coast, have in many ways already freed themselves industrially from the North. This can especially be said of cotton and the amazing progress of that industry in the last few years. I predict what may look like a pipe dream. Let the future be my witness.[11] The South, not long hence, will displace Great Britain and New England as the leading producer of cloth for the American market. Above all, does it make sense that Americans should raise cotton on their own ground, send it to Britain for processing, and buy it back at high prices?[12] Americans

---

9. Chinese lasted but "a few weeks in the furious sun" and left for easier work. White labor of various kinds did not stay, either. "The planters found they must continue dependent upon the Negro" (Kane, *Deep Delta Country*, 72). "The movement to import Chinese [which began in 1869] soon collapsed and no great number were brought to Louisiana" (Sitterson, *Sugar Country*, 238). The "Chinese movement," a fad to begin with, soon lost support in the North as well as the South. Southerners feared their pouring in by the millions, to be used politically by demagogues. Northerners feared their use politically by the South against the North (Coulter, *Reconstruction*, 105–6).

10. For the growth of the South compared to other regions, see Johnson, *Domestic and Foreign Commerce*, 266.

11. Hesse-Wartegg was not alone in these predictions, which came true in "a rapid growth of the Southern cotton-textile industry," without "parallel in the annals of American industry" (Cohn, *King Cotton*, 213). Probably unwittingly but nonetheless accurately, he perceived a new status for cotton in the South. Forty years later there was "every reason for selecting the year 1880 as the beginning of the cotton manufacturing development in the South" (Broadus Mitchell, *The Rise of the Cotton Mills in the South*, 59).

12. What first "inspirited cotton mills" in the South was the "presence of the raw material" (Mitchell, *Cotton Mills*, 137).

have the machines and southerners the best waterpower in the greatest quantities. Materials to build factories cost less than in any other country. Cotton is at least $100 less than in Britain or the North (and better besides because baling, shipping, and other handling reduce quality), and labor is twenty-five to thirty percent less than in the North. To all those reasons add this one: capital invested in the cotton industry [in the South] pays no taxes.[13]

An American newspaper has the following to say about the industry in the South. Its mills are returning about twenty percent more profit than mills of the North. The reason? Northern mills must sustain costs that do not exist in the South: packing, storage, insurance, and freight. In Augusta, Georgia, $800,000 has been invested in mills. Last year they paid a twenty-eight percent dividend. A new mill costing $500,000 should be erected besides, so lucrative is this business here. The mills of Columbus, Georgia, return twenty-two percent. People everywhere in the South, realizing cotton's profitability, have begun to invest in mills when and where they can get the capital.[14] Here is a list of southern states and the number of spindles in each.

Arkansas	1,700
Alabama	63,000
Georgia	137,000
Kentucky	11,264
Louisiana	6,200
Mississippi	70,000
Maryland	113,000
Missouri	26,300
North Carolina	93,000
South Carolina	92,000
Texas	9,300
Tennessee	40,500
Virginia	52,000
Total	715,264

---

13. To these reasons for the success of the cotton industry, add that people worked for success with a sense of moral mission and a desire for social betterment. See Cohn, *King Cotton*, 213–15; and Coulter, *Reconstruction*, 266–67. On tax relief and other inducements to investment, see Mitchell, *Cotton Mills*, 238–42.

14. On the profitability of the mills, see Mitchell, *Cotton Mills*, 244 and passim.

American mills process 1.76 million bales, up from the modest 1.25 million of only a few years ago in 1875.

There is more to this success story. Notices have been making conspicuous way through the newspapers. A machine invented by W. Clement spins cotton immediately, if not in the field where picked, then close to the plantation! Inventions, Eli Whitney's *"cotton gin"* for example, have turned the world upside down. Clement's at present seem incredible yet suggests we may be near another revolutionary device.[15] The *Freie Presse für Texas* describes it as a combination of the original *"gin"* and a spinning mill. In the old way, fast-moving combs separate fiber from seed, leaving the fiber tousled [and resistant to processing]. In this condition it is baled. In the new system, the gin moves more slowly and plucks fiber off the seed rather than ripping it apart [leaving it readier for processing]. A cylinder takes it and spins it then and there. Baling, opening the bales later, readying the fiber afterward for spinning: these tasks disappear, and with them a large part of the cost. One machine does the work of several. It also finishes more of the raw cotton; the old created much waste—nine percent.

One more advantage. A pound of cotton done the old way brings eight cents and not a fraction more anywhere. Thread from the Clement is worth seventeen cents. A bale of cotton from the gin, $50; the equivalent in thread from the Clement, $100 on the spot. This year's harvest, estimated at five million bales, would bring the South by the old system $225 million; by the new, $500 million and of it, $100 million profit. (A Clement does three gins' work for a third the cost.)

A revolution in the cotton industry has begun. The South is taking the first—a giant—step down the road to agribusiness.[16]

---

15. Lewis T. Clement (not W. Clement), a Tennessee cabinetmaker, patented in 1869 an attachment to spin the cotton as it left the gin. (Coulter, *Reconstruction,* 267). See also Harriet L. Herring, "The Clement Attachment: An Episode of Reconstruction Industrial History," 186–88. The attachment neither was so different nor would be so successful as Hesse-Wartegg claims. Part of the old process, it did not bring the gin to the field. See a picture of it and a description in the *Atlanta Constitution,* 23 January 1880. Enthusiasm for it was at a peak in 1879 but waned when the machine did not live up to promise, though the idea struggled along for years afterward (Herring, "Clement Attachment," 186–89, 190, 193–98). One forecast would have it work "greater revolutions in the South than the cotton gin has done in the last half century!" It did attempt to combine ginning and spinning, and try to improve both, but proved "makeshift, a partial solution," not "a real industrial development" (Mitchell, *Cotton Mills,* 154).

16. The term *agribusiness,* though unknown in English in 1880, seems the best translation of Hesse-Wartegg's *Ackerbau-Industrie.* If southerners lacked the word to describe it, they were nonetheless hell-bent on the industrialization of agriculture. See Mitchell, *Cotton Mills,* 144–59.

Lumber follows cotton in importance. The South's vast forests in Alabama, Mississippi, Georgia, and other states supply the North and send abroad the finest of woods. Along the Gulf and Atlantic coasts, hundreds of sawmills run at capacity, turning out boards, beams, and masts [or poles] in millions of feet.[17] Unfortunately, a lumber industry of this magnitude does the South more harm than good! Sooner or later such destruction of forests must end. Individuals benefit, true, but the South shall suffer beyond calculation.[18] The northern Sahara—yes, even that dead and sunbaked desert—flourished with forests a few hundred years ago, the equal of the Mississippi valley now. Saharan forests disappeared; with them, water, rivers, and agriculture. May the southern people consider before it is too late what harm will come of the ruin of their forests! Let newspapers take up the cause and not rest until Congress legislates to protect the forests!

Third in importance is the mining of coal and iron ore. The south-Atlantic states may have much coal, but Alabama, Arkansas, and Tennessee take first place with practically unlimited wealth of this ultra-important mineral. One to three feet thick, Alabama's "*Warrior Coal Field*" spreads across 3,000 square miles. The Cahawba region in the center of the state has 700 square miles of six-to-eight-foot beds. In all, Alabama has 5,500 square miles of coal, in many places fifteen to twenty feet thick. Geologists speak of equal deposits of iron. Large iron mines have been dug and big smelters built.[19]

We can see how Nature has bestowed almost too many advantages on the South. There may be no other place anywhere at this latitude on earth with such fertility of soil and so much mineral wealth. Old-time southerners did not comprehend the value of what they had. The war has taught them a lesson. Sad though the aftermath was, the war may prove beneficial to a corresponding degree for the next generation. The

17. By 1900 the South would surpass the Lake states in lumber, the South's yellow pine "comprising more than a fourth of the production of the entire country" (Johnson, *Domestic and Foreign Commerce,* 263).

18. Quoting an article in the *Chattanooga Tradesman* (1886), Woodward notes that "early warnings against denuded forests and irreparable waste were brushed aside as 'immeasurably stupid. . . . Taken seriously [they] would leave all nature undisturbed'" (*New South,* 118). Early in this century, J. F. Duggar wrote that twenty years of lumbering had produced "probably the most rapid and reckless destruction of forests known to history" ("Areas of Cultivation in the South," quoted in Woodward, *New South,* 118). For Hesse-Wartegg's ambivalence about the limitations of natural resources, see chapter 15, note 5 above.

19. "The business revival of 1879 opened the way for the Southern iron industry," especially in Alabama (Woodward, *New South,* 126). "By the late eighties the South was producing far more pig iron than the nation produced before the war; [and] investment in blast furnaces was mounting faster than in any northern state" (127).

South stands higher than before in prosperity and culture. Abundance no longer occurs as sporadic wealth; the people partake of it. The South's condition leaves much to be desired, as we have seen. But the South has entered upon the course that will lead steadily to social improvement and economic prosperity.

28. The Lives of Women in Creole Land: Louisiana and the Caribbean

Where is "the land of the Creoles"? The vague and uncertain Orient can be more readily located. We know that the Orient begins about where European culture ends, and ends about where India begins. What, then, of Orientals—where is their country? We find Orientals in Europe, Asia, and Africa; they can be Christian, Muslim, or Jew. If "Oriental" is therefore hard to define, "Creole" is harder.[1] Geographically, Creoles can be located—on the east coast of Africa, the west of South America, in the West Indies as well as Mexico, and in North America—but ethnologically they remain a riddle. Some say, "We are French and born in the West Indies." Others, "We are Spanish and born in the West Indies." Again, "We are birthright Americans with fathers and mothers born in Europe." North Americans label Louisianians of Latin extraction *Creoles.* According to German-language newspapers of states along the Gulf, Creole can as readily fit Germans as Frenchmen and Spaniards.[2] French people on Mauritius and Bour-

---

1. *Creole* remains a problem in definition. In the Caribbean and southern United States it usually refers to descendants of Spanish, Portuguese, and French settlers. "The word Creole, as used in Louisiana, applies to white descendants of early French and Spanish settlers. It connotes also a high native quality—Creole furnishings, Creole vegetables, Creole manner" (Kane, *Deep Delta Country,* 21). George Washington Cable, often cited as an authority on Creoles, introduces vagueness when he contends that they are the French-speaking people of the Mississippi delta (*The Creoles of Louisiana,* 1-8). Cable admits French, Spanish, "colored," and other Creoles only if they have become Creole by unusual intermarriage and been "thoroughly proselyted" (*Creoles of Louisiana,* 41-42). In fact, Creoles are to be distinguished by language, culture, heritage, and even attitude, from Yankees, Anglo-Saxons, and others of north-European origin. For a discussion of the confusion over who is a Creole, see Joseph C. Tregle, "Early New Orleans Society: A Reappraisal," 20-36.

Recognizing the difficulty of defining *Creole,* Hesse-Wartegg perceives it as encompassing many kinds: Cable's "native born"—whites, blacks, and mixed; the poor and illiterate; the greedy and money-grubbing along with the aristocratic—as well as Adrien Rouquett's whites of native French and Spanish stock, and Grace King's and Kate Chopin's polished aristocrats and genteel souls. See Jackson, *New Orleans in the Gilded Age,* 14-15, 283-84. Hesse-Wartegg seems to favor the genteel and the polished as essential to *Creole.*

2. It could fit the descendants of Germans, some of them Alsatians, who arrived

bon, and Negroes on Santo Domingo also call themselves Creoles. A Creole society can thus be assembled of all nations and races, of whites and mestizoes and quadroons and Negroes. They represent all languages and cannot understand one another, yet all are Creoles. Some speak French, but French people cannot understand them.

Creole, then, cannot be defined by race, language, or heritage. Those criteria produce contradictions. One criterion distinguishes Creoles: their nature; that is, character or bearing, an infallible sign. In Louisiana, on Cuba, on Guadeloupe—wherever you please—Creoles stand out in the crowd. A foreigner may migrate to those places but never become Creole or even learn the language. He will use the words but never speak the tongue. He will turn brown under the southern sun. He will assume some of the carefree attitude. But the imperturbability, the elegant nonchalance, the lack of constraint, the composure, the [calm] exterior that masks fire within—these he will never learn. He can become refined, open, hospitable, but never be able to express refinement or offer hospitality with a Creole's courtliness and grace. Let me illustrate. Every American, from President to servant, is sovereign, so the saying goes. Someone helps us; we offer him a tip and he rejects it with the slogan "I'm a free man." A black Creole slave polishes our shoes in Cuba; we offer a few pennies and he takes them. Who shows greater dignity, the American who rejects the pittance or the Creole who accepts it? The Creole, by far!

Descending the Mississippi, you reach Creole country at New Orleans. Indeed, you arrive at the Creole capital. New Orleans has been esteemed from the first, not only as Queen of the Mississippi and chief city of Louisiana, but also as the center of Creole life. Because of the war, however, New Orleans verges on the end of its Creole status. The most valuable Creole property, slaves, went free after the war. So much for Creole wealth. Plantations lost value accordingly, sinking to a third or fourth of real worth. Many Creole millionaires became little more than beggars. What a change, then, in the Louisiana of old. It had been a slaves' hell and a whites' paradise. Hell vanished and took Paradise with it.

Creole society, impoverished, withdrew from the best parts of New Orleans. Only the French quarter has them now. Other elements of old Creole society languish in Louisiana's remote regions. Look in vain for Creoles in the streets, in the public life of New Orleans. Proud ladies

---

before 1720 and settled on what became the German Coast. They often gallicized their names and became indistinguishable from the French. See Carter, *Lower Mississippi,* 36–37. For a discussion of Germans as Creoles after drifting from their native language to English, see Deiler, *German Coast,* 111–29.

ruled as princesses on their plantations and journeyed to New Orleans for Carnival. Slaves made these planters' wives royal. As princesses they could rule; they could wield the power of life and death over their subjects. But they could do nothing else. They could not work. So, losing their slaves, they lost everything. They have been deposed. The republic has dethroned them. They rarely appear in society anymore.[3]

I wanted nevertheless to hunt up and study Creole life in New Orleans. I found little of it in the streets. True, in the French Market or of a Saturday evening on the city's Corso (Canal Street), I spied now and then a Junoesque form alone.[4] She would be wearing something dark, perhaps a good cloth well cut. But it seemed to me negligently donned and without the brisk and casual elegance the French so trenchantly call *chic*. The feet were delicate, small, shapely, instep coquettishly high, shoes of the French style, delicate too, and equally coquettish. Only they had long since lost the charm of being new. She herself? Tall. Well developed. Breasts of a Venus. The fact was plain; she had lost all but the best: beauty.[5] A profound sorrow had left every inch with a charm beyond words. She seemed to cling to sorrow even as she cherished memories of what she had lost. On the promenade, in the cafe, in the park listening to music, she kept silent and, with pride and resolve, held herself aloof from Northerners, Yankee and carpetbagger alike.

Everything about these women aroused my interest to the full. I put it to my friend and host. "Get me an introduction to Creole society."

The time was ripe, the middle of Carnival. (With flowering trees at the full, Carnival? With the fine homes of Rampart and Esplanade streets already hidden among the green of leaves, Carnival? In this heat, Carnival? Yes, this is February in the American South!)

I had already made the request of several acquaintances. Some answered evasively, especially Anglo-Americans. Germans laughed in my face. "There are no more Creoles!" Only then did I learn that Creoles avoid Yankees like the plague. Even the best of Yankees thus seek in vain for entry into Creole society.[6] (I am using *Yankee* as short-

---

3. The end of the old Creole civilization began with the Civil War. "A long time in the dying . . . their aged and high culture crumbled very slowly," chiefly under financial ruin (Davis, *Louisiana,* 319).

4. For the Via del Corso, see chapter 21, note 13 above and for Canal Street, chapter 19, note 20.

5. "Newly arrived Americans and foreigners in Louisiana generally thought Creole girls extremely beautiful, though some New Englanders considered some of them a bit plump" (Davis, *Louisiana,* 325).

6. "Every effort was made to keep out most Americans." Barriers tightened over the years. "Creole balls became increasingly exclusive," shrinking "to small affairs" of the same "families and carefully selected friends" (Tallant, *Mardi Gras,* 102-3).

hand for people who have moved here from the North—New York and Pennsylvania, chiefly—and from the West.)

At last I got the desired invitation to the city's premier Creole ball.[7] (My illusions had already been shattered. The worst yellow-fever epidemic had raged not long before; thousands were in mourning, yet there was Carnival. In summer, the Grim Reaper; in winter, Prince Carnival. In summer, Death; in winter, Life! So it goes in the South, whether in America or Europe.)

The gala evening arrived. The old French-colonial *grandezza* came in carriages, usually borrowed.[8] Members of the committee [of arrangements], wearing ribbons and cockades, greeted guests at the door and did the honors—not as would be expected in an American city, but at a European court. With further surprise I looked at a ballroom where masters of ceremonies directed introductions and supervised dances. The old *noblesse,* brought to Louisiana by families of former colonial dignitaries, had lost much glitter; but, I observed, it had retained its essence.[9] Maybe on no other occasion do these people permit themselves a certain splendor: the one night of the year to evoke the *ancien régime* in its majesty and the only time Creole society presents itself as it used to be. Never before at an American ball had I seen all the men in formal attire. As for the women's luxurious, gorgeous gowns, make no mistake of provenance. They came from Paris. Here indeed you can learn why the beauty of Creole women has become proverbial. Look elsewhere in vain for so much loveliness in so little space.

Women had come only to dance and enjoy themselves. And they had transformed themselves. In the morning I witnessed languish and gloom. In the evening I saw belles of the ball, lionesses. Their blood steamed. Young, voluptuous, they exhibited Junoesque pulchritude at its brightest. Scarcely pausing to rest, they wanted only to dance. Their passionate rhythms made them all the more beautiful.

At intermission when the music stopped, they threw themselves on couches, exhausted. Their partners surrounded them. Conversation began. Balls, dancing, entertainment, pleasure—these topics prevailed. Any reference to literature, to this or that author or novel, American or European, brought no response. The world at large seemed

7. Creole balls, dating to eighteenth-century French times, had been modeled on grand balls of Paris. A "social institution of paramount importance then," they retained at least a nostalgic significance at the time of Hesse-Wartegg's visit. See Davis, *Louisiana,* 150. Certain Carnival balls, Creole balls of long standing, remain as important in the 1980s as Creole balls of the 1780s.

8. *Grandezza,* Italian for grandeur or greatness, especially of manner or appearance, here refers to people who look grand: high society.

9. For the panoply of what it was, see Davis, *Louisiana,* 237–39, 319–20.

as remote as these women to the world at large. Reading and learning are to the mind of a woman what clothes are to her body: facades. Unattractive women need clothes for the body and learning for the mind. Women like these Creoles need neither. They wore ignorance so gracefully, they made it so lovely and congenial, you would think perforce: "What foolishness for women to read books or learn anything of science, here in the South!"

The ball neared its end. In adjoining rooms, men indulged the Creole addiction: roulette, rouge et noir, and the infamous "*poker.*"[10] I believe no other American city gambles as much as New Orleans. Many of its Creoles have no other means or pastime. Of course. Reared on plantations, masters while still in the cradle, they wielded from that time the power of life and death over slaves. Creole mothers—warm, tender, loving—showered upon children a devotion near worship. Children got what they wanted. A wave brought a dozen slaves to each little master's feet. Creole children therefore grew up loafers. They barely learned to read. Then the masters lost their slaves. Indeed, the war took their wealth and knocked all from under them. Can they recover their losses? Even if they could, they would not. Being "*gentlemen,*" they detest, they loathe work. Furthermore, ignorant, they are unfit for politics—Yankees have pushed them out of it. Arriving from the North, alien opportunists have spread a good name for themselves among blacks, and finagled every public office, even of governor. So Creoles pass the time gambling and making love.[11] Is nothing left to this generation but to die out? Their children will fare better.[12]

I received much-welcomed invitations from several families at the ball. One afternoon I called on the M——y family.[13] The two daughters had been the ball's loveliest of the lovely. Their "palace" was in the French quarter. The quarter, beautiful days gone, might as well be the

10. "The dominating vice of Creole New Orleans," and "a trait of Creole character," was "a passion for gambling" never equaled on this side of the Atlantic (Asbury, *French Quarter,* 212, 213).

11. Creoles had long suffered a bad reputation. "Most contemporary descriptions [at the time of the Louisiana Purchase] of the French Creoles were not flattering, characterizing them as an indolent, pleasure-loving class, for the most part adventurers and not a few ex-criminals, who lived principally for their balls and their gambling" (Davis, *Louisiana,* 166).

12. This cryptic remark seems to mean that, as the parents have sunk to the depths, so the children must be better off: nowhere to go but up.

13. Only one prominent Creole family's name fits: Marigny. If this is the one Hesse-Wartegg means, he went to the top. "The name . . . stands first . . . in the chronicles of the old Creole families of New Orleans" (Grace King, *Creole Families of New Orleans,* 9). Louisiana's first Marigny arrived with the discoverers. Thereafter the family was a leader in society, business, and politics. See 10–58.

slums of St. Louis! Streets are dead—pavements torn up, rubbish scattered about—and piles of manure block the way. Row upon row of houses stand vacant. Tenants occupy many, gratis, to keep them from ruin. Remnants of the old splendor do exist. I saw them, now and then, in the better streets. But the quarter remains America's Faubourg St. Germain.[14]

A black servant opened the door. When he saw the stranger he snatched a pair of white gloves from his coat pocket and put them on. His hands were dirty, the gloves patched. After he had taken up my card, he led me into the salon. I heard doors opening and shutting. Steps. Voices. Scolding rose to a screech, then subsided to a whisper.

The salon had been furnished in tasteful opulence. These carpets and curtains, this wallpaper torn here and there, this rococo furniture: they must have endured many upon many a year. Old pictures on the walls, mostly portraits. Heavy silver graced the table yet, but upon dirty linen. A corset on an old sofa, a pair of women's shoes by the door, and clothing hanging from chairs. The prevailing disorder and neglect in other circumstances would have seemed charming, even seductive. Here I had to see it otherwise.

One of the women appeared at last. In the ballroom's bouquet she had been the loveliest flower. I presumed with Alphonse Kerr that at home she would be the bouquet itself.[15] To my disappointment the slovenliness included *her*. What she wore indoors would do for encounters with relatives, but the adequacy did not extend to meetings with strangers. She lacked an important item. It lay, as I have said, on the sofa. The second woman came in later. She had dressed with greater care and spent more time on the toilette.

I did not stay long. Even the supreme beauty can become unpleasant when she makes herself unattractive.

I heard everywhere that Creole women, quarrelsome by nature, raise hell at home and become unbearable. I am, of course, unable to speak to this point. Louisianans say that the Creole is his wife's wife. She wears the pants and he takes a bad second. The man for his part prefers mulattoes—so much that his wife is to be pitied.[16] Creole men, in fact, have given rise to a new race, the half-castes: mulattoes, quadroons, and octoroons.

14. The Faubourg was Paris's aristocratic and fashionable quarter.
15. Hesse-Wartegg's "Kerr" is probably Alphonse Karr (1808–1890), the French writer whose reminiscences appeared in 1879 and 1880. See *Chambers's Biographical Dictionary*, s.v. "Karr, (Jean Baptiste) Alphonse."
16. Davis thinks the obsession with "young girls of the mixed-blood group" has been sensationalized. Nevertheless they "dressed and acted the part of courtesans so effectively and aspired to white association so successfully as to make necessary [the] special regulations regarding their dress and personal actions" (*Louisiana*, 132).

As the hereditary [Creole] planter-aristocracy dies out, however, so shall the half-castes. In the first place, the taboo against black-white intermarriage has been set to law in the South. Moreover, both blacks and whites hate and shun the half-caste. Even black plantation workers take pride in being "*pure sang*,"[17] and prize their ancestry no less than Creoles theirs.

Negroes who pride themselves on blood and heritage are Creoles, too, albeit of another color.[18] Even Germans born in New Orleans call themselves Creoles, gladly, though bearing little resemblance to French and Spanish counterparts. German Creoles number nowhere near as many as the Creoles of the French quarter. Yet these Germans constitute the most prosperous element in New Orleans.

Many times I traveled out from New Orleans and across plantation Louisiana. I went into areas away from principal lines of communication, away even from bayous, themselves little known to the world outside. I read of this region first in Bernardin de Saint-Pierre, Gerstäcker, and Sealsfield—what enchantment, what romance it seemed to hold then![19] So seldom is it visited, so infrequently described that any account rouses interest in Europe. The plantations are still romantic. But the sinister, savage ennui has meddled here, too, and leavened the romance.

In the shade of two tall old magnolias the Creole lady, mistress of the plantation, idles in her hammock. Her long housedress trails out and down from it. The little bright clouds of her cigarette disappear in the

17. "Pure blood" or purebred, in the sense of ancestry or race.

18. Louisiana had numerous "free people of color," many from Santo Domingo, former slave-owners and wealthy. They were called *Creoles de coleur,* to distinguish them from slaves, *nègres creoles* (Davis, *Louisiana,* 132). Thus the term *Creole* acquired layer upon layer of complication. See also Jackson, *New Orleans in the Gilded Age,* 276, 277, 285, 302.

19. Jacques Henry Bernardin de St. Pierre (1737–1814), French novelist and botanist, wrote *Paul et Virginie,* one of the most popular books of all time (300 editions). The reference here is unclear. He was not known as a writer on America in the way that Gerstäcker and Sealsfield were, or as was his countryman and contemporary, Chateaubriand. See Stanley J. Kunitz and Vineta Colby, *European Authors, 1000–1900,* 821–22; and P. E. Charvet, *A Literary History of France: The Nineteenth Century,* 60–66. Friedrich Gerstäcker (1816–1872), prolific author of novels and travel books, many about America and widely read in German-speaking Europe, taught many Europeans what they knew of America. He spent time on the frontier and in the "wild West," describing them with color and verve that have kept him in print. The reference here is probably to his *Pirates of the Mississippi* (1848). See *Oxford Companion to German Literature,* s.v. "Gerstäcker, Friedrich." Karl Anton Postl (1793–1864) wrote under the name Charles Sealsfield. This Austrian novelist and short-story writer traveled in America and described it colorfully and with forceful style. He portrayed America as the "golden land of freedom." The reference here could be to any of several of his travel books. See Kunitz and Colby, *European Authors,* 856–57.

trees' dark foliage. A Negro runs up to announce the guest's arrival. "Haho, Diana! Ceres!" The negresses, thus called, bound from the house and help mistress out of the hammock. Slowly she shuffles into the house and welcomes us. In this oppressive heat I feel comfortable only in the dim expanses of the old salon of the house. The many spacious rooms and old pictures, the antique furniture and tall fireplaces suggest chateaux of French feudal lords.

Why, then, her melancholy? The planter, her husband, has left for the fields. Continual isolation, summer heat, and far-reaching silence together have brought despondency to her and her kind. They do not live, they vegetate. They revive for a short time during the season in the city, during Carnival. So they adore guests who tell of the world and nourish their fantasies of Paris and Europe's grand and elegant haute monde. Painfully they yearn for the company, the amusement, the favors they must miss from their husbands. Should we wonder that hospitality lasts and lasts? That days lengthen to weeks before the guest is allowed to leave?

Do you think the Creole woman loses her youth early? She does not. She matures young but keeps for many years her beauty in full. One sign reveals her as past her prime: she gains weight. Her husband, often indifferent, does not care about her. He chases the plantation's young Negresses. Early in marriage she feels passion for him, like a lioness. It soon expires. She repays neglect in kind. She bestows tenderness on her children.[20]

People of neighboring plantations visit but rarely. Towns, villages, hotels: nothing of the sort hereabouts. Visitors, therefore, are always welcome in plantation houses and at the tables. When neighbors do call, they arrive in old carriages, relics of colonial times. The assembly observes a certain ceremony, a definite *grandezza*. They sit down to a table served by Negroes in white gloves. The waiters' livery, however, often reveals large areas of—nakedness. Everything breathes sensuousness and decay.

In Cuba, where Creoles are Spanish, those conditions also prevail, only translated into Spanish. There, however, summer pours more heat upon our backs, mosquitoes bite deeper, and hoteliers prove worse bandits than New Orleans counterparts. Havana lives by hotels nonetheless. The city's finest apartments are in them.

Cuban Creole women dwell in homes with uncarpeted marble floors, wicker furniture, rocking chairs, and a few tables. Though less beau-

20. In the novel *Homoselle* "the handsome quadroon was really the daughter of the head of the house. . . . Behind [the popular and literary conceptions of the plantation woman's character] are the shadows of deep grief that give cause for wonder" (Gaines, *Southern Plantation,* 181).

tiful than their French counterparts, these Creole women seek pleasure more readily and are more relaxed and more sincere. They spend the days at home, evenings in the streets and the parks and on the promenades. There they smoke cigarettes and sip Jicarra.[21] They eat little and seem to subsist on chocolate, Narangada, and other sweets.[22] On the promenade and in the home you can feel an eerie chill in their relations with their husbands; as if with every couple, ill-will festers between man and woman. (Spanish etiquette from the days of the Conquistadores has devolved upon them.)[23] An invisible iron grate seems to divide man from wife in conversation. Toward the stranger the women act happier and more natural. They flirt. The fan is the instrument, their toy, their true tongue. When it comes to the fan, Spanish women themselves cannot outdo Creoles. Understand the language of the fan and you win at that game.

I have already said that the Creole women of Cuba are less beautiful than their Louisiana counterparts: darker, less regal of form, and indulgent of an ugly practice. They powder face and shoulders with carcarilla, a preparation of eggshell.[24] You can scarcely imagine how, for example, it makes a woman look when she dances a criolla or a lanza, Havana's popular Carnival dances. On beautiful European women the white powder can be compared to the pollen of a flower. On dark faces of Creoles—repulsive!

At present the "Pearl of the Antilles," as Cuba is called, finds itself in a condition not to be envied, having suffered civil war and a slave insurrection. Civil war thus took away the wealth and devastated the plantations of Creoles in Louisiana and Cuba both. Yet in Cuba the Creoles must remain planters, pay heavy tribute to the Spanish captain-general and the government, and suffer continued depletion of wealth. The insurrection did them further damage.

French Creoles, their fate sealed, shall give way to Anglo-Saxons. In Louisiana without doubt, dispersal and destruction await the Creoles. With this generation passes the last of a truly hereditary aristocracy there. Creoles in Cuba, being descendants of the conquerors of New Spain, have the best of old Spanish blood in their veins. But Creoles no more dominate Cuba than they dominate Louisiana. They have been forced low; the Cubans and their Spanish masters hate and shun them. Creoles never dominated Cuba nor even so much as won political

---

21. Probably a drink from the fruit of the calabash tree.
22. Narangada may be naranjilla, the richly flavored acid fruit of the naranja (orange).
23. The meaning may be that the Conquistadores brought conjugal ill-will from the Old World.
24. *Cascarón* is the usual word for eggshell.

office. Spaniards, the "foreigners," have always been the political choices.

Cuban Creole culture has managed to survive on its plantations. War did leave Creoles in Cuba one thing it took from them in Louisiana: slaves.[25] Everywhere else [in the Caribbean], when slaves were freed, they made short work of Creole society. Consider as good examples Santo Domingo, Haiti, and the French colonies of Guadeloupe and Martinique.[26] In the first two, Negroes drove the Creoles out. In Martinique the Creoles are likewise headed for destruction. In Cuba, Negroes remain slaves and Creoles maintain their culture unspoiled by Negroes.

What lies behind the downfall of Creoles on Martinique? Female mulattoes. Their existence shows the weakness of Creole men for Negro women, their former slaves. Dark-skinned beauties, offspring of Creole-Negro unions, inherited the warmth and the well-developed figures of their mothers as well as something of the elegance and advanced intellectual development of European fathers. Then, just as their black mothers proved seductive to their fathers, so must mulatto daughters and their undeniably profound beauty prove all the more seductive to Creole men.

Mulattoes thus displaced the aristocratic element in the [Spanish] colonies. White women remain the crown of society, true, but in the smallest number. The mass of female Creoles are dark.

In general, whites and mulattoes avoid one another in society and private life, interacting only in business. Female mulattoes live as parasites on whites. Yet, because born higher (even though bastards), mulattoes consider themselves better than lowly black Negroes and spurn marriage to them. They look longingly upward at white Creole men, the cultured and well-to-do element. The social standing of the men, however, prevents their legitimate union with mulattoes. But the men, attracted by seductive charms, seek the company of these women. You can readily imagine what the lives of women must be, in consequence, on these Creole islands. Such mulatto baggage rarely marry. They constitute their own society, and the members—merry, contented, easily satisfied, spare of diet, temperate of drink—live a life devoted to coquettishness and love in their definition of paradise. On Martinique, two or three children of every four hundred are legitimate. Martinique is the paradise of apples and the daughters of Eve, where the archangel of the flaming sword never meddles.

25. Probably the Ten Years War (1868–1878) in Cuba is meant.
26. Perhaps Hesse-Wartegg's reference to Santo Domingo (Dominican Republic) alludes to the expulsion of the Spanish in 1821. His mention of Haiti probably refers to the expulsion of whites in 1804, when Dessalines, an ex-slave, proclaimed himself emperor.

I could say more about life on Martinique, plenty to delight and amuse but (with respect to decency) at the same time *sad*. This is not the place to tell such tales. In the much better situation on the Danish St. Thomas, the two races keep their distance, to the good fortune of both. Likewise on British Jamaica: a model in this regard. Wherever whites mingle with Negroes—Mexico, Peru, Central America—whites incline to the ways of the lower races without those races taking a notable step up in civilization. Unfortunately, the women especially do not rise. They remain on the lowest levels of society in the land of the Creoles.

A hot and tropical climate, indolence, a lack of purposeful action, and the absence of a life of the mind contribute to the sad state among Creoles. But mulattoes and quadroons are the chief problem. If Creole men had the strength to resist them, Creoles would enjoy better prospects than the one they face now: RUIN.

29. The Mouths of the Mississippi

Luxurious gardens and orange groves, and plantations of sugar and rice extend almost without interruption along the great river for sixty to seventy miles below New Orleans. Then the expanses of delta begin, too low even for rice and therefore useless. The river widens to a lake of several miles across. In effect the river ends by branching in several directions. The easternmost branch divides again, once, several miles below the first. The river thus diverges into several *"passes"* on the delta, each emptying into the Gulf. Here they are, beginning at the northeast:

> Pass a l'Outre
> Northeast Pass
> Southeast Pass
> South Pass
> Southwest Pass

In the Gulf the infamous banks or *"bars"* of Mississippi mud lie square in front of the mouths of these passes: obstacles to be removed. They arise because the river loses declivity and therefore speed, and cannot carry farther the load of sediment. With its last momentum, the river spreads its water slowly over the heavier salt water of the Gulf. Whereupon the bits of earth and sand sink and become the bars that so threaten shipping.

River water, while thus being cleaned, travels a distance past the mouth without mixing into the Gulf. Saltwater green comes to light only in the wake of steamships: churned to the top by wheels or screws. The Gulf's waters, for their part, remain below the river's because of specific gravity but penetrate upstream with the tides as far as New Orleans.

Bars grow most during high water because the river carries the most sediment into the Gulf then. In addition, *"mudlumps"* change the configuration of the bars. These conical mounds often form in a few hours into an obstacle to shipping. Today the pilot finds depth for a ship of the greatest draft; tomorrow in the same place, too little for a ship of the least. The day after tomorrow the cone of mud may have crumpled and disappeared, while elsewhere lumps rise and accumulate gradually into islands. I assume that these Mississippi shores—long, narrow strips of land—took shape in this way.

Mudlumps—how do they form? According to one explanation, as lava and steam seek ways out of Earth's interior, so gases formed by the rotting and fermentation of organic matter erupt in the riverbed, forming cones as they escape. It is likelier, especially when the river runs high, that masses of water exert pressure on the thin layer of gray and watery mud beneath the lax and uncertain surface of the bottom, forcing the mud to seek outlets [as if being squeezed until it squirts out the weakest place]. Lumps, like miniature volcanoes, occur where mud escapes.[1] Cones of them soon wash away in moving water. In calm places they grow and grow as mud and sand accumulate on them. They become the advance guard as it were for land moving in behind and among them. Hence the continual and considerable variations in depth, imperiling navigation.

For centuries up to the present, therefore, ships have needed pilots when negotiating the navigable Southwest and Northeast passes. Consequently, little port towns have risen on marshy, reedy, unstable land along bayous—towns with pilot boats and lifesaving apparatus. Several lighthouses have been built at the mouths of passes. "The Balize," a small settlement on Northeast Pass, even gained importance by becoming a port-of-entry, where ships often had to wait weeks before they could clear the bar and proceed to New Orleans itself. The French fortified the site and built an arsenal. The great *"hurricane"* of 1870 smashed the place and carried everything off. The old port-of-entry has lost importance.[2] Its role has passed to Pilot Town, the village on Southwest Pass. The American government maintains customs houses for incoming ships at Southwest Pass and Pass a l'Outre.

Efforts of many kinds to deepen the mouths have failed.[3] Those cannot be of interest to my readers. The latest, however, has been the most successful. The St. Louis engineer, Captain James B. Eads, suggested it after much study of the mouths of the Danube and else-

1. Nothing like the lumps occurs anywhere else on Earth. Theories include volcanic action, gas and oil bubbling up, and upheavals of the kind that produce mountains and underground rivers. Hesse-Wartegg favors the one held by "many geologists," that sediment weighs upon soft clays beneath, and "the clays 'flow' under this pressure and break through the surface" (Kane, *Deep Delta Country,* 133).

2. "Today the Balize [once a village of 800 and the cynosure of Mississippi shipping and pilotage] is no longer marked on most maps. The Delta has reclaimed it from man. All that remain are a patch of reeds only slightly higher than the surrounding wastes, and a narrow waterway overgrown with wild grass. The former path of empire has become a stagnant ditch" (ibid., 124).

3. In one effort the surface of the bar would be agitated "in the hope that the current would carry away the loosened mud and thus deepen the channel" (Sinclair, *Port of New Orleans,* 174).

where.[4] Embankments along the river, "*jetties,*" now create a man-made extension of the river into the Gulf.

Except for the last three and a half miles, the width of South Pass remains the same from the point of divergence, the "Head of the Passes," to the point of exit into the Gulf. Observations for this purpose indicate that above the last three and a half miles shores remain the same, subject to no changes. Along those last miles, a constant addition of sediment occurs together with an unfailing extension of shoreline—eight inches a day, on average.

The river thus builds as it were its own jetties, two natural strips of land that now accompany the river 100 miles into the Gulf. That is, when the river has escaped the shores that hem it in, it slows and at a rate in proportion to the rate of slowing, loses its cargo of sediment. The sediment settles on the bottom, except in the center of the current, where greater speed carries it along. In calm water, to the right and left, sediment collects along shores and extends them, as already noted, eight inches a day into the Gulf.

Hence the question of particles still suspended and moving in the current. How much farther does the river carry them? Declivity stops at the true mouth. Water advances from there by inertia alone. Slowing to a halt in the Gulf, it can no longer bear sediment, which sinks. There rise the banks or bars.

According to precise observations by General Humphreys, the river can move sediment three miles beyond the mouth.[5] A bar, in fact, occurs three miles beyond the mouth. Were man to hasten natural processes by helping the river extend its shores into the Gulf, the water would be kept together for the length of the artificial shores. Current would then be maintained and with it the power to carry sediment. Instead of three miles out from the natural mouth, the bar would be deposited three from the man-made one. Push that mouth seven miles into the Gulf: the bar will occur ten miles from the present, true

---

4. Kane, *Deep Delta Country,* 135–43, narrates most concisely the story of Eads and his jetties. See also Dabney, *One Hundred Years,* 272–73. The fuller story is in Florence Dorsey, *Road to the Sea: James B. Eads and the Mississippi River,* 166–223. In *A History of the Jetties at the Mouth of the Mississippi River* (1881), E. L. Corthell gives a contemporary account of Eads's work. Corthell, a civil engineer, was "Chief Assistant and Resident Engineer During Their Construction" (title page). The book's 384 pages show how Hesse-Wartegg has simplified a complex subject. See also Mathews, *Remaking the Mississippi,* 102–50. For Hesse-Wartegg on Eads Bridge in St. Louis, see chapter 1 above and note 2 there.

5. Captain Andrew Atkinson Humphreys wrote, with Lieutenant Henry L. Abbot, *Report upon the Physics and Hydraulics of the Mississippi River.* Humphreys, a Civil War topographical engineer, opposed Eads and his theories (Dabney, *One Hundred Years,* 273). Humphreys' attack was "the most violent" of several against Eads (Dorsey, *Road to the Sea,* 172–73). See also Corthell, *Mississippi Jetties,* 41–49.

mouth. Ten miles out into the Gulf is so deep that a bar would not appear for hundreds of years.

This theory has often been verified. On it Captain Eads based his proposal to Congress for eliminating bars at the mouth of the Mississippi. He suggested specifically the mouth of Southwest Pass. At that time, only that pass would accommodate large ships; people hesitated to expose it to a project of uncertain outcome. Eads was ordered to build jetties at South Pass, running at that time (1875) a depth of seven to nine feet. Thus the shores have been extended artificially by two jetties or embankments. Built on the bed of the river and out into the Gulf, they extend the natural shores at about 1,000 feet apart and parallel.

Let us consider their construction. They were done out of fascines and wickerwork, the only suitable constituents, because river-bottom mud lacks the solidity to sustain stone walls. As for wooden jetties, or the ones built on pilots [or piles], they stand in peril of attack and destruction by wood-devouring worms, "*tenedoes*."[6] The pests have already begun their dirty work even on the wicker bundles of jetties in the river. It may be necessary to coat the bundles with concrete.

When building these jetties, "*pilots*" came first, driven into the bottom along the line of jetty to follow.[7] Next a tug towed into place the prefabricated "mattresses" of wicker, each seventy feet long and forty wide. These became the foundation, sunk by large stones to apply equal pressure at all points. A second, narrower mattress followed on top of the first, a third on the second, and so forth until the wall reached about to the surface. Pegs and stones anchored each to the other as well as to the bottom. Boulders at the base further reinforced the whole. (More to come.) A layer of earth to each side now: another reinforcement. The river, thus enclosed, must also be deepened. Short crossdams, so-called "spurs," created the depth in a surprising fashion. That is, spurs fastened to the jetty project into the river. Sediment quickly fills the space along the jetty between two spurs. The consequent narrowing speeds up the water. This acceleration gradually deepens the bed.[8]

---

6. This unclear reference could be a misspelling of Tenebrio, a family of beetles, some of which attack wood. See Donald J. Borror and Richard E. White, *A Field Guide to the Insects of America North of Mexico,* 186–88. No similar word occurs in literature about the jetty. Hesse-Wartegg, without benefit of historical distance, discusses a significant topic many later authors have failed to discuss: the jetties' durability.

7. Hesse-Wartegg several times uses *pilot* in the sense meant here. As a German and an English word, it would seem plausible for the thing indicated; but dictionaries assign it no such meaning, nor does it occur in the literature. He might mean it as the equivalent of *pile,* but the German for *pile* is not usually *Pilot*.

8. Hesse-Wartegg's description of the jetties and their effects, though briefer,

One thing more. Jetties' ends out in the Gulf must be reinforced to withstand waves. Wide caps, reinforcements, slope gradually into the water.

According to the latest reports to reach me [in Europe] from America, the jetties' purpose has already been achieved.[9] The bar has been eliminated, a navigable channel created: 200 to 300 feet wide and a constant 30 feet deep. New Orleans has been made accessible to the largest oceangoing vessels, its vital interests thus secured. The cost up to now of jetties has been $4 million.

Another question arises. Will they last? Flimsy wickerwork cannot long tolerate the flow of the river, nor contain its outward pressure, nor yet endure tempestuous waters that rise in this part of the Gulf. And the worst threat of all has appeared, the woodworm, the most dangerous enemy to wickerwork and all wooden materials. Inspections already reveal damage on an important length of the jetties. In some places considerable sections have been eaten away. It must be asked: how long before the structure is ruined?

The jetties face two other threats. Because of increased depth between jetties, currents may undermine them and they may crumble. (2) The flimsy wickerwork may be unable to bear long the winter storms of the Gulf and may be gradually torn away. Therefore, the authorities cannot be urged too much. *Strengthen the jetties! Reinforce them thoroughly!*

Besides that admonition I have nothing but congratulations for the authorities and New Orleans. The mouths of the Mississippi have been opened. If after this excellent work a rational and well-applied system of navigation, including canals, can be brought to the valley, a crying necessity will have been met for the renaissance of the South. Moreover, this improvement will continue to contribute to the prosperity of the prairie states and the West.

---

compares favorably with Corthell's in *Mississippi Jetties,* 147–53. Corthell uses the older *willow* and *willow work* for what I have translated as *wicker* and *wickerwork.*

9. Hesse-Wartegg must have procured these reports in Europe when he was finishing this book. He probably left the South in March of 1879. In July, Eads realized the requisite thirty-foot depth of a clear channel from Head of Passes to the Gulf.

30. To Mobile

I have taken many railway journeys in my several years' travels around this continent. But scarcely another etched itself deeper in memory than the one from New Orleans to the capital of Alabama. (How poetic this name Alabama, how euphonious and scintillating compared to America's Smithsville and Brownsville! Alabama, an Indian word, means "We shall rest here.")[1] Going to the station of the Mobile Railroad on the levee in New Orleans, I knew I had ended my Mississippi-valley travels. I wanted the most direct route to New York and to return to Europe from there. But in America, fresh surprises never fail, day after day! The traveler covers hundreds and thousands of miles. Hundreds and thousands more stretch ahead, unseen, unknown, so new, so exotic. The traveler cannot keep his portfolio shut. Involuntarily he slips back into what he has pursued for months: the exciting enterprise of study and observation. When the pilgrim to America finds himself once more on the grand and open ocean, only then does peace of mind, so sorely missed, come to him at last. Only then is he sure no herds of buffalo will cross his path, no alligators shadow him, no flaming steamboat loaded with cotton demand his attention. He rests assured he can enjoy a few days of absolute peace and quiet—impossible as long as he remains on American soil.

People may call this country the home of conformity and repetition. The opposite is true. My journey to Mobile and from there through the south-Atlantic states to the North confirms it. The train's every mile and every stop presented new scenes and things I had never seen before. The journey by rail between New Orleans and Mobile, being one of the sights of the South, offers 141 miles of cypress swamps and virgin forests, charming little seaside resorts, Negro villages with names that betray Indian or French origins, and dramatic river crossings. The train also crosses miles-wide inlets from the Gulf—goes right through them!

The first few miles follow the sliver of land that divides two salt lakes, Borgne from Pontchartrain. Tall, ancient cypresses, branches

---

1. According to the *Encyclopedia of Southern History,* the name comes from an Indian word meaning "thicket clearers" (s.v. "Alabama").

trailing the characteristic moss, abide in dim swamps also covered with moss. Here and there, banks of reeds spring up. Turtles, snakes, and alligators—and a few water birds, now here, now there—animate the gloom. Swamp and scenery extend to the Rigolets, Lake Pontchartrain's outlet to the Gulf.[2] Miles of wooden bridge span the river here. A gap of 100 feet at the center: open, it lets ships pass; closed, trains. A flagpole rising from dark walls announces Fort Pike to the northeast. Even after we go over the bridge we cannot be sure whether we are on a water-indented part of the mainland or a lake strewn with islands. The train hurries through green land, nothing but savannah, water, and primeval forest. The expanses look to us like free-floating islands. Lagoons have the name *"trembling prairie."*[3] Piles must support the roadbed to prevent the trains' sinking into a water-soaked meadow that floats.[4] Glances through interstices in the forest reveal endless spreads of savannah and water to the north and the island-dotted Gulf to the south. Small houses and plantations surrounded by forest occur in places of elevation.

The train stops at lonely stations, arriving at last at Bay St. Louis, the favorite seaside resort among the Creole community of New Orleans. Attractive villas on either side of the tracks. Hotels with wide verandahs. Finally the beach and a number of *"piers,"* or wooden palisades, extending into the Gulf. They have small bathhouses at the far ends. The owner of every villa and cottage, for the simple reason that tides run the extreme from high to low, has built one of the piers of strong stakes and wooden crosspieces. Else when the ebb leaves so much beach high and dry, swimmers would have to go a distance [over disagreeable ground] to reach the water. The unusual setting suggests a Japanese rather than an American resort. The train pauses a few minutes, then proceeds.

Where? Straight into the Gulf? Whoa! Back! The cars race—it's enough to scare us to death—down the beach toward the surf! Yes, we can see on the horizon a tentative strip of land, but ahead, below, behind us nothing but the Gulf's salty waves! I look out the window: waves seem to be breaking on the wheels of the train while the train seems to glide along the surface of the water! We cruise like a boat; we even seem to feel the disagreeable rocking of a boat.

We are on a bridge barely above the water. We can see the bridge not

2. The lake and Gulf are connected by the Rigolets via Lake Borgne.
3. "Quaking surfaces have been found to overlap deep pools of oil in the alluvium" (Kane, *Deep Delta Country,* xix).
4. "There is just enough solidity to support piling, and thus piling is what every man-made thing here is built upon; otherwise it must of necessity float" (Sinclair, *Port of New Orleans,* 2–3).

at all. (Winds must raise waves that a train cannot pass, so low is this bridge.) It began as a double row of piles, fashioned from the largest and stoutest firs cut hereabouts. Often the piles had to be set by driving as much as eighty feet into the bottom. Beams fastened by pegs to the tops of piles join the piles one to another in each row. Rails laid across the row complete the *"trestle-work"* bridge. Quite the simple structure, yet over two miles long. Should one or another pile give way, the train will plunge into the water! All hold and we happily gain the other side—of course, back to the prairie of jelly, but at least to land!

At Mississippi City, Ocean Spring, Biloxi, Pascagoula, and other, places, we must traverse similar structures perhaps equally long: bridges to span arms of the Gulf that reach inland. Half the time on land, half on water, this amphibious role earned our hurrying locomotive the name Steam Alligator rather than Iron Horse. The tall and gloomy primeval forest accompanied us on the north. Small *"shantytowns"* have taken shape on its edge. Their many steam-powered sawmills cut up those splendid trunks. At last we crossed the border at some nameless point, leaving Mississippi for Alabama, soon to enter Mobile, the capital.

Besides being the capital, this peaceful and downright lovely town of 35,000 is a port, the major one for the abundance of Mississippi and Alabama cotton. No other southern city shows so strikingly the effects of the Civil War. Quiet streets seem dead. In Government Street and others, many beautiful homes of the old, planter aristocracy have been abandoned. Grand hotels are empty, business slack, industries absent. Of the last decade's nineteen large French emporiums, one remains. Only the cotton trade is still here, but the 900,000 bales shipped annually before the war are reduced to barely half. The harbor had been silting up, a principal cause of commercial stagnation. Levees and barricades erected for the war contributed to the loss of depth. Transatlantic ships and even the smaller coasting vessels cannot reach Mobile. They must anchor out in the bay twenty to thirty miles and be loaded by barges.

The national government has thus committed a sin. A seaport must be a seaport or die. Besides, it is the main port of the state. Dredging, blasting, and the removal of wartime impediments would have stimulated not only Mobile, but also Alabama. Furthermore, Mobile could be one of the *nation's* prosperous ports. To begin with, the state constitutes a large hinterland. In addition, railroads and navigable rivers spread into it in all directions from Mobile. Moreover, the nation's chief cotton-growing region lies near, along with northern Alabama's concentration of iron and coal. No doubt Mobile would regain eminence were the harbor made navigable for deep-drawing ships and they were able to dock at the waterfront.

At present, however, Mobile suffers straitened circumstances for the reasons stated, plus repeated epidemics of yellow fever. And now, as a way of eliminating debt, Mobile has followed the example of Memphis and given up corporate status. Mobile has stopped being a city, in other words. A commission of eight, a "port authority of Mobile," has taken the place of city government. The commission can levy taxes for current expenses, but such monies cannot be used to retire debt.

Creditors can do nothing about such measures. Were the issue adjudicated, a federal court would doubtless award creditors every cent that could be raised. Action would end with the decision, however, because it could not be enforced. The Supreme Court of the United States ruled four or five years ago that federal courts do not have power to impose taxes on states, counties, or cities, and therefore have no right to use United States marshals to collect taxes. So where local officials or legislatures refuse to tax for these purposes [of retiring public debt] creditors have no means of obtaining a court order that will settle their claims.

In recent years [in consequence of Mobile's problems] commercial activity in the port has left for Pensacola, a small Florida town. The Louisville, Nashville & Great Southern Railway wants to make Louisville an emporium of the South and in a big step toward the goal, lately chose Pensacola as its southern terminus. A steamship for Havana departs Pensacola's splendid harbor every Saturday; thus the railroad has brought much of Alabama, Tennessee, [and Kentucky] into communication with the Antilles. Pensacola, furthermore, enjoys the largest timber market on the Gulf coast, shipping annually sixty-five to seventy million feet of lumber, six million of logs, and fourteen of lath [or staves].[5] During the winter, 150 to 200 ships lie at anchor in the harbor, to take on this cargo. It is yellow pine, every last foot of it: taken from local forests that extend practically to infinity.

These being mostly national forests, at least two-thirds of the timber has been cut in them. Unfortunately, much has been cut illegally, stolen, that is, by so-called "*logmen*" or timber thieves.[6] They used to take possession of any 160 acres of federal land [by virtue of the Homestead Act.][7] They had to pay an insignificant registration fee, something like $14, and live on the land for five years. They did not respect boundaries, nor do they yet, preferring to seek the largest and choicest

5. This large export of lumber out of Pensacola after the Civil War was in full swing by 1870 (Coulter, *Reconstruction,* 271).
6. Neither Craigie and Hulbert, *Dictionary,* nor Mathews, *Dictionary,* defines *logman* as thief. Ordinarily the word designates a lumberer.
7. Hesse-Wartegg does not say why this "used to" happen. So much land may have been taken by 1880 as to prohibit ready access to "any 160 acres."

trees, wherever they may be. Nine-tenths of the people of [Escambia] county live by the lumber business—as logger, transporter, exporter, or thief.

Mr. J. S. Gainey, special agent of the Department of the Interior, works full-time in prosecuting. Always he faces the ordeal of getting a verdict of guilty, because jurors by and large spend their free time stealing timber. He offers as a prime example the trial of thieves in Pensacola of late. (I have it from the *Belletristisches Journal* of New York.) He brought forty-seven witnesses. The jury found none of the accused guilty. When trials can be moved to Tallahassee or elsewhere in the state, then—and only then—will thieves be convicted.

Settled [by farmers], every inch of the area could be transformed into a garden. Any male over the age of twenty-one can claim 160 acres and, as I have said, need pay only the $14 and live there five years. The sandy soil proves excellent for sweet potatoes and oranges. Ships that come for lumber in winter, go to Quebec in summer. Hence a slack time for business [when farmers might be busy] during the hot months. The climate is described as mild and salubrious.

Pensacola quickly rebuilt its burnt-out business district, seventy-five commercial establishments having recently gone up in flames. Yet Pensacola seems less than an agreeable place to live. "There are churches enough, and some schools, and two newspapers—but far more saloons of the lowest sort, and gambling halls, frequented by seamen. The waterfront is nothing but a concourse of gambling halls, honky-tonks, keno shops, and houses of ill fame. Banners flying from buildings wave at you the word '*keno*.' You will see them at night, too, and from a distance, illuminated. Only women serve drinks in saloons. Many a seamen spends in one night all he has earned in six months at sea." Thus the *Belletristisches Journal*. It ends with the cliché that follows every description of American cities: "But because of its location, the city has a bright future."

From Mobile the best route to New York crosses Alabama, Tennessee, and Virginia. After several months in the South, I left on that route [probably the Alabama & Great Southern] to return to the North American metropolis.

Bibliography

Ames, Charles Edgar. *Pioneering the Union Pacific.* New York: Appleton-Century-Crofts, 1969.

Arndt, Karl R. J., and May E. Olson. *German-American Newspapers and Periodicals, 1732–1955: History and Bibliography.* Heidelberg: Quelle & Meyer, 1961.

Arvin, Newton. *Longfellow: His Life and Work.* Boston: Little, Brown, 1962.

Asbury, Herbert. *The French Quarter: An Informal History of the New Orleans Underworld.* 1936. Reprint. New York: Capricorn Books, 1968.

Athearn, Robert G. *In Search of Canaan: Black Migration to Kansas, 1879–1880.* Lawrence: Regents Press of Kansas, 1978.

Atyeo, Don. *Blood and Guts: Violence in Sports.* New York: Paddington, 1979.

Ayers, Edward L. *Vengeance and Justice: Crime and Punishment in the 19th-Century American South.* New York: Oxford University Press, 1984.

Barbé-Marbois, Marquis François de. *The History of Louisiana.* No translator named. Philadelphia: Carey & Lea, 1830.

Baughman, James P. "The Evolution of Rail-Water Systems of Transportation in the Gulf Southwest, 1836–1890." *Journal of Southern History* 34 (1968): 357–81.

Bettelheim, Bruno. *Freud and Man's Soul.* New York: Knopf, 1983.

Board of Experts on Yellow Fever and Cholera. *Conclusions . . . [on] the . . . Epidemic of 1878.* Washington: Judd & Detweiler, 1879.

Boatner, Mark Mayo. *The Civil War Dictionary.* New York: David McKay, 1959.

Bonner, James C. "Plantation Architecture of the Lower South on the Eve of the Civil War." *Journal of Southern History* 11 (1945): 370–88.

Borror, Donald J., and Richard E. White. *A Field Guide to the Insects of America North of Mexico.* Boston: Houghton Mifflin, 1970.

Boskin, Joseph. *Sambo: The Rise and Demise of an American Jester.* New York: Oxford University Press, 1986.

Botkin, B[enjamin] A. *A Treasury of Mississippi River Folklore.* New York: Crown, 1955.

Boyle, James E. *Cotton and the New Orleans Cotton Exchange: A Century of Commercial Evolution.* Garden City, N.Y.: Country Life, 1934.

Brown, Maria Ward. *The Life of Dan Rice.* Long Branch, N. J.: The Author, 1901.

Brown, William G. *The Lower South in American History.* New York: Macmillan, 1902.

Büchmann, Georg. *Geflügelte Worte.* 32d ed. Edited by Gunther Haupt and Winfried Hofmann. Berlin: Haude & Spenersche, 1972.

Bull, Jacqueline P. "The General Merchant in the Economic History of the New South." *Journal of Southern History* 18 (1952): 37–59.

Cable, George W. *The Creoles of Louisiana.* New York: Scribner's, 1884.

Capers, Gerald M., Jr. *The Biography of a River Town: Memphis.* Chapel Hill: University of North Carolina Press, 1939.

———. "Yellow Fever in Memphis in the 1870s." *Mississippi Valley Historical Review* 24 (1937–1938): 483–502.

Carter, Hodding. *The Angry Scar: The Story of Reconstruction.* Garden City, N.Y.: Doubleday, 1959.

———. *Lower Mississippi.* New York: Farrar & Rinehart (Rivers of America), 1942.

Cash, W[ilbur] J. *The Mind of the South.* New York: Knopf, 1941.

Castellanos, Henry C. *New Orleans as It Was.* New Orleans: Graham & Son, 1895.

Chambers, Julius. *The Mississippi River and Its Wonderful Valley.* New York: Putnam's, 1910.

Charvet, P[atrick] E. *A Literary History of France: The Nineteenth Century.* London: Ernest Benn, 1967.

Child, Mrs. [Lydia Maria]. *An Appeal in Favor of That Class of Americans Called Africans.* 1833. Reprint. New York: Arno, 1968.

Childs, Marquis W. *Mighty Mississippi: Biography of a River.* New Haven and New York: Ticknor & Fields, 1982.

Clark, Dan Elbert. *The West in American History.* New York: Crowell, 1937.

Clark, John G. "New Orleans and the River." *Louisiana History* 8 (1967): 117–35.

Clark, Thomas D. *Frontier America.* New York: Scribner's, 1959.

———. "The Mississippi River in History." *Mississippi Quarterly* 16 (1963): 181–90.

———. *Travels in the New South: A Bibliography.* 2 vols. Norman: University of Oklahoma Press, 1961.

Cohn, David L. *The Life and Times of King Cotton.* New York: Oxford University Press, 1956.

Commager, Henry Steele, ed. *Documents of American History.* 9th ed. New York: Appleton-Century-Crofts, 1973.

Connell, Evan S. *Son of the Morning Star: Custer and the Little Bighorn.* San Francisco: North Point, 1984.

Corthell, E[lmer] L. *A History of the Jetties at the Mouth of the Mississippi River.* New York: Wiley, 1881.

Coulter, E[llis] Merton. *The South During Reconstruction, 1865–1877.* Baton Rouge: Louisiana State University Press, 1947.

Craigie, William A., and James R. Hulbert. *A Dictionary of American English.* 4 vols. Chicago: University of Chicago Press, 1944.

Dabney, Thomas E. *One Hundred Great Years: The Story of the Times-Picayune.* Baton Rouge: Louisiana State University Press, 1944.

Davis, Clyde Brion. *The Arkansas.* New York: Farrar & Rinehart (The Rivers of America), 1940.

Davis, Edwin Adams. *Louisiana: A Narrative History.* 2nd ed. Baton Rouge: Claitor's Book Store, 1965.
Davis, Susan Lawrence. *Authentic History of the Ku Klux Klan, 1865–1877.* New York: Susan Lawrence Davis, 1924.
Dayton, Fred E. *Steamboat Days.* 1925. Reprint. New York: Library Editions, 1970.
Deckert, Emil. "New Orleans, the Mississippi, and the Delta Through a German's Eyes." Edited and translated by Frederic Trautmann. *Louisiana History* 25 (1984): 79–98.
Deiler, J[ohn] Hanno. *The Settlement of the German Coast of Louisiana and the Creoles of German Descent.* 1909. Reprint. Baltimore: Geneological Publishing Company, 1970.
Destler, Chester M. "David Dickson's 'System of Farming' and the Agricultural Revolution in the Deep South, 1850–1885." *Agricultural History* 31 (1957): 30–39.
Devèze, Jean. *An Enquiry into . . . Epidemic Disease . . . in Philadelphia . . . 1793.* Philadelphia: Parent, 1794.
Dickens, Charles. *American Notes.* 1842. Reprint. London: Oxford University Press, 1957.
Dodd, Donald B., and Wynelle S. Dodd. *Historical Statistics of the South, 1790–1970.* University: University of Alabama Press, 1973.
Dodd, William E. *The Cotton Kingdom.* New Haven: Yale University Press, 1919.
Dorsey, Florence. *Master of the Mississippi: Henry M. Shreve.* Boston: Houghton Mifflin, 1941.
―――. *Road to the Sea: James B. Eads and the Mississippi River.* New York: Rinehart, 1947.
Du Bois, William E. B. *Black Reconstruction.* 1935. Reprint. Cleveland: World Publishing Company (Meridian Books), 1964.
Ellis, L. Tuffly. "The New Orleans Cotton Exchange: The Formative Years, 1871–1880." *Journal of Southern History* 39 (1973): 545–64.
Faust, Patricia L., ed. *Historical Times Illustrated Encyclopedia of the Civil War.* New York: Harper & Row, 1986.
Fitz-Barnard, Lawrence. *Fighting Sports.* London: Odhams [1921].
Fleming, Walter L. "Immigration to the Southern States." *Political Science Quarterly* 20 (1905): 278–94.
Foner, Eric. *Reconstruction: America's Unfinished Revolution, 1863–1877.* New York: Harper & Row, 1988.
Fox, John A. *Mississippi River Flood Problem: How the Floods Can Be Prevented.* Mississippi River Levee Association, 1914.
Frank, Arthur DeWitt. *The Development of the Federal Program of Flood Control on the Mississippi River.* New York: Columbia University Press, 1930.
Franklin, John Hope. *Reconstruction: After the Civil War.* Chicago: University of Chicago Press, 1961.
Gaines, Francis Pendelton. *The Southern Plantation: A Study in the Development*

and the Accuracy of a Tradition. 1924. Reprint. Gloucester, Mass.: Peter Smith, 1962.

Ganzel, Dewey. "Twain, Travel Books, and *Life on the Mississippi.*" *American Literature* 34 (1962): 40–55.

Gayarré, Charles. "A Louisiana Sugar Plantation of the Old Regime." *Harper's New Monthly Magazine,* March 1887, 606–21.

Genovese, Eugene D. "Ulrich Bonnell Phillips & His Critics." In Phillips, *American Negro Slavery,* vii-xxi.

"A German Traveler on the Mississippi." Review of *Mississippi-Fahrten,* by Ernst von Hesse-Wartegg. *New York Times,* 30 January 1882.

Gilbert, Felix. *A European Past: Memoirs 1905–1945.* New York: Norton, 1988.

Graham, Philip. *Showboats: The History of an American Institution.* Austin: University of Texas Press, 1951.

Green, Fletcher M. "The South in Reconstruction, 1865–1880." In Clark, *Travels,* vol. 1.

Hammond, M[athew] B. *The Cotton Industry: An Essay in American Economic History.* New York: Macmillan (for the American Economic Association), 1897.

Hauk, Minnie. *Memories of a Singer.* 1925. Reprint. New York: Arno, 1977.

Havighurst, Walter. *Voices on the River: The Story of the Mississippi Waterways.* New York: Macmillan, 1964.

Henry, Robert Selph. *The Story of Reconstruction.* Indianapolis: Bobbs-Merrill, 1938.

Herring, Harriet L. "The Clement Attachment: An Episode of Reconstruction Industrial History." *Journal of Southern History* 4 (1938): 185–98.

Hesse-Wartegg, Ernst von. *Nord-Amerika: Seine Städte und Naturwunder, sein Land und seine Leute.* Leipzig: Weigel, 1880.

———. *Prairie-Fahrten.* Leipzig: Weigel, 1878.

Highsmith, Richard M., Jr., J. Granville Jensen, and Robert D. Rudd. *Conservation in the United States.* Chicago: Rand McNally, 1962.

Hildreth, Peggy Bassett. "Early Red Cross: The Howard Association of New Orleans." *Louisiana History* 20 (1979): 49–75.

Hole, Christina. *English Sports and Pastimes.* London: Batsford, 1949.

Howard, Perry H. *Political Tendencies in Louisiana.* Rev. ed. Baton Rouge: Louisiana State University Press, 1971.

Huber, Leonard V. *Advertisements of Lower Mississippi River Steamboats, 1812–1890.* West Barrington, R.I.: Steamship Historical Society, 1959.

Humphreys, A[ndrew] A., and H[enry] L. Abbot. *Report upon the Physics and Hydraulics of the Mississippi River.* . . . Philadelphia: Lippincott, 1861.

Hunter, Louis C. *Steamboats on the Western Rivers: An Economic and Technological History.* Cambridge: Harvard University Press, 1949.

Jackson, Joy J. *New Orleans in the Gilded Age: Politics and Urban Progress, 1880–1896.* Baton Rouge: Louisiana State University Press (for the Louisiana Historical Association), 1969.

Johnson, Emory R., et al. *History of Domestic and Foreign Commerce of the United States.* Vol. 1. Washington, D.C.: Carnegie Institute, 1915.

Jordan, Weymouth T. *Hugh Davis and His Alabama Plantation.* University: University of Alabama Press, 1948.
Judge, Joseph. "New Orleans and Her River." *National Geographic,* February 1971, 151–87.
Kane, Harnett T. *The Bayous of Louisiana.* New York: Morrow, 1943.
———. *Deep Delta Country.* New York: Duell, Sloan & Pearce, 1944.
———. "Land of Louisiana Sugar Kings." *National Geographic,* April 1958, 531–67.
———. *Queen New Orleans: City by the River.* New York: Morrow, 1949.
Keating, J[ohn] M. *History of the Yellow Fever.* Memphis, Tenn.: Howard Association, 1879.
Keir, Malcolm. *The March of Commerce.* Pageant of America, vol. 4. New Haven: Yale University Press, 1927.
Kelly, Howard A. *Walter Reed and Yellow Fever.* New, rev. ed. Baltimore: Medical Standard Book Company, 1906.
King, Edward. *The Great South: A Record of Journeys.* 2 vols. 1875. Reprint. New York: Burt Franklin, 1969.
King, Grace. *Creole Families of New Orleans.* New York: Macmillan, 1921.
———. *New Orleans: The Place and the People.* New York: Macmillan, 1892.
Klibanoff, Hank. "Stroke by Stroke." Review of *Mississippi Solo,* by Eddy L. Harris. Philadelphia *Inquirer,* 6 November 1988.
Kruse, Horst H. *Mark Twain and "Life on the Mississippi."* Amherst: University of Massachusetts Press, 1981.
Kunitz, Stanley J., and Vineta Colby. *European Authors, 1000–1900.* New York: Wilson, 1967.
Lantz, Herman R. *A Community in Search of Itself: A Case Study of Cairo, Illinois.* Carbondale: Southern Illinois University Press, 1972.
Loewenberg, Bert James. "Efforts of the South to Encourage Immigration, 1865–1900." *South Atlantic Quarterly* 33 (1934): 363–85.
Lowrey, Walter M. "The Engineers and the Mississippi." *Louisiana History* 5 (1964): 233–55.
Marquette, C. L., ed. "Letters of a Yankee Sugar Planter [Daniel Thompson]." *Journal of Southern History* 6 (1940): 521–46.
Mathews, John Lathrop. *Remaking the Mississippi.* Boston: Houghton Mifflin, 1909.
Mathews, Mitford. *A Dictionary of Americanisms on Historical Principles.* 2 vols. Chicago: University of Chicago Press, 1951.
Matthes, Gerard H. "Paradoxes of the Mississippi." *Scientific American,* April 1951, 18–23.
Mitchell, Broadus. *The Rise of the Cotton Mills in the South.* Studies in Historical and Political Science, no. 2. Baltimore: Johns Hopkins University Press, 1921.
Morison, Samuel Eliot. *The Oxford History of the American People.* New York: Oxford University Press, 1965.
Morison, Samuel Eliot, and Henry Steele Commager. *The Growth of the Amer-*

ican Republic. 3rd ed. 2 vols. New York: Oxford University Press, 1942. 7th ed. (with William E. Leuchtenburg), 1980.

Morrison, John H. *History of American Steam Navigation*. New York: Stephen Daye, 1958.

Mott, Frank Luther. *A History of American Magazines*. Vols. 2 and 3. Cambridge: Harvard University Press, 1938.

Naipaul, V. S. "A Reporter at Large: The Old South." *New Yorker.* 1988. 3 pts. 24 October, 56–76, 89–102; 31 October, 60–78; 7 November, 109–32.

Nau, John Fredrick. *The German People of New Orleans, 1850–1900*. Leiden: E. J. Brill, 1958.

Nevins, Allan. *American Social History as Recorded by British Travellers*. New York: Holt, 1923. New ed. *America Through British Eyes*. New York: Oxford University Press, 1948.

New Orleans Progressive Union. *New Orleans—What to See and How to See It: A Standard Guide*. New Orleans, 1913.

Nichols, George Ward. "Down the Mississippi." *Harper's New Monthly Magazine*, November 1870, 835–45.

Painter, Nell Irvin. *Exodusters: Black Migration to Kansas After Reconstruction*. New York: Knopf, 1977.

Parsons, Coleman O. "Down the Mighty River with Mark Twain." *Mississippi Quarterly* 22 (1969): 1–18.

———. "Steamboating as Seen by Passengers and River Men, 1875–1884." *Mississippi Quarterly* 24 (1970–1971): 19–34.

Patterson, Carolyn Bennett. "Mardi Gras in New Orleans." *National Geographic,* November 1960, 726–32.

Paxson, Frederic L. *History of the American Frontier, 1763–1893*. Boston: Houghton Mifflin, 1924.

Percy, William A. *Lanterns on the Levee*. New York: Knopf, 1941.

Phillips, Edward Hake. "The Gulf Coast Rice Industry." *Agricultural History* 25 (1951): 91–96.

Phillips, Ulrich Bonnell. *American Negro Slavery*. 1918. Reprint. Baton Rouge: Louisiana State University Press, 1966.

———. *Life and Labor in the Old South*. New York: Grosset & Dunlap, 1929.

———. "Plantations with Slave Labor and Free." *Agricultural History* 12 (1938): 77–95.

Powell, John H. *Bring Out Your Dead: The Great Plague of Yellow Fever in Philadelphia in 1793*. Philadelphia: University of Pennsylvania Press, 1949.

Price, Willard. "The Lower Mississippi." *National Geographic,* November 1960, 681–725.

Prichard, Walter. "The Effects of the Civil War on the Louisiana Sugar Industry." *Journal of Southern History* 5 (1939): 313–32.

Pridgen, Tim. *Courage: The Story of Modern Cockfighting*. Boston: Little, Brown, 1938.

Rankin, David C. "The Origins of Black Leadership in New Orleans During Reconstruction." *Journal of Southern History* 40 (1974): 417–40.

Riegel, Robert E. *America Moves West*. Rev. ed. New York: Holt, 1947.

Ripley, Eliza. *Social Life in Old New Orleans: Being Recollections of My Girlhood.* New York: Appleton, 1912.
Rousey, Dennis C. "Black Policemen in New Orleans During Reconstruction." *Historian* 49 (1987): 223–43.
Rowland, Dunbar. *Encyclopedia of Mississippi History.* 2 vols. Madison, Wis.: Brant, 1907.
Saloutos, Theodore. "Southern Agriculture and the Problems of Readjustment, 1865–1877." *Agricultural History* 30 (1956): 58–76.
Schmidt, Paul. "River vs. Town: Mark Twain's 'Old Times on the Mississippi.'" *Nineteenth Century Fiction* 15 (1960): 95–111.
Schmier, Louis. "The Letters and Southern Jewish History." In *Reflections of Southern Jewry: The Letters of Charles Wessolowsky, 1878–1879,* edited by Louis Schmier, 157–75. [Macon, Ga.]: Mercer University Press, 1982.
Scott, George Ryley. *The History of Cockfighting.* London: Skilton, n.d.
Searight, Sarah. *New Orleans.* New York: Stein & Day, 1973.
Shannon, Fred A. *The Farmer's Last Frontier: Agriculture 1860–1897.* New York: Farrar & Rinehart, 1945.
Shelton, Jo-Ann. *As the Romans Did: A Source Book in Roman Social History.* New York: Oxford University Press, 1988.
Shugg, Roger. "Survival of the Plantation System in Louisiana." *Journal of Southern History* 3 (1937): 311–25.
Sigafoos, Robert Alan. *Cotton Row to Beale Street: A Business History of Memphis.* Memphis: Memphis State University Press, 1979.
Sinclair, Harold. *The Port of New Orleans.* Garden City, N.Y.: Doubleday, 1942.
Sitterson, J[oseph] Carlyle. *Sugar Country: The Cane Sugar Industry in the South, 1753–1850.* [Lexington]: University of Kentucky Press, 1953.
Somers, Robert. *The Southern States Since the War, 1870–1871.* London: Macmillan, 1871.
"The South from Alligator to Zydeco." Prepublication review of the *Encyclopedia of Southern Culture. U.S. News and World Report,* 3 October 1988, 57–58.
Spalding, Thomas. "Observations on the Method of Planting and Cultivating Sugar-Cane in Georgia and South Carolina." In *Georgia's Disputed Ruins,* edited by E. Merton Coulter, 227–63. Chapel Hill: University of North Carolina Press, 1937.
Stackemann, Julius H. "Ein Negerexodus." *Aus allen Welttheilen* 11 (1880): 129–32.
Stuart, Charles B. *The Naval and Mail Steamers of the United States.* New York: Norton, 1853.
Swearingen, Mack. "Thirty Years of a Mississippi Plantation: Charles Whitmore of 'Montpelier.'" *Journal of Southern History* 1 (1935): 198–211.
Tallant, Robert. *Mardi Gras.* Garden City, N. Y.: Doubleday, 1948.
Taylor, Joe Gray. *Louisiana Reconstructed, 1863–1877.* Baton Rouge: Louisiana State University Press, 1974.
Thompson, John R. "Southern Sketches." *Appleton's Journal.* 1870. 4 pts. 2 July, 12–13; 9 July, 44–45; 23 July 108–10; 6 August, 164–66.

Tregle, Joseph C. "Early New Orleans Society: A Reappraisal." *Journal of Southern History* 8 (1952): 20–36.
Trelease, Allen W. *White Terror: The Ku Klux Klan Conspiracy and Southern Reconstruction.* New York: Harper & Row, 1971.
Twain, Mark. *Life on the Mississippi.* Stormfield Edition. New York: Harper, 1929.
———. *Mark Twain, Business Man.* Edited by Samuel Charles Webster. Boston: Little, Brown, 1946.
———. *Mark Twain–Howells Letters: The Correspondence . . . 1872–1910.* Vol. 1. Edited by Henry Nash Smith and William M. Gibson. Cambridge: Harvard University Press, 1960.
United States. Bureau of the Census. *Historical Statistics of the United States: Colonial Times to 1970.* Washington, D.C.: Government Printing Office, 1975.
———. Department of the Interior. Census Office. *Report on the Social Statistics of Cities.* Pt. 2. Vol. 19 of *Tenth Census of the United States.* Washington, D.C.: Government Printing Office, 1887.
———. Treasury Department. Bureau of Statistics. *Report on the Internal Commerce of the United States: Commerce of the Mississippi and Ohio Rivers.* Washington, D.C.: Government Printing Office, 1888.
Van Hise, Charles Richard. *The Conservation of Natural Resources in the United States.* New York: Macmillan, 1922.
Vietmeyer, Noel D. "Our 90-Year War with the Boll Weevil Isn't Over." *Smithsonian,* August 1982, 60–68.
Vincent, Charles. *Black Legislators in Louisiana During Reconstruction.* Baton Rouge: Louisiana State University Press, 1976.
Vogeler, E. Jerome. "Cock Doom Makes Everybody Equal." In *Esquire's First Sports Reader,* edited by Herbert Graffis, 274–82. New York: Barnes, 1945.
Wager, Willis. Appendix "Suppressed Books." In Mark Twain, *Life on the Mississippi,* edited by Willis Wager. New York: Heritage, 1944.
Watkins, James L. *King Cotton: A Historical and Statistical Review, 1790–1908.* New York: James L. Watkins & Sons, 1908.
Williamson, A. M. Preface to Hauk, *Memories,* 5–8.
Woodman, Harold D. *King Cotton & His Retainers.* Lexington: University of Kentucky Press, 1968.
Woodward, C[omer] Vann. *Origins of the New South.* Baton Rouge: Louisiana State University Press, 1951.
Work Projects Administration. American Guide Series. *Arkansas: A Guide to the State.* New York: Hastings House, 1941.
———. *Illinois: A Descriptive and Historical Guide.* Chicago: McClurg & Co., 1939.
———. *Indiana: A Guide to the Hoosier State.* New York: Oxford University Press, 1941.
———. *Louisiana: A Guide to the State.* New York: Hastings House, 1941.
———. *Mississippi: A Guide to the Magnolia State.* New York: Viking, 1938.

———. *Missouri: A Guide to the "Show Me" State.* New York: Duell, Sloan & Pearce, 1941.
———. *New Orleans City Guide.* Boston: Houghton Mifflin, 1938.
———. *New York: A Guide to the Empire State.* New York: Oxford University Press, 1940.
———. *Tennessee: A Guide to the State.* New York: Viking, 1939.
Young, Perry. *The Mystick Krew: Chronicles of Comus and His Kin.* New Orleans: Carnival, 1931.
Zeichner, Oscar. "The Transition from Slave to Free Agricultural Labor in the Southern United States." *Agricultural History* 13 (1939): 22–32.

Index

Abeille de la Nouvelle Orleans, newspaper, 161, 188
Acadians, 127
Agribusiness: as term, 216*n16*
Agriculture: procedures in, 72, 108–9, 123–24, 206, 207–10 *passim*; machinery in, 195, 209, 213–14; changes in, 205, 205*n22*, 213–214; labor in, 213, 214; crops grown in, 214. *See also* Blacks: as agricultural labor; Chinese; Cotton; Machinery; Plantations; Rice; Sugar
Alabama: future of, 72; size of, 72; as cotton state, 107; name of, 235; Gulf coast of, 237–38
Alabama & Great Southern Railroad, 239
Alcorn University, 75
America: foreign travelers on, 2–3; available land in, 127; size of, 127; diversity of, 235
American Notes (Dickens), 2; quoted, 39
American River Transportation Company, 148. *See also* Steamboat lines
Amité, Louisiana, 81
Anchor Line, 17–18, 24. *See also* Steamboat lines
Anti-Semitism, 74*n2*. *See also* Jews
Anzeiger des Westens (newspaper): cited, 146
Architecture: on plantations, 107–8, 123, 136, 184, 192–93, 226; in New Orleans, 153, 158, 159, 163
Arkansas: future of, 95; black migration to, 105; misinformation about, 116; history of, 116, 117; law and order in 116, 117, 118–19; social conditions in, 116, 117, 118–19; described, 116–17, 118; dueling in, 117*n4*; transportation in, 117–18; economic conditions in, 118; blacks in, 119
Arkansas River, 117
Atchafalaya, Louisiana, 127
Atchafalaya River, 135–36
Attakapa Indians, 126–27
Aus allen Welttheilen (magazine): quoted, 101–2, 103

Balize, 231
Barges, 91–92, 148. *See also* Boats and other craft
Baton Rouge, Louisiana, 124, 165*n3*, 201
Bayou Teche, Louisiana, 127, 128
Bay St. Louis, Mississippi, 236
Bell, Jack, 83, 84, 85
Belletristisches Journal, (New York magazine): quoted, 52, 149, 239
Black migration: causes of, 99–104 *passim*; ideas about, 105
Blacks: Hesse-Wartegg on, 6–7; social status of, 6–7, 13, 28, 77; as free people, 6–7, 27–28, 72, 85, 98–101, 104, 193–94, 195, 213; character of, 6–7, 82, 87, 99, 100–101, 104–5, 109, 110–11, 194, 203; migration of, 13, 96, 98–106; as subservient, 6–7, 85; morals of, 27–28; described, 27, 28, 65, 66–67, 69, 87, 101–3 *passim*, 113, 166, 167–68, 184, 185–86, 187, 189–90, 193–94, 206, 209; family life of, 28; in Cairo, Illinois, 35; in Memphis, Tennessee, 52; in govern-

251

ment, 52, 72, 75, 77, 160, 165–68; and yellow fever, 55, 57, 208; in occupations, 66–67, 94, 111*n17*, 190, 197, 198, 224, 226; and their dead, 71; cemeteries of, 71; economic state of, 74, 75, 99, 100–106 *passim*, 109–11, 119, 203–4; in Jackson, Mississippi, 75; in Natchez, Mississippi, 77; numbers of, 77; in Vicksburg, Mississippi, 77; KKK and, 78, 79; as criminals, 78–85 *passim*, 79*n7*, 87*n4*; in St. Louis, 98, 99; as farmers, 99–105 *passim*; as slaves, 100–101, 109*n7*, 111*n14*, 152, 153, 165, 166, 167, 208, 213; as agricultural labor, 100–103, 104, 109–14 *passim*, 194, 195, 199, 203, 207, 208, 209, 213, 214*n9*; exploitation of, 100–105 *passim*, 100*n10*, 203–4; and Jews, 101; future of, 103–6 *passim*; homes of, 109, 110, 127, 193–94, 194*n6*; songs of, 113; in Arkansas, 119; in New Orleans, 151, 152, 153, 159, 160, 165–68; and Creoles, 225, 228, 229; mulattoes and, 228. *See also* Race relations; Segregation; Stevedores

Blackville, Kansas, 96

Black women, 35, 183, 185–86, 189, 194, 207

Blood sports, 176–77

Boatbuilding, 23–24

Boats and other craft, 18, 19, 22, 23, 24, 26, 86–87, 88–91, 138, 148, 185, 190, 199, 206. *See also* Mississippi River: traffic on; Snag boats; Steamboats

Bobolink, 208–9

Boll weevil, 113*n20*

Bollworm, 113

Bonnet Carré, Louisiana, 133, 134

Borgne, Lake, 134, 235, 236*n2*

Boston Mountains, 116*n1*

Bottomland, 76, 94–95, 116

Brazil, 149–50

Buffalofish, 88

Bullfighting, 176

Butchering, 112

Cairo, Illinois, 23, 33–35, 148

Calcasieu River, 134

Calypso (black woman), 184*n3*, 186–187

Canada Bill (cardsharper), 94

Canal Street, New Orleans: importance of, 156, 175; as boundary, 156, 162–63; described, 156–58; parade on, 173; women on, 175

Cape Girardeau, Missouri, 30–32

Cardsharpers, 93–94, 181

Carnival: and yellow fever, 54; history of, 169–70; where celebrated, 169–70; defined, 169–70, 175; described, 169–75; king of, 169–75 *passim*; importance of, 170–72, 175; preparations for, 170–72; visitors at, 172–73; parade of, 173–74; of 1879, 174; organizations in, 174; costume balls of, 175; as social event, 175*n15*; Creoles at, 222–23. *See also* Mystik Krewe

Carondelet, Missouri, 20, 29–30

Carpetbaggers, 7–8, 48, 168, 187

Carroll, George, 81, 82

Catfish, 88

Cathedral of New Orleans, 163

Cemeteries, 71, 159, 164, 191

Charitable institutions, 57

Chicago, St. Louis & New Orleans Railroad, 49*n14*

Chickasaw Indians, 153, 161

Chinese, 212*n5*, 214

Choctaw Indians, 153

Churches, 162, 191

Cincinnati, Ohio, 22, 23, 184

Cities: beginnings of, 32

City of Vicksburg (steamboat), 26, 43, 45

Civilization in United States: beginnings explained, 32
Civil War: horrors of, 13; consequences for blacks, 27; in Vicksburg, 76, 77, 96*n25*; and Mississippi River traffic, 93; effect on planters, 93; effects on agriculture, 99–100, 124, 127, 137*n3*, 204*n18*, 205, 207; and architecture, 108*n3*; and Mississippi River control, 132*n8*; and New Orleans, 138*n7*, 142, 158–59, 162; and Creoles, 193, 196*n9*, 220; aftermath in South, 217–18; and Mobile, Alabama, 237. *See also* Blacks: as free people
Clement, Lewis T., 216*n15*
Clement attachment, 216
Cleveland, Cincinnati, Chicago & St. Louis Railroad, 33–34*n3*
Coal, 217
Cockfighting, 176–81; and betting, 179–81 *passim*
Coffee, 150
Conservation, 126*n5*, 217
Corruption: in Memphis, 47–48; in New Orleans, 161, 165*n3*, 166–67; in Louisiana, 165*n3*, 166–67, 168, 177. *See also* Carpetbaggers; Reconstruction
Cotton: in St. Louis, 20; in Memphis, 49; importance of, 77, 201; as crop, 101–2, 112–14 *passim*; described, 112–13; pests of, 113; byproducts of, 114; processing of, 114–15, 115*n25*, 214–16; prices of, 115; amounts produced, 115, 216; in New Orleans, 138, 149, 158; value of, 216; in Mobile, 237
Cotton belt, 107
Cotton gin, 114, 216
Cotton industry, 214, 215; profits in, 215; spindles in, 215
Cotton worm, 113
Cowden, James A. (or John), 133

Creoles: in New Orleans, 162, 165, 166, 178, 220–25; and Carnival, 170, 222–23; hospitality of, 192, 196; and blacks, 194, 228, 229; ways of life, 199; nationalities among, 219–20, 225; definition of, 219–20, 225*n18*; in Louisiana, 220; economic status of, 220–21; described, 220, 221–24; dances and balls of, 222; as husbands, 224, 226, 228, 229; inter-racial marriage of, 224–25, 228, 229; blacks as, 225; Germans as, 225; decadence of, 226; in Cuba, 226–28; as slaveowners, 228; in the Caribbean, 228, 229; character of, 229; future of, 229; in Latin America, 229
Creole women: described, 174–75, 196, 220–28 *passim*; as mothers, 223, 226; hospitality of, 226; as wives, 224, 226; ennui of, 225–26; daily life of, 225–26, 227; in Cuba, 226–27
Crevasses, 132, 188. *See also* Mississippi River: control of, power of
Crime, 77–85 *passim*, 93–94, 95, 127, 181. *See also* Law and order; Lynching; Rowdies
Criminal News (magazine), 31, 32*n9*
Crozat, Antoine, 152
Cuba: life in, 226; civil war in, 227. *See also* Creoles: in Cuba
Cursing, 73–74

Deeves, J. F., 60
Delta. *See* Mississippi Delta
DeSoto, Arkansas, 96
Deutsche Zeitung (New Orleans newspaper), 62, 161, 188; quoted, 60–61, 82, 144, 160
Devèse, Jean, 60*n13*
Dickens, Charles, 2, 3; quoted, 39
Dickinson, Dr. (plantation owner), 43
Dogfighting, 176, 181

Domestic Manners of the Americans (Frances Trollope), 2–3
Drummers, 75
Dueling, 117*n4*

Eads, James B., 17*n2*, 231–32, 233, 234*n9*
Eads Bridge, 17, 19
Eclipse (steamboat) 26*n15*
Economic conditions, 212, 212*n3*, 213*n8*, 214–15, 217–18. *See also* Agriculture; Cotton industry; Industry; New Orleans: as port; Plantations; Mississippi River: importance of, traffic on; Railroads vs. steamboats and river craft
Emancipation: in New Orleans, 162. *See also* Blacks: as free people
Exodusters, 98*n1*

Fevers, 208. *See also* Yellow fever
Fires, 123–24, 206
Flatboats, 86–87, 88. *See also* Boats and other craft
Floods, 125–26. *See also* Mississippi River: floods of
Florida, 238–39
Foreign travelers: on America, 2–3
Forests, 72, 118, 126, 235–36, 237, 238; conservation of, 217
Förster, Georg, 62
Fort Pike, Louisiana, 236
"Forty acres and a mule," 100
Frank Leslie's (magazine), 31, 32
Freie Presse für Texas (newspaper): cited, 216
French language, 162–63, 186–87
French market, New Orleans, 163–64
French quarter, New Orleans, 153*n13*, 223–24
Furnishing merchant, 110*n10*. *See also* Storekeepers; Supply merchant

Gainey, J. S., 239
Gambling, 21, 45, 93–94, 162, 179–81 *passim*, 223. *See also* Cardsharpers
General merchants, 110*n10*
Germans, 13, 19–20, 21, 161, 225
German-American press, 10, 62
German Coast, 161*n39*
Gerstäcker, Friedrich, 86, 225
Gins, 114, 216
Golden City (steamboat), 24
Golden mountain, 100
Golden Rule (steamboat), 24
Grain trade, 147
Grand Republic (steamboat), 24*n9*
Grangers, 148–49
Great Eastern, (ship), 37, 183
Great Republic (steamboat), 24, 24*n9*, 25, 26
Great South, The (Edward King): cited, 117
Grenada, Mississippi, 64, 65, 66, 67–70, 71
Grenada Sentinel (newspaper), 69–70, 71
Gulf coast, 235–37

Half-castes, 225. *See also* Blacks: and Creoles; Mulattoes
Harper's (magazine), 31, 32*n9*
Hauk, Minnie, 3–5 *passim*, 128
Helena, Arkansas, 89, 95
Hercules, coachman and boatman, 190, 206
Hesse-Wartegg, Ernst von: as writer, 1, 3–4, 5–10, 13, 62, 160; as traveler, 1, 3–4, 6, 9, 10, 13, 65; and America, 1, 6–10 *passim*, 13; and Mark Twain, 1–2, 38–39; described and evaluated, 1–10 *passim*; life and times of, 3–8; attitude toward blacks, 6–8, 10; opinions of, 6–8 *passim*, 10, 62, 160; and slavery, 7; and *Travels on the Lower Mississippi (Mississippi-Fahrten)*, 8–10; and languages, 10; perspicacity of, 10, 62, 160, 216; essay

on sanitation and yellow fever, 62, 160
Higgins, Jim, 83*n14*
Hog butchering, 112
Hogshead, 124, 201
Holiday, George, 103
Holt, Dr. (writer on yellow fever), 60, 62
Homestead Act, 238, 239
Hopkinsville, Tennessee, 82, 83
Hot Springs, Arkansas, 119
Howard Association, 57–58
Humphreys, Andrew A., 232–33
Hurricane of 1870, 231

Ice gorge, 18
Illinois Central Railroad, 33*n3*, 148
Immigration: and agriculture, 115; to Arkansas, 116; United States and, 119, 120; to Louisiana, 127, 204–5; amount of, 212; efforts for, 212*n5*; and steamship lines, 213
Indians, 126–27, 151, 198. *See also* tribes by name
Industry, 211, 214–16; in New Orleans, 160. *See also* Cotton industry; Iron industry; Lumbering; Rice: production; Sugar: planting sugarcane
Insects, 76, 202
Iron-clad cudgel, 69
Iron industry, 217*n19*
Iron ore, 217

J. M. White (steamboat), 24*n9*
Jackson, Andrew, 154, 163
Jackson, Mississippi, 74–75
Jamieson, Arch, 83, 84, 85
Jeffersonville, Indiana, 23–24
Jefferson, Joseph, 128
Jetties, 146, 232, 233, 234
Jews, 74, 101; Hesse-Wartegg on, 6, 204
Johnson (criminal), 81, 82
Judge Lynch, 80, 81, 85

"Jumping the bar," 41

Kansas: black migration to, 96–97, 105
Kansas Landing, Louisiana, 97
Kansas Pacific Railroad, 64
Keating, John M., 58
Kellogg, William P., 211*n2*
Kerr, Alphonse, 224
King, Edward, 117
Kountz Line, 17. *See also* Steamboat lines
Ku Klux Klan, 77–79, 80

Labor. *See* Agriculture: labor in; Blacks: as agricultural labor; Chinese; Industry; Plantations
Land speculation, 95, 127
Laprade, Lee, 82, 82*n13*, 83
Law and order: in St. Louis, 21; in early Reconstruction, 78–81, 85; in Napoleon, Arkansas, 95; in Arkansas, 117, 118; in Louisiana, 127; in New Orleans, 178. *See also* Cardsharpers; Crime; Lynching
Levees, 131–32, 134, 198–99, 208; at New Orleans, 136, 137*n4*, 138. *See also* Mississippi River: control of
Lien system, 110*n10*
Life on the Mississippi (Mark Twain), 1–2, 19*n5*
Little Rock, Arkansas, 119
Liverpool Southern Steamship Line, 149. *See also* Steamship lines
Logmen (timber thieves), 238–39
Longfellow, Henry W., 39
Louisiana: as cotton state, 107; sugar produced, 124, 125; economic conditions, 124–25; slavery in, 124–25, 162; described, 126, 127, 128, 137, 235–36; and immigration, 127, 204–5; size of, 151–52, 154; history of, 151–54; population of, 154; corruption in, 165, 166–

67, 168, 177; Reconstruction in, 166–67, 168; future of, 168; Yankees in, 168. *See also* Baton Rouge; Cockfighting; New Orleans; Mississippi Delta; Mississippi River
Louisiana Country Visitor (newspaper), 188
Louisville, Kentucky, 23, 238
Louisville & Great Southern Railroad, 67, 238
Louisville & Nashville Railroad, 49$n14$
Lumbering, 87–88, 217, 237, 238–39
Lynching, 70, 71, 77, 81–85 *passim*

Machinery: in agriculture, 195, 209. *See also* Clement attachment; Cotton Industry; Gin
Magazines, 31–32. *See also* by title
Magnolia Plantation, 190, 191, 206
Mail, 187–88
Male chauvinism, 186$n7$
Manners, 94
Mardi Gras, 170, 171$n4$, 174,
Marigney family, 223–24
Marion, Mississippi, 74
Mark Twain. *See* Twain, Mark
Mason, Samuel, 93$n17$
Massere Mountains (Ouachitas), 116
Memphis, Tennessee: as port, 23; described, 45–50 *passim*; corruption in, 46–47, 50, 51; economic conditions, 46–48; yellow fever in, 46, 49, 50–52; government of, 47–48; people of, 48; Reconstruction in, 48$n11$; as commercial center, 49; sanitation in, 49, 50, 51–52; cotton in, 49, 114; future of, 51, 53; blacks in, 52; as transportation center, 52–53; as gateway to South, 64
Memphis & Charleston Railroad, 49$n14$
Memphis Appeal (newspaper), 52, 62

Memphis Avalanche (newspaper), 52, 88
Mercier, Alfred, 58
Meridian, Mississippi, 70, 74
Meschacébé, (weekly journal), 58
Mineral deposits, 211, 217, 237. *See also* Coal; Iron
Mississippi: future of, 72; development in, 72, 73; described, 72–74 *passim*, 236–37; transportation in, 73; economic conditions in, 74; crime in, 74, 77; wildlife of, 76; as cotton state, 107. *See also* Meridian; Mississippi River; Natchez; Vicksburg
Mississippi & Dominion Steamship Line, 149. *See also* Steamship lines
Mississippi & Tennessee Railroad, 64–65, 67
Mississippi bottom, 76, 177
Mississippi Central Railroad, 49$n14$
Mississippi Delta: described, 182, 184–85, 190–91, 192, 196–99, 230. *See also* Mississippi River; Mississippi Valley
Mississippi River: traffic on, 13, 17–19, 22–24 *passim*, 26–30 *passim*, 86, 87, 125, 136, 137, 185, 188, 190, 199, 206, 209; control of, 13, 125, 131–35, 191, 199, 231, 232–34; described, 17–18, 33$n1$, 37–40 *passim*, 123, 131, 188, 198, 199–200, 206; at St. Louis, 17–21 *passim*; importance of, 22, 23, 86, 87, 148–49, 154, 234; cities and towns of, 23, 24, 30–31; damage by, 30, 45, 95–96, 129–30, 188, 199; flow of, 33, 129–35 *passim*, 206; power of, 37, 130, 131, 132, 188, 191, 198, 199, 206, 208; debris in, 37, 188; navigation of, 38, 40, 41, 43, 44, 92, 230, 231, 233, 234; dangers of, 38, 40, 41, 43–44, 92, 191, 199, 208, 231; shape of, 39–40, 86$n2$, 129, 133,

187; floods of, 40, 43–44, 45, 72, 76, 130–35 *passim*, 199; bars of, 41, 230, 232; size of, 86, 130, 132, 138, 206, 234; discharge of, 86*n1*, 230, 232, 233; future of, 92; history of, 129; length of, 129, 133, 232, 233; government policy on, 131, 132–34 *passim*, 135; sediment in, 132–33, 184, 230, 232, 233; outlets of, 132–35; depth of, 138, 233, 234, 234*n9*; at New Orleans, 146–47; levels of, 147, fear of, 199; tides in, 207–8, 230; mudlumps in, 230–31; passes of, 230–33 *passim*; jetties of, 232–34 *passim*. *See also* Boats and other craft; Crevasses; Levees; Mississippi Delta; Mississippi River Commission; Mississippi River system; Snags; Steamboats; tributaries by name
Mississippi River Commission, 134*n17*, 135*n18*
Mississippi River system, 23, 86*n1*
Mississippi Southern Railroad, 74*n1*
Mississippi Valley: described, 13, 65–66, 76, 92, 94–95; people of, 87–88; swamps of, 123, 126. *See also* Mississippi Delta; Mississippi River
Mississippi Valley Transportation Company, 148
Missouri Pacific Railroad, 49*n14*
Mister Judge (cardsharper), 93–94
Mobile, Alabama, 235, 237–38
Mobile & Ohio Railroad, 33*n3*
Morgan Line, 138
Morgan Railroad Company, 144
Moselle (steamboat), 92–93*n16*
Mudlumps, 230–31
Mulattoes, 228
Mules, 157, 195, 207
Mystik Krewe of Comus, 174. *See also* Carnival

Napoleon, Arkansas, 95–96

Nashville, Tennessee, 23
Nashville American (newspaper): on crime, 83–85
Nast, Thomas, 167*n8*
Natchez, Mississippi, 77
Natchez (steamboat), 92*n16*
Natchez Indians, 153
National cemetery, 77
National Grange, 148*n20*
Natural resources, 217. *See also* Forests; Mineral deposits
Negroes. *See* Blacks
New Iberia, Louisiana, 128
New Orleans, Louisiana: as commercial center, 22, 23*n6*, 138, 141–43, 144–50, 158, 164; as port, 23, 137–39 *passim*, 141–50; and grain trade, 23*n6*, 145–46, 150; sanitation in, 68, 159–60; as Crescent City, 136, 137; described, 136, 137–39, 151, 153, 154–64 *passim*, 161, 162–63, 173, 177; railroads in, 138, 143–44; importance of, 138, 148, 149–50, 151, 156, 157; cotton in, 138, 149, 158; future of, 138, 150, 154; economic conditions in, 141–46 *passim*, 147*n18*, 158, 159, 164; and Civil War, 142, 158–59, 162; yellow fever in, 142–43; access to Gulf from, 143; renewal of, 144; Mississippi River at, 146–47; navigation at, 146–47; shipping news of, 146–47; steamship lines at, 149; languages in, 151, 157, 162–63; history of, 151–54; people of, 151, 156, 161–62, 163–64, 173, 178–79; blacks in, 151, 159, 160, 165–68; slavery in, 152, 153, 165; architecture in, 153, 158, 159, 163, 164*n48*; French quarter of, 153*n13*, 162–63; low life in, 154*n16*; Rampart Street in, 156*n20*, 160; streets of, 156–61, 162–63; Creoles in, 157, 162, 165, 166; women in, 157, 164, 170, 174–75; streetcars in, 157–58, 160; buri-

al in, 159–60, 164; Reconstruction in, 159–60, 166–67, 168; industry in, 160; corruption in, 160, 161, 166–68 *passim*; Custom House in, 161; newspapers in, 161; cultural life in, 161–62; pastimes in, 162, 177, 178; Cathedral of, 163; tourists in, 163*n43*, 172–73, 178–79, 181; French market in, 163–64; attitude to money in, 164; social life in, 165; state capitol in, 165–68; cockfighting in, 177–81; law and order in, 178. *See also* Canal Street; Carnival; *Deutsche Zeitung*; Pontchartrain, Lake; St. Charles Hotel; St. Louis Hotel; Yankees: in New Orleans

New Orleans & Jackson Railroad, 49*n14*

Newspapers: in Cape Girardeau, Missouri, 31; importance of, 31; numbers of, 31, 69; role of, 51, 60, 88, 181, 217; nature of, 88; shipping news in, 146–47; in New Orleans, 161; in Louisiana, 188. *See also* by title

New York Herald, 67

New York Times, 3, 9

New York Tribune, 62

Nicholson wooden pavement, 49

Nicodemus, Kansas, 98*n4*

Nigger (crane), 25, 187, 189

Nigger trash, 87

North German Lloyd Steamship line, 149, 190, 213

Notrebe, Frederick, 95*n24*

Ohio River, 33, 37

Opera, 35 *passim*, 88–91 *passim*, 128, 162

Orange Island, Louisiana, 128

Ouachita Mountains, 116*n1*

Ouachita (Washita) River, 117, 130, 134–35

Outlet system, 132–35

Overstolz, Henry, 98*n3*

Ozark Mountains, 116*n1*

Pain Court, 19

Paper towns, 95*n22*

Parish, meaning of, 206

Park Mountains (Ozarks or Bostons), 116

Passes of the Mississippi, 230–33 *passim*

Paul et Virginie (Saint-Pierre), 185

Peigneur, Lake, 128

Pensacola, Florida, 238–39

Phillips, Mr. (crime victim), 81

Pigs, 112

Pilot Town, 231

Pilots, jetty construction, 233

Pilots, riverboat, 41–43

Pinchback, Pinckney, 105

Piracy, 93

Pittsburgh, Pennsylvania, 22, 23, 184

Plantations: slaves and, 72; value of, 72, 204*n18*, 205, 220; life on, 107–8, 109–14 *passim*, 185, 192–96, 202–3; described, 107–8, 123, 125, 136–37, 184, 192–93, 201–2, 206, 207–10 *passim*, 225–26; agricultural practices on, 108–9, 112; immigrants on, 111–12; white employees of, 111–12, 194, 195; livestock on, 112; hospitality at, 192, 196. *See also* Blacks: as agricultural labor; Cotton; Plantation legend; Plantation system; Rice: production; Sugar: planting sugarcane

Plantation legend, 107*n2*

Plantation system, 205*n22*

Planter aristocracy, 68, 75, 77

Planters, 93, 108, 210, 211, 237

Plaquemine Parish, Louisiana, 182

Poems of Places (Longfellow), 39

Point Coupé, Louisiana, 133

Poker (card game), 93

Police Gazette (magazine), 31, 32*n9*
Police News (magazine), 31, 32*n9*
Poll tax, 110
Pontchartrain, Lake, 134, 155–56, 235–36
Poor colored trash, 87*n5*, 105
Poor whites, 211–12
Poor white trash, 87, 212
Pork, 112
Port Hudson, Louisiana, 129
Progress, 217–18
Pucket, Orange (farmer), 101–3

Quarantine, 142–43
Quarters (homes), 108, 109*n7*, 123, 125, 193

Raccourci Cut Off, 129
Race relations: Hesse-Wartegg and, 6–7; in transportation, 65, 103; interracial marriage and, 70–71, 225, 228, 229; as friction, 77; in Mississippi, 77; unfairness in, 85; harmony in, 106; in Arkansas, 119. *See also* Segregation
Racism, 6–7, 186*n7*
Rafts, 88. *See also* Boats and other craft
Railroads: travel by, 17, 64–67, 73–74, 75, 235–39; in Memphis, 49; described, 64–65; importance of, 73; *vs.* steamboats and river craft, 92, 126*n3*, 142*n4*, 142–43, 144–45, 148–49, 150; in Arkansas, 117–18; interstate net, 117–18; routes of, 117–18, 141–42, 143–45, 147–49, 150; U.S. policy on, 118; in New Orleans, 138, 143–44; monopoly of, 145, 147–49; regulation of, 148*n20*; as local transportation, 201; on Gulf coast, 236–37; mentioned, 96. *See also* lines by name
Ramsey, Joe, 84
Reconstruction: ideas during, 6, 7, 8; Hesse-Wartegg's definition of, 8;
effects of, 13, 27–28; in Memphis, 48*n1*; in New Orleans, 159–60, 166–67; in Louisiana, 166–67, 168. *See also* Blacks: as free people, in government; Carpetbaggers; Civil war: effects of; Corruption; Race relations
Red River, 107, 117, 125–26, 130, 134, 135
Rice: production, 207–10; monetary return for, 210
Rice, Dan, 88–91
Richardson (steamboat), 24
Rigolets, 236
River rats, 87*n4*
Rivers. *See by name*
Robert E. Lee (steamboat), 24, 92*n16*
Roustabouts, 43. *See also* Stevedores
Rowdies, toughs, and riffraff, 21, 74, 75, 77, 85. *See also* Crime; Law and order

Saddlersville, Tennessee, 82, 84
St. Charles Hotel, New Orleans, 161, 165, 173
St. Charles Parish, Louisiana, 182
St. Francis River, 117
St. Louis, Missouri: Eads bridge at, 17; waterfront of, 18, 19, 21, 22, 25, 28, 29; described, 18–21 *passim*, 29; French in, 19; history of, 19; commerce of, 19, 20, 22, 23, 24; Germans in, 19–20, 21; as industrial center, 20, 21, 29–30; low life in, 21; transients in, 21; as port, 23; black migrants in, 98, 99; as cotton center, 114
St. Louis Hotel, New Orleans, 165–67, 165*n3*
St. Louis Southern & Iron Mountain Railroad, 117
St. Pierre, Jacques, 225
St. Vrain, Colonel (saloon owner), 70
Salesmen, 75
Sawmills, 237

Schools, 110, 162, 239
Sealsfield, Charles (Karl Anton Postl), 225
Sediment. *See* Mississippi River: sediment in
Segregation, 55, 75, 103, 119, 195
Servants. *See* Blacks: occupations of
Shakespeare, Joseph, 160*n3*
Sharecropping, 109*n8*. *See also* Lien system
Share system, 109–11
Ships. *See* Boats and other craft; Mississippi River: traffic on; Steamboats; Steamship lines
Shreve, Henry, 36*n6*
Slavery, 6–7, 72, 162, 220. *See also* Blacks as slaves
Smith, Dick, 81, 82
Snag boats, 35–36
Snagbooks, 36
Snags, 36
South, the: condition of, 64; poverty in, 72; economic conditions in, 99–103 *passim*; agriculture in, 99–106 *passim*; future of, 104, 218, 234; climate of, 190; life in, 190, 200
South Carolina: sugar produced, 124
Southern Pacific Railroad, 49*n14*
Southern Transportation Line, 23
Springfield, Tennessee, 83*n15*, 84
Squad: as a word, 111
Staatszeitung (New York newspaper), 62; on crime, 82–83; cited, 160
Steamboat lines: Kountz, 17; Anchor, 17–18, 24; Southern Transportation, 23; Morgan, 138; American River Transportation Company, 148
Steamboats: numbers of, 18, 92; importance of, 18, 30–31, 137; range of, 18, 52–53, 126, 127, 137, 138, 182–83; described, 19, 22, 23–27 *passim*, 139, 140, 173, 184; accidents among, 24, 25, 26; cargoes of, 25, 26–27, 28, 30, 36–37, 187; food on, 26; crews of, 26, 27, 28; arrivals of, 30–31; landings by, 30–31, 43, 45, 139–40, 189; loading of, 36–37, 183–84; travel on, 41, 45, 94, 127–28, 183–90 *passim*; gambling on, 45; future of, 92; races of, 92–93; dangers of, 92*n16*, 126; whistles of, 125, 140, 173; *vs.* railroads, 142–43, 142*n4*, 143*n7*, 144–45, 148–49, 150; as mail carriers, 187–88; damage by, 188. *See also* boats by name
Steamship lines: at New Orleans, 149; enumerated and evaluated, 213
Stevedores, 26–28 *passim*, 30, 36–37, 43, 184, 187, 189
Storekeepers, 110*n10*
Sugar, 124, 201, 202–3, 205; planting sugarcane, 202, 204, 205, 210*n3*
"Sunny South," the, 64
Supply merchant, 110*n10*
Swamps, 123, 126, 196–98

Tallahassee, Florida, 239
Tangipahoa, Louisiana, 81
Texas, 107, 124
Theaters, 88–91, 162
Thompson, Daniel, 205*n19*
Timber thieves, 238–39
Town-booming, 95*n22*
Transportation, 73. *See also* Boats and other craft; Railroads; Steamboats; Steamship lines
Travels on the Lower Mississippi (Hesse-Wartegg), xi-xii, 1–10 *passim*, 13
Trembling prairie, 236
Trollope, Frances, 2–3
Truck system, 204
Tugboats. *See* Boats and other craft
Twain, Mark, 1–2, 8, 9, 38–39
Twitchell, Marshall H., 211–12*n2*

Under the Gaslight (magazine), 31, 32*n*9
Union Pacific Railroad, 64*n1*
Universities, 75, 119
University of Mississippi, 75

Vacheries, 127
Vicksburg, 23, 68, 73, 76–77, 96
Vigilance committees, 80

Wage system, 109*n8*, 110–111
Walker (criminal), 81, 82
Warmoth, Henry C., 7, 183–84, 186, 187, 190, 211*n*2
Washington Parish, Louisiana, 81
Washita River. *See* Ouachita River
Whistling Dick (cannon), 77
White River, 117
Whitewashing, 70
Whitney, Eli, 114
Wildlife, 76, 182, 197, 198, 202
Williamson, A. M.: quoted, 4–5, 5–6
Wilson (Samuel Mason, pirate), 93*n17*
Women: on transportation, 65; in New Orleans, 157, 164, 170, 174–75; in Louisiana, 170; in New Orleans, 174–75; absence of, 178; as steamboat passengers, 184*n3*, 185, 186, 187; manners of, 193; plantation life of, 196; status of, 229. *See also* Black women; Creole women
Woodard, Warren, 84

Yalobusha River, 68
Yankees: Southern penetration by, 125, 128, 205, 211, 221–22; in New Orleans, 151, 157, 158–59, 178; in Louisiana, 168; defined, 221–22
Yazoo River, 64, 68, 71, 72, 76
Yellow fever: knowledge of, 9; measures against, 9, 56, 58; Hesse-Wartegg and, 9, 62; described, 13, 54–59, 62–63; at Memphis, 45–46, 49, 50–53, 56–57; origins of, 54; and Carnival, 54, 222; attitudes toward, 55, 60, 62, 63; heroism and, 57–58; causes of, 58–62; threat of, 62; in Grenada, 64, 66, 67–68, 71; economic effects of, 142–43; in New Orleans, 142–43, 174, 222